A Practical Guide to Minicomputer Applications

A Practical Guide to Minicomputer Applications

Edited by
Fred F. Coury
Minicomputer Section Manager
Hewlett-Packard Company

A volume in the IEEE PRESS Selected Reprint Series, prepared under the sponsorship of the IEEE Computer Society.

The Institute of Electrical and Electronics Engineers, Inc. New York

Copyright ©1972 by

THE INSTITUTE OF ELECTRICAL AND ELECTRONICS ENGINEERS, INC.
345 East 47 Street, New York, N.Y. 10017
All rights reserved

International Standard Book Numbers:

Clothbound: 0-87942-005-7
Paperbound: 0-87942-006-5

PRINTED IN THE UNITED STATES OF AMERICA

Contents

Part IV: General Applications

Part V: Specific Applications

A Practical Guide to
Minicomputer Applications

Introduction

The purpose of this volume is primarily to acquaint the prospective user with minicomputer applications rather than to serve the computer professional as a textbook or state of the art document.

I assume that the reader is an engineer or student whose expertise is in a field other than minicomputers. He has a problem in his field that he understands and can describe in a problem-oriented language. He has heard much about minicomputers and wants to know if a minicomputer can help solve his problem.

He needs to know: 1) if minicomputer techniques can be applied to his problem, and how well they apply, 2) what is involved in actually bringing a minicomputer to bear on his problem, and 3) if a minicomputer is indeed a reasonable solution, how to go about the selection and connection process.

This volume, then, is a collection of recent papers intended to provide the reader with sufficient background information and examples for him to answer the above questions concerning his own particular situation.

There are several factors that the reader must keep in mind in order to really get the most from these articles. The first is the dilemma involved in the selection of papers on minicomputer applications. The minicomputer industry has been characterized by rapid change and growth over the last decade. The tendency, then, in a publication regarding such a dynamic phenomenon, is to speak in generalities, concentrating on the basic characteristics of the devices and neglecting details that are subject to change.

On the other hand, a treatment of real-world applications of any practical value requires specific details. Indeed, the closer one gets to the solution of his particular problem, the more specific must be the information he needs. Papers on applications tend to be very specific, causing two kinds of problems.

First, they become dated very rapidly. As a matter of fact, by the time a problem is defined and a minicomputer system is selected, installed, programmed, debugged, and finally published, it may no longer be state of the art; it may even be obsolete.

Second, minicomputer applications are, by nature, very practical. Minicomputers are specific pieces of hardware manufactured and sold by real live companies. Papers on real applications usually refer to the minicomputer and its peripheral equipment by make and model number. This detailed information is very valuable to the reader who is trying to benefit from the author's experience. However, the inclusion of such a description in a publication of this nature might be construed as an endorsement of, or preference for, a particular manufacturer or his products. This, of course, is not the case.

Papers have been chosen on the basis of their value to the reader previously described. Application papers, especially, have been selected on the basis of providing practical, detailed information on the solutions of problems from several areas. The articles that cite specific details, although dated, were chosen because only through specific details can the reader fully understand the author's problem and its solution, and from this understanding, extrapolate to his own problem.

This book is divided into five parts: I. An Introduction to Minicomputers, II. Peripheral and Software Considerations, III. Selecting a Minicomputer, IV. General Applications, and V. Specific Applications.

No attempt is made to teach the reader about minicomputer hardware, software, or peripheral design except as it applies to his solution of the problem at hand. It is hoped that the reader, upon completing this book, will feel, not that he has learned a lot about minicomputers, but that he now knows how to go about solving his problem.

With this in mind, the following papers have been selected and are included herein.

Part I
An Introduction to Minicomputers

This part consists of a single paper by R. A. Kaenel of Bell Labs. It is a brief but comprehensive survey of all aspects of minicomputers, intended to provide a background for the non-computer-oriented reader. History, technologies, architectures, software, and even some applications are covered. It also defines in context several terms that will be encountered in later articles and in future minicomputer dealings. A bibliography is included in the article for those interested in pursuing any one topic further.

Minicomputers–A Profile of Tomorrow's Component

REG A. KAENEL
Bell Telephone Laboratories, Inc.
Murray Hill, N. J. 07974

Abstract

There has been an explosive rate of growth of the types and the applications of minicomputers. This growth is a result of employing small computers in a new set of applications that were previously unexploited by the manufacturers of larger computers. To place the emergence of minicomputers in significant perspective, the following analysis is attempted: 1) typical minicomputer characteristics are outlined, 2) technological reasons for the emergence of minicomputers are suggested, 3) the architecture of contemporary minicomputers is given in terms of hardware structure, instruction format, and input/output configuration, 4) a software system that implements a shared environment on a typical minicomputer system is described, and 5) the advantages of using minicomputers are discussed and representative applications are sketched in the area of testing, control, communication, and laboratory experimentation.

I. Introduction—The Emergence of the Minicomputer

The Minicomputer Growth Rate [1]

Over the past five years, the computer arena has witnessed the emergence of low-cost computer systems (see Fig. 1) which have been named "minicomputers". As a matter of fact, the greatest growth in the computer industry in this period has been in minicomputers.

The first minicomputers were introduced in 1962 for aerospace applications. They included such machines as the Arma Micro Computer, the Burroughs D210, the Hughes HCH-201, and the Univac Add-1000. Commercial minicomputers by such manufacturers as Honeywell, Scientific Control Corporation, Xerox Data Systems, and Systems Engineering Laboratories appeared on the scene about 1966.

Today, some 10 000 systems have been installed representing over 100 different minicomputer types manufactured by more than 50 companies (not counting an additional 15 varieties by 10 foreign companies).

Minicomputer shipments grew approximately 75 percent between 1968 and 1969, reaching about 6000 units per year. The industrial and data communications sectors paced this growth. Continued expansion in these sectors combined with that in the business and laboratory sectors is sufficient to support the anticipated growth shown by the median of Fig. 1, indicating an increase in total shipments from 6000 units in 1969 to a probable 40 000 in 1975. If the education and transportation markets become significant, production could reach the upper bound of Fig. 1—over 45 000 units in 1975.

Fig. 2 indicates substantial growth for the industrial market—from approximately 2500 units in 1969 to over 15 000 units in 1975. Other areas with strong potential are data communications (650 to about 5000) and business (less than 100 to over 9000). Growth in the laboratory market will continue (2000 to about 5000 units), but this will become a less significant portion of the total market. Only moderate applications are anticipated for typesetting and education.

Market studies indicate a significant downtrend in average costs for the central processor unit (CPU). New technologies should begin to reduce CPU costs significantly in the not too distant future. Thus, although unit shipments are expected to rise perhaps fivefold, their dollar value should increase only about threefold, from about $100 million in 1969 to about $300 million in 1975. The ratio of total system to central processor value is expected to advance from about 2:1 in 1969 to about 4:1 in 1975, reflecting the growing value of the peripheral devices of the system. Total system value will rise from about $200–$250 million in 1969 to $2–$5 billion in 1975.

Over the past five years, the number of minicomputers in use at Bell Telephone Laboratories has grown to some 120, comprising 34 different types from 12 manufacturers. About half of these systems are employed in some sort of testing application, most of the other half are for laboratory systems and communication experiments.

Manuscript received August 13, 1970.

Reprinted from *IEEE Trans. Audio Electroacoust.*, vol. AU-18, pp. 354–379, Dec. 1970.

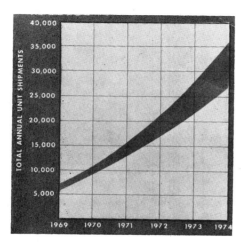

Fig. 1. Projection of the annual delivery growth rate of minicomputers (after Arthur D. Little, Inc. [1]).

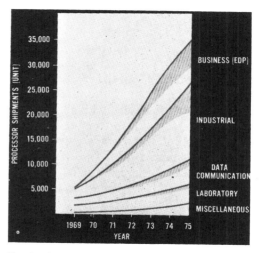

Fig. 2. Projection of the use distribution trend of minicomputers. The application categories are defined as follows (after Arthur D. Little, Inc. [1]).

1) Industrial: management control, such as data collection; and manufacturing including production control.

2) Data communication: batch terminal controllers; store-and-forward message switching and preprocessing equipment; and data concentrators.

3) Laboratory applications: physical sciences, e.g., gas diromatography and acoustics; medicine, e.g., clinical analysis.

4) Business applications: fiscal management, e.g., payroll and invoicing.

Today's Minicomputer Industry

The Industry Structure: Early in its development, the minicomputer industry was dominated by a few mainframe manufacturers. The supporting software sector was comprised essentially of small firms; the larger software companies tended not to cater to this market. More recently, the industry has expanded to include many computer and system manufacturers, suppliers of peripherals, independent software suppliers, and systems houses which supply turnkey systems. Let us briefly characterize these industries.

The Mainframe Manufacturers: Today, Digital Equipment corporation, Varian, Hewlett-Packard, and the Computer Control Division of Honeywell, in order of importance, lead the industry, accounting for about 80 percent of total unit sales during 1969. Original equipment manufacturers (OEM) represented about 50 percent of total sales for Digital Equipment, the Computer Control Division of Honeywell, and Varian, and 20 percent for Hewlett-Packard. The remaining sales are for applications where the end user is purchasing a system in which the minicomputer is only a component rather than buying the minicomputer as such to incorporate in a system of his own design. Hewlett-Packard's greater emphasis upon end user systems is due to its activity in the industrial instrumentation market through its other divisions.

Other companies in the minicomputer business include large enterprises like Xerox Data System, which possess the resources necessary for penetration of this market. Additional firms will undoubtedly decide that this market is sufficiently compatible with their other corporate activities to address themselves to it for either OEM, end users, or both. Some companies aiming for the end user market attempt to enter it by initiating their own devel-

opments or by becoming associated with a significant system and service capability.

The Peripheral Manufacturers: Until recently, the input, output, and storage devices used with low-cost central processors were those developed for large systems, and in many instances their performance, capacity, and cost were not compatible with the requirements of systems using minicomputers. In fact, only a few of the minicomputer manufacturers have supplied peripheral devices of their own make.

During the last two years, a new class of peripherals for use with minicomputer systems has been emerging. The class includes lower cost and lower performance secondary storage media—disks, drums, and magnetic tapes; data entry storage using magnetic tape cassettes or cartridges which compete in cost and convenience with paper tape and card equipment; line printers; and alphanumeric cathode-ray displays. Higher performance serial printers are also now available.

In the next few years, more of the larger suppliers of minicomputers are expected to develop a strong capability for manufacturing their own line of components with broad performance and cost ranges, while a number of new companies specializing in subunits for minicomputers will offer limited product lines. The impetus for such a development is the ratio of total system cost to computer cost, which ranges from 2:1 to 10:1.

The Software Suppliers: System software and application programs are developed by computer manufacturers, end users, programming firms, and original equipment manufacturers (OEM) customers. Typically, computer manufacturers supply system software for their product line, and the larger firms assist with application programming and supply programs for tunkey systems. In general, however, application programming falls to the users rather than the manufacturers. The application libraries of established manufacturers are largely the product of user group associations.

Programming staffs of manufacturers tend to be small (with the exception of the major suppliers); therefore, independent software firms are important to both computer manufacturers and their customers. Expenditures for all software development have been estimated at about $100 million in 1969 and could reach about $1 billion by 1975 when the total population of machines in this class will be more than 100 000. The greatest number of these will be smaller machines in dedicated applications. These machines will utilize modularly constructed software systems that consist largely of a specialized combination of general-purpose software packages whose development cost can be amortized over many applications. This tends to keep the average software expenditure per machine on the low side.

The System Suppliers: Independent system suppliers offer a capability based primarily upon knowledge of specific application areas. These independent system companies compete with minicomputer manufacturers selling directly to end users. A typical company in this class will develop, or have developed for itself, the software for an application, but will purchase virtually all equipment from established computer suppliers, preferring a single source for all equipment, if possible.

These companies face the usual service problems of the equipment manufacturers as well as a few that are unique. To grow, they must recruit personnel with a strong combination of technical skills and the ability to apply them. In addition, the development of workable, integrated "turnkey" systems requires the selection of applications with a sufficiently broad market that the development costs can be amortized over a reasonable number of sales. Services demanded by customers, such as maintenance of software and hardware and training programs, are usually supplied by the combined efforts of personnel from both the systems firm and the computer manufacturer.

Profile of Contemporary Minicomputers

What is a Minicomputer?: Minicomputers are having a remarkable impact on the computer industry since in some respects their performance is even better than that of their big brothers which have built up the computer industry over the past 20 years. For instance, many minicomputers have core cycle times and peripheral transfer rates which are considerably higher than the conven-

Fig. 3. Typical ranges of minicomputer characteristics [2].

CHARACTERISTICS	FEATURES AVAILABLE		
	MINIMUM	AVERAGE	MAXIMUM
MEMORY			
WORD LENGTH (BITS)	EIGHT	EIGHT OR 16	18
SIZE (WORDS)	1024 TO 4096	4096 TO 32,768	1024 TO 65,536
INCREMENT SIZE (WORDS)	1024	4096	8192
CYCLE RATE (KHz)	125	571 TO 1,000	2000
(CYCLE TIME, μSEC)	EIGHT	(1.0 TO 1.75)	(0.5)
PARITY CHECK	NO	OPTIONAL	STANDARD
MEMORY PROTECT	NO	OPTIONAL	STANDARD
DIRECT ADDRESSING (WORDS)	256	256 TO 4096	ALL OF CORE
INDIRECT ADDRESSING	NO	SGL/MULTILEVEL	MULTILEVEL
CENTRAL PROCESSOR			
GENERAL-PURPOSE REGISTERS	ONE	ONE, TWO, THREE, OR FOUR	128
INDEX REGISTERS	NONE	ONE	15
HARDWARE MULTIPLY/ DIVIDE	NO	OPTIONAL	STANDARD
IMMEDIATE INSTRUCTIONS	NO	HALF YES	YES
DOUBLE-WORD INSTRUCT	NO	MOSTLY YES	YES
BYTE PROCESSING	NO	HALF YES	YES

tional large-scale computers. Core cycle times of less than 1 μs are common and some machines are in the region of $\frac{3}{4}$ μs. Maximum I/0 transfer rates are frequently determined solely by memory speed, and with 16-bit machines transfer rates of over two million 16 bit-characters per second are quite common.

It is interesting to compare these parameters with an IBM System 360/50 which has a core cycle time of 2 μs and a maximum I/0 data rate of 800k bytes per second on the selector channel (which is the fastest channel). The 360/50 could in no sense be classified as a minicomputer and, of course, in other areas such as core size, instruction repertoire, range of peripherals, standard software markup, etc., it is far more powerful than any minicomputer. Nevertheless, this does indicate that for those applications where high-speed minimum-complexity processing is required and rapid I/0 transfers are needed, minicomputers may well be more effective than their large counterparts.

How, then, are minicomputers defined?

It appears that any attempt at defining minicomputers must be in terms of their price, performance, and applications. Let us, therefore, consider these factors.

Characteristics of Minicomputers: Minicomputers have often been defined by their price rather than by their performance. As recently as early 1969 some observers were classifying minicomputers as those with a minimum-system cost of less than $50 000. Today a more reasonable figure would be $20 000 and some people may press for $15 000 or even $10 000.

Nevertheless, considering the performance of minicomputers offered today, it is found that they typically have fast processing rates, relatively short word lengths, and versatile input–output structures [2] (Figs. 3 and 4). Their cost is generally related to word length, scope of the instruction set, and the degree of versatility of the input–output structure.

CHARACTERISTICS	FEATURES AVAILABLE		
	MINIMUM	AVERAGE	MAXIMUM
INPUT/OUTPUT			
PROGRAMMED I/O CHANNEL	ONE	ONE	ONE
I/O WORD SIZE (BITS)	EIGHT	EIGHT OR 16	18
PRIORITY INTERRUPT LINES	ONE	ONE STD, UP TO 64 OPTIONAL	TWO STD, UP TO 256 OPT
DIRECT MEMORY ACCESS	NO	OPTIONAL	OPTIONAL
I/O MAXIMUM TRANSFER RATE (DMA)	125,000	400,000 TO 600,000	1,000,000
OTHER FEATURES			
REALTIME CLOCK	NO	OPTIONAL	STANDARD
POWER FAIL/RESTART	OPTIONAL	OPTIONAL	STANDARD
LARGEST DISK (MEGABITS)	NO	2.1 TO 9.0	183.6
ASSEMBLER	YES	YES	YES
COMPILER	NO	BASIC FORTRAN	BASIC FORTRAN, STD FORTRAN, ALGOL
OPERATING SYSTEM	NO	NO	REALTIME, FOREGROUND/ BACKGROUND
PURCHASE PRICE			
COMPUTER WITH 8K WORDS OF CORE AND TELETYPE ASR-33	$8200	$12K TO $15K	$24K

Fig. 4. Typical ranges of minicomputer characteristics.

The central processors are single-address binary processors with negative numbers expressed as two's complements. The processors vary the most with respect to the number of accumulators provided, the instruction sets implemented, the instruction decoding technique, and interrupt handling capability. Most processors have an instruction set of 64 to 100 instructions; some have many more, to a maximum of over 200. Many of the hardware features of larger processors have been carried over to minicomputer designs and can be recognized in the tabulation of Figs. 3 and 4.

Examining the typical applications of minicomputers, it is discovered that the minimal system is usually dedicated to control functions, data acquisition, and display. Typically, these systems are used for monitoring and control of a process, or monitoring a process and displaying appropriate data for manual control. The data reduction and analysis capabilities of the average equipment imply longer word lengths, a more comprehensive instruction set, larger primary memory, and usually a need for a secondary store as well as more sophisticated display equipment. The display equipment may be a printer, an x-y plotter, or a cathode-ray tube to generate hard copy and/or on-line interactive displays. The maximal equipment is usually dedicated to perform all of the functions of the lower-type systems and is programmed to operate in a time-sharing mode, supporting foreground and background modes. Thus, an operator may interact with the system in the background mode, e.g., for program development, as it monitors and controls instrumentation in the foreground mode.

It is clear that no simple definition of minicomputers exists. Even the characteristics of contemporary minicomputers have a wide range. Still, computers whose characteristics fall within the ranges summarized in Figs. 3 and 4, and which are used in dedicated real-time type of applications, are generally classified as minicomputers.

II. The Impact of Component Technology on Minicomputers

Technological Background

In the years since World War II, electronics has passed through two distinct periods and has entered a third one, namely that of integrated electronics.

The first period centered on the vacuum tube. It reached its culmination and simultaneously its economic limitations in the 1950's. The second period was introduced by the invention of the transistor. The basic building blocks of the transistor-based technology are transistors, diodes, resistors, capacitors, and inductors. These discrete components are mounted by mass-soldering on the ubiquitous printed circuit board.

Transistor technology developed at a rapid rate in the decade beginning in 1950, but leveled off in subsequent years. For example, frequency response increased from 10 to 10 000 Mc, failure rate per billion element hours decreased from 50 000 to about 1, and the cost per transistor dropped from about $10 to about $0.10.

The ensuring lower rate of improvement in transistor technology has been offset by the great strides made by integrated electronics, which requires extensions and refinements in the processes of transistor technology. A side-by-side comparison of discrete silicon transistor manufacture and silicon integrated circuit manufacture may best illustrate the significance of contemporary integrated electronics.

Both fabrication processes start with a slice of epitaxial silicon. For discrete silicon transistors this slice may pass through about 88 consecutive steps of diffusion, etching photolithography, and various cleaning operations. The fully processed slice will then contain some 3000 transistors that are separated to produce 3000 individual chips. Each chip is then further processed to produce a hermetically sealed discrete transistor. This "packaging" process is very costly compared to the intrinsic cost of the transistor chip.

In the fabrication of silicon integrated circuits the same kinds of processing steps are performed except that the number of steps is about 50 percent larger. The processed slice will typically contain 20 000 devices (i.e., 400 integrated circuits each containing about 50 elements). It is separated into individual integrated circuits each of which contains integral leads that permit easy attachment to thin-film substrates. Each integrated circuit is fully protected both chemically and metallurgically against the atmosphere and does not require an expensive protective can. Integration, in addition to reducing size and cost, also reduces the failure rate by orders of magnitude.

The level of integration of digital electronics has moved from one functional circuit, such as a gate or an amplifier, per chip to the dozen circuits per chip now found in computers. Several tens of circuits per chip are already a proven reality, and serious work is progressing towards the 100 or more circuits per chip area. The projected number of circuits per chip available commercially appears to grow at the rate of one order of magnitude every six years.

The statistics are even more impressive when expressed in terms of actual components per chip. Considering the logic in delivered machines, the density today is of the order of 100 components per chip, and is growing at the rate of about an order of magnitude every four years. Production announcement represents a density of about an order of magnitude higher and advanced development is attempting still another order of magnitude of higher density. Expressed in circuits per square inch, the level of integration used today is about 100 and has grown about two orders of magnitude over the past ten years, starting with a density of 0.1 circuit/in² in 1960 with discrete components, and progressing through a density of 2 circuits/in² with hybrid integrated circuits[1] (1964), 10 circuits/in² with integrated circuits (1967), and is expected to reach 200 circuits/in² with larger scale integration in 1972. Regardless of the degree of integration eventually reached, this approach already offers the possibility of reducing circuit costs to a few cents per circuit, of improving reliability, and of offering the ultimate in high-speed performance.

However, to obtain low-cost integrated devices, production must reach sufficient volume to make the startup cost insignificant. These startup costs include design and debugging, generation of test procedures, paperwork for production control, and the effects of initial inefficiency in making a new product. Today, for example, it can easily cost between $10 000 and $100 000 to develop a 50-circuit chip and put it into manufacture. Unfortunately, however, the greater the number of circuits on a chip, the more difficult it becomes to obtain multiple usage of this chip and thus achieve high production levels. This implies the existence of an optimum scale of integration for a given situation.

Two approaches are being pursued to enhance the potential of integrated devices. The startup cost is being reduced by computer-aided design methods and simplified/automated fabrication techniques, thus reducing the prove-in volume requirement. The other approach aims at defining standardized generic functional components from which logic systems can be constructed. Memories are one such standardized component. The benefit afforded by applying integrated electronics to such a standardized component is very substantial, especially where the restriction imposed by such a standardization is negligible or ignorable.

The significant improvements in digital electronics have been the key contributors to bringing down the cost of the early compact aerospace minicomputers, and thus opening up the explosive commercial market for minicomputers which we are currently witnessing.

Functional Minicomputer Devices

Which Functional Devices?: Since the advent of in-

[1] This term is often used to mean the combination of silicon ICs and thin-film components.

tegrated electronics technology, several schemes have evolved for the utilization of large arrays to their full potential. In a common and straightforward approach the designer restricts himself to the equipment under consideration at the moment. Faced with only a limited set of problems, he has little difficulty specifying the integrated array types that will efficiently complete the design. While the results are quite encouraging for specific cases, the drawbacks of any mass adoption of these techniques are obvious. This, the so-called "custom approach," would require the semiconductor manufacturer to be responsive to each customer by making numerous low-output production runs of highly specialized devices. The per-unit cost to the user, for his own efforts as well as those of the manufacturer, would be quite high because of the latter's inability to spread initial costs over many devices. Also, the complexity of 100-gate-plus arrays is such that it is difficult to substitute one for another (with efficient results). This would severely limit the off-the-shelf capabilities for both user and manufacturer.

An obvious solution to these problems is the introduction of a small set of standard, integrated, functional components. Semiconductor suppliers, making tentative advances into integrated circuits product marketing, have already proposed such devices as adders, counters, and shift registers. However, this represents the solution to only part of the overall problem. A design heavily committed to the use of these devices must fall back on hybrid circuitry using elementary integrated circuits for the large remainder of the circuitry. The reason is that adders, counters, registers, and other orderly, well-defined functions represent the regions of the system with the highest ratios of logic gates to the number of pins through which the functional unit is accessed (i.e., gate-to-pin ratios). After these portions are lifted out of the system, the remainder is characterized by very low gate-to-pin ratios, notably within the control and data routing functions. Unable to continue satisfying the integrated electronics design criteria of high gate-to-pin ratios, the designer must look to more standard (i.e., discrete) components. Unfortunately, for the problem of partitioning logic systems to make best use of integrated electronics, any proposed solution that lacks a total system approach tends to drift toward this pitfall.

Two conceptually different approaches to partitioning are being pursued today: bit slicing and functional partitioning. To illustrate the difference, consider the data portion of the computer. In functional partitioning one may specify an adder as one integrated array, registers as another, a shift register as a third, and so forth. On the other hand, in bit slicing one would design an integrated array consisting of a combined one- or two-bit adder, registers, shift registers, etc., then build up his system from this chip type according to the desired word length.

The bit-slice approach has resulted in some notable advantages, particularly the ability to achieve very high gate-to-pin ratios and implement systems using a small number of different array types. However, bit-sliced modules appear to be quite system-dependent [3]. Functional partitioning has also been applied successfully. Combining bit slicing and functional partitioning gives the approach the versatility to implement both complex and simple systems of different word lengths with equal efficiency [3].

There appears to be general agreement that control functions are more difficult to modularize than functions related to data operations. Micromemory control techniques using READ-ONLY memories with built in sequencer and instruction registers lend themselves well to being partitioned into the large modules necessary for integrated implementations. These modules have a well ordered structure that makes them easier to produce than complex circuit arrays. Control functions in this form are then amenable to reproduction in large quantities of identical units.

A representative set of functional devices for minicomputers then could be: register storage, general logic, arithmetic logic, input/output, micromemory counter, microinstruction register, microarray, scratch pad memory, up/down counter, switch, and mainframe memory. Which set of functional devices will eventually form the staple components of minicomputer manufacturers remains to be seen. In any case, the assumption that integrated functional devices will be used in large quantities, and produced with improved manufacturing techniques, suggests a declining cost trend. As the costs decrease, the speed range of bipolar integrated circuits will continue to improve. The benefit from this speed improvement is likely to be small since present bipolar circuit speeds are more than adequate for most minicomputer applications. Typical MOS integrated circuit speeds, which generally are significantly lower than those of bipolar circuits, can be expected to improve by about a factor of 2 to 5 during this period. As the speed of MOS circuits increases, the construction of all-MOS high-performance processors will become feasible. However, present MOS circuit performance is already adequate for many applications.

Partititioning of minicomputers for the most effective use of integrated electronics illustrates the economic criterion underlying the engineering design for integrated embodiments. The conventional criterion of minimizing the number of components is changed by the introduction of the integrated electronic technology, with modularity (or commonality) becoming more important and with component count becoming less important.

Mainframe Memories: It turns out that more than half of the cost of the central processing unit of most contemporary computers is attributable to primary memory. Usually, the more sophisticated computers come with a larger minimum size of primary memory. Historically, the technology used in memory systems (magnetic devices) has been sufficiently different from the technology used in the rest of the mainframe of computers (semiconductor devices) that memory systems have become important functional devices.

Three memory technologies appear to be of greatest importance at this time. They are core, thin film (including plated wire and planar thin film), and semiconductor (including bipolar and MOS integrated circuits). Core memories will be challenged by plate wire and semiconductor memories in the immediate future.

Semiconductor memories promise to offer both cost and performance advantages over core memory. They also offer the potential for higher speed and smaller size than magnetic thin-film memories. However, the power level will generally be higher, although not excessively so. For the near term, the performance of semiconductor memories will be the most important consideration. The costs initially are higher than those for core memories, but are expected to drop rapidly.

Magnetic Memories: Through all of the 1960's, magnetic storage elements have been the predominant memory devices in all classes of digital computers. The speed/cost ratio improvement of several hundred to one that has been accrued during the 60's by system designers using ferrite core systems makes the core a rapidly moving target for any new technology. Core memories remain an elusive cost target due to continued improvements, foremost of which are trends toward two- and three-wire stack designs, radical unitized packaging, and the use of integrated circuits.

Core memories achieve about 0.5- to 5-μs cycle times and are expected to realize a factor-of-two improvement over the next five years. The cost per bit is a strong function of the size of the memory; it is halved for every order-of-magnitude increase in bit capacity (e.g., 3 cents/bit for 100 000-bit capacity in 1970).

The higher speed, nondestructive READ-OUT (NDRO) capability, and lower power offered by plated wire provide a flexibility for accommodating a variety of system storage needs which cores cannot match. Plated wire has the greatest advantages relative to ferrite cores in applications requiring less than 500-ns cycle time. It is in these areas that the initial growth of plated wire will be concentrated.

Neither plated wires nor ferrite cores adequately satisfy the economical integrated-circuit compatibility requirement today. The plated wire bit current, 40 to 50 mA for 5 mil diameter wire, will drop to 15 to 25 mA as 2- to 2.5-mil diameter wire is introduced. The plated wire word drive current, 800- to 1000-mA turns today, can be reduced to 250- to 350-mA turns by several means. The length of the bit will be reduced from 50 to 60 mils to 20 to 25 mils. Ferrite core memories have a decided advantage in bit packing density compared to production plated wire memories. Ferrite core mats achieve 2500 bits per square inch relatively easily, while production plated wire memory planes are 550 to 1000 bits per square inch. Plated wire memories exhibit a temperature coefficient (approximately -0.07 to -0.1 percent per degree centigrade) that is substantially less than the temperature coefficient of standard ferrite cores.

In the past, commercial magnetic memories have not been designed to minimize power consumption. However, power consumption will become increasingly important as memory system prices continue to decrease and storage capacity increases. It has been estimated that the lifetime cost of providing power to the system and removing the heat from the system and from the room ranges from $2 to $10 per watt.

This is no longer a negligible cost factor. For example, if extended main memory prices drop to 0.5 cent per bit, then 1 mW per bit raises the total cost to twice the acquisition cost. In this context, the reduced power consumption of plated wire memories compared to that of core memories (typically 1/25) may become a significant advantage for plated wire memories.

Semiconductor Memories: Improved processing, outstanding photolithography, and refined circuit configurations have resulted in active semiconductor memory cells having array densities outstripping both core and plated wire. The advantages of semiconductor memories include exceptional speed, nondestructive READ-OUT operation, smaller size, (possibly) lower power, compatibility with processor electronics, and realization of low-cost memory modules. These are the stepping stones for the adaptability to provide a universal memory potential that magnetics cannot meet.

Semiconductor technology offers a single-technology approach which can combine storage, decoding, and sensing on the same chip. This feature promises to have significant advantages in terms of cost, reliability, and flexibility.

Probably the strongest single argument that exists for the single technology realization is that by this means the total number of off-chip interconnections in the memory system is minimized. Such interconnections not only make a major contribution to failure rate, but contribute significantly to integrated circuit operating costs today. Their minimization thus is a long step toward lower initial cost and improved realiability of operation— probably the two most important measures of merit for a mainframe memory system once adequate speed is achieved.

Reliability has been one of the big problems of semiconductor memory. Field data are becoming available to indicate that 10^8 hours or more of mean time-to-failure for interconnected integrated-circuit chips can be assured. Store reliability appreciably greater than actual device reliability is possible through the use of error-correcting codes.

Store volatility is another aspect of the system reliability problem. Information is lost from a semiconductor memory when the power supply is interrupted. This limitation may eliminate semiconductor memories for certain applications, but appropriate system design may satisfy the recovery requirements of many applications. One solution is a backup power supply; another solution is the provision of a nonvolatile backup store; still another solution may be the development of nonvolatile semiconductor memories such as the experimental metallic nitride semiconductors (MNOS) memories.

Thus, it appears that the overall system reliability may be comparable for magnetic and semiconductor memories of comparable storage capacities.

READ-ONLY Memories: READ-ONLY memories find two dominant applications in computer mainframes: microprogramming and macroprogramming applications.

In the microprogramming application a READ-ONLY memory is used to interpret the instruction set by controlling the sequence of logical operations required (for example, for an add operation or a shift operation).

Fast READ-ONLY memories, at a cost comparable to or less than that of the much slower READ-WRITE memories, offer the capability of implementing sophisticated instruction sets, arithmetic routines, and major service programs in minicomputers using standardizable register banks and transfer gates. Bipolar READ-ONLY memories of 1024-bit size and with access times of less than 50 ns are now available. They permit implementations of instruction sets that have performance speeds comparable to those realizable with the more costly, fully customized handwired approach. Testing of computers whose instruction set is realized through a micropogrammed READ-ONLY memory is greatly facilitated.

In the macroprogramming application a READ-ONLY memory essentially replaces a portion of the main memory with a fixed rather than an erasable memory. The READ-ONLY memory then contains instructions in the same sense as would an erasable memory.

There are many variations for implementation of READ-ONLY memories. One possibility, which is applicable to both magnetic and semiconductor technologies, is to have the wiring pattern for input and output fixed to reflect the appropriate macro- or microprogram. This approach requires a new ROM if programming changes are made, and represents a disadvantage if frequent program changes are expected.

This problem can be avoided by using HARD-WRITE memory, such as the piggy-back twistor. In this approach new micro- or macroprograms are electrically written into memory and, once they are written, permit the memory to be operated in a READ-ONLY mode. Another possibility is the capstor-type memory where a removable mask contains the program.

Implementation of all of these types of ROM in semiconductor form is being pursued. The most important candidates at this time appear to be READ-ONLY diode matrix memories and semiconductor memories.

The Technological Impact

The rapid advances in component technology have had a spectacular effect on computer technology. Over the last decade, computer speeds have increased by a factor of 1000; costs of computation have decreased by a factor of the order of 500; and the memory capacity of digital computers has gone up by some three orders of magnitude. This remarkable technological progress has made possible the construction of low-cost and stripped-down computers, i.e., minicomputers, whose performance characteristics still make them most suitable for a wide range of applications and, despite their very general capabilities, highly competitive with specialized digital controllers in terms of both cost and performance.

Since their introduction, the cost/performance ratio of minicomputers has itself improved by two orders of magnitude as a result of advances in integrated circuit, core memory, and packaging technologies. There is little doubt that the trend toward even more cost-effective minicomputer processor hardware will continue in the foreseeable future.

The potential of integrated electronics will have an increasingly beneficial effect on the cost/performance ratio of minicomputers as 1) the fixed costs associated with circuit designs are reduced, 2) the minicomputer manufacturers become larger so as to justify increasingly automated production facilities, and 3) an increasing standardization of product and functions is achieved.

In particular, the impact of semiconductor memory upon machine architecture will be great. As a result of the higher performance of semiconductor memory, the need for general registers which serve primarily as speed buffers for processors will be diminished. Also, in those instances where input/output buffers have been incorporated into the channel controllers, it will be feasible for many systems to make a direct data transfer to main memory. For minimum-cost systems it may also be possible to incorporate various control registers into the main memory. Thus it appears that integrated electronics may remove the designation of the mainframe memory as a historic distinct functional computer device.

It has been speculated [4] that an entire processor may be fabricated on a single chip in the not too distant future. The ultimate cost of such a processor, utilizing MOS technology with 1000–16 000 components per chip, may be in the $10 range. A computer can then be constructed from such a processor chip by combining it with a READ-ONLY memory and a semiconductor READ/WRITE memory.

Before a fully integrated processor is produced, however, there will appear an ever-increasing number of minicomputers [5] which will employ varying degrees of integration based on the availability of a rapidly growing number of integrated circuit devices which challenge the ingenuity of the system designer.

In the meantime, however, the rapid and significant advances in integrated component technology also appear to be causing a profound change in the structure of the component suppliers and computer manufacturers. The use of increasingly sophisticated integrated circuits has made the computer manufacturer increasingly dependent on proprietary integrated circuits to produce unique computer systems; the computer systems differ less in the combination of components used and more in the types of components employed. This has the effect that computer manufacturers tend to build up their own integrated electronics capabilities (this trend is sometimes referred to as a downward integration). Concerned by the gradual erosion of the dependence of their customers, the integrated circuit suppliers are expanding their systems development efforts, going even as far as developing their own computers, which puts them in direct competition with their customers (this is sometimes called upward integration). The big question today is how the computer manufacturers will deal with the suppliers-turned-competitors. It is quite conceivable that both computer manufacturers and components suppliers will gradually become largely self-sufficient suppliers of integrated systems of increasing sophistication that are aimed at different market segments.

III. Systems Architecture for Minicomputers

Functional Description of Minicomputers

General Sequence of Events: A typical mainframe consists of a memory section, a processing section, and an input–output (I/O) section. Each of these sections contains several registers; in particular, the processing section includes a program counter, an accumulator, an accumulator extension register, and one or more index registers. All of these registers are connected by several data buses.

During program execution, an instruction is moved from the location pointed to by the program counter into the instruction decoder. Depending on the instruction fetched, a data item is moved from one register (or memory) to another register (or memory) via the data buses; also, the instruction decoder may cause the data to be modified or combined with previously moved data. The instructions recognized by the instruction decoder are executed by the processor control unit which sequentially operates a set of transfer gates and thus implements the instructions. When the execution of the instruction has been completed, the program counter is advanced and the next instruction is fetched for execution.

The traditional control units are fixed wired. The use of microprogrammed control units is relatively new in minicomputers though old in concept. Microprogramming is the employment of a stored program module for the control unit of the CPU rather than the traditional fixed wired control unit. Within the stored program control unit, a set of microcommands is stored. These microcommands, when addressed from either a microprogram location counter or from a microcommand register, are decoded and executed. The microcommands normally perform elementary processing operations and are each executed in one machine clock cycle.

Stored Program Control Unit: In computers which use the microprogram technique, basic operations are determined by a stored program rather than by hard wiring. Since the stored program can be easily changed or expanded to suit the application, the hardware of the computer need never be altered. The result is a more flexible system at a lower cost.

Microprogrammed computers generally operate from two levels of stored programs: 1) a microlevel stored control unit, and 2) a macrolevel using commands in core to specify the microcommands performed by the control unit. In the latter a macrolevel instruction that can be

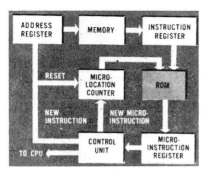

Fig. 5. Lower cost, more versatile computers are feasible through expanded use of ROMs for microprogramming. Computer instructions and counter supply address inputs to ROM, whose outputs are used as microinstructions.

user-generated calls a set of microcommands in the stored control unit to perform a specific function of subroutine. Hence, a microprogrammed computer is emulating the operation of a fixed control unit.

While the microprogram technique can be applied to the entire computer operation, present usage is a combination of hard-wiring and stored programs. The microprogram storage unit typically consists of a READ-ONLY memory (ROM) since the stored program usually need not be electrically alterable during normal operation.

Minicomputers that use ROM to store microprograms attain a high degree of flexibility but sacrifice some speed in conventional instruction execution. Despite the high speed of ROM (typically 100-ns cycle time) and the high speed of microinstruction execution times, the total instruction execution time increase since a conventional instruction consists of several microinstructions. However, the user can define an instruction set specific to his application. This may mean that the overall throughput for the specific job may be increased and the core storage requirement decreased. Microprogramming is a technique for gaining faster execution of compound instructions without paying the price of linkages, jumpsave, and other features required in traditional general-purpose software.

Use of a ROM in a microprogram is illustrated in Fig. 5. Here, the combination of the computer instruction and a counter are used as the address inputs to a ROM and the resulting outputs are used as microinstructions. The full microprogram sequence begins with an instruction that has been read from memory at the location specified by the address in the address register. The operations code of the instruction selects the required microprogram by addressing a particular portion of the ROM. The first output word of the ROM (the microinstruction) is gated into the microinstruction register and an operation is performed in the control unit. If the result of the operation is incomplete, the control unit advances the microlocation counter and the new address selects a second microinstruction, and so on.

When the control unit completes its operations, it requests a new instruction by advancing the address in the

address register, then resets the microlocation counter so that it is prepared for the next microprogram sequence.

Program Execution Interrupts:

Interrupt Capabilities: Interrupt systems equip minicomputers for quick response to input/output demands or other events that require immediate attention. A priority interrupt system provides immediate response, conserves memory space, and improves program running speed. The alternative technique of scanning (polling) devices in sequence is much more expensive in terms of program length, memory space, and program running time, and does not provide immediate response.

Interrupt systems for minicomputers are quite extensive and consist of internal and external interrupt levels. The internal interrupt levels include power fail-safe, memory parity, memory protect, and real-time clock interrupt levels. Usually, the memory protect level can be inhibited from the operator's console, but the other internal interrupt levels cannot. The basic external interrupt system usually consists of one or two levels; additional interrupt levels can be added in modules of two, four, or eight levels providing maximums from 16 to 256 levels.

External interrupt levels are under program control and can usually be disarmed or inhibited individually. A disarmed interrupt level ignores an interrupt signal; an inhibited interrupt level stores an interrupt signal but does not cause an interrupt until the inhibition has been removed.

Interrupt Sequence: Usually the interrupt procedure implemented in the hardware consists of suspending processing and completing a set of instructions out of sequence; the interrupt level provides the core address of the first instruction to be executed out of sequence. If the interrupt servicing subroutine consists of only one instruction, the contents of the program counter are not changed, and the interrupted program is continued after the interrupt instruction is finished. If the interrupt servicing subroutine consists of several instructions, however, the instruction stored at the location addressed by the interrupt instruction must be a transfer of control to the interrupt servicing subroutine. The interrupt procedure then executes a transfer of control instruction to an indirect address in a core location selected by the interrupt level. Sometimes the procedure includes storing the processor status before transferring control to the interrupt servicing subroutine.

Some hardware provision is made to block out all interrupts until the interrupt servicing subroutine has stored the status of the processor, contents of the accumulator, index register, program counter, overflow, etc. In addition, hardware provision is made to block out all interrupt levels of an equal or lower priority until the current interrupt level is released by instruction.

Functional Description of the Minicomputer Sections

The Memory: Contemporary machines use core memory exclusively for implementation of the memory section. Memory sizes range from 1000 to 65 000 words and memory speeds from 0.5 to 8 μs. Options offered for memory include a parity check bit per word, which serves to detect read errors, and a memory protect bit, which prohibits writing into selected memory sections except when the computer operates in a restricted supervisory mode. The memory protect method is used to permit partitioning memory into separate banks, each containing a separate program, so that execution of a program in one bank cannot affect the program located in an adjacent memory bank. Another implementation of the memory protect feature is by upper- and lower-bound registers that define the protected core area. This feature also includes a set of instructions that is effective only if the machine operates in its supervisory mode and that permits setting up the protective fences. An associated interrupt level signals a protect violation or a parity failure.

Three memory addressing modes are customarily made available: 1) direct addressing by which the memory location specified in a memory reference instruction is accessed, 2) indirect addressing by which the location specified in a memory reference instruction contains a pointer to (i.e., address of) the location to be accessed, and 3) indexed addressing by which the content of an (index) register is added to the direct or indirect address to establish the effective address of the location to be accessed.

The entire core is usually addressable via indexing and/or indirect addressing. In some cases, an address extension register or double word length instruction permits direct addressing of all of core. Indirect addressing is usually recursive (chaining of indirect addresses) with indexing allowed at each level.

Because of the short wordlengths, most minicomputers use a paging technique to address core by a one-word memory referencing instruction. The length of the pages is defined by the number of core locations that the address field can specify. These instructions can directly address the local page that contains the instruction and/ or a specified base page in core. This base page is usually the first page in core. Some machines permit specifying the location of this page by a page register. Despite the paged use of memory, overlapped timing for the pages is not used nor is it used for the banks of partitioned memories.

The 8-bit minicomputers differ little in addressing capabilities from the 16-bit machines because the memory reference instructions of the 8-bit machines use two words per instruction instead of one.

Several minicomputers include a READ-ONLY memory (ROM) either as basic hardware or as optional equipment. ROMs have a shorter cycle time than core memories or even semiconductor READ/WRITE memories. The ROMs are used in two different ways: 1) to store, protect, and decrease the execution time of real-time programs, executive routines that allocate the processor time to different application programs, and frequently used subroutines, and 2) to store microprograms that define the processor's instruction set.

The Processor: As mentioned before, the processor section typically consists of general registers, the arithmetic logic, and a control section which can use either microprogrammed or hardwired logic hardware. The principal variations in contemporary processors are in the number of registers provided, the instruction set implemented, the instruction decoding technique, the interrupt handling capability, and the bus arrangement. The general registers may vary from 3 to 256. In most cases the processor operates in a word mode, but in some machines the unit processed is a byte with the unit stored in a memory register being one or two bytes. Instruction sets implemented by the control unit in combination with processing units range from a very rudimentary set with functions such as multiplication, division, and floating point available only in software to a complex set which is a subset of that for the IBM 360 system. The instruction sets provided are discussed in more detail in the section on processor operational capabilities.

Two distinct bus structures are used. In the type I structure [6] a multiplicity of buses interconnect memories, accumulators, arithmetic units, instruction and index registers, and other key elements (see Fig. 6). In the more recently introduced type II structure [7], [8], often referred to as a Unibus structure, all the key elements are attached to two buses, i.e., the source and destination buses (see Fig. 7).

The type I structure is not as functionally oriented as the type II structure. In the former structure, the processor is primarily oriented to accumulate data from a subsystem, perform arithmetic calculations on it, and return

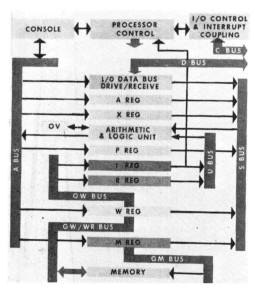

Fig. 6. Typical type I architecture using four buses. The following seven registers are provided in this example. The accumulator (A) and index register (X) are the principal registers used for working storage. Most instructions which operate on data (operands) make use of these two registers and the arithmetic logic unit. The instruction counter (P) holds the instruction address. Registers R, W, and M work in connection with the memory.

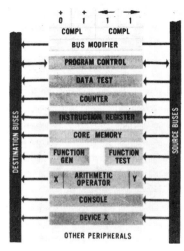

Fig. 7. The elements are brought outside the actual processor, and all computer devices are connected across the same bus structure as the devices to be controlled [7]. The bus modifier provides a programmable path that permits taking data from any input device and moving to any output device, and performing operations on the data as they pass from one device to the other. Program control provides the signals that indicate when a source device is to send data, sets up the route the data are to follow, and specifies the destination device that is to receive the data.

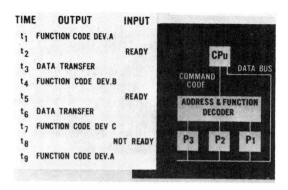

Fig. 8. Fully sequential I/O scheme. The left side of the illustration functionally indicates the sequence of events for a typical I/O operation. The right side shows a representative implementation. The peripheral devices (P_i) are enabled for I/O by the decoder circuitry. Data transfer takes place by the data bus.

the results. It was not conceived in terms of controlling and sequencing activities that may not involve mathematics at all. In fact, the user of a type I minicomputer must program control systems function in terms understood by the more arithmetically oriented structure despite the fact that these terms may bear little relationship to the functional requirements. The actual programming of the control function is then often turned over to a programmer specialist who relates the systems requirements to equivalent terms that can be translated as instructions to the computer. However, in so delegating system development tasks, project control becomes more difficult and development cost increases. The type II structure has been chosen to facilitate the functional programming for control applications. This will be illustrated in the section on processor operational capabilities.

The I/O Structures:

Responsiveness of the I/O Schemes: In the many applications of minicomputers, the input and output of data is a dominant factor. Minicomputers are being used extensively for process control, data multiplexing, communication line concentration, switching, and other areas in which data are continuously transmitted between the computer and external devices. Requirements for minicomputer systems in even one I/O application area can vary greatly. For example, when multiplexing communi-

cation lines, a typical small-scale system might consist of an in-house time-sharing computer with a minicomputer front end. The minicomputer would be used to handle the communication line processing for say 10 to 30 low-speed lines, each connected to a single teletypewriter, or it can serve as a line concentrator for up to 64 full duplex lines at speeds up to 4800 bits per second.

The basic facility for transferring data between the computer and the I/O device is generally referred to as the I/O bus.

Signaling on the I/O bus may be either nonresponsive or responsive (handshaking). Nonresponsive signaling may be simpler and less costly; signals remain on the lines for a preset time (dictated by the worst anticipated conditions), and are then removed under the assumption that they have been detected at the receiving end of the bus. Responsive signal systems present data to the receiver, continuously or repetitively, until an "acknowledge" signal is returned. Advantages of the latter approach are: 1) less strict tolerance, or faster operation, 2) greater control, and 3) flexibility in adapting to variations in controller speeds or in bus lengths. Virtually all minicomputers use a responsive I/O scheme.

Two categories of responsive I/O schemes can be distinguished. They will be referred to as 1) fully sequential schemes, and 2) overlapped schemes. Most minicomputers use a combination of these schemes to match their intrinsic speed with the response rate of the I/O device.

In the fully sequential schemes (e.g., Fig. 8) an I/O operation is fully executed before the next operation is initiated. As a result the required handshaking sequence associated with a specific I/O operation is completed before the next sequence is activated. Because of the rigid handshaking protocol, most sequential I/O schemes use a hardwired I/O interface to perform the handshaking sequence within a computer instruction cycle.

The handshaking sequence associated with some I/O operations can be intrinsically slow. For example, acknowledgment of a "start I/O device" may take several

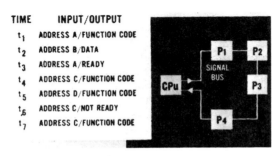

TIME	INPUT/OUTPUT
t_1	ADDRESS A/FUNCTION CODE
t_2	ADDRESS B/DATA
t_3	ADDRESS A/READY
t_4	ADDRESS C/FUNCTION CODE
t_5	ADDRESS D/FUNCTION CODE
t_6	ADDRESS C/NOT READY
t_7	ADDRESS C/FUNCTION CODE

Fig. 9. Overlapped I/O scheme. The left side of the picture functionally describes a typical I/O sequence of events. The right side suggests a representative implementation comprising a set of peripheral devices (P_i) connected in series along a signal bus.

milliseconds, which is very long compared with the microsecond cycle rate of most contemporary minicomputers. In these instances it is preferable to initiate the I/O operation and determine the success of the execution of the I/O instruction at a later time.

Using an implementation similar to that used by a fully sequential I/O scheme, the processor can determine the I/O device response by querying a register associated with the device under program control. Thus, the handshaking sequence is broken down into programmed distinct I/O operations.

The implementation of an overlapped I/O scheme shown in Fig. 9 is assuming increasing importance in communications oriented systems. All I/O devices are serially located on a common I/O bus. Each device is equipped with circuitry that recognizes the operation codes that are addressed to the device; each device is also equipped with circuitry that associates the responses with an identification code designating the device from which the response originated. In some systems, the device addresses are explicitly given (serially coded or transmitted along a parallel bus); in other systems each device is associated with a distinct time slot (time multiplexing), simplifying the decoding circuitry.

The data stream to the peripheral I/O devices is placed into an output queue from which it is transmitted to the I/O devices. The inputs from the devices are placed into a response queue from which they are fetched to be analyzed by the processor and related to the proper I/O operation instruction.

Some overlapped I/O schemes provide means for rapidly detecting specific response codes which can cause a processor interrupt. These responses can thus be promptly recognized and the proper action immediately taken. Other schemes provide means for automatically ignoring codes that merely represent a standby condition (idling codes).

Sequential I/O Schemes: The most widely used I/O schemes are of the fully sequential type. Several schemes of this type are currently offered with virtually all minicomputers. Because of their importance, these schemes will be briefly discussed.

In the sense that overall system operation is under control of the program, it may be said that all input/output transfers are also under program control. However, there are wide variations in the amount of program control necessary to effect a transfer.

Fully Program-Controlled I/O: The standard method used is a programmed party line channel. This method is under full program control. Each word is transferred on the I/O bus between a working register and the I/O device, and stored in memory by means of program instructions. Thus, the maximum data transfer rate over a programmed party line I/O channel is limited by the program overhead for servicing the I/O devices requesting service.

Data transfers performed on the standard I/O bus require program intervention for each word transferred. There are two methods for using the program to control transfers. In the first method, the transfer of each word is effected by means of a program request. The program addresses the desired I/O device and then waits until the device is ready to transmit or receive data. This delay leads to processing inefficiency. Therefore this method is resonable only in cases where the I/O data is highly disciplined (predictable and program synchronized), or where processing requirements are low.

To free the program for other tasks during the waiting period, the interrupt method is used. After the I/O device is instructed on the function to be performed, the program may continue processing until an interrupt signal is received, indicating that the device is ready for the next instruction. With this method an interrupt followed by an interrupt processing sequence are still required for each word that is transferred.

Memory Access I/O: The throughput can be increased by reducing I/O interrupts and program control of I/O transfers, i.e., both direct-processing time for the transfer and the time required for program interrupts. This reduction is obtained by employing additional equipment in which I/O transfers between peripheral devices and mainframe memory are controlled by hardware instead of by the stored program. When data is transferred directly between an I/O device and memory, program intervention is required only at the beginning and end of the transfer, or when there is a detected error. Dedicated locations in memory provide the beginning and final core addresses that define block length. Thus, it is possible to transfer large blocks of information while simultaneously processing other data. This allows relatively high-speed devices to interface to the channel for data transfer.

Three methods are used for transferring data directly between the main memory and the peripheral devices. In the first method a direct memory access channel (DMA) provides a direct data path to the memory. It permits the high-speed transfer of a contiguous block of data. Control and addressing logic are in the external device which requests service, and connection is made directly to the main memory rather than through processor registers. The DMA connection permits stealing of main memory cycles from the processing unit when the appropriate peripheral device demands service. One of two modes may be used for performing cycle stealing. One is to switch control to the DMA interface and perform a block transfer. The other is for the input–output control logic to check for a peripheral "ready" status; if the peripheral is not requesting service, control is returned to the processor until a peripheral transfer is ready. Because most minicomputers have only one memory bus, transfers via DMA suspend processing if the processor and DMA try to access memory simultaneously; the DMA channel has priority. Several devices can usually interfere to a DMA channel, but only one device can use the channel at a time.

A second interface method is direct multiplexed memory access (DMC). With this arrangement a number of peripheral devices are serviced by a hardwired input/output program that is executed when a data transfer is to occur. This program effects the data transfer by way of the standard input/output bus and associated processor registers in which the data are assembled and buffered. The multiplexor channel consists of a number of subchannels that are scanned in sequence for service or can request service by an interrupt. A priority channel is usually used to support high-speed devices.

Two pairs of core locations are dedicated to each subchannel to provide initial (or current) and limit addresses for continuous block transfers. The subchannels usually share a data buffer and current address and limit address registers.

Thus, several memory cycles are required to transfer each byte of data because the channel must automatically access memory to load the current address and limit address registers, to pack the current byte in the current word, and to restore the current address in memory. Up to six memory cycles may be required depending on the number of subchannels active, the order in which the subchannels require service, and the design of the channel. This causes the DMC to have a data rate noticeably below that of a DMA arrangement.

The third method is a block-multiplexed access method (selector channel). At any one time, only one I/O unit can access memory. The other units can gain memory access only at the end of a block transfer.

It is clear from the foregoing discussion that the hardware for memory access I/O must automatically perform memory addressing. The current address and the end of the data block must be stored and accessed. As each word of data is transferred, the current memory address is updated, and a check is made to determine if the final address has been reached. If so, an interrupt must be generated. The current address is initialized by the program at the beginning of the transfer operation as the starting address of the data transfer.

Current and final memory addresses may be stored in reserved locations of core memory or in separate external registers. The latter case results in more expansive but faster throughput. Those devices which are capable of interlacing transfers by word require a set of current and ending addresses for each device connected, or for the maximum number of devices capable of simultaneous operation.

Other registers are often provided, especially in communications oriented computers, to detect special control codes embedded within the data stream.

Since the register is associated with a control unit and is program loadable, the user has wide flexibility in his selection of criteria with which to end a data transfer and interrupt the program.

Priority Control: When a number of units are connected together on a common bus, several techniques are available for establishing priority and resolving contention between two or more units. If I/O data are disciplined, transfers can, with reasonable efficiency, be under program control. Then the selection of the I/O unit may be by any appropriate algorithm. Alternatively, if control is by means of interrupt, three basic techniques are employed, as follows.

1) A single common line is used by all I/Os to signal an interrupt. When the interrupt is allowed, the program polls each device, according to a polling table, to determine which devices are bidding. The priority is implicit in the order in which I/Os are listed in the polling table.

2) A single interrupt line is used, and a single go-ahead is used. I/O devices are connected in a daisy-chain arrangement on the go-ahead line, with priority assigned in the order of connection to the line. Higher priority units obtain access first, and when not bidding, relay the go-ahead signal to the lower priority devices in order; the device which is successful in obtaining an interrupt sends its identity on the address lines.

3) Separate interrupt lines and separate go-ahead lines are provided for each device. Contention is resolved on a priority basis by some type of hardware.

In a number of computers, priorities are program controlled by what is usually referred to as a masking instruction. This type of instruction can selectively prevent an I/O unit from generating an interrupt until the instruction is negated. This facility provides an efficient means for allowing only higher priority interrupts to interrupt lower priority interrupts.

Operational Description of Minicomputers

The Minicomputer Instructions:

The Instruction Set: Most of the operation codes of the instruction set are used for memory referencing instructions. Nonmemory referencing instructions use additional bits of the instruction word as part or all of the operation code, so the number of instructions is not necessarily small. The modification field further qualifies the instruction by defining the addressing mode (direct, indirect, and/or indexed) or specifying that the address field contains a constant (i.e., the address field contains a literal).

As discussed earlier, because of the short instruction word length, most minicomputers use a paging technique to address core. Memory-referencing instructions can directly address the page that contains the instruction and/or a base page. In this case, the address field provides an address increment. The effective address is calculated in accordance with the address mode; usually a base address of zero or the content of the program counter specify the page number (i.e., the base address) and the address field specifies the core address relative to that page. The entire core is generally addressable via indexing or indirect addressing. In some cases, an address extension register or double wordlength instruction enables directly addressing all of core.

Most contemporary processors are single-address binary processors with negative numbers expressed as two's complement. The basic instruction set of type I structure machines usually includes the arithmetic operations of fixed-point add, subtract, multiply, and divide, although multiply and divide are frequently available as optional features. Double-precision fixed-point add and subtract are frequently provided. A few of the larger machines offer floating-point hardware as an optional feature. All offer some form of logic, compare, and shift operations; many also offer byte manipulation instructions. The I/O instructions are usually very general and complex. Commonly, the I/O instruction also provides control for operational features, which are addressed as I/O devices.

General-purpose machines have a greater number of instructions available, and therefore generally have a more traditional fixed-wired processor. The controller-type machines have a more limited number of instructions and frequently rely more on microprogrammed organization to permit specialized instruction sets and user-generated macroprogrammed languages.

When a minicomputer is equipped with a memory protect feature, the instruction set includes a protected set of instructions, such as those that load the upper- and lower-bound registers or change the interrupt status and I/O instructions.

Type II structure machines could specify an instruction set akin to that of type I machines. However, recognizing the capability of transferring data directly between the various processing units of type II machines and to orient these machines more toward control applications, the instruction set consists of one main instruction: "Device X to Device Y". Provision of this type of instruction has been found to greatly facilitate certain control application programs, and provides a natural environment for recognizing the numerous I/O devices connected to type II machines.

The Instruction Format: Most 16-bit processors of type I architecture use one-word instructions with the following format (see Fig. 10): a 4- to 6-bit operation code, a 2- to 4-bit modification field, and an 8-bit address field. The 8-bit minicomputers differ little in addressing capability from the 16-bit minis because the memory

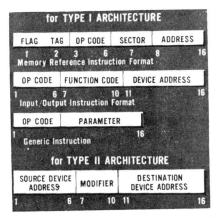

Fig. 10. Instruction formats of machines of type I and type II architectures.

referencing instructions of the 8-bit machines use two words per instruction instead of one.

Some 8-bit processors operate similar to the 16-bit processors by using two words per instruction. Others, however, require only one programmed byte for many instructions by using a byte-sharing technique. These instructions also use two bytes per instruction but only the first byte is stored as part of the program. The second byte is stored as a constant (shared byte) in a dedicated core area and is referenced by the first byte. The 8-bit instruction word format uses three or four bits as the operation code, none or one bit as a modification, and four bits as the address field.

The operation code specifies an instruction class, such as compare, and a dedicated core area of 16 locations. The address field of the instruction selects a location within the dedicated core area; the accessed core location contains the shared byte that further defines the instruction, such as type of compare and addressing technique. The shared byte does not increase the number of operation codes available, nor does it decrease the instruction execution time; it does decrease the amount of core storage required to store programs.

The instructions for machines of type II architectures have the single format shown in Fig. 10. The actual operation performed by an instruction is dependent on the unique combination of source address, destination address, and modifier. This type of format appears to naturally and meaningfully represent the typical control computer environment with its characteristically large I/O control devices. All internal and external system elements are thus directly addressable by use of a compiler-like functional language rather than a mathematically oriented language. The programmer does not have to develop the involved command sequences that will translate process data into a language that the computer can understand, and then back again into instructions that the equipment can react to. The unimpeded flow of data from device to device saves temporary storage locations for bookkeeping purposes and provides the de-

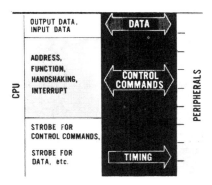

Fig. 11. Simplified I/O interface structure from the processor I/O interface to the I/O device.

signer with modularity and flexibility to adapt the computer to specific system requirements.

The Minicomputer I/O Interface Systems: Since virtually all minicomputers are used within an environment that is strongly dominated by I/O devices, the I/O interface has an operational significance similar to that of the instruction repertoire. It is through the suitable application of the instruction repertoire in combination with a properly configured I/O interface that a minicomputer is made to perform a useful function.

Functionally, the I/O bus permits the transfer of data between I/O units and the working registers of the computer. Some computers have dedicated registers for I/O transfers, reducing housekeeping requirements. The number of devices which may be connected is determined by the size of the address field of the computer's I/O instruction, and correspondingly, the number of address lines in the I/O bus. Thus, a one-byte addressing structure will accommodate 256 individual I/O units. This is, of course, a theoretical maximum and does not imply that the logic devices can be contained in one cabinet, nor that the computer has the capability of accommodating the throughput of any combination of 256 devices working simultaneously.

The I/O bus will contain communication lines for the following purposes (see Fig. 11).

1) Data output lines for transferring data from the computer to the device, and data input lines for transferring data from the device to the computer. Transfers may be one word at a time or in multiples or submultiples of a word.

2) Output address lines for enabling the computer programs to select one of the I/O devices connected to the bus, input address lines for enabling an I/O device to identify itself to the program, function lines with which the program designates the functions to be performed by the selected I/O device, status lines whereby the device indicates to the computer program its status of busy, ready, etc., program interrupt lines with which devices signal the program to request an interrupt, parity error lines whereby a device indicates to the program the detection of an error, and various miscellaneous control func-

tions such as setting and clearing of interrupt mask, system reset.

3) Timing lines whereby the device operations are synchronized.

To reduce costs, some of the above functions may be combined on the same lines. For example, the data lines are often used also for the device address and the function information. Additional signal lines are then used to indicate the type of data present. The time-multiplexing of lines by different pieces of information achieves lower cost at the expense of slower operation.

To connect an I/O device to the computer I/O interface, a device controller is required. Quite a large set of signal leads may have to be connected to facilitate the handshaking sequences of a responsive I/O scheme [9].

IV. Software Systems for Minicomputers

Overview of System Software

System software is designed to assist the user in program preparation and in system initialization and operation. For program preparation, an assembly language plus various aids to the programming of the machine are usually available including trace, editing, breakpoint, debug, and linkage routines. Quite a few manufacturers also supply a basic FORTRAN compiler to aid the user in developing arithmetic programs, and some also provide a standard FORTRAN compiler. For system initialization and operation, the manufacturers customarily make available such aids as peripheral operating systems, real-time monitors, partitioned (multiprogramming) operating systems, loader and utility routines, machine diagnostics, and restart/fallback routines.

Assembly languages vary in structure from one machine to another. Most assembly languages are indications of the specific machine's overall hardware architecture and logic. An increasing number of assembler systems for minicomputers that run on large general-purpose computer systems are becoming available. This avoids the necessity of equipping the minicomputer systems with general-purpose I/O devices that are usually not needed except for program development. Some of these systems are simulator packages for larger machines which permit program development for the minicomputer directly in the assembly language of the large machine, and thus make conveniently available the sophisticated macro-assembler capabilities of these large-system assemblers. Many of these systems have been derived from the compiler systems used for programming the large computer by providing suitable pre- and post-processors.

Efficient compiler operation is difficult to realize in small machines, and virtually impossible in 4000 words of core. Most minicomputer compilers require 8000–12 000 words of core. This represents a greater cost to the buyer for the use of a compiler facility, and makes more attractive the use of compilers that are operational on large machines of computer centers. It should be noted that while many of the translators are termed compilers, many are actually interpreters; in these the input code is translated to an intermediate language that is interpreted during the execution of the program. The advantage of this approach is that less time is required during compilation and less storage is necessary for intermediate and final forms of the translated code. However, the storage and compilation time savings are paid for by the increased execution time characteristic of interpretive systems.

Applications Software

Today, application libraries contain program modules or subroutines written for control of certain laboratory instruments, I/O interface routines, typesetting machines, graphic displays, and specific industrial processes. Despite the contribution of the large manufacturers, most application libraries are user generated and supplied through user associations.

Many application programs are supplied as part of a total "turn-key" package which consists of a completely self-contained hardware/software system. Offerings exist for laboratory, data communication, industrial instrumentation, and specialized business systems.

Real-Time Monitor Systems

Motivation for a Monitor System: For many of the applications of minicomputers an operating system that supports the use of the computer is superfluous. These systems comprise program routines that aid in the preparation of application programs (i.e., assemblers and compilers), facilitate the performance of input/output operations (i.e., input/output control systems), assist in the debugging of programs (i.e., debug routines), and control the execution of individual program subsystems (i.e., executive systems, often also referred to as monitors). However, when the system operates in a real-time environment and must respond to interrupts from a number of sources, then some type of an executive system is needed.

Some recently described executive systems have advanced capabilities. Of particular interest are several systems which include a limited form of multiprogramming. Some of these permit foreground operation in real time while other activities occur in the background. For computers intended for both process control and other activities, the foreground is generally used for the control application while the background may include the compilation of programs.

The desirability of using a real-time monitor system is based on the economic advantage of sharing resources among different tasks, if possible. Considering the cost/performance tradeoff of storage devices (see Fig. 12) makes it quite apparent that whenever tasks become inactive for more than some specific time, they should be moved from the expensive high-speed mainframe memory to a much lower cost bulk storage device. Most real-time applications are structured to permit this type of reallo-

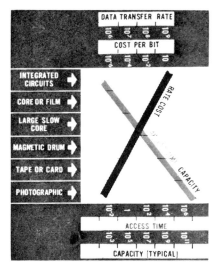

Fig. 12. Typical cost/performance relationship of store systems.

cation of task resources; the real-time monitor system is the instrument that controls the reallocation operation. The performance characteristic of such monitor systems are perhaps best outlined by a specific example.

Example of a Multiprogramming, Virtual Memory System for Minicomputers:

Overview: The system described here for illustration supports a virtual-memory addressing scheme and a multiprogramming user environment on a Honeywell DDP-516 minicomputer. The system supports virtual addressing by providing a mechanism to convert virtual addresses to real mainframe memory addresses, a task that requires memory management if the addressed data are not currently in the mainframe memory. It manages memory by moving programs and data between the mainframe memory (core storage) and bulk storage (disk) on demand; it also provides a low-level interrupt handler for I/O. The multiprogramming support is provided in the form of the tables and memory management required to automatically switch control from one user to another without interference [10].

The various programs to be executed on the computer system are stored on disk as segments. The program segments are moved to core by the monitor system whenever they become active and are to be executed.

A segment is a contiguous block of storage which cannot be subdivided. It is the basic building block of programs and data. There are eight sizes of segments from 64 to 768 words, although 64 is the most common since all data files are organized into strings of 64-word segments. When a segment is allocated, it is assigned a unique name (ID) which is used to reference this segment. To implement the system, a segment also contains words of header or overhead for memory management purposes. This includes the type of segment, such as data, program, etc., its size, and an indication of usage to determine

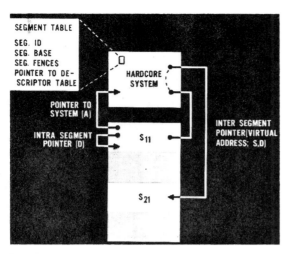

Fig. 13. Memory addressing requirements: intrasegment, absolute, and virtual addresses.

SEGMENT TABLE
SEG. ID
SEG. BASE
SEG. FENCES
POINTER TO DE-
SCRIPTOR TABLE

HARDCORE
SYSTEM

POINTER TO
SYSTEM (A)

INTRA SEGMENT
POINTER (D)

S_{11}

S_{21}

INTER SEGMENT
POINTER(VIRTUAL
ADDRESS: S,D)

which segments to throw out of core when more space is required.

The process of dynamically moving the segments from disk to core as they are referenced and back to disk when they are no longer needed is not apparent to the users, who get the impression of having a large virtual memory available. Of course, time is the price paid for not having all of a user's program and data in core at once. But in a multiprogramming environent, while one user is waiting for a referenced segment to be transferred into core, another user will be making use of the processor.

There are problems associated with this type of dynamic memory management. For example, if a segment contains a program, its internal addresses must be relocated relative to the slot it occupies (relocation) after it is transferred into core. Also a mechanism must be provided to permit one program segment to call or address another (linkage). There are also memory management problems. For example, fetching a segment from disk requires that one or more segments be pushed out of core to make room for it. These pushed segments may not be adjacent, so the system shifts the segments in core until all holes obtained by pushing segments are adjacent and can be merged. The new segment can then be transferred into core.

It has proved convenient to provide four distinct addressing modes for segments (see Fig. 13).

1) Intrasegment addresses provide a method for program segments to reference themselves.

2) Absolute addresses allow segments to reference the system.

3) Virtual addresses are the generalized intersegment linkages.

4) Direct addresses are a specialized form of intersegment linkage.

Let us discuss these addressing modes in turn.

Addressing Modes: The *intrasegment address* is the normal type of intraprogram reference—a reference to data assembled into a program or a transfer of control within the program. The problem arising from the use of segments is address relocation—the addresses must be correct wherever the segment happens to be located within core at the time it is executed. Relocation difficulties have been avoided by using the index register as a base register. The index register is loaded with the address of the currently executing segment. Thus, all memory-reference instructions and indirect addresses which point within the segment are assembled using the relative address within the segment and have the index bit set. Notice that this scheme works since indirect addresses contain the index bit which are automatically set by the assembler.

The fact that a memory-reference instruction has a 9-bit address field makes it convenient to limit program segments to 512 words, which is quite a reasonable limit considering the small size of core memory. However, larger segments may be written by making appropriate use of indirect addresses.

The *absolute address* points to a fixed core location in sector O which is part of the area of the monitor system. To reach sector O, the index bit is simply set to zero. Absolute addresses are used to identify frequently referenced information. This use will be discussed below.

Virtual addresses provide intersegment linkage. They are interpreted by software routines and consist of two words. For example, assume that segment A contains a subroutine call to segment B. At assembly time the call statement is converted into a subroutine transfer to a system CALL program, followed by a two-word virtual address. The first word of the virtual address is the identifier (ID) of segment B. The second word contains the relative address (RA) within the referenced segment and the LL field (seven bits wide). The LL field is a "loose link" which speeds up the process of locating the referenced segment; its function will be explained below. The ID contains the address where the segment is stored on disk (13 bits; $2^{13} \times 16 = 500k$) and the segment size (three bits; designating one of eight possible sizes).

The *direct address* is a more privileged addressing mode. It also acts as an intersegment link, but it is simply an absolute pointer to a segment. Hence, it must be updated each time the referenced segment is removed. This requires that the referenced segment be held in core as long as any direct address points to it. This address mode is desirable because it is much faster than virtual addresses (software interpretation), even though it is substantially more difficult to set up and take down (greater system overhead). It is, therefore, used for linkages to data which are referred to frequently.

Direct addresses are explicitly set up by the program. By command within the program, a specified virtual address is interpreted to produce a direct address that is stored in a specified location in the thread block. Simultaneously, the direct address count of the referenced segment is augmented by one. This direct address count is stored in the descriptor table which is physically located at the top of every segment (see Fig. 14). The program can then refer indirectly to the virtual address location via the address stored in the known location in the thread table. Whenever an existing direct address is removed, the direct address count in the descriptor table of the segment containing the address is decreased by one. Thus, whenever the direct address count is zero, there is no reference to that segment by direct address and therefore nothing that would require the segment to remain in core.

The Memory Management Routines of the Monitor System: The segments that currently reside in core are listed in the segment table of the monitor system (see Fig. 13). When a virtual address reference is made, a system routine searches this segment table to determine whether the particular segment (identified by its ID) is in core. This routine begins its search at the location pointed to by the LL field of the virtual address block. If the actual entry is different from that pointed to by the LL field, then the LL field is updated with the new location. The virtual address (consisting of ID and RA) is converted to the proper core location by adding the relative address (RA) to the base address found in the segment table. If control is to be transferred to this new segment, the base register is loaded with the base address, and control is transferred to the relative address within the segment. If the LL field points to the correct entry in the segment table, then the conversion from virtual address to physical core address is relatively rapid (in the order to 20 μs).

If the corresponding ID of the desired segment cannot be found in the segment table, then the segment is not in core and must be fetched from disk. Remember that the ID is a segment identifier and also contains the information required to fetch a segment from disk (location and size). This greatly facilitates the fetching operation. Upon moving the required segment into core, the proper segment table entry is made in a vacant table location.

When core is filled with segments and a new segment is required, one or more of the in-core segments must be pushed (written onto disk or discarded) to make room for the new segment. The algorithm for choosing the segments to be pushed out of core is simple and uses the descriptor tables. A sequential scan of the descriptor tables produces push candidates. The scan begins where the last push scan ended and ends when successful pushes have yielded the desired amount of space. A candidate is pushed if and only if the direct address and interrupt address counts of the descriptor table are both zero. The leading bit of the segment-type entry tells whether the segment must be written on disk when it is pushed or can be simply discarded.

When enough segments have been pushed out of core to make the desired amount of space, the holes left by the pushed out segments are gathered at the top of core. This is accomplished by moving all the segments above the holes down over the holes. Moving the segments in core requires that all direct addresses be changed to reflect the core shift. These include the segment addresses in the

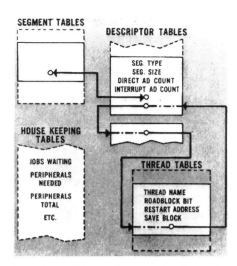

Fig. 14. Additional tables used by the monitor system for implementing a virtual memory and multiprogramming environment. The descriptor table contains such items as the segment type, segment size, direct address count, and interrupt address count.

segment table, the users' call pushdown lists, the direct addresses in the thread table, and various pointers to system subroutines which are relocatable. Since this is a long list and shifting the segments down is a long task (about 50 ms), an attempt is made to free a large block of space instead of just the amount requested. This makes the next few space requests easier to fill since a segment push and core shift are not required.

When a call to a subroutine is made, the return direct address of the calling segment and the direct address to the called segments are pushed on a list contained in the thread table, and the direct address count for the called segment is incremented. The direct address of the called segment is pushed to store the base address of that segment. This base address may be needed in combination with the return address of that segment should this segment execute a call to still another segment. Upon execution of a return, these direct addresses are retrieved from the list to find the return address from which point processing is to resume, and the count is decremented. Hence, all segments on user pushdown lists are locked into core, as are all segments pointed to by direct addresses established by the user. I/O interrupt handlers are also allowed to be segments; when in use, they are locked into core by incrementing the interrupt address count. This technique for keeping track of the return path of a series of subroutine calls intrinsically permits the use of reentrant subroutines.

At assembly time, programs refer to external segment locations by name. During load time, a name versus ID table is first constructed (during the first load pass); this table is then used to insert the virtual address into the segments (during the second load pass) and to construct the proper descriptor table entry.

Routines for Multiprogramming: Processor control is automatically allocated to various users in a multiprogramming environment. In general, time can be allocated either by roadblocks or by interrupting events such as a timer. When allocating time by roadblocks, a user is processed until he needs I/O, such as a message from a teletype, or an out-of-core segment from disk. Then he is roadblocked until I/O completion, and the monitor sequentially scans the list of inactive users until it finds one ready for further processing. Thus, service is granted on a round-robin basis, not according to some priority scheme.

The heart of the multiprogramming routines in general is a thread table (Fig. 14) which is continuously present in core. It contains an entry for each of the possible threads. Thus, a user is defined by his thread table entry. This forms the basis for the processor allocation described above.

Part of the thread table is moved into a predesignated area in core sector zero whenever a thread becomes active. The "thread save" block contains all the data and pointers required by system and user to implement pure procedure programs. Before a thread save block is moved into core sector zero, the save block in core sector zero is restored to the previous thread save block. This data movement constitutes most of the overhead involved in changing threads (in the illustrative example it takes about one ms). However, most of the roadblocks that occur when a thread is using hard-core system programs require only four of the data cells in the thread table entry to be in core sector zero. Thus, moving the thread table by parts can reduce the thread changing time by a factor of 20.

A thread can roadblock for several reasons. If the thread requests input or output, a roadblock occurs and the I/O proceeds under interrupt control. When the I/O is complete, the thread is no longer roadblocked. A thread can also address a segment which is not in core, which causes a roadblock until the segment is brought in from disk. If a thread is still roadblocked (I/O not completed yet) when its turn comes around again, it will be skipped. Thus a thread is given control only when its roadblock is removed and its turn comes around.

The desirability of moving the thread table by parts into core sector zero is shown by the following example. When an out-of-core segment is addressed, a thread could be roadblocked three or four times for things like reading the disk ID table, making space for the segment, and finally transferring the segment into core. Only after the segment is in core and the address is about to be computed is the complete thread save block required to be in sector zero.

There are several other interesting roadblocks which can occur. For example, a low-usage program may be more compact and simpler if it is not pure procedure (required by multiprogramming). This is allowed by using a GATE statement at the start of the program. The gate allows only one thread to be in the program. Any other threads that tried to enter would be roadblocked until the first thread opened the gate on its way out.

When the system is otherwise idle it scans the thread tables for a thread that is not blocked (roadblock bit = 0). When such a thread is found, its four temporary data cells are transferred to core sector zero, and the thread is restarted at the address specified by the thread table entry. This restart address is always within the hard-core system; before control is passed to an outside program segment, the thread save block is moved into core sector zero.

Routines for I/O: It is customary to perform all input/output operations under the interrupt system with the aid of the I/O table. This table contains an entry for every I/O device attached to the computer, specifiying the interrupt handler address for the device, the buffer address, the buffer size, the buffer cursor (current character pointer), escape character, the initial character, and the link to the thread using the I/O device.

When input or output are desired, the appropriate program is called with the buffer segment and the escape character supplied as arguments. The called I/O program then fills in the I/O table entry, primes the I/O device, and roadblocks the thread. When an interrupt occurs, the system gives control to the location specified by the interrupt handler address in the I/O table entry for the interrupting device.

On interrupt, a character is transferred between the I/O device and the buffer specified in the I/O table, using the buffer address and the current character pointer. When an escape character match or full buffer are encountered, the thread table pointer in the I/O table entry enables the program to clear the roadblock, and the I/O function is complete.

To accommodate a large number of different I/O devices, with only a few of them active at one time, interrupt handlers are allowed to be program segments. When an I/O device becomes active its interrupt handler segment is fetched and locked into core for the duration of its activity.

The key I/O routine for the system is the disk handler. Disk I/O is controlled by the disk I/O queue which contains a maximum of twenty entries, one for each disk I/O request. Each entry contains information such as the disk address, the core address, and the thread table pointer. A disk transfer is initiated by finding an empty queue entry and inserting the address of the appropriate disk transfer program and its arguments. The requesting thread is then roadblocked.

The disk I/O handler is an autonomous process which goes on in the background of thread processing. When a disk I/O task is finished, the current disk rotational position is read and the disk addresses on the disk I/O queue are scanned to pick the I/O operation that can be performed most immediately (i.e., the task with the least latency). Control is then given to the chosen entry's disk transfer program, which sets up the disk I/O. Upon completion of the task, the thread is unblocked using the thread table entry address in the queue entry.

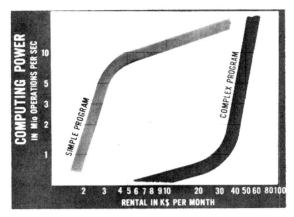

ADVANTAGES of Using a Programmable Computer Instead of Hardwired Logic

- ACCELERATED SYSTEM DEVELOPMENT
  (concurrent hardware and software design)
- HIGH GROWTH POTENTIAL
  (flexibility)
- LONGER USEFUL LIFE
  (also flexibility)
- LOWER COST
  (timesharing of and use of mass produced components)

Fig. 15. The merits of a stored program controlled system.

Fig. 16. Illustrative cost per computation for simple and complex data-processing tasks as a function of the computer system size (expressed in terms of rental cost).

V. Application Areas of Minicomputers

The Merits of Minicomputer Applications

The explosive growth of the minicomputer market is a result of employing minicomputers in a new set of applications that were previously unexploited by the larger computer manufacturers.

In the past the larger computer companies first focused most of their attention on commercial uses for data processing. These companies pioneered the application of computers in finance, manufacturing, and marketing. More recently, they have made the computer encroach progressively into the engineering design process. Initially, the computer was merely put to the task of analytical computing, taking advantage of its most obvious capability; then it was more initimately linked into the total engineering design cycle with the introduction of improved man–machine communication techniques such as graphic input devices and problem-oriented languages.

Still, the larger computer manufacturers, while they have great computer experitise, have in general had neither the knowledge nor inclination to automate real-time processes such as the control of chemical plants, the control and acquisition of data from scientific experiments, and the automation of test processes. These applications, for the most part, have been served by companies who have an understanding of the process. It is this type of organization that has pioneered the bulk of the minicomputer applications, predominantly in the area of real-time applications.

There are five compelling motivations for using a programmable minicomputer instead of specialized hardwired logic (see Fig. 15).

One of these motivations is the possibility of developing the hardware portion of the application system concurrently with the software portion through a clearly definable interface, i.e., instruction repertoire and timing diagrams. This can significantly accelerate the development of the system. Often written for a computer data installation is a simulation program that permits extensive debugging and system testing long before the hardware system is operational. This capability is a highly effective development aid, since the software system usually contains the details of the application which are always subject to substantial changes during the system

definition stages. Such a simulation program also permits the writing of diagnostic programs that can be used for the efficient debugging of the hardware system.

As a result of this limited yet crucial interdependence between the hardware and the software portions of a system, the system offers a high potential for growth, and associated with this, a much longer useful life. Experience has shown that most real-time applications are dynamic in their capabilities. Each successful application reveals other associated applications that are economically, technically, or administratively desirable. Programmable systems provide the flexibility to economically accommodate these ever-changing system requirements.

Despite their flexibility, contemporary programmable systems often even represent the lowest cost implementation. This is probably the most important motivation of all for using minicomputers. The possibility of sharing resources with a programmed system (as was discussed in Section IV) and the use of general-purpose integrated components made in large quantities (as discussed in Section II) are the two main reasons for this cost advantage.

The Economics of Minicomputer Applications

The relationship of the economy of size in computer systems has been widely discussed [11], [12]. It is generally agreed that the cost effectiveness increases with the size of the computers (see the trends depicted in Fig. 16). What is interesting to note are the points of diminishing and increasing returns. For complex programs, such as accounting, it has been shown that a minimum configuration is needed to reach a region where the economy of size is significant. However, it can be argued that for simple programs, such as that for communication which uses an elementary instruction set and few peripheral devices, a point of diminishing return clearly limits the realizable economy of size. For these applications it appears that minicomputers clearly offer the most economical solutions, since they lie below the point of diminishing return.

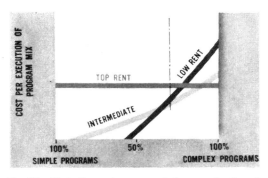

Fig. 17. Illustrative cost per computation as a function of the complexity-mix of the data-processing tasks, shown for different size computer systems.

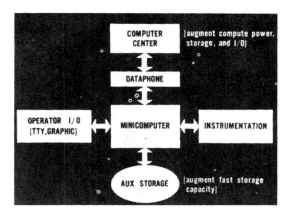

Fig. 18. Components of the most general minicomputer system configuration. The components include a minicomputer, I/O devices for man–machine communication, I/O devices for control applications (sensors and controllers), bulk storage devices, and devices for communicating with other computers.

What are the consequences of these economy-of-size trends in a data processing environment? Let us consider a hypothetical example (refer to Fig. 17).

Assume that a "low-rent" computer is operating with a program mix of which 20 percent are simple programs. Assume next that the program load doubles, requiring either two "low-rent" computers or one "intermediate-rent" machine. If the program mix ratio remains the same, then it is more economical to trade up to the larger computer. However, if the program mix increases in simple programs (e.g., 50 percent), then it is clearly preferable to add a second "low-rent" computer. In fact, it may be even more economical to replace one of these computers with a minicomputer and the other by a slightly more powerful machine specifically designed to process complex programs only. Most minicomputers handling the communication tasks of large data processing installations (i.e., front-end communication processors) are doing just that.

Typical Minicomputer Applications [13], [14]

It is useful, for discussion purposes, to group the minicomputer applications into the following categories: communication, control, laboratory, and data processing. In all of these applications the minicomputer operates in an environment where real-time responses are important. This is evident in the application of minicomputers to operating departments where these systems are already used to transact routine business (e.g., inventory control or credit verification).

Generically speaking, all minicomputer systems comprise a combination of the following elements (see Fig. 18): 1) one or a multiplicity of minicomputers that provide the central system control, 2) input/output devices that furnish an effective man–machine communication facility for such uses as operator control, 3) bulk storage, such as disk files, to augment mainframe memory so as to permit the economical implementation of effective system-operating and application software, 4) communication equipment for gaining automated access to other computer systems for such purposes as augmenting

the compute and storage capabilities of the minicomputer system, and 5) instrumentation that couples the system to other systems such as a manufacturing plant. Consideration of a few specific examples within the applications areas listed before will illustrate the use of these elements.

Data Communications Applications: The cost of small computers is decreasing faster than the cost of data communication facilities. Notwithstanding this, the utility of centralized data bases and extensive program libraries available only with large computer systems offsets the added communication line charges of using large remote-access computer systems instead of using small, locally installed systems. However, most large computers were designed basically for batch processing, and the concept of high-speed real-time interaction with these machines often has been added as an afterthought. Thus, when it is attempted to use these machines for systems such as airlines reservations, time sharing, and message switching, it is found that it is relatively easy to burden the large processor with the simple tasks of handling communication lines, attending to external interrupts, and interrogating large data files, thereby leaving no time for the basic computation that may need to be done and for which these computers were specifically designed. The realization of this has led to the off-loading of the simple jobs handled by large machines onto minicomputers which can be economically dedicated to the high-speed but relatively simple tasks and which provide a system of greater cost effectiveness.

Data communication applications can be meaningfully grouped into pure telecommunication applications where minicomputers operate as an integral part of a communication network, and preprocessing (front-end) applications where minicomputers provide a flexible interface between input/output devices and a data processing facility. In some configurations the two applications are integrated into the same minicomputer systems [15], [16].

One telecommunication application is for message switching. Available telephone communication systems using line switching facilities appear to be economically and technically inefficient to meet typical communication requirements of interconnected computer systems. The traditional method of routing information through the common-carrier switched network establishes a dedicated path for each conversation. With present technology, the time for this task is in the order of seconds. For voice communication, this overhead time is negligible. But in the case of many short transmissions, such as may occur between computers, this time is excessive. To meet the requirements for burst-type communication profiles, it is preferable to employ wideband leased lines over which messages are routed by computer-controlled switching equipment according to the address that each message carries. Minicomputers have been effectively used for implementing message-switching networks of this type.

Another telecommunication application is for data concentration, which is often made an integral part of message-switching networks. Data concentrators subdivide a high-speed communication channel into several low-speed communication channels to realize some of the economy of size in the telecommunication field. Minicomputers have been found to be an effective method for multiplexing in time several low-speed channels onto one high-speed channel.

Still other telecommunication applications use minicomputers for controlling switching matrices of private branch exchanges (i.e., private switchboards), and for the digital processing of signals for such uses as reduction of data redundancy. In all telecommunication applications the minicomputers are often used for such auxiliary tasks as converting codes and data rates, inserting error control information, formating and assembling characters and messages, performing echo check control, conducting traffic accounting, and accumulating network statistics.

Let us now turn our attention to the preprocessing type of minicomputer applications. Several functions must be provided at the remote-access computer site facility to control data communication. They include means for assembling bits to characters and then the characters to messages, means for converting character codes (e.g., EBCDIC to ASCII), means for controlling the communication lines and the input/output devices attached to them, and means for buffering the messages to smooth out the processing workload. This is particularly necessary when the messages arrive in a random fashion and in fluctuating quantities, as in commercial time-sharing systems. These functions are increasingly delegated to preprocessor minicomputers which communicate only completed messages to the data processing computers.

Additional functions, which benefit neither from a complex and extensive instruction repertoire nor from the considerable bulk storage devices available on the large data processing computers, are often also delegated to a minicomputer preprocessor. These functions include

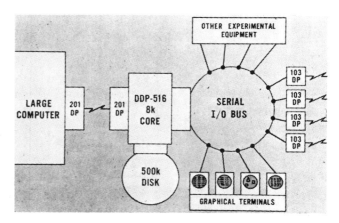

Fig. 19. A typical minicomputer system providing a flexible interface between I/O devices and a general-purpose computer center.

editing capabilities, interactive compilation systems, and centralized control functions for sophisticated input/output devices.

The use of minicomputer preprocessors not only increases the cost effectiveness of most systems, but also greatly facilitates interfacing equipment from different manufacturers. Without preprocessors the technical problem of interfacing is usually a very difficult one, involving both hardware as well as software incompatibilities. Today minicomputer preprocessors for all major data processing systems (e.g., IBM 360, Univac 1108, Burroughs B-5500, and Control Data CDC-6600) are available commercially.

A rather effective and advanced use of a minicomputer configured to interface graphical terminals to a large batch-processing computer is shown in Fig. 19. It uses a system software system of the type described under the section on real-time monitor systems. The small computer can provide the graphical terminals with real-time processing for generating, editing, and manipulating graphical or text files. The small computer passes requests along to the large computer for large tasks and provides access to the data base in the large computer. The configuration also provides remote concentration. The terminals are connected to the system directly or through several low-speed data sets (300 bits/second). The small computer then is connected to the large computer through a single higher speed data set (2400 bits/second). This configuration reduces communication costs for a group of terminals located remotely from the large computation center. Thus, the system appears as a large autonomous file facility to the minicomputer systems which can also be attached to the system.

A minicomputer system of this type has been constructed [10]. In its present form it consists of a 16-bit Honeywell DDP-516 with 8k of core, and a 500k fixed head disk. The system accommodates up to eight simultaneous users and allows them to access program and data segments on disk as if they were in core. Thus the core memory appears to the user to be very large. The DDP-516 with its disk connected through a high-speed direct memory access port provides the hardware foundation for a virtual memory system. A 201 Data-Phone® set with automatic calling unit provides communication with the large computer, which is a General Electric 635 operating under the GECOS III operating system.

Laboratory Applications: The automation of laboratory instruments by computers is an accomplished fact. Whether the automation computer is a minicomputer dedicated to a specific application, or a large time-shared system that services several experiments simultaneously, depends on such factors as the rate at which data are taken, the accuracy required, and the computational complexity of data reduction. It also depends on such managerial questions as budgets, the willingness (and desirability) of scientists to learn simple programming, the availability of support personnel, and the rate of change of the laboratory environment. In either case the system requires an effective man–machine communication interface that facilitates control of the automated laboratory.

A properly automated laboratory leaves the scientist or engineer more free time to spend on truly creative parts of his job, i.e., research and development. Such a system can free people from the time-consuming chores of collecting data. At the same time it can improve the accuracy of the data by removing human errors resulting from the performance of repetitive operations. In addition to speeding up the acquisition of data, the data reduction process can be expedited and facilitated to become a real-time process. Techniques of information theory can be applied to the data in real time to immediately produce results that are mose meaningful and lend themselves best to interpretation. These techniques include filtering, spectral analysis, correlation analysis, signal-to-noise enhancement, and statistical estimation.

The automated laboratory can open up new experimental dimensions. It makes possible experiments with more variables, faster measurement rates, and more data. This permits the investigation of phenomena heretofore inaccessible by classical instrumentation.

There is a growing acceptance of dedicated minicomputers for controlling the instrumentation of laboratories. These computers are usually more economical than large time-sharing systems which require costly executive monitor systems, involve sophisticated input–output devices, and necessitate complex interfaces. Also, dedicated minicomputer systems allow the user complete freedom of action within the limitations of his computer. They do not impose the limitations of large time-sharing systems, such as timing interferences between different experiments, and programming restrictions associated with the executive monitor.

Most programs of dedicated systems are written in assembly language. To enhance the computational capabilities of these systems, there is a growing tendency to interface them to a large time-sharing computer which provides computational capabilities from high-level languages, as well as large secondary data stores and powerful input/output capabilities. This hierarchical structure of interconnected computers appears to offer immense potentials.

The applications of minicomputers for automating laboratory systems are many. In the physical sciences they include facilities for research in signal processing, for speech and visual research [17], for chemical analysis (e.g., gas chromatography), for nuclear physics studies (e.g., nuclear magnetic resonance), and for seismographic investigations (e.g., probing for oil sources). In the medical sciences they include facilities for the clinical laboratory (e.g., autoanalyzers), for automated waveform analysis (e.g., EKG and EEG), and for patient monitoring (e.g., in the intensive care units). The dedicated automated laboratory even has found its way into the arts for such applications as musical composition and choreography, and will probably establish its place in areas not conceived of today.

Industrial Applications: Minicomputers have been controlling production facilities for some time. In some applications they are used strictly as a data source that transmits sequences of commands to hardwired numerically controlled (N/C) machines. These machines perform such tasks as metal working, assembling (e.g., bonding or robot-type assembling), and mask-making (i.e., photolithographic semiconductor device fabrication). In other applications minicomputers send actuating pulses directly to the servomotors attached to the machine tool. At the same time they may perform calculations for contouring and interpolating, and they may even control another machine tool.

Extensive computational power may be required to prepare the sequences of instructions for the N/C machines (e.g., for contouring N/C machines or N/C mask-making machines), and large amounts of core storage are usually required to implement higher level programming languages (as for APT and XYMASK). It is then customary to produce a compact instruction sequence on a large general-purpose computer and submit this sequence to a minicomputer for post-processing. The results may be retained in the minicomputer system which then directly controls an N/C machine; often the results are punched out on paper tape which is then mounted on the N/C machine for execution.

Virtually all computer-controlled test facilities employ a minicomputer for generating the sequences of test instructions that control the instrumentation (e.g., voltage sources, current sources, pulse generators, and voltmeters). In these applications the minicomputers also analyze the results, which may determine the subsequent test steps to be executed and automatically produce a log of the items that have been tested.

Minicomputers are also extensively used to regulate the flow in continuous operations, such as the flow of material in chemical processes and the flow of electricity in power systems. Two approaches are used—set point control and direct digital control. In set point control, which is the traditional approach, the computer serves only as a supervisor for the analog controllers, adjusting the desired values for the process (i.e., the set points). If the minicomputer or one of its associated peripherals fails, the process can continue operation under manual control, since the analog controllers are present. In the more recently introduced direct digital control approach, the analog controller functions are performed by the minicomputer via software programs executed by the computer. The minicomputer drives the process actuators directly, using operational amplifiers to maintain the proper driving condition between successive output calculations for each loop. In this approach, if the minicomputer or an associated peripheral fails, the entire process is without control unless extensive backup facilities have been provided.

The required computer performance depends on the rate of process variation. High rates of variation require higher measurement sampling rates and higher rates of control commands than slow rates of variation. Also, the direct digital control approach places a much larger computational load on minicomputers than does the set point approach, since the computer must simultaneously serve a multiplicity of control loops. To implement this multiple control loop environment, each control loop comprises the control programs and a status table that contains a listing of the control parameters for that loop, intermediate values which are carried forward from previous control calculations, and branch codes that indicate which of several control algorithms is being applied. However, there is an increasing trend toward implementing the more sophisticated control systems by the direct digital control approach, thereby avoiding the expense of complex analog hardwired controllers and affording the flexibility which permits the control systems designer to adjust the control methods and parameters to obtain a more efficient process operation at minium cost. Contemporary direct digital control systems may have typically from 50 to 1000 control loops.

Still another increasingly important industrial application of minicomputers is in the area of material handling and warehousing. For example, minicomputers are now used to control the full operation of a fleet of forklifts and picking vehicles. Each vehicle communicates automatically with a centralized control minicomputer up to several times a second, reporting its exact position in the warehouse. The control computer sends the traveling and operation commands directly to each vehicle via completely buried cables. The cabling both guides the vehicles accurately and allows two-way data communication between the control computer and each vehicle. Such an automated system offers several advantages; they include faster and more accurate order processing, higher vehicle usage, possibility for better inventory control, and improved space utilization.

Similar material movement systems exist using stacker cranes and rail-based carrier vehicles. Each carrier is marked so that a control computer can activate the proper switches for each carrier.

The use of minicomputers in industrial applications promises to facilitate the administration of industrial activities by automatically supplying timely and accurate production and inventory data to administrative systems (i.e., mangement information systems). These systems can be programmed to initiate routine acitivties automatically and single out significant or exceptional data on which management must act.

Administrative Applications: The administrative applications, as understood here, include computer-based systems for production management (e.g., activity scheduling, activity reporting, order processing, inventory control, and material management), personnel managment (e.g., payroll, status reports, vacation and sick leave, personnel inventory, labor distribution, turnover statistics, schedule of hours report, and audit reports), fiscal management (e.g., invoicing accounts receivables, general ledger accounting, nonoperating expenses, operating expenses, and budget control), and statistical analysis (e.g., sales analysis, sales forecasts, production planning and simulation). Using minicomputers for these applications has been only a recent development, largely for two reasons: 1) the minicomputer manufacturers are just beginning to commit resources to the provision of training, product servicing, and software support as required by small commercial data processing installation, and 2) low-cost peripheral equipment for business applications that make minicomputer business systems economically attractive are only now becoming available. In most business applications the price/performance ratio of the peripherals, the software provided, and the I/O speeds of the central processor are far more important than the computation features of the central processing unit.

The chief advantages in the use of minicomputer systems for administrative applications are their low cost and rapid response time, provided the systems come equipped with the applications programs that completely meet the user's needs. Many organizations that could not justify a large data processing center find that they can easily afford a minicomputer installation that comes as a turn-key package where the program development cost is amortized over many customers. Such a dedicated minicomputer system located directly in a user department usually can then be made much more responsive to that department's needs than a centrally operated computer center run in the batch mode ever could. Time-shared systems will eventually be capable of providing the kind of responsive service obtainable with dedicated minicomputers. However, the use of minicomputers promises to facilitate the evolution to large, integrated computer networks. This is based on two opposing applications that have recently emerged.

There is an increasing trend toward centralizing data processing in large and sophisticated computer centers that are staffed and operated quite autonomously by exceedingly capable specialists. These centers strive to increase their processing efficiency by making best use of the most modern equipment available and by developing highly sophisticated program systems. Eventually, the minicomputer centers will probably want to tap the sophisticated resources available only at these large computer centers and to make increasing use of them. They will gain access to these resources by highly efficient data communication networks designed to meet the specific needs of computer-to-computer communication. Thus, minicomputer systems can be viewed as rather autonomous system elements of large scale computer networks which permit the evolutionary installation of complex computer systems.

In the process of attaching minicomputer systems to large computer centers, the actual data processing load of the minicomputer system will probably decrease. Still, it will probably be advantageous to maintain some files locally so as to not swamp the central computer with excessive details, which could make the composite file unmanageable, and limit the data flow between computers. Thus, minicomputer systems will probably assume increasing importance in the area of data communication and data base management, and gradually lose some importance in the area of actual data processing.

Despite the gradual loss of the functional importance of minicomputer centers, their use promises to make the realization of complex management information systems practical. The reason is that the use of minicomputer centers permits breaking the total data processing job into manageable proportions. It permits the development of a modular information system where the interaction between modules can be minimized and where each module can be made to pay for itself before the next module is added. One benefit of this modularity is the possibility of using individual applications long before they have been perfected and completely integrated into the total system, thus facilitating a think-do–think-do cycle which enhances the controlability of a project. Another benefit is a reduction of the total capital investment required to achieve a flexible information system, since individual applications can be made to pay for themselves as soon as they are operational. Still another benefit is a reduction in the probability of failure of the system development, since the individual modules can be carefully tested and individually debugged.

Other Applications: A rapidly increasing number of dedicated systems for a variety of other applications where minicomputers play an integral part are now being developed.

For example, minicomputers are used to control key-tape and keydisk systems in the preparation of data-processing data through keyboard entry devices. Instead of punching the data on cards on these systems, the data are directly assembled on magnetic tapes or disks from which point they are then transferred to the data-processing system. Minicomputers are usually used to control several keyboards in combination with one bulk storage device.

They are also part of large data-processing systems where they increase the throughput for such functions as computation of the fast Fourier transform and data sorting.

Furthermore, minicomputers are being applied to typesetting tasks where they control the justification and hyphenation of text, and the preparation of input media for typesetting machines such as photocomposition equipment.

VI. Epilog

Minicomputers are here to stay. They represent a new and powerful building block in their own right and will find increasing use. In fact, this trend will be accelerated because of the continuing decrease in the cost of minicomputers as a result of progress in semiconductor and memory technology fields.

Eventually, many minicomputers which are now external units will become an integral portion of the system, actually built right into many of the individual devices. And because of the increasingly higher efficiency of the central processing unit, many of these minicomputers will be operated in a multiprogramming mode to make the best use of the peripheral devices attached to them.

Minicomputers will also have a profound effect on the component technology. They permit the definition of functional blocks of increasing complexity without making these blocks narrowly specialized, and thus unlikely to reach large production levels where the startup costs become insignificant. Minicomputers, because they are usually sold in larger quantities, generally offer more integrated electronics part numbers than do the conventional large computers. This helps realize the economies of integrated electronics even more, even for nonmemory components. This will result in minicomputer structures that are even lower in cost. One day an entire processor will be fabricated on one chip at a cost of perhaps $10–$20. With from 1000 to 5000 MOS devices per chip, this is completely within the realm of possibility today. Combining this processor with a ROM with less than 50-ns access time will make the resulting minicomputer also substantially faster than present models.

Thus, minicomputers are becoming the embodiment of tomorrow's functional devices. In fact, people will eventually wonder how they ever did without them. To make this happen is one of the great challenges of the 1970's.

Acknowledgment

This paper reflects the very valuable discussions held with W. F. Chow, C. Christensen, A. D. Hause, and H. S. McDonald of Bell Telephone Laboratories; G. C. Henry and C. B. Newport of the Honeywell Computer Control Division; N. S. Zimbel of Arthur D. Little, Inc.; S. A. Goldstein and R. Denzau of the Diebold Group, Inc.; and many others with whom the author has had the privilege of interacting. The author would also like to acknowledge the valuable comments received in the preparation of this paper from K. M. Poole, the editorial help from Mrs. E. Blair, and the patient typing assistance from Mrs. N. Firestone.

References

[1] N. S. Zimbel, "Outlook for minicomputers, 1969–1974," Service to Management Report, Arthur D. Little, Inc., March 1970.
[2] J. J. Bartik, "Minicomputers turn classic," *Data Processing*, p. 42 ff, January 1970.

[3] M. E. Hoff, "Impact of LSI on future minicomputers," presented at the 1970 IEEE Convention.
[4] F. J. Langley, "Small computer design using microprogramming and multifunction LSI arrays," *Comput. Design*, April 1970.
[5] F. D. Erwin and J. F. McKevitt, "Characters—universal architecture for LSI," in *1969 Fall Joint Computer Conf., AFIPS Proc.*, vol. 35. Montvale, N. J.: AFIPS Press, 1969.
[6] *A Pocket Guide to HP Computers*, Hewlett Packard Inc., and *Small Computer Handbook*, Digital Equipment Corporation.
[7] S. B. Dinman, "The direct function processor concept for system control," *Comput. Design*, March 1970.
[8] G. Bell *et al.*, "A New architecture for minicomputers," in *1970 Spring Joint Computer Conf., AFIPS Proc.*, vol. 36. Montvale, N. J.: AFIPS Press, 1970.
[9] *A Pocket Guide to Interfacing HP Computers*, Hewlett Packard, Inc.
[10] C. Christensen and A. D. Hause, "A multiprogramming, virtual memory system for a small computer," in *1970 Spring Joint Computer Conf., AFIPS Proc.*, vol. 36. Montvale, N. J.: AFIPS Press, 1970.

[11] K. E. Knight, "Evolving computer performance 1963–67," *Datamation*, January 1968.
[12] B. Schwab, "The economics of sharing computers," *Harvard Bus. Rev.*, vol. 46, no. 5, September–October 1968.
[13] F. F. Coury, "A systems approach to minicomputer I/O," in *1970 Fall Joint Computer Conf., AFIPS Proc.*, vol. 36. Montvale, N. J.: AFIPS Press, 1970.
[14] C. B. Newport, "Applications and implications of minicomputers," in *1970 Fall Joint Computer Conf., AFIPS Proc.*, vol. 36. Montvale, N. J.: AFIPS Press, 1970.
[15] L. G. Roberts and B. D. Wessler, "Computer network development to achieve resonance slicing," in *1970 Fall Joint Computer Conf., AFIPS Proc.*, vol. 36. Montvale, N. J.: AFIPS Press, 1970.
[16] F. E. Heart *et al.*, "The interface message processor for the ARPA computer network," in *1970 Fall Joint Computer Conf., AFIPS Proc.*, vol. 36. Montvale, N. J.: AFIPS Press, 1970.
[17] P. B. Denes, "On-line computers for speech research," this issue, pp. 418–425. See also other contributions on the use of computer-based laboratory systems in this issue.

Part II
Peripheral and Software Considerations

The next five papers treat various aspects of applying minicomputers to real problems. J. J. Morris provides valuable insight into the nature of minicomputers by contrasting them with large-scale general-purpose machines. Spencer et al. address themselves to what is available and what is involved in software for minicomputers. Denes and Mathews discuss minicomputer operating systems, an extremely important consideration in many applications. They also present two specific examples of mini operating systems. A comprehensive bibliography is also included. The last three papers in this part deal with peripheral equipment for minicomputers, the integration of this equipment into the total system, and the impact of minicomputers on the design and utilization of sensors.

Because the large-scale computer has been on the scene much longer than the minicomputer, most engineers tend to use it as a basis of reference in viewing the minicomputer. Since one of the greatest problems in evaluating a mini is determining its software potentials and weaknesses, it is useful to see how this software compares with that of a large computer. The author cautions that there is usually not a one-to-one correspondence between minicomputer and large-scale instructions, and that it is in this area where many evaluators are misled. Nevertheless, he stresses the weaknesses of the mini compared to its bigger brother only to point out the pitfalls. Actually, he considers small computers to be "a really great boon" to the control field, provided they are fully understood and properly utilized.

What to Expect
When You Scale Down to a Minicomputer

J. J. MORRIS, Custom Computer Systems

Prior to the minicomputer, many computer users concentrated on centralizing computing activities in large central processors tied to remote input-output stations or time-sharing systems, to take advantage of the economy of scale inherent in the larger systems as well as to consolidate programming skills. The advent of the low-cost minicomputer has caused a reexamination of this approach and a new appreciation of its many problems, especially the sometimes catastrophic consequences of the failure of a single machine. But while the mini is the apparent answer to some of these problems, it is not without its own difficulties, particularly in the programming area.

Perhaps the most common characteristic of the great majority of minicomputers is that they are wholly dedicated to a particular task. The LSGP (large-scale general-purpose computer), on the other hand, is often used for a great variety of purposes. This difference, perhaps more than any other, dictates the architecture of the two types of machines and the corresponding software support required for each.

Initial considerations

Initially, an application must be validated from both an economic and feasibility standpoint. In the case of the mini, it is easy to be misled by the low cost of the basic cpu. This cost is only the cost of the basic unit, including 4K or less of memory, and does not embrace a number of necessary options, such as power fail, direct memory access, and so on. Often it does not even include the cost of a teletypewriter—the standard minicomputer I-0 unit. Larger memories. more peripherals, and interfacing to the application, can easily double or triple the cost of minicomputer hardware.

The major difference in programming between a minicomputer and an LSGP is that the mini requires a good deal more programming effort. If a programmed mini is too "small" or too "slow," the system it controls will be either inefficient or incapable of doing its task. If it is too "large" or too "fast," the initial costs plus running maintenance could prove to be an expensive luxury. In general, a mini application is a dedicated application, and there are no service bureaus or second shifts to handle the overloads. There are also no set rules to assist in matching the task to the computer. It can be safely said that the minicomputer user will be more deeply involved in five computer areas than an LSGP user, so that it becomes imperative that these areas be examined in more than a cursory fashion by anyone considering a mini. The balance of this article will be concerned with the differences between minis and LSGP's in:
■ Memory size
■ Arithmetic capability
■ I-0
■ Programming languages
■ Addressing and paging

Memory size

The first order of business is to determine the total storage requirement of the minicomputer. Because of

Reprinted with permission from *Contr. Eng.*, pp. 65–71, Sept. 1970.

Table I—Basic Programming Steps, Memory Requirements, and Execution Time for $A = X + YZ$

Approach	Program steps	Memory locations (instructions plus data)	Time
Floating-point hardware	1. Load multiplier register Z. 2. Floating multiply by Y. 3. Floating add X. 4. Store A.	7 locations	43 microsec
Fixed-point arithmetic, double-precision	1. Jump to double-precision multiply routine. 2. Form and store least significant sum. 3. Check overflow. 4. Form and store most significant half of sum.	145 locations	1,438 microsec
Floating-point software	1. Jump to enter floating-point package. 2. Pseudo load Y. 3. Pseudo multiply Z. 4. Pseudo add X. 5. Pseudo store A.	1,050 locations	2,500 microsec

needs that arise while programs are being developed or while "It-would-be-nice-if-we-could" computing functions are being evaluated, it is difficult to make this judgment while the system is on paper. More will be said on memory estimation shortly. The point to keep in mind is that, unlike the LSGP environment, the environment of the mini may prohibit peripheral mass storage devices—because of excessive cost or lack of addressing capability on the part of the mini—which means the programmer cannot always be bailed out by adding overlays or employing other schemes of piecemeal program operations.

Minicomputer memory requirements may be broken down into three basic categories, each of which must be separately considered in estimating total memory requirement:

(1) Stored program and fixed data.
(2) Buffer area for data in process.
(3) Safety factor.

The most difficult problem in estimating memory requirements for the program is that the programmer cannot rely on past experience with other computer architectures, particularly the typical LSGP—instead he must intimately know the instruction repetoire, accuracy (determined by word length), and addressing (paging) characteristics of each computer under consideration. All of these parameters can have a significant effect on program size.

Taking the instruction repertoire as an example, several minis do not have a variable shift instruction (i.e., shift left or right N places). If the program requirements are such that shifting operations of a variable nature are frequently required, several extra memory locations must be utilized to offset a variable shift with fixed shift instruction.

As for the safety factor, this margin is a function of experience. Under the assumption of a well-defined problem, the uninitiated designer should dou-

ble or triple his basic estimate to obtain an adequate margin. For the experienced engineer, a safety factor of 25 percent would probably prove adequate.

There may be some temptation to arbitrarily up the safety factor without regard to cost. This can have a dramatic effect on the cost of a minicomputer. For example, one of the more popular minis today sells for $8,000 for the basic computer, including teletypewriter. The cost of adding an additional increment (minimum 4K) of memory and the memory expansion unit is about $6,000 or a 75 percent increase. Also, it should be remembered that many minis cannot be expanded above certain levels (e.g., 8K or 32K).

Arithmetic capabilities

Frequently the arithmetic capability of a computer is measured by its basic cycle time, or in terms of microseconds per addition. This method of measurement can be misleading for minicomputers, since on the surface the minicomputer compares favorably with respect to cycle times with its big brother. Typically, the range is from less than 1 up to 4 microsec cycle time.

When programming the mini, word size and instruction set can have serious consequences on both the memory and timing requirements of the system. The typical small computer has a word size of 12 to 16 bits, whereas a large-scale computer may have a word size of 36 bits. This means that in many cases arithmetic on a mini must be carried out in at least double precision to obtain accuracies equivalent with the large-scale machine. This in turn requires at least a doubling of the data storage capacity for such variables. Also, since the smaller machine usually has only a very basic order complement, it should also offer a complete set of subroutines, such as double-precision add and double precision subtract, to be

Table II—Memory and Time Requirements for Various Arithmetic Operations

Arithmetic operation	Large-scale general-purpose computer		12-bit mini with minimum hardware instruction repertoire		16-bit mini with moderate hardware instruction repertoire	
	Required locations	Execution Time	Required locations	Execution time	Required locations	Execution time
Fixed-point single-precision multiply	1	23	44	350 microsec	40	720 microsec
Fixed-point double-precision add	1	4	30	68 microsec	23	54 microsec
Floating add	1	13	250	300 microsec	149	403 microsec
Floating divide	1	26	450	1,600 microsec	133	600 microsec
Floating cosine	50	500	650	20,000 microsec	581	2,880 microsec

NOTE: Different ratios between the times and the number of locations for the routines listed for the two minicomputers may seem inconsistent. However, the development of such routines is a function of at least three parameters: required accuracy, desired speed, and programmer skill. The results shown are based on actual operating results obtained in various programming situations. Requirements for low speed, high accuracy or high speed, low accuracy, for example, can greatly alter these figures.

capable of the more sophisticated computations found as instructions in LSGP's, though at an additional cost of storage and time. For a large amount of double-precision arithmetic, it is conceivable that overall execution time could be increased by a factor of three or more.

Floating-point hardware is generally not available to the minicomputer programmer except in a few machines where it comes at additional cost. Therefore, the programmer has the choice of writing his program in fixed-point arithmetic with its attendant scaling problems, or utilizing floating-point software packages in the implementation of his program. In the first case the programming becomes a chore, and in the second there are additional memory requirements of up to 500 words or more, along with a tenfold increase in execution time. Perhaps a simple example can best illustrate the differences among the three courses of action, namely: programming a simple function for floating-point hardware, utilizing fixed-point arithmetic on a small machine, and employing the floating-point software package on the small machine.

Consider the simple function $A = X + YZ$. Table

Table III—Frequency of Program Errors

Type of error	LSGP	Minicomputer
Data	Occasional	Moderate
Scaling	Rare	Moderate
Logical	Occasional	Occasional
Format	Occasional	Moderate
Sequencing or timing	Rare	Many
Allocation of storage	Rare	Many

I describes the basic programming steps, gives the memory requirements for these steps, and lists the approximate times for execution in the three examples. Note that the figures given in the table are only typical, since differences exist among the various computer models—primarily because of the different word lengths, instruction repertoires, and speeds. These differences are broken out further in Table II, which lists the requirements for performing relatively comparable functions on a large-scale machine, a 12-bit mini with minimum hardware instruction capability, and a 16-bit mini with a moderate hardware instruction capability.

Input-output devices

The typical minicomputer system usually has a teletypewriter as the standard peripheral device. A number of other peripherals, such as tapes, discs, card readers, printers, etc., are also offered by minicomputer manufacturers, as well as by independent peripherals makers.

The major difference distinguishing the I-0 sections of big and small machines relative to programming is the manner in which the special devices attached to a mini are "talked" to. It is perhaps here more than anywhere else that the role of the programmer has changed. The change is reflected in the programmer's involvement in the systems design.

The nature of the problem is that in an industrial application, external devices generate or receive data in the form of voltages, pulses, and the setting of relays while the data in the computer must be in a binary format. The link between the two types of equipment may be referred to as the computer interface, and it performs the task of translating data between the external device and the computer.

At the outset, the rules are not clearly set as to the delineation of function between the hardware inter-

FIG. 1. Touch-tone truth table. The codes associated with each digit on the dial are shown to the right of the digit column. Since these codes are not conventional binary numbers, the resulting character representations cannot be computed directly on a minicomputer and must first be converted before processing can take place.

Digit	Receive Data Leads			
	RD1	RD2	RD3	RD4
1	1	0	1	0
2	1	0	0	1
3	1	0	1	1
4	0	1	1	0
5	0	1	0	1
6	0	1	1	1
7	1	1	1	0
8	1	1	0	1
9	1	1	1	1
0	0	0	0	1
*	0	0	1	0
#	0	0	1	1
Unassigned	1	0	0	0
	0	1	0	0
	1	1	0	0
	0	0	0	0

face and the program. Hardware-software trade-offs must be performed if an effective system is to be developed—and the programmer's involvement is considered a necessity in this area. A successful effort here can result in significantly lower total systems costs as well as a great deal more flexibility in system operation.

Once these ground rules have been established, and the format and timing of the data to be processed are known, the programmer can proceed with the programming task itself. Here he will recognize two relatively new constraints not often encountered with the LSGP, namely:

(1) The form the data must take.

(2) Timing constraints to be incorporated in the program.

As an example, we might look at the minicomputer processor that interfaces to a telephone data set (modem), in particular the Data Set 403D5, a binary coded matrix (four-level) voltage interface designed for multiple-data-set installations. Figure 1 shows the digits on the touch-tone telephone and their equivalent codes. The character representation itself is not amenable to calculation, and must be converted before processing can take place. Furthermore, receipt of a character in the computer is not sufficient; the interpretation of its meaning must also take place. For instance, the first character received may be an identifier, the next two a code, and the next four may be data. These characters must be formated within the computer before meaningful processing can take place.

Figure 2 illustrates the timing sequence in the above example. The timing constraints indicated in the figure become an integral factor in the design of the program. Thus, after the data-carrier-detect-start signal is received by the computer and interpreted by the program, the program has approximately 40 millisec to assimilate the data. If the program does not direct the computer to pick up the information in this interval, the message is lost. Therefore, the program must be designed to poll the multiple data sets, determine if data is ready, and process the data—all within the indicated time interval.

Programming languages

When one thinks of programming languages the first ones that come to the mind are FORTRAN or PL/I

for general problem solutions, or special-purpose languages such as GPSS or Simscript for the solution of simulation problems. Assembler language has been proclaimed "dead" for some time now in LSGP's, although the majority of programs written for the minicomputer applications are indeed written in assembler language.

In some cases, this has been a matter of necessity rather than choice, since many of the minicomputers available today do not offer a compiler such as FORTRAN. On the other hand, even when a higher level language like FORTRAN is available, the choice is still frequently made in favor of assembler language. The reason is that most industrial minicomputer applications involve logical decisions and interactions between the computer and instruments, actuators and I-0 devices rather than formula calculations. The FORTRAN language can be best utilized when high-volume mathematical operations must be done on a "number-crunching" basis. Thus, only if the application is for general scientific calculations is FORTRAN a consideration.

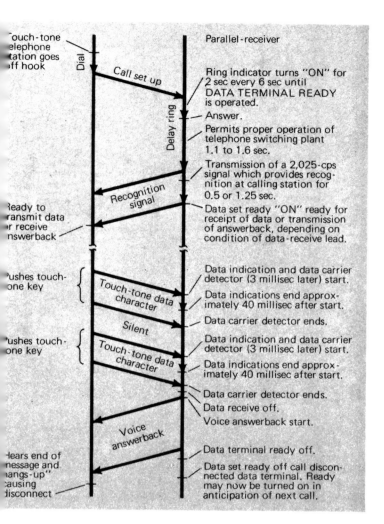

Touch-tone telephone station goes off hook

Dial

Call set up

Delay ring

Parallel-receiver

Ring indicator turns "ON" for 2 sec every 6 sec until DATA TERMINAL READY is operated.

— Answer.

Permits proper operation of telephone switching plant 1.1 to 1.6 sec.

Transmission of a 2,025-cps signal which provides recognition at calling station for 0.5 or 1.25 sec.

Recognition signal

Ready to transmit data or receive answerback

Data set ready "ON" ready for receipt of data or transmission of answerback, depending on condition of data-receive lead.

Pushes touch-tone key

Touch-tone data character

Data indication and data carrier detector (3 millisec later) start.

Data indications end approximately 40 millisec after start.

— Data carrier detector ends.

Silent

Pushes touch-tone key

Touch-tone data character

Data indication and data carrier detector (3 millisec later) start.

Data indications end approximately 40 millisec after start.

Data carrier detector ends.
Data receive off.
Voice answerback start.

Voice answerback

Hears end of message and "hangs-up" causing disconnect

Data terminal ready off.

Data set ready off call disconnected data terminal. Ready may now be turned on in anticipation of next call.

FIG. 2. Timing sequence for touch-tone telephone. Timing constraints must be considered in programming, in that the computer must input or output the data in synchronism with the peripherals. In this example, following receipt and decoding of the carrier detect signal the computer has 40 millisec to assimilate the data.

or page of memory which is to be accessed by the specified address. For example, if the sector bit is a 0, the primary sector or base page (page 0) is selected; if the sector bit is a 1, the address is in the page from which the instruction was taken. Therefore, a memory reference instruction can only directly address the page in which it is located or the base page. To reference other pages of the memory, it is necessary to jump to another part of the program and read out a memory reference instruction from the desired page.

This addressing scheme imposes restrictions on the addressability of data and the transferring of control within the total program. Attention must be paid to the segmentation of the program in this environment. The following rules can simplify the addressing or paging problem:

■ Programs should be organized into subroutines, each of which is a logical entity.

■ Each subroutine should be entirely contained in a single sector of core memory.

■ Small subroutines which use common data should be grouped in sequence and contained in the same or an adjacent sector.

■ All data common to routines in a number of sectors should be contained in the base page or pointed to from the base page.

■ Each page should contain some margin of safety to ensure having a sufficient number of locations. A good rule of thumb is to reserve 10 percent of the locations in a page for debugging.

For the most part, minicomputer assemblers do not differ in concept from those available on the larger machine, as will be described later in this article, and the major problem is understanding the machine itself and not the assembler.

Addressing and paging

Any discussion of programming for a minicomputer would not be complete without a few words on memory organization.

On most minis, each 4K memory module is logically divided into pages. A page is defined as the largest block of memory which can be addressed by the address bits of a memory reference instruction. The size of the page is therefore machine-dependent. The page size for machines having eight or ten bits allocated to specify a memory address within an instruction word are 256 and 1,024 locations, respectively.

To improve efficiency in accessing a given page, the pages of a memory are functionally related in pairs. Associated with each memory reference instruction is a sector bit, which determines the sector

Debugging programs

For the most part, LSGP systems have sufficient I-0 capabilities to perform debugging through the submission and resubmission of test cases and the obtaining of "dumps" (printouts of all or selected memory locations). This mode of operation is not practical when utilizing a minicomputer-teletypewriter combination due to the excessive time involved. Consequently, program debugging for the typical minicomputer system requires many hours at the console. It usually consists of stepping through the program, instruction by instruction, while examining on the console readouts, the contents of the various registers which display the binary form of the current instruction, the contents of the accumulator, etc. This procedure may be speeded up with hardware and software aids that enable the setting of halts or breakpoints

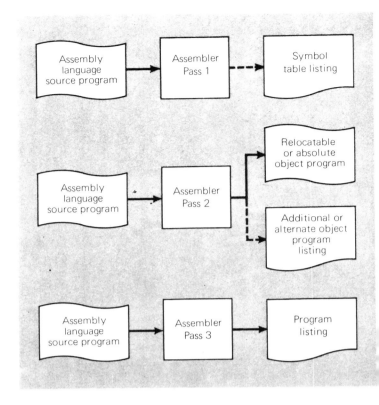

which automatically initiate printouts from selected areas of memory or stop the machine to facilitate tracing portions of the program.

The preceding discussion represents the more obvious aspects of debugging minicomputer programs. A less obvious consideration is the realistic use of time scales. For real-time applications, the slow execution of sophisticated instructions has made optimum management of time an important goal in programming minis. This has lead to the establishment of priority interrupt systems and the logical sequencing of programs, both of which make debugging of a single program a difficult task.

In a real-time environment the procedure of stepping through the program is inadequate because it only is capable of checking the arithmetic and logic independently of time. Such a test cannot check operation with the multitudes of combinations that are possible at a given time. Dynamic tests that incorporate the time constraint must be devised to fully test the typical minicomputer control system program. Table III shows some of the common program errors that occur and their relative frequency for the two types of systems.

Assembling and compiling

The assembling and compiling processes in the large computer installation might be said to be "transparent" to the programmer. Whether the programmer submits his job through a standard I-0 or some remote entry device, all that is required is the filling out of one or more control cards that precede his program and data. The full processing power of the LSGP computer is then brought to bear with tapes or discs containing the compiler and library. The procedure may call for several passes (a pass being defined as a processing cycle of the source program input) to ultimately assemble or compile the program into machine-executable steps. The programmer is generally uninvolved and most times unaware of the details of the process. The process itself requires usually not more than a few minutes of cpu time.

The situation when using a minicomputer and a single teletypewriter is considerably different, not only in the amount of time required for assembly and compiling but also the degree of the programmer's involvement in the process.

In the case of the assembly of a program for example, both types of machines handle the problem in basically the same manner in that the assembly process is a two-pass operation, where the symbol tables are generated on the first pass and the program is actually assembled on the second pass. In the case of a large machine this appears to the programmer as a one-step operation; but with a minicomputer, the programmer becomes involved in the actual process itself and must be knowledgeable about its operations.

For both types of machines, a third physical pass is usually required to obtain a printout of the program as shown in Figure 3. Since the ten-character-per-sec teletypewriter serves as the I-0 device, the process outlined in Figure 3 no longer takes only a few minutes of machine time but can require up to a day for a moderate-sized program. Additionally, the programmer must operate the equipment himself and become intimately involved in each step of the process. While in some cases an operator may be provided to perform these functions, this luxury is usually too expensive for minicomputer environments.

The typical assembly process first requires the programmer to turn on the equipment and see that it is in working order as a prerequisite to running his job. Subsequently, he must place the assembly tape in the reader and then depress several register and control switches to read in the program. When the machine halts, he must verify that the process was completed

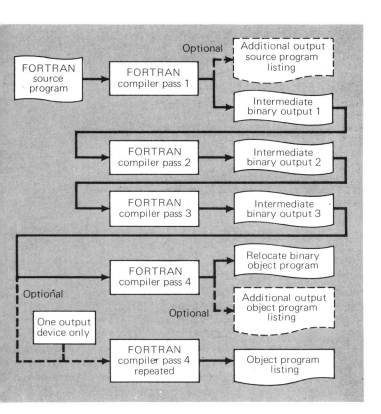

FIG. 4. Compiler program. Compilers such as the 4K memory FORTRAN program shown here may require four or more passes. In addition to reloading the source program data at each step, the program representing the pass of the compiler presently being worked on may also have to be separately loaded at each pass.

successfully by examining the binary contents of a register. He has now prepared the minicomputer to actually assemble his program as outlined in Figure 3. Each pass will require procedures similar to those outlined above.

The procedure for compiling, as shown in Hewlett-Packard's *Guide to Computers* handbook and considered to be typical, is outlined in Figure 4. The compiling process for the minicomputer represents an essentially similar procedure as far as the programmer is concerned. The main difference is that four or more passes may be required. Also, in addition to reloading the source program data at each step, the program representing the pass of the compiler presently being worked on may also have to be separately loaded at each pass. For example the program steps might be:

(1) Load pass 1 of compiler.
(2) Load source program.
(3) Load pass 2 of compiler.
(4) Load source program (or equivalent output from pass 1).

The major effect on the programmer in the minicomputer environment is that the ability to recompile or reassemble is diminished due to the time required for this process. The programmer is therefore required to turn back the pages of history to the early days of the LSGP and make what are called "binary patches" to his program at the console, during the course of the debugging, rather than reassembling or recompiling when program errors are encountered. This requires something more than a cursory knowledge of the machine on the part of the programmer. He must be completely cognizant of the instruction repertoire and the detailed internal workings of the computer.

Some final thoughts

After examining some of the major differences in the programming process on the mini and the LSGP, it should be evident that the engineer utilizing a minicomputer requires a significantly more detailed knowledge at the machine level than his counterpart utilizing the LSGP. This knowledge is hard to come by and is best gained by actual "hands-on" experience for an extended period of time. Such experience, while being quite costly the first time around, can prove invaluable on subsequent evaluations of the mini and is perhaps the only way the engineer can know whether a mini can solve his digital control or data-acquisition problems. This involvement can come in several forms, including:

(1) **Utilization of an in-house group.** If several minicomputer systems are being developed within a company, it is natural to assume that an in-house capability already exists. Working with an experienced group not only expedites the learning process of the engineer user but also represents the most economical path of implementation.

(2) **Utilization of the systems house.** This alternative is essentially the same as, and offers all the advantages of, the first category—as long as the choice of the systems house is made with great care. It represents the preferred alternative when an in-house systems group does not exist.

(3) **Reliance on the vendor.** A word of caution should suffice to the engineer choosing this alternative. The level of manufacturer support for a $10,000 computer is not the same as that for a $1-million machine.

In summary, and regardless of the path of implementation, the development of a low-cost minicomputer system is feasible (evidence the 5,000 to 7,000 such systems in the field), but it takes expertise to make "everyman's computer" work for every man. □

SMALL COMPUTER SOFTWARE

by Henry W. Spencer, Harlan P. Shepardson, and Larry M. McGowan, Digital Equipment Corporation

This paper discusses the current status of software for mini (or small) computers, and attempts to give a feeling for the potential of small computer software.

INTRODUCTION

It is generally true for large computers that software technology is not as advanced as the hardware technology. This statement is even more applicable to small computers, and software technology is still advancing less rapidly than hardware technology. There are many reasons for the existence of these conditions, but the following are probably major:

1) Since small machines have small sales prices, unit profit is much less than for a large machine. This pricing picture has not encouraged small computer manufacturers to spend large sums of money for software development.

2) Until the last few years, small computer suppliers had not found software to be a necessary element for sales.

3) Small machines have historically embodied limited instruction sets. Thus the programming effort required to produce a given major program has been considerably greater for a small machine than for a large machine.

Manufacturer supplied software was not originally found to be a necessary item because small computers were used largely for very special purpose applications. In fact, a large proportion of small computers have been sold to Original Equipment Manufacturers (OEM's) who resold them with their own special purpose hardware and software. This original buyer used some minimal assembler to generate his software and the end user had no need to concern himself with software at all.

This special applications programming by OEM's as well as by many single machine purchasers has led to the existence of a large body of highly sophisticated special purpose software. General purpose software such as operating systems, advanced, high level languages, etc., is not as readily available for small computers as for large computers. However, small computer software is beginning to close the gap. With the increased popularity of the small computer, increasingly sophisticated, general software is becoming available. The current state of general purpose software will be covered in a later section.

Because of the large number of models of small computers now available in the marketplace and the nearly equally large number of organizations currently manufacturing small computers, it is impossible to even make a list of the software available from each supplier. This paper will, therefore, attempt to give the reader a feeling for the types of software in use on small computers. This feeling will be gained by examining in some detail a few examples of software rather than covering a large number of examples only lightly.

Four areas of small computer software will be discussed. The areas to be treated are special applications software, general applications software (for solving classes of problems), general purpose software and future possibilities for small computers.

SPECIAL PURPOSE APPLICATIONS SOFTWARE

Special purpose applications software is a field of software that covers virtually every use of computers. The term "special purpose" means the software was developed to perform a particular function or to solve a particular problem. In many cases, special hardware other than the computer is involved. Sometimes, although the application may be quite simple, a computer is used to provide the desired flexibility, speed and/or consistency. Often the experimental environment may be too hostile for sustained human participation. In any case, because of the low cost and programming ease of a small computer, it is often advantageous to include a computer in the system.

Small Machine Applications

A simple application in Computer Assisted Instruction (CAI) and a sophisticated real-time, time-sharing clinical laboratory system will now be described.

Reprinted from *IEEE Comput. Group News*, vol. 3, pp. 15–20, July/August 1970.

The CAI system consists of a central computer and five small satellite computers. The central computer, which has a large disk containing the entire set of lessons, produces tapes for each satellite containing the lessons for one day's operation. The tapes may be physically transported or transmitted over telephone lines to the satellites, which operate independently of each other and of the central computer. The satellites are used throughout the school day to provide lessons for up to 24 students. During the day they compile information about student progress which is put on tape and sent back to the central computer at the end of the day for analysis. This results in teacher reports on the progress of the class and of individual students. The analysis also allows a tape for the next day's lessons to be prepared which is dependent on the progress of the student that day This allows the student to proceed at his individual rate. The lessons consist mainly of sets of short examples and quizzes of varying degrees of difficulty. Each student is given a pre-test to determine the level of the student before the lessons begin. At the end of a set of lessons a final test is given and reports are created for the teacher.

The lessons are stored in a language which is executed through an interpretive process. The language allows a problem along with correct and incorrect answers to be easily described. Actions to be taken upon the receipt of an answer are specified by whomever generates the lesson. The interpreter also allows time limits for an answer to be set with appropriate actions occurring if the limit is exceeded.

The general procedure for a lesson is for a student, on a scheduled basis, to log on a teletype with identification information. A search of the disk is performed to determine which lesson the student is to receive. If the lesson is not on the disk, which is not the normal case, the lesson is transferred to the disk from tape and then the lesson proceeds.

As an example of a fairly sophisticated application of a small computer, a real-time, time-sharing operating system will now be discussed. The level of detail will be quite shallow, but it is hoped that the flavor of the system will be gained by the reader.

This operating system provides for the acquisition and processing of data in real-time while simultaneously providing control and utility functions for a group of non-computer oriented users. The environment is a clinical laboratory where the main tasks to be performed are to accept requests for tests, to set up the requested tests for the technologist and/or automatic devices, to gather the results and to prepare reports on the tests.

The basic hardware configuration is a 12 bit minicomputer with 4K of core[1], a 360K word disk and a 12 channel I/O multiplexer. All I/O other than the disk I/O goes through the multiplexer which provides for quick identification of the interrupting device.

Examples of the kinds of devices which would be attached through the multiplexer in a configuration would be: teletypes, automatic instruments (SMA-12, Coulter Model S, etc.), line printer, magnetic tape, and a special peripheral processor maintaining 16 interactive data consoles.

The acquisition and verification of test results make up the majority of the tasks performed in the foreground of the system. When there are no tasks for the foreground, background tasks are initiated by the system. These consist mainly of the printing of reports which have been requested.

The letter K will be used to indicate the numeric value 1024 in this paper.

Foreground processing occurs on several levels of priority. Level 1 (highest) consists of the interrupt handlers for the disk and multiplexer. Level 2 is a set of overlays called by the system as the result of actions performed by the interrupt routines. The only I/O performed by these overlays is disk I/O and therefore they do not go into long wait states Thus, once an overlay is called in, it runs to completion. This restriction simplifies the context switching from one overlay to another since the overlay's status need not be saved (they always run to completion) and common resident routines will not be re-entered. Level 3 in the foreground consists of segments (overlays) explicitly called by the users or by the scheduler when it wants to swap users. The purpose of user segments is to make up for lack of core. Usually the user segments spend most of their time waiting for low speed I/O to complete. Thus the scheduling of users is based upon I/O interrupts, that is, a segment is suspended whenever it is awaiting completion of a nondisk transfer. If a level 2 overlay can be started it will be read into the overlay area and run to completion. If no overlays are ready, a ready user segment may be started or continued.

The segments described above perform functions requested by operator commands from the teletypes. Each teletype is considered a user and each teletype may be running a different segment in a time shared mode.

As can be seen from the brief description given above, the system is quite sophisticated and relies heavily on the disk for overlays and swapping. This is mainly the result of running in a 4K machine. However, these techniques make it possible to perform various functions for multiple users and to simultaneously control automatic testing instruments with a small computer with only 4K of core. Without using overlays much more core memory would be required. If time sharing were not employed, the machine would be idle most of the time and only one function could be performed at a time. The use of a foreground/background arrangement allows the high speed devices and high priority processes to be operated in the foreground in real-time with low priority tasks performed in the background when there is nothing else to do.

GENERAL PURPOSE APPLICATIONS SOFTWARE

The previous section detailed some special purpose applications software created specifically to solve particular problems. Such software had to be written from the ground up, and required the user to provide himself with the necessary skills in computer technology, a field not necessarily related to the problem at hand.

It has, therefore, become an economic necessity for small computer manufacturers to encourage and participate in the development of generalized applications software. This software can take many forms, ranging in generality from programming languages aimed at the needs of a single class of users, to programs which perform a specific data manipulation task common among a class of users. The goal in providing such software is to minimize the amount of time, effort and knowledge required for a user to arrive at a point of useful return from his small computer.

One runs the risk, of course, of getting more generality than is needed. A physics experiment, for example, may be a simple one and require only 3 of the 17 kinds of reports that can be requested from the accelerator control program supplied with the computer. Generality always comes

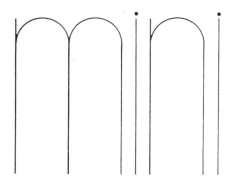

at a price, and in this case it might have been the price of an extra core memory module. However, the added cost is very likely to be less than the cost of making up a special package and fitting it into the minimum available configuration. Maintenance responsibility is a long-term cost which must also be included in making this kind of a trade-off.

Specific examples of general purpose applications software will now be described. This is a rather wide field, and the distinctions which separate it from the special applications discussed earlier and the general purpose software discussed later are sometimes cloudy. However, an attempt is made to show examples which have wide relevance in distinct market areas.

Data Acquisition

The area of industrial data acquisition and control systems has probably received more careful attention concerning the application of small computers than nearly any other. Small computers can cheaply provide the speed and accuracy required in these applications, and are frequently used to gather and partially process data into a form which simplifies complex analysis by a larger computer.

One available compiler and operating system for a 12 bit minicomputer designed to facilitate the development of such applications is an example of a special-purpose programming language. It is designed for industrial data acquisition, and includes a compiler-level real-time language and an operating system which performs scheduling, interrupt control, storage management and input/output operations to standard peripherals and process devices. Many capabilities commonly required in this area are provided. Data gathering, conversion and output provide operational records. Process monitoring is achieved by checking data against limits and sending alarms to the operator or taking action directly in case of out-of-tolerance conditions. Control programs can adjust set points to regulate the process based on acquired data and operator inputs. Libraries of standard functions and I/O handlers are provided to support these capabilities.

This real-time language is syntactically similar to FORTRAN or BASIC and provides many of the same features. In addition, provisions are made for handling the special requirements of the real-time situation. An EQUIP-MENT statement allows I/O parameter specification. GET and SEND are simplified real-time I/O statements which can be applied to any device. The AT and EVERY statements allow multiple program scheduling, and the TIMER statement allows clock control. SYSTEM, PHASE and SNAP allow the user to organize and segment his programs to achieve effective use of system facilities.

It is obvious that a considerable degree of programming sophistication and a detailed knowledge of the application are required to make use of such a system. Its advantages are that the programming is done in a higher-level language, and that many recurring details are taken care of, such as interrupt and priority control and core overlaying. Thus a system of probably less than optimum efficiency can be up and producing results considerably sooner than a completely hand-coded system.

Control

Numerically controlled (N-C) machine tools are generally thought of as belonging in the domain of larger computers; however, an example of a small computer software system for parts programming, designed to run on a 12 bit computer will be described. The system comprises a simple parts program compiler which allows direct input of information supplied on conventional parts drawings. Input is via Teletype keyboard or paper tape, and some editing functions are provided. Basic arithmetic capabilities, a shorthand to define common geometric patterns such as bolt holes, and common machine tool functions are also provided. Some "subroutine" capability is made available by the ability to store and repeat recurring pattern definitions. Special post processors are used to punch output in the format recognized by the machine tool control unit. Printouts containing input data, parts program instructions and machine operator instructions may also be obtained.

Although the interaction between the system and the operator is much greater than in the previous example, such a software package also requires very little computer knowledge of its users. Here again, the user is concerned about the end product rather than the computer or the program.

Laboratory Applications

An area in which small computers have had wide acceptance and a long history is in the laboratory, running and monitoring test equipment of all descriptions. These users have traditionally been an independent lot and are knowledgeable in both hardware and software aspects. It has been only relatively recently that general-purpose laboratory packages have come into being. These are typified by a GLC (Gas-Liquid Chromatography) package and a Spark Chamber On-Line Data System package. In both of these, the computer is interfaced to a piece of special equipment. It is possible to add methods of data analysis, but the most commonly used reports, histograms, etc. are built into the system. Via the console teletype, the experimenter sets up parameters, specifies the control he wants to exercise, the data he wants collected and the form in which to display it. The GLC package controls the operation of one or several chromatographs, analyses results and prints the requested reports on-line. The Spark Chamber package is primarily a monitoring and data collection system. A CRT display is used to present histograms showing the progress of the accelerator experiment, and, if desired, the data is identified and written without editing on magnetic tape for later analysis.

Communications

A major area of small-computer utilization, with more of a future than a past, is that of communications processing. Because of the breadth of this application area, a brief general discussion of some of its many aspects will be given, rather than a specific example.

The main requirements of communications processors are the ability to switch rapidly between program states, to randomly access entries in large core resident lists and tables, and to conveniently handle character data. Thus the important system features are a good interrupt structure, some form of direct, indexable access to large blocks of memory and byte manipulation capability. "Number crunching" is usually of secondary interest.

Communications applications take many forms, and the roles of hardware and software are sometimes not clearly delineated. A typical example is a multiplexer which connects up to 64 low-speed asynchronous devices to a medium speed modem. Hardwired systems to do this are relatively inexpensive, but a software system in a small computer offers much greater flexibility.

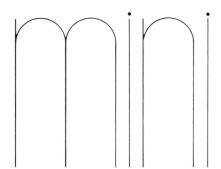

Other examples of communications processing are preprocessing, where inputs from a number of lines are gathered and passed to a local computer; message switching, where a number of lines are connected and messages are routed from source to destination; and remote batch terminals, where a remote station has batch I/O equipment such as card readers and line printers, and jobs are transmitted to and from a central large computer.

Business

The last area of small-computer applications to be touched upon here is that of business packages. As in communications, the use of small computers in this field is only now gathering headway and will expand greatly in the future. This field includes business data processing, administration, report generation, forms control, etc. These applications have traditionally been the domain of large computers. However, easy access and low cost coupled with imaginative systems design make the use of small computers more attractive and economical as a solution of the needs of small businesses. A recent paper[2] by V.L. Rosenberg, of the Chesapeake Life Insurance Co., Baltimore, Maryland, describes a system which gathers information from insurance applications and calculates costs. The use of this system enables the job to be done 80% faster with a reduction in required skills from the assistant supervisor level to the lowest clerk level. To quote Mr. Rosenberg, "Our company wants a machine that it can make an integral part of its operations, working alongside its personnel and eliminating the many small, repetitive functions of day-to-day work." Mr. Rosenberg has abandoned the traditional approach and adopted a solution designed for a set of real needs which may be found in any small business.

Multi-user Language Processors

A number of examples of small-computer applications are characterized by multiple consoles, allowing several users to be simultaneously doing more or less the same thing. Many such applications are built around the notion of time sharing because of scheduling and access problems, and because simpler applications don't come near taxing the limits of processing power of even a small computer. This same technique is used to broaden the availability of general purpose problem-oriented programming languages. This has led to the development of multi-user higher-level languages systems, in which several people at a time are able to use the computer to develop programs of a general nature.

Such systems are typified by multi-user BASIC and similar languages developed in the last few years. They offer the advantages of low-cost-per-terminal computing power of a very real nature, and, via the relatively simple higher level language, allow access by the problem-solver who may be unschooled in the ways of programming. These systems are also finding wide acceptance in education, where the easy language and easy access provide a way of teaching about programming without getting involved in the usual morass of extraneous details.

As popularity of multi-user language systems increases and the market grows, more small-computer manufacturers are making plans to provide

them. Systems are currently under development which will provide multiple access to several higher level languages concurrently. Besides the expected BASIC and conversational FORTRAN, these will soon include languages oriented toward administration and report generation. Special-purpose languages will undoubtedly be added to the list before long.

Multi-user language systems operate in a "friendly" environment, and complex hardware or software to protect users from each other is not needed. This is because all machine code is executed under control of the operating system, which takes the responsibility for always doing the right thing. This differs from a usual timesharing system in that assembly language is not allowed at all, and some limits are placed on flexibility of using the system. The extent of these limits depends on the sophistication of the operating system and the languages provided.

GENERAL PURPOSE SOFTWARE

For the purposes of this paper, general purpose software will be considered to be those programs which are provided as an aid to all computer applications rather than as support to any particular application or class of applications. Examples of general purpose software would be assemblers, compilers, input/output executives, etc. It should be noted at this point that the more general a given program becomes (i.e. the more problems for which a given piece of software attempts to give an adequate solution), the more inefficient the program becomes. On a large machine, a general program with all of its inefficiencies can often be tolerated because of the termendous computing power available. On a small machine, however, even slight inefficiencies are often immediately obvious to the user. Thus the general purpose software available for a smaller computer is often considerably less general than that available for larger models.

Often the only software available for a small computer is a limited set of program development software. This type of software will be discussed first below and more complex general purpose software will follow

Program Development Software

The type of general purpose software which is most readily available and probably most useful is program development software. The purpose of this software is to aid the user in developing programs for his particular applications. The essential ingredient of a program development system (and hence the simplest possible system) is a program loader which transfers data from some input device to the computer's core memory. The user must then prepare his program by hand (e.g., hand punching a paper tape) or prepare it on another computer.

The obvious drawbacks have resulted in very few computers being marketed without at least the next level of program development software. This next level consists of the loader mentioned above along with an assembler and often a text editor. This assembler, editor and loader package is popular for small machines with very limited (paper tape only) I/O devices. The assembler produces absolute code after two or three passes over the input data and the loader is used to load assembler output into core. The text editor gives the user the capability to modify his assembler source (input) easily so that entire tapes do not have to be regenerated from scratch to make a minor (or major) change.

The programming environment for small computers generally involves on-line, console debugging. However, small computers do not usually have very sophisticated operator control consoles. For this reason debug-

[2]V.L. Rosenberg. "Efficient Use of Personnel with a Computer." *DECUS Proceedings.* Fall 1969. p 259-266

ging aids have been often included in basic software packages. The most common type of debugging aid allows the user to set stop points, examine specified core locations, and modify selected core locations. The user then generally has the capability to output (usually punch a paper tape) his corrected program to save himself frequent reassembly.

This software consisting of an assembler, loader, text editor, and an on-line debugging aid forms a basic, simple, useable package for the user with a very minimal machine configuration.

Each of the elements of the package discussed above is generally a "stand alone" program; that is, each program performs all of its own I/O at the machine language level, and few standards for program user communication exist. The next level of software, "systems", provides for more standardization of its programs as well as providing at least a minimal set of subprograms which have some common value.

A software system generally requires some type of bulk storage hardware for storage and retrieval of the subprograms it provides. Generally a small disk or a simple, reliable magnetic tape device is used. The software system is usually based on a set of common I/O processing routines which have the function of handling the basic activities of the various I/O devices supported by the system. A simple system will provide only I/O handlers for issuing orders to a device and servicing device interrupts. More complex systems provide full file-type I/O capabilities which remove from the user any need for consideration of I/O device characteristics.

The software system usually provides an assembler, editor and debug capability as discussed above, except that they make use of the common I/O processing routines and also are more standardized in their external appearance. The program loader provided will load programs from the bulk storage device as well as from external media.

Management of the system subprograms and user programs on the bulk storage device is performed by some type of librarian provided by the system. This librarian generally has the capability to catalogue (store) programs on the device and then locate them for later retrieval. Many systems also provide the capability to link together separately assembled programs to make one large executable program. Higher level languages such as FORTRAN, BASIC and FOCAL are also often provided in either compiler or interpreter form to run under the environment of the software system.

Two examples of general purpose software systems will now be given. The first will be an example of a very simple system and the second will be a more general and complex system.

A good example of a fairly simple software system for a small computer which provides the user with a comprehensive capability is the Disk Monitor System for a small 12 bit computer. The basic hardware requirement for this system is a computer with 4K words of core, a teletype console, and a bulk storage device which may be either a fixed head, 32K word disk or a simple, small magnetic tape unit. This system provides several services for the user as well as providing a unified approach to the use of the various services.

User interface to all services of the system is through use of the teletype console. The user has the capability to save and recall programs from the system resident device. The user may also request the loading and execution of various system programs. The interface between the system programs and the user is through a common command string interpreter. This command string interpreter determines the user's input, output and possible optional files in the same way no matter what system service is being used. Thus the user is spared the trouble of learning separate command sequences for each program.

The disk monitor also provides a common I/O handler for the system device. This handler can be used by both system programs and user generated programs. Programs which reference other devices must include their own I/O handlers, however.

The system provides several services to aid the user in the development of his programs. These include the following:

1) Editor - An editor enables the user to generate and edit symbolic (source) programs on-line at the teletype console.
2) Assembler - An assembler allows the user to build his machine language programs in a symbolic language. The assembler also provides various pseudo-operations to allow the user to direct the assembler in its code generation.
3) Debugging - A Dynamic Dubugging Technique allows the user to control the execution of his program and make changes to it while it is running on the computer. The user may refer to locations in his program symbolically through the use of tags from the assembly listing or absolutely by octal core address. The user may then save his altered program for later recall.
4) FORTRAN - A FORTRAN compiler is provided.
5) Files - A Peripheral Interchange Program can be used for file copying and other file oriented functions.

The Disk Monitor system currently under development for a new 16 bit computer will be used as an example of a more extensive program development system. This system offers extensive services for both program development and execution of the developed program. To illustrate the increased capability offered the user, the input/output area will be discussed first. Whereas the disk monitor discussed above offers a single device oriented handler, the disk monitor supports completely device independent I/O processing for all I/O devices. The user writes his program as if a given I/O operation were performed on a particular type of device. When the program is actually run, the operation may be assigned to any device available on the machine. The user also has a choice of several "modes" for performing I/O in his program. These are enumerated below.

1) Logical Level - The user may request the Monitor to perform blocking and deblocking of device oriented physical blocks into a more convenient format.
2) Physical Level - The user may request a physical block transfer either to a monitor buffer (dynamically allocated) or to a user buffer.
3) Direct Access Level - The user may access the basic device handler directly and thereby bypass all system overhead.

I/O levels discussed in 1) and 2) above may be used in conjunction with a comprehensive file structure system for bulk storage devices.

Other system services are similarly more comprehensive; for example:

1) The assembler provides macro and conditional assembly capabilities as well as providing relocatable output.
2) A linkage editor is provided which will combine relocatable output of several language processors (or previous linkage edits) to produce a single execution module.
3) Execution time facilities include restart capability, request for allocation of free core, etc., in addition to I/O service.
4) The hardware makes provision for re-entrant coding. The system makes use of this feature to provide greater efficiency.
5) Most system routines are written so that they may be either permanently core resident or swapped from disk whenever needed. Each user can determine and get the best monitor configuration for his particular uses.

The modular design which allows the swapping in 5) above to be implemented also allows simple extension and updating of the system by either the user or the supplier. The user may also incorporate any of the system modules into his own specialized system (e.g., I/O handlers would be good candidates for such use).

The minimum hardware configuration for this system is slightly larger than for the previous system. A more powerful, 16-bit processor is required, with 8K words of core. A disk is required for system residence and either high-speed paper tape or a small magnetic tape unit is required.

Only a few specific areas of this new monitor have been discussed, however, the wide variation in available program development software should be readily apparent.

Real-Time Software

It was mentioned earlier in this paper that small computers have been used extensively for control and process control applications. These applications generally have the common requirement that stimuli from external devices require responses from the control computer within a specified maximum time interval for each device. This time interval requirement gave rise to the term real time to describe this class of applications. The fact that some external devices are more time-critical than others necessitates a priority scheme for sequencing the tasks of the control computer.

Since there is a very wide range of real-time applications, the general purpose software available in this area usually consists of a monitor (now usually called an Executive) system, which is designed to support a real-time environment and perhaps some extensions to a common language (like FORTRAN) to make it more suitable for generating code for a stimulus/response situation. The Executive Control System available from one major minicomputer manufacturer is described in the following paragraphs.

This executive provides the framework upon which the user can construct his applications for his own specific real-time needs. The user structures his program as several "tasks". Each task may be initiated at run time by either an executive scheduler or by a hardware priority interrupt. Interrupt servicing programs are run in interrupt mode, that is, another interrupt is stalled until the current interrupt routine has completed. When no interrupt service routine is in execution and no hardware interrupt is pending, the scheduler places the highest priority noninterrupt program (as determined by a fixed table) into execution.

A noninterrupt routine can be interrupted by a hardware interrupt. The executive routine saves the status of the noninterrupt program so that it may resume execution upon completion of the interrupt service routine (and possibly some higher priority noninterrupt routine).

An interrupt mode program may request the execution of a noninterrupt program. The requested program will then become a candidate for execution governed by the executive scheduler. The most efficient manner of using this type of system is to separate the servicing of any hardware interrupt into two sections; a time critical section and a time independent section. The time critical portion will be run as an interrupt mode program. The interrupt mode program performs its function and then places a request for the executive scheduler to run the less critical portion on a time-available basis.

The executive provides the following support functions:
1) Either an interrupt mode program or a noninterrupt program may request the execution of a noninterrupt program as discussed above. The program may be entered at any point stated.
2) Any program can request the execution of a program at a specified clock time or after a specified interval.
3) Cyclic execution (continued rescheduling after a specified interval) may be requested for a program.
4) A program can request an I/O device for its exclusive use. This causes internal linkage for the device to be set up for the requesting program. The program then becomes an interrupt mode program.
5) A program may suspend itself indefinitely or wait for a specific interrupt.

The user may use this system as a basis for constructing any real-time application such as those discussed in prior sections. Other real-time executive systems currently available provide both simpler and more sophisticated capabilities than those presented here, but since their purpose is similar, the services they provide are similar.

FUTURE DIRECTION

The reader has now been exposed to the current state of small computer software in the areas of special applications packages and general purpose software. The natural question is "What will small computer software be in the future?" The writers can only make guesses as to software directions but there appear to be several software and hardware trends that can be noted. Their effect on future software development can be fairly confidently conjectured.

1) Price Trends
   Small computers are becoming cheaper and cheaper. It is possible for more new processes to become "computerized" with each reduction in price. Thus, one should expect to see many "simple" processes under computer control as the price reduction trend continues. A computer recently marketed as a kitchen aid is an example of the effect of reducing prices.

2) Hardware Trends
   The rapid hardware development will continue so that eventually small computers will have capabilities which are now reserved only for the giant computers. User demand will result in software to match so that small computer software technology will be at least equal to large computer software technology. The time sharing systems (software and hardware) currently available for very inexpensive small computers are an example of this trend. Microprogramming for small computers is another example.

3) Software Trends
   As software technology strains to catch up with hardware technology the trend is toward more flexible software. This flexibility trend is apparent in the general applications software and the general purpose software discussed earlier. The trend will lead to more modularity and flexibility in future software and better management of hardware resources.

After noting these trends, the writers will leave further prognosticating to the reader.

The reader should be reminded again that large areas of small computer software have been omitted in an attempt to give a more "in-depth" survey. Illustrations were chosen because of their general interest and because information on them was readily available to the authors.

Laboratory Computers: Their Capabilities and How to Make Them Work for You

PETER B. DENES AND M. V. MATHEWS, MEMBER, IEEE

Invited Paper

Abstract—A laboratory computer is a small- or medium-sized general-purpose machine which has been specially selected to do a particular job. Important economies as well as great computing power are achievable by matching not only the kind of machine, but also the particular set of components to the tasks at hand. For this reason, laboratory computers have become very popular. In addition to selecting the hardware, advantages can be achieved by tailoring the operating system and other general software to the situation. Enough operating systems for such computers have now been written to show how a specific system may be developed by modifying and incorporating features of existing systems and by modifying standard programs supplied by computer manufacturers. In this way, special systems can be implemented using a reasonable amount of time and effort.

This paper provides an introduction to laboratory computer operating systems to serve as a starting point for someone intending to create his own system. Specific systems for a LINC computer, and for the Honeywell DDP-224 and DDP-516 computers are described in some detail. These systems illustrate many features that have been found useful. The documentation needed to use the computer, the size of the user group, and some of the history of development are mentioned. Similar systems can be created to focus new machines on new tasks. Only current state-of-the-art programming is needed. The benefits of such specialization far outweigh the effort and costs.

I. INTRODUCTION

What is a Laboratory Computer?

LABORATORY computers are general-purpose digital machines whose configuration is specially selected to suit a particular application; such applications frequently involve direct connection to a variety of laboratory instruments and close, rapid control by the user. The computers are usually, but not invariably, smaller than those used for batch processing. Their chief competitor is the remote access, time-shared, central machine. However, powerful time-sharing systems have proven to be harder to develop and are more complicated than was anticipated. As a result of these difficulties, the computing load at many institutions is shared by numerous laboratory computers and by a separate center that employs a large machine working both in batch processing and in time-sharing modes.

Advantages of Laboratory Computers

The rapidly increasing popularity of special-purpose laboratory computers is due to a variety of reasons. For certain applications they offer capabilities not obtainable in any other way. For example, in some tasks the computer is so intimately connected with other equipment that it is almost part of the apparatus, and such tasks cannot be done by traditional central computers operated in either a batch processing or a time-sharing mode. Similarly, the use of special laboratory machines is a necessity in other applications for which convenient interaction with human operators requires fast response from the computer. In addition, laboratory computers offer considerable economies in operating costs. Certain jobs for which either laboratory machines or conventional computer systems are suitable can be done much less expensively with the right laboratory computer.

Why are these machines less expensive? The most important reason is that their size and complexity is tailored to the requirements of the job they are intended for. Compared with the general batch processing machine that has to cater to the needs of a great variety of jobs, the laboratory computer may—depending on what job it is intended for—have a shorter word length, smaller memory, fewer instructions, fewer peripheral devices, or any combination of these economies.

The economies of specially tailoring "general-purpose" computers for particular applications were pointed out by Mathews [1] in a study in which he compared certain cost measures of 14 machines ranging in size from a PDP-8 to an IBM 360/65. He found large differences in costs—as much as 20 to 1 in the extreme case. Even greater economies can be achieved by tailoring the hardware of the digital processor to the special requirements. Cox [2] has argued that macromodular systems [3]—an assemblage of modules such as memory units, adders, multipliers, etc., which are physically patched together to do a given job—can carry out certain tasks 500 times less expensively, compared with a general-purpose batch processor.

As a consequence of their specialization, many laboratory computers are smaller and cannot do larger problems; hence, a comparison with large machines for these problems is hardly fair. However, for problems within their capabilities a valid comparison can be made. These problems often utilize the large machines inefficiently and in such cases great savings can be achieved with the right laboratory computer.

In addition to pure economies, laboratory computers have the advantage of simplicity compared with the large batch processing machines. Perhaps the best measure of simplicity is the number of pages of documentation which the normal user must know or refer to. The user's manual

Manuscript received December 5, 1969; revised January 29, 1970.

This invited paper is one of a series planned on topics of general interest.—The Editor.

The authors are with Bell Telephone Laboratories, Inc., Murray Hill, N. J. 07974.

Reprinted from *Proc. IEEE*, vol. 58, Apr. 1970, pp. 520–530.

46

for the DDP-224 computer, which we will shortly describe, has a total of 250 pages which can easily be carried home in a briefcase. By contrast, the corresponding manual for the Bell Labs GE-635 central computing facility consists of 1600 pages residing in five large binders.[1]

II. OPERATING SYSTEMS FOR LABORATORY COMPUTERS

The "operating system" of a computer is a package of fundamental and frequently used programs essential for the smooth and effective utilization of the machine. A satisfactory operating system is not usually available as an off-the-shelf item when the laboratory computer is delivered. This is because the operating system, just as the computer itself, must be specialized to the needs of the user and it is almost impossible for a manufacturer to supply a ready-made system which will serve all applications. This lack of an acceptable operating system may attenuate the attractions of laboratory computers and a certain amount of planning and programming effort will be required to provide such a system and thereby make the laboratory computer really effective. In the past, making a good system required creative genius. Today, enough patterns exist so that copying and adapting their features demands only competence and a reasonable effort. Often, the most satisfactory way of producing a good system is by substantially modifying an existing system—provided by the manufacturer or by another user of a similar machine. Such a system can then exactly fit the needs of a particular application.

Our objective is to familiarize a potential user with laboratory computer operating systems so he will be willing to make his own. The best way to learn this art is to study examples. This paper presents three examples of user-written systems for different sized machines and for different applications. We will attempt not only to describe the systems technically but also to recount some of the history of their development in terms of hours of work and the skill of the programmers.

The Basic Functions of an Operating System

Almost all computer users carry out the following fundamental processes which the operating system must either tolerate or facilitate.

1) *Writing a program:* Classically a handwritten program is converted to a machine readable form by punching it on computer cards. Alternative input media for machines without card readers are punched paper tape or a typewriter. The operating system must provide a program for accepting one or more of these modes of input.

2) *Editing or changing a program:* Classically this is done by the manual process of replacing cards in a deck. However, if the program to be edited resides on a magnetic tape or disk memory, then an editing program is an efficient and convenient alternative which must be provided by the operating system. The program will be one of the most frequently used parts of the system and it must be well human engineered.

3) *Storing programs:* Classically programs are stored as decks of cards in a drawer. Paper or magnetic tape are alternatives. A secondary storage device such as a disk file is an attractive way of keeping a library of programs. The operating system must provide ways of adding programs, removing programs, and retrieving programs from such a library.

4) *Assembling or compiling a program:* All machines have assembly programs to convert statements as written by the programmer to the correct form for execution in the computer. All except the smallest machines have compilers such as FORTRAN which compile machine-language instructions from compiler language statements written by the programmer.

5) *Loading programs:* In order to be executed, programs must be read from the medium on which they are stored and placed in the computer core memory. A loader accomplishes this task. Usually several programs must be loaded together and executed together. A relocating and linking loader automatically loads a set of programs into contiguous blocks of memory locations (relocating) and supplies certain addresses so one program can communicate with another (linking). One program may call a number of other programs. An advanced loader will automatically search through a library of programs and load all those called by any other program.

6) *Debugging programs:* The classic debugging aid is the memory dump which prints the contents of the core memory at some stage in the computation such as the computer's unexpected halt. Printed memory dumps are the heritage of large batch processing installations and cannot be conveniently provided by those laboratory computers which do not have fast printers. The operating systems of laboratory computers must exploit the unique capabilities of these machines and offer other equally effective debugging aids. Programs for conveniently displaying on a cathode-ray tube (CRT) the content of selected memory locations and of program listings must be available. Easy methods for changing the contents of the memory are also vital. Facilities for halting the program at selected key locations and for conveniently inspecting core and special registers at such halts are very useful.

7) *Executing programs:* The simplest way to start a program is to manually set the instruction counter on the computer to the first instruction of the program and press the start button. This method is adequate for most laboratory applications. Large computer operating systems automatically execute a "batch" of programs. Much complexity in the operating systems of

---

[1] Incidentally, it does not seem necessary that a large machine have a complex system although almost all present large computers are so afflicted. A small, simple operating system could conceivably make a large machine attractive, even to a small machine addict. The size of the operating system is more a function of the variety of tasks facing the machine rather than its size. Specialization of operating systems would be worthwhile.

small computers can be avoided by using manual sequencing.

8) *Bootstrapping:* All machines must provide a start-up procedure to load an initial program into core memory and then execute this program. The program is usually a loader which loads other programs. In laboratory computers, the initial instructions are often put into the memory manually. These load a loader which in turn loads the start-up portion of the operating system.

Operating systems do more than these fundamental operations. Most systems have routines to perform a great variety of algebraic operations and to communicate in a simple manner with complex peripheral devices such as disks, typewriters, and scopes. Also, each user will insert programs for his own special purposes. These we will mention only in passing.

When designing or considering a new system or computer, it is useful to ask how each of the above functions are realized, and to think about the speed, convenience, and general human engineering of each process. For example, many computers have been purchased with only a slow (10 character/second) paper tape reader as an input device. Although these machines may have an adequate FORTRAN compiler, the compiler program requires 20 minutes to load in to memory via the paper tape reader. This slowness makes frequent compiling painful and limits the uses of the machine to relatively fixed programs that are infrequently recompiled. The limitation can be beautifully cured with a disk file from which the compiler (and other programs) can be loaded in seconds. We will try to make clear how each of these operations is done in the examples to be discussed.

Examples of Operating Systems

We shall now describe and discuss the operating system of three different computers.

The first example is the LAP6 operating system for the LINC computer written by Mary Allen Wilkes and her associates at Washington University, St. Louis, Mo. The LINC is one of the smallest computers in general use and is used primarily in medical and biological fields for jobs such as processing neurological signals, monitoring data from cardiac patients, handling data from hospital laboratories, and collecting medical histories from patients; it is by far the best known machine in this field. The computer and several earlier operating systems were developed [4]–[9] over a period of more than five years incorporating the experience of many users. As a result, LAP6 is outstandingly well human engineered.

The second example is a system for the DDP-224 computer written by Barbara Caspers and Peter Denes at Bell Laboratories. The DDP-224 computer was purchased especially to carry out studies of speech synthesis and analysis. It is large and fast according to laboratory computer standards, having a 32 000 word, 24 bit, 1.9 μs memory. The construction of this system is a good example of how a powerful system focused on a particular use may be created

by writing certain parts and modifying other existing programs.

The third example is a DDP-516 computer which is intermediate in size between the LINC and the DDP-224. It was obtained to run psychoacoustic experiments, such as presenting sounds to a subject and recording his response. Its system was constructed in a manner similar to that for the DDP-224 and illustrates a smaller system. It was designed by J. L. Flanagan, C. H. Coker, and their associates at Bell Laboratories.

The LAP6 Operating System

1) *The LINC Hardware and LAP6*

The LINC computer is shown in Fig. 1. The basic machine has a 4096 word, 12 bit, 1 μs memory, and hardware to multiply but not to divide (this must be done by a program).[2] In one form the machine has neither paper tape facilities nor hard copy output. All input comes via a keyboard; all output is either displayed on the scope or is an electrical voltage. External electrical equipment may be easily connected to eight digital-to-analog converters built into the machine. Likewise, a built-in analog-to-digital converter allows digitizing external electric signals. The cost of this configuration is about $45 000.

The two LINC tape drives are an essential part of the basic machine and make possible the operating system which we shall describe. Unlike most computer tapes, any section of a LINC tape can be overwritten without affecting the preceding or succeeding sections; thus, they are ideal for editing purposes. Such a tape drive was described as early as 1958 [10]. The tapes function as removable disk packs which are cheap, if slow. The tape reels are about four inches in diameter and, thus, easy to store. One tape reel holds 130 000 words. The operating system, programs, and data are all kept on these tapes.

The essence of the operating system consists of nothing more (or less) than a manuscript editing and filing system which enables manuscripts to be typed on the keyboard, filed on a tape, retrieved from the file, and modified. A manuscript can be anything, but is typically a source language program which will be assembled into a LINC machine-language program.

2) *Detailed Description of LAP6*

The structure of the information on a LAP6 tape is shown in Fig. 2. LINC tapes are organized into 512 blocks each containing 256 words of information. Up to eight blocks may be read into computer memory by a single computer instruction which gives the number of the block (0 to 511) and the number of blocks to be read. This powerful tape communication instruction greatly facilitates several LAP6 operations.

The first 184 and the last 232 blocks on a tape are used to file manuscripts. The file is divided into two sections to reduce the time needed to reach a manuscript. A list occu-

---

[2] The original LINC only had 2048 words of memory and this was a factor influencing the design of LAP6.

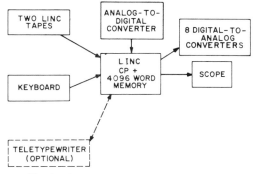

Fig. 1.   Basic LINC computer configuration.

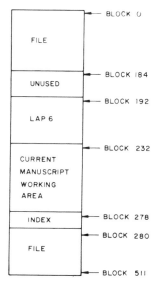

Fig. 2.   Standard LAP6 tape organization with file. (This drawing is a modified version of Chart I in the *LAP6 Handbook* [11].)

NAME	BN	#BLKS
GEORGE	M 430	12
	B 262	2
2345678	B 442	3
DP-MAR 20	M 445	27
	B 474	6
DP2 APR 2	M 264	4
DISPLAY	B 502	3
MNEMONIC	M 505	11

Fig. 3.   Index of LAP6 file displayed on CRT.
(From *LAP6 Handbook* [11].)

56		ADD 9J
57	#6K	STC p+5
60		JMP 3Y−2
61		LDA i
62		MTB
63		STA

Fig. 4.   Current manuscript displayed on CRT for editing purposes.
(From *LAP6 Handbook* [11].)

pying two blocks contains the names of the manuscripts, their block numbers, and their length. The list may be displayed on the CRT as illustrated in Fig. 3. The first column gives the manuscript name. the second, whether it is a user-written manuscript (M) or machine instructions (B). the third gives its starting block, and the fourth gives its length. Users refer to manuscripts by names which they assign. The LAP6 system occupies 32 blocks. When a manuscript is assembled. the machine-language instructions are put in the eight blocks denoted "current binary." From there they can be loaded into the LINC memory for execution.

In order to edit a manuscript, it is transferred to the scroll (current manuscript) area of 45 blocks. Up to 15 lines of the current manuscript may be displayed on the CRT. Fig. 4 shows a sample display of six lines. Lines of a manuscript are sequentially numbered by LAP6 and the numbers are shown in the left-hand column. The user may display any 15 lines by "scrolling" through the manuscript. Editing is accomplished by deleting or inserting lines at any point in the manuscript, new lines being typed at the keyboard. Changes are shown on the scope as they are made, thus, the display is always current.

The user instructs LAP6 as to what he wants done simply by typing "meta" commands at the keyboard, each command being uniquely identified as starting with a "→". The current command is shown at the bottom of the CRT. For example, "→ SM GRAPHIC,1" saves the current manuscript in the file on tape unit 1 under the name GRAPHIC. If a manuscript named GRAPHIC already exists on the file. the user will be asked whether he really wishes to overwrite the old file before the command is executed.

Some of the other LAP6 commands perform the following functions:

1) Position the current manuscript to a given line number in preparation for inserting or deleting lines.
2) Combine two manuscripts by inserting a manuscript from the file after a given line number in the current manuscript.
3) Copy manuscripts from the file on one tape unit to the file on another.
4) Convert a manuscript to machine language—a process usually referred to as assembling the program.
5) Load a machine-language file into the LINC memory.
6) Transfer control from the LAP6 system to a user program in order to execute the program. Procedures also exist for returning to LAP6.
7) Type a manuscript (if the LINC has a teletypewriter).

The assembly process creates absolute rather than relocatable programs in that they are always loaded into the same memory locations by the loader. Also. the loader will not combine or link several programs. In order to combine programs. the original manuscripts are combined using instruction 2) and the composite manuscript is assembled. LAP6 manuscripts contain symbols (as do the assembly language manuscripts for most computers) which are eventually associated with specific memory locations. Combining manuscripts may cause an error if the same symbol is used in two manuscripts. Another LAP6 instruction displays the symbols from a manuscript to simplify checking for this error.

Another way of effecting the interaction of separate programs is based on the powerful tape reading instruction which we mentioned earlier and is called *layering*. Various programs are stored in machine-language form in blocks on the LINC tape. The single tape reading instruction will read up to eight of these blocks into the LINC memory, replacing the program already in memory. If desired, the next instruction executed by the LINC comes from the incoming layer. Thus, the tape reading instruction is equivalent to a "transfer to subroutine instruction" in many other computers. Layering has the additional advantage that the subroutine is read into the same memory locations as the program which calls it, thus conserving memory space which is vital in a machine with as small a memory as the LINC. As an example of layering, LAP6 itself has 11 layers.

3) Discussion of LAP6

We might now review how the eight fundamental operations listed in a preceding section are accomplished with LAP6. Facilities for writing, editing, and storing programs have been discussed and are the crowning glories of LAP6. The keyboard language for writing and editing is very well human engineered. One objective was to make catastrophic mistakes, such as destroying the file, almost impossible. The user is encouraged to guess if he forgets the exact form of a command. LAP6 will reject most mistakes and inform him of errors. The data transfer rate from the LINC tapes is fast enough and much thought has been given to the arrangement of the information so most reading or writing processes do not delay or harass the user. A tape may be spun from one end to the other in about 25 seconds. The entire memory of the computer may be loaded from tape in about 0.5 second. The speed of these operations are good landmarks to keep in mind when laying out an operating system and considering storage media.

Assembling is much simplified and becomes almost a subpart of manuscript editing. Compiling is not available. It is difficult to make a good compiler for a machine with so little core memory and so short a word length. Users of LAP6 often state they prefer assembly language although such statements are skeptically received by users of compilers.

Program loading is also simplified by avoiding relocation and linking and becomes a subpart of manuscript handling. Some inconvenience, if not limitations, are imposed by the simple loader.

Program execution is initiated from the keyboard by the user.

Bootstrapping is elegantly done with the tape reading instruction. Using switches on the console the user manually executes one instruction to read in the first eight blocks of LAP6 and manually transfers control to a starting location in LAP6. All subsequent operations can be done from the keyboard.

Almost no debugging facilities are provided by LAP6.

However, the computer hardware contains powerful built-in debugging tools. Program execution can be halted at any prespecified location. Programs can be executed one instruction at a time or at a slow rate. The contents of the LINC memory locations may be viewed on the console by setting switches to the desired memory address.

One other special instruction in the LINC machine has greatly influenced LAP6. Much use is made of the CRT for displaying manuscripts and alphanumeric information. A display instruction allows the presentation of a letter by executing only two instructions. In addition, the shape of the letter is described by only two memory words. Thus, the 63-character font needs only 126 memory locations. Without this simple display, the CRT programs would have been much less attractive.

LAP6 contains a total of 4600 instructions. The LINC computer was first used in 1963 and the experience of many users is incorporated into the present system. Wilkes estimates that five months were spent on planning, two on documenting, and thirteen on programming and algorithm study.

Perhaps a more useful figure is a time of about three months needed by three "computer enthusiasts,"—Richard Lary, Leonard Elekman, and Henry Maurer—at the Polytechnic Institute of Brooklyn to create a very similar system for a PDP-8. Their system includes the more exotic languages of LISP, SNOBOL, and BASIC, but uses essentially the same editing and filing scheme.

Documentation for LAP6 and the LINC consists of one 40-page handbook [11] for LAP6 and one 130-page instruction manual for the LINC computer, [9] a delightfully minute library.

Perhaps the best testimony to the outstanding success of LAP6 is the fact that almost none of a wide range of users has felt a need to modify the system. The editing and filing procedures are universally acclaimed and are worth emulating in computers of any size. The most frequently suggested modifications are simply extensions that handle more than two LINC tapes or a version which uses a disk instead of a tape.

A DDP-224 Operating System

Our second example is the operating system of an intermediate-sized computer, a Honeywell DDP-224, which is in use at Bell Laboratories. It has a 32 000 word, 24 bit, 1.9 μs memory, floating point arithmetic, and cost $300 000. The operating system was designed for self-service operation by a variety of users. Many of these users are not expert programmers, some cannot program at all, and most of them have little technical knowledge of the peripheral devices attached to the computer. These peripherals range from standard digital tape and disk drives to special laboratory instruments such as microphones, graphical input devices, control knobs, display oscilloscopes, loudspeakers, and speech synthesizers.

The operating system of such a machine must be both simple and powerful. It must be simple so that the nonexpert users can operate it themselves in a trouble-free manner. The system must also be powerful enough to offer, in a

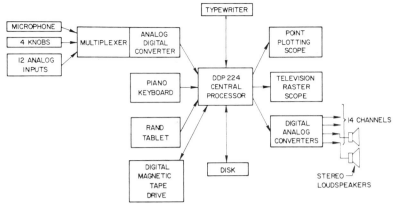

Fig. 5.   Block diagram of peripheral devices connected to DDP-224.

convenient manner and without reliance on larger machines, at least some of the features of a larger system. A good assembler, a FORTRAN, and other more application-oriented languages must be available. There must also be subroutines for controlling the computer's peripheral devices in a simple manner; these subroutines must be usable in either assembler language or FORTRAN. Finally, effective debugging aids are required: the users need programs for memory displays and for updating programs, and those who have to maintain the computer need effective machine diagnostic programs.

1) The DDP-224 Hardware

The hardware configuration of our DDP-224 is shown in Fig. 5. The core memory locations are accessed by two data channels which can read and write independently of the central processor. A typewriter, a magnetic tape drive, a disk, and simple interrupt facilities came with the machine. We added circuitry of our own to connect the computer with control knobs, a microphone, a Rand tablet, a piano keyboard for composers of computer music (or for subjects' responses in computer-controlled tests), loudspeakers, speech synthesizers, and two display cathode-ray tubes, one with point-plotting facilities and one with a television-like scanned display.

A number of devices share the same data channel. It was made a rule that no user would ever have to, or be allowed to, mechanically connect or reconnect laboratory devices with the computer. All devices are therefore permanently connected to the computer and are switched into action electronically by program-initiated signals. We found that effective maintenance, and orderly succession of users who needed varying configurations of peripheral connections, were possible only with a strict "hands-off" policy for the users. This enabled the person in charge of maintenance to have a clear picture of the status of connections between peripherals and computer; it also helped the users because the automatic selection of peripherals by program eliminated human errors in making these connections.

There is no card equipment and no line printer. Most of our programs, however, are still punched on cards and printed program listings are also readily available. This is possible because the assembler and FORTRAN compiler of our system read their source programs from magnetic tape and record their listings on tape. These tapes are hand-carried to a batch processing computer down the hall that performs the card-to-tape and tape-to-printer conversions. This arrangement avoids the high cost of printers and of card equipment.

An important feature of the hardware system is the disk which allows highly flexible storage and retrieval of data or programs. The disk drive which we selected is a moving head drive with removable disk packs and a storage capacity of 2.4 million 24-bit words. It provides the means for random storage and retrieval of a great number of separate files. In this way, it is an essential factor in making our operating system fast, convenient, and easy to use. Many users have their own disk packs.

2) A Short Introduction to the DDP-224 System

The principal constituents of the operating system are shown in Table I together with their size and the time required to develop them.

As an introduction to describing them, let us see how the system appears to a typical user. The user sits at a console and starts by manually transferring control to the system executive. The executive permanently resides in the uppermost 256 core memory locations which is the only core memory preempted by the system. In case they have been erased, the bootstrap starting procedure consists of manually executing six instructions at the console which reads in the system executive from the disk.

Upon transferring control to the system executive, the computer writes "READY" on the typewriter. The user types the name of one or more system programs which are loaded into core memory by the system executive. They are obtained from the system library stored on the disk. Our user will call for the frequently used loader. He will manually transfer control to the loader. It will load his routines from a tape or disk, it will relocate and link together his programs and subroutines, and it will search through the subroutine library (on disk) for any programs not already supplied. Upon successfully finding all programs, the loader will type a map showing where each program is located in core memory. In order to begin execution the user now manually transfers to the starting location of his first program. The

TABLE I
PROGRAMS OF THE DDP-224 OPERATING SYSTEM

Program Function	Approximate Programmer-Weeks for Writing and Documentation	Number of Instructions
System executive	6 weeks	256
Disk store: 1) by code name	5 weeks	217
2) by disk track address	5 weeks	111
System editor—including editing of subroutine library	5 weeks	416
Loader*	4 weeks	1300
Symbolic assembler*—DAP	4 weeks	6800
FORTRAN IV compiler*	3 weeks	6530
(extension of READ/WRITE statements for disk operation)	3 weeks	
(modifications and debugging of manufacturer's library subroutines)	9 weeks	
File editor	5 weeks	1750
Display and modification of selected core locations	5 weeks	1532
Memory dumps—for hard copy	1 week	147
Subroutine library:		
Disk I/O	9 weeks	240
Tape/disk storage by speech sample number or by word count	8 weeks	1008
Graphics package	6 weeks	1375
Bit manipulation	2 days	76
Adaptation of fast Fourier transform algorithm	1 week	2212

* Time to modify manufacturer's program for disk operation.

whole process might take 30 seconds to five minutes depending on whether tapes or disks must be mounted.

As an alternative to invoking the loader, our user may have previously named his program and stored it on disk as part of the system library. In this case, he would merely type the name and the system executive would load his program as any other system program.

If instead of loading and executing, our user wishes to assemble (or compile) a new program, he will call for the assembler and transfer control to it. The user-written source program to be assembled was previously written on tape which was mounted on the computer. The source program could have been written on the computer typewriter using the file editor, but typically it will have been punched onto computer cards and transferred to tape with a card-to-tape conversion in the nearby batch processing computer. The file editor program is often used to modify an existing tape.

The assembled machine-language instructions are automatically stored on disk and are available to the loader to be put into core and executed. Alternatively, the machine instructions can be copied onto a separate file on tape and loaded on a subsequent occasion. A listing file may also be put onto tape and printed in the batch processing computer center.

3) *Details of DDP-224 System*

Having viewed the machine as a user, let us now discuss the programs listed in Table I. The system executive also

contains a debugging aid which operates from the console. It displays and allows modification of the contents of successive memory locations.

The disk store programs place absolute programs identified by name onto the system library (for retrieval by the system executive) or places them at a given numbered disk track (for manual retrieval via the disk store program). Only absolute programs or core images are handled, no relocation or linking is done by these programs. Relocation or linking is done only by the loader. Input material for the loader consists of either an output file from the assembler or compiler or a file on the subroutine library.

The system editor is used to add or delete programs on the subroutine library. It is also used to delete programs from the system library and to make tape or disk copies of the system library and the subroutine library.

The file system for the DDP-224 lacks some of the elegance of the file system for LAP6 in that the several kinds of files—absolute, relocatable, source programs, and listings—are treated slightly differently. Some can be named, others not; some are typically kept on tape, others on disk. Different editing and manipulating programs are used for each kind of file. In LAP6, all files are treated alike. Part of the DDP-224 multiplicity arose historically, particularly in making use of the manufacturer-supplied loader; part arises because the DDP-224 file system is conceptually simpler. No automatic restructuring of the files is done. The DDP-224 system is probably closer to what most people will create starting from manufacturer-supplied programs; systems written from scratch might aim for the LAP6 unity. However, both are very effective file systems.

The loader, symbolic assembler, and FORTRAN IV compiler are a frequently used part of the system.

The file editor operates from the typewriter and allows modification of source files which are typically read from and written onto tape. Lines in the files are sequentially numbered by the editor. The program operates by line to print, to insert, or to delete lines.

The two main debugging programs display the contents of core memory on the scope or write the contents of core memory on a tape for subsequent printing on the batch processing computer. The display program allows easy scrolling through memory and allows modification of memory locations.

The programs so far discussed carry out the eight fundamental operations listed earlier. In addition, there is an extensive subroutine library consisting of several sections. There is the usual selection of mathematical function subroutines. There are the subroutines for data transfer to and from the computer's numerous peripherals, including the disk. One set of these subroutines are "low level," that is, they require detailed specification of track address (e.g., for the disk routines), or record size, and of similar information. They are seldom used, except by those writing system programs. Most programmers use another set of input–output subroutines that require practically no technical familiarity with the peripherals. To write on disk or tape, the user needs only to specify the starting address of the block of data to be transferred and the number of words to be transferred (in either assembler or FORTRAN symbols). These data words can be as easily retrieved. Control knobs can also be read by a subroutine in which only the reference number of the knob and the address in which the reading is to be stored need be specified. There is an equally simple set of graphics subroutines for producing cathode-ray screen displays; there are point-by-point and vector plotting subroutines for both the point-plotting cathode-ray tube and the television-type display.

4) Evolution of DDP-224 System

The main use for our DDP-224 is to aid research on speech analysis and synthesis. Speech research has used computers extensively since the late 1950's [12]-[17]. First, this was done in the conventional batch processing mode, but in the mid-1960's we decided to supplement these facilities by obtaining a small dedicated computer [18], [19]. A DDP-24 was obtained in January 1965, and a DDP-224 in May 1967. Both machines are now in operation. Although very similar, they differ in certain details. In particular, the DDP-24 operating system was based on a magnetic tape file system while that of the DDP-224 is based on a disk file. We have described only the latter. Previous experience with the DDP-24 facilitated the design of the DDP-224 system and also reduced the programmer-weeks needed for its completion.

DDP-224 was accepted in February, 1968 after Honeywell's customer engineers remedied a number of hardware bugs; since then, it has been almost trouble-free. One of our own engineers spent about one year designing and building the digital circuitry for linking laboratory peripherals with the computer and working with the customer engineers. The digital interface includes a fairly elaborate electronic switching system for connecting peripherals to data channels under program control and for switching these peripherals from one data channel to another.

On the software side, the manufacturer delivered a loader, a symbolic assembler, a FORTRAN IV, a subroutine library for calculating mathematical functions and for the control of standard peripherals, certain file editing programs, and a set of computer diagnostics. No software at all was initially available for the disk. Some disk programs were delivered at a later stage but we found them cumbersome and inconvenient to adapt for our requirements, and they were never used.

The disk-oriented executive program was written entirely by ourselves and so were the subroutines for reading and writing on disk. The manufacturer's loader and symbolic assembler were substantially trouble-free but we had to rewrite their input–output sections in order to adapt them for use with the disk. FORTRAN also had to be changed to output its object programs and listing to disk; in addition, we also extended the scope of the FORTRAN READ/WRITE statements to include access to the disk. The FORTRAN compiler itself gave us no trouble but we made major revisions of its library subroutines. We eliminated the recursive and dynamic storage features as well as a number of bugs.

The manufacturer's programmers gave very valuable advice in making some corrections; still, several programmer-months of our own effort were needed to make FORTRAN operative.

The FORTRAN we now have uses the fast hardware floating point arithmetic, has no known bugs, and is used extensively. In fact, most users now write all their programs in FORTRAN. This trend has been reinforced by the numerous and convenient additional FORTRAN subroutines we have made available for bit manipulation, for graphical display, for control knob and Rand tablet operation, and for calculating Fourier transforms.

The file editing program that came with the DDP-224 was not used. Instead, we took the editing program we have used for years on the DDP-24 and adapted it to the DDP-224 by providing the program with disk capability.

The bulk of this programming was done by Mrs. B. E. Caspers who spent about one year on this project. In addition, several other programmers spent a total of about eight programmer-months on writing certain parts of the system. Information about the time needed to prepare various sections of the system is given in Table I.

5) The DDP-224 System and Its Users

The DDP-224 currently has about a dozen regular users. There are separate manuals for FORTRAN, for the assembler, and for the operating system; there is also a reference manual for the machine itself. The four volumes have a total of about 250 pages. Users get an initial demonstration of the machine and of the operating system, and have easy access to the four manuals. After the first few weeks, they normally require very little additional help.

Individual users are on the machine for not less than one hour and not more than two hours. Between 9:00 AM and 6:00 PM on weekdays, time is allotted according to the needs of individual research projects; schedules are revised weekly after consulting the users. After 6:00 PM and on weekends, time is available on a sign-up basis. Users cannot sign up for more than two hours although, of course, they can stay on the machine for as long as they like in case there is nobody waiting to get on. Not turning up for times reserved by sign-up is actively discouraged. The machine is normally in continuous use from 9:00 AM to about 11:00 PM on weekdays and typically for about four to five hours on weekends.

A DDP-516 Operating System

1) The DDP-516 Hardware

The DDP-516 is intermediate in size between the LINC and the DDP-224. The computer has a 16-bit word length and the particular machine 16 000 words of 1 μs core memory. Of our three examples it is probably most typical of the majority of laboratory machines. Sixteen- or eighteen-bit word length is very popular. A diagram of the configuration is shown in Fig. 6. The central processor has fast fixed point multiply and divide instructions built into the hardware. Two data channels access the memory, independently of each other and the central processor. Program interrupts

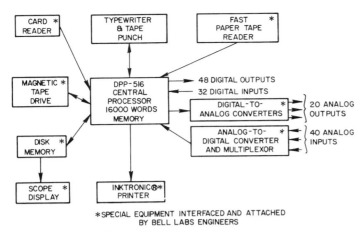

*SPECIAL EQUIPMENT INTERFACED AND ATTACHED BY BELL LABS ENGINEERS

Fig. 6.   DDP-516 computer system.

TABLE II
NONSTANDARD EQUIPMENT ATTACHED TO THE DDP-516

Item	Hardware Cost (dollars)	Labor to Attach
Common overhead for design of interface system to which all the peripheral devices are attached		2 man years*
Fast paper tape reader	600	1 man week
Card reader	1800	1.5 man weeks
Magnetic tape drive	14 000	6 man months
Disk	12 000	6 man months
Scope		1 man month
Inktronic[R] printer	5600	3 man days

* This figure is more than twice that required for the DDP-224 because some of the peripherals that were specially interfaced to the DDP-516 were obtained as manufacturer-supplied options for the DDP-224.

TABLE III
PROGRAMS OF THE DDP-516 OPERATING SYSTEM

Program Function	Approximate Programmer-Weeks for Writing and Documentation	Number of Instructions
System executive	2 weeks	48
System and subroutine library editor	8 weeks	2400
Loader*	8 weeks*	2000
Symbolic assembler*—DAP	8 weeks*	6000
FORTRAN IV compiler*	8 weeks*	6000
Memory dump—hard copy*	2 weeks*	900
General scope display	4 weeks	300 FORTRAN Statements
FORTRAN callable input–output subroutines	12 weeks	

* The main program supplied by manufacturer. The time given was used to make minor modifications.

and digital clocks are included. The configuration, as shown in Fig. 6, cost $100 000 excluding the digital–analog converters.

As is evident from Fig. 6, much of the equipment is not supplied by the DDP-516 manufacturer but was especially attached. Table II indicates the cost of the special items and labor to attach them. That they could be used at all testifies to the effectiveness of the data channels. The wisdom of making special attachments depends on many factors such as the cost and quality of available engineering help. The magnetic tape and disk proved difficult to attach, and we are now inclined toward manufacturer-interfaced items. The rest of the equipment is connected easily.

The disk is a fixed-head machine by the Data Disc Corporation, which gives rapid access to 394 000 words secondary storage. The scope display is a special device[3] which can be controlled directly from one of the 64 disk tracks; hence, no computer time is required to maintain the display. The Inktronic[R] printer manufactured by the Teletype Corporation provides a moderate speed output (120 characters/second) at a moderate price ($6000).

Forty-eight digital outputs which operate relays, 32 digital inputs from switches or relays, 20 analog outputs, and 40 analog inputs connect the computer to a wide variety of experimental apparatus.

2) Description of DDP-516 Operating System

Table III lists the principal programs in the operating system. The bootstrap consists of 15 instructions which are located in a nonerasable section of core memory. Execution of these instructions loads the 48-instruction system executive from the disk. The system executive is loaded afresh each time it is used since the memory locations which it occupies are overwritten by most other programs.

The executive is used to load other system programs from disk into core memory. Systems programs are numbered rather than named. To load a program the user enters its number into a console register and transfers control to the executive.

[3] This is an incremental scope developed by H. S. McDonald and his associates at Bell Telephone Laboratories.

Editing the system is accomplished manually. When a new system program is to be added, the user must locate a blank disk space large enough to accommodate it, load the program into core and transfer it to disk. Compacting the system would require moving the system programs by hand. Consequently, this is rarely done. The system executive transfers programs from disk to core memory. Three other programs used in editing transfer material from magnetic tape to disk, from core to disk, and from one part of disk to another. Copies of the system on magnetic tape can be made.

The system has a library of relocatable subroutines located in a protected area of the disk. Tape copies can be made. Users can also have private subroutine libraries on other parts of the disk. The loader will refer to these libraries. A subroutine editor deletes or adds subroutines to these libraries, the source of the subroutine being a paper tape.

Three manufacturer-supplied programs, an assembler, a FORTRAN IV compiler, and a loader do the bulk of the translation from human to machine language. The assembler and compiler output two files on the disk, a machine-language file to be loaded by the loader or punched onto paper tape and a listing file which can be printed by the Inktronic[R] printer or viewed on the scope.

The loader is a complicated program. In addition to relocating, linking, and finding programs in subroutine libraries, it readdresses programs where necessary. The DDP-516, in common with many other 16-bit machines, can only directly address 512 words of memory. The assembler and compiler generate instructions which address the entire memory. The loader uses special addressing procedures (indirect addressing) where necessary. Hence, it provides a final pass of the assembly process.

All three of the manufacturer-supplied programs were modified only by a short machine-language patch to accommodate disk input–output. They were not even reassembled.

Source programs are punched onto cards. Consequently, no editing programs for source files are needed and program writing and editing is done away from the computer, thus saving computer time.

A memory dumping program prints out the contents of the core memory and provides other, infrequently used, debugging aids. Another program displays memory contents on the scope.

The subroutine library includes input–output programs which allow FORTRAN I/O to be directed toward any device—the Teletype® teletypewriter, the paper tape, the Inktronic® printer, the disk, the magnetic tape, and the scope. This was simply accomplished with subroutines which make all the devices appear to be teletypes to FORTRAN. Other levels of input–output exist including bit-oriented, character-oriented, and word-oriented routines.

Documentation for the operating system consists of a ring binder with 40 pages. The users group contains about 15 people whose offices are close together and have easy opportunity to exchange information.

3) Development Schedule of DDP-516 System

The DDP-516 described here was delivered in April 1967. An effective system based on a tape secondary storage became operational in six months. Work on the disk interface started in December 1967 and was working in April 1968. A basic disk executive was operative a few weeks later and the full system listed in Table III was developed during the following year in response to the experience of users. The hardware was constructed and maintained by two full-time engineers and a wireman. The systems programs were written by one of the engineers and one programmer. At present, two identical systems are used to study hearing and certain speech coding problems.

III. Conclusions

We have reviewed three operating systems for laboratory computers. One system (LAP6) was programmed in its entirety by a single person. It contains many features worth considering for copying into other systems. The LINC machine is by a factor of two the smallest of the examples and the sophistication of its system in such a small environment is truly an achievement. The other systems (DDP-224 and DDP-516) were assembled from some manufacturer-supplied and some home-written programs. They are excellent examples of how commercial programs can be customized to serve specific needs. In one machine (DDP-516), many of the peripheral devices were "home-attached" thus demonstrating the ultimate flexibility inherent in current computers. All the machines and systems interact well with the external world through analog–digital converters or data channels.

The great diversity of uses of these machines make it impossible to point to universally desirable features. Thus, a LINC user may be admirably served by its simple assembly program, whereas many DDP-516 or DDP-224 users do not even know machine language and write only in FORTRAN. Instead of rigid recommendations, one must say that the features of a computer and its operating system must fit the task and users for which the system is intended. This is the recapitulation of the theme of specialization which was announced in the introduction. Perhaps the only generalization that can be safely made is to again point out the basic processes of program writing, editing, storing, assembling or compiling, loading, debugging, executing, and starting. These must be accommodated by the system and the accommodation should be well human engineered. Well-designed library subroutines and utility programs for controlling the special laboratory instruments can significantly extend the utility of the machine by making it available to users with little computer experience—as was demonstrated by the DDP-224 system.

One of the prominent differences between the systems we have described and the stripped-down little computers widely advertised for $4000 to $15 000 is the presence of an adequate secondary storage system. A disk is almost always the best secondary storage, but as LAP6 demonstrated, the right kind of tape drive will also serve. The secondary storage makes possible adequate speeds and good human engineering for many of the system programs as well as enhancing the computer's potential for the users' programs. It is worth its substantial cost.

The other, almost universal feature shown by the examples is the usefulness of a good editing and filing program. There is need to both keep and revise source programs, machine-language programs, and user data (although this was not discussed). The one contradiction to the need for editing occurred on the DDP-516 where a card reader provided good manual editing via cards.

Two notable features missing in these systems are any automatic sequencing to execute a series of programs and any multiprogramming or time sharing. Automatic sequencing is replaced by manual transfers to start the various programs. The time needed seems consistent with the cost of the machine, with the block of time a typical individual user has on the machine, and with its use in a laboratory environment. Manual sequencing avoids much operating system complexity and preserves maximum flexibility. Time sharing has introduced difficulties and rigidities which are as yet incompletely solved in big computer centers and we feel it had best be avoided in laboratory computers except in very special and circumscribed conditions.

One highly desirable feature we have not mentioned is an electrical communication network attaching small computers together and attaching them to large computers. In this way, common use could be made of expensive peripheral devices such as fast printers and large secondary storage files could be shared. We have avoided these attractive possibilities because networks giving good service do not yet exist. The main stumbling blocks are not the electrical connections to the computers, but rather the difficulty of modifying the systems in the larger machines to accommodate this kind of service, and the difficulty of batching together messages to efficiently use expensive long distance communication channels. We hope these obstacles can be overcome. If so, we envision even more effective use of laboratory machines. Computing power will be distributed among many different kinds of machines, each selected for a particular application. The machines will be spatially distributed to be convenient to the people and equipment with which they interact. The machines will be able to call upon other machines through the network where such operations are economically desirable or where information must be exchanged.

We have claimed that it is practical for users to put together their own computer configuration and their own operating system specially tailored to their application. But it is not as clear how much effort is involved. The DDP-224 and DDP-516 give some idea of what was involved in specific cases. In the process of creating the system and configuration, at least one expert systems programmer and one engineer who understands the computer will be needed. One would be optimistic to expect many systems to give good service sooner than a year after delivery of the computer. On the other hand, a system taking more than two years to develop is probably over-ambitious.

Enough good operating systems for small computers have been made so acts of creative genius are not necessary to make a new system. Competent programming is required along with the knowledge of existing systems so as to adapt the available techniques to the specific demands of a particular application. The self-reliance and bravery necessary to get one's own small computer and to write one's own operating system will be greatly rewarded both by economical computing and by flexibility in fitting the computer and programs to the tasks at hand. In this way many applications can be done which are either too expensive or impossible with other approaches.

ACKNOWLEDGMENT

The authors wish to thank Miss M. A. Wilkes for her essential help in supplying information about LAP6. In addition, the authors are indebted to Mrs. E. Kippel, F. R. Moore, and Miss M. Southern, who did the programming, A. M. Noll who wrote the graphics package, and G. D. Bergland [20] whose FORTRAN-written fast Fourier transform program was adapted for use in the DDP-224 system. O. C. Jensen, who designed and built the DDP-224's digital interface, also contributed to the programming effort.

REFERENCES

[1] M. V. Mathews, "Choosing a scientific computer for service," *Science*, vol. 161, p. 3836, July 5, 1968.
[2] J. R. Cox, Jr., "Economies of scale and specialization in large computing systems," *Computer Design*, November 1968.
[3] W. A. Clark et al., "Macromodular computer systems," *1967 Spring Joint Computer Conf., AFIPS Proc.*, vol. 30, Washington, D. C.: Spartan, 1967.
[4] "Convocation on the Mississippi," *Proc. Final LINC Evaluation Program Meeting* (Washington University, St. Louis), March 18–19, 1965. (Held in conjunction with the National Aeronautics and Space Administration under NIH contract PH 45-63-540.)
[5] M. A. Wilkes, *LAP3 Users' Manual*, Center Development Office, Mass. Inst. Tech., Cambridge, Mass., (informal report), 1963.
[6] M. A. Wilkes, "LAP5:LINC assembly program," *1966 Proc. DECUS Spring Symp.* (Boston, Mass.), May 1966.
[7] W. A. Clark and C. E. Molnar, "A description of the LINC," in *Computers in Biomedical Research*, vol. 2, R. W. Stacy and B. Waxman, Eds. New York: Academic Press, 1965.
[8] G. P. Hicks, M. M. Gieschen, W. V. Slack, and F. C. Larson, "Routine use of a small digital computer in the clinical laboratory," *J. Am. Med. Assoc.*, vol. 196, no. 11, June 13, 1966.
[9] M. A. Wilkes and W. A. Clark, *Programming the LINC*, 2nd ed. St. Louis: Computer Systems Laboratory, Washington University, January 1969.
[10] R. L. Best and T. C. Stockebrand, "A computer-integrated rapid-access magnetic tape system with fixed address," *Proc. Western Joint Computer Conf.* (Los Angeles, Calif.), 1958.
[11] M. A. Wilkes, *LAP6 Handbook*, Computer Research Laboratory, Washington University, St. Louis, Mo., Tech. Rept. 2, May 1, 1967.
[12] E. E. David, M. V. Mathews, and H. S. McDonald, "Description and results of experiments with speech using digital computer simulation," *1958 Proc. Natl. Electronics Conf.*, pt. 1, pp. 766–775.
[13] E. E. David, M. V. Mathews, and H. S. McDonald, "A high-speed data translator for computer simulation of speech and television devices," *Proc. Western Joint Computer Conf.* (San Francisco, Calif.), March 1959.
[14] M. V. Mathews, "The effective use of digital simulation for speech processing," *Proc. Seminar on Speech Compression and Processing*, USAF Cambridge Research Center, September 1959.
[15] P. B. Denes and M. V. Mathews, "Spoken digit recognition using time-frequency pattern matching," *J. Acoust. Soc. Am.*, vol. 32, no. 11, pp. 1450–1455, November 1960.
[16] E. E. David, M. V. Mathews, and H. S. McDonald, "Digital computer simulation as a tool in speech research," *Proc. 3rd Internatl. Congr. Acoustics* (Stuttgart, Germany), 1959.
[17] M. R. Schroeder, "Computers in acoustics: symbiosis of an old science and a new tool," *J. Acoust. Soc. Am.*, vol. 45, pp. 1077–1088, May 1969.
[18] P. B. Denes, "Real-time speech research," *The Human Use of Computing Machines*, Bell Telephone Laboratories, pp. 15–23, 1966.
[19] P. B. Denes, "Computers in speech research," *Proc. Kyoto Speech Symp.*, 1968.
[20] G. D. Bergland, "A radix-eight fast Fourier transform subroutine for real-valued series," *IEEE Trans. Audio and Electroacoustics*, vol. AU-17, pp. 138–144, June 1969.

PERIPHERAL EQUIPMENT FOR MINICOMPUTERS

L. W. Vincent
Data Products Division
Lockheed Electronics Company
Los Angeles, California

Peripheral equipment requirements for minicomputers are often misunderstood. Because the computer is minimal and low in cost, peripheral equipment requirements are assumed also to be minimal and low in cost. Although cost is an important consideration, requirements certainly are not minimal, neither in performance nor diversity. Minicomputers are not restricted to minisystems. Requirement for any system, small or large, is application dependent, and there is a diversity of applications for minicomputers. Minicomputers are being used in every application conceived for major computers, and in some unique applications where, for the first time, cost goals can be achieved. A significant change has occurred in the application development with minicomputers. Often someone other than the minicomputer vendor is responsible for the application development, casting a new aspect upon the definition of the peripheral equipment requirements: what equipment should be offered versus who should offer it.

Minicomputer applications can be considered in three categories:

I. A Low Cost Computer System - Concept of a traditional computing system with all functional features, yet cost is paramount.

II. A Low Cost Element in a Computer System - The ultimate goal is to increase the performance of a total computer system. A batch terminal is an example.

III. A Low Cost Element in a System - A controller element only within a system developed by the user.

A number of common system requirements are within these three categories that can be considered computer system options. Three of the most common are Direct Memory Access, I/O interface line drive capability, and memory expansion such as disc or drum. Demand is made upon the computer vendor both to fulfill the needs of these common requirements and those of category I. The needs of category II can be filled by either the computer vendor or the user. Category III requirements are almost totally filled by the user.

Consider the forms of peripheral equipment, regardless of application category as Memory, Input, and Output. For each, a quick tabulation includes such devices as shown in Tables I, II and III. Each item has a particular utility for a given application. The utility function choice usually is based upon obtaining the highest reliability for the lowest cost within the bounds of the minimum acceptable performance level. The Model ASR33 teletype is a keyboard, printing mechanism, paper tape reader and punch with the capability to transmit and receive data electrically over a pair of wires. At a selling price of less than $800 from the Teletype Corporation, this is a remarkable machine. Performance is minimal and reliability acceptable. This model is used universally, and all users would like something better; but, at the same cost.

All items in Table I act as extensions of main computer memories. The utility of an individual device depends upon the access requirements versus cost. Ideally, a memory device would be limitless in capacity with all information immediately available. A magnetic tape system is effectively limitless in capacity because the storage medium is low in cost, but access is slow. High speed but costly bulk core is available. A disc or drum is a satisfactory compromise between cost and capacity for most applications. The disc pack has become quite successful because of removable memory media. The total storage can be considered limitless as with magnetic tape, yet with much more rapid access. Devices such as the RCA RACE units or NCR CRAM offer memory files comparable to the magnetic tape system, but with the ability to access massive data files by automatically manipulating the file medium, magnetic cards. Low cost magnetic tape and head-per-track disc or drum units are category I items that are also commonly requested for category II and III applications. High performance and capacity units, and special items such as RACE or CRAM fall into categories II or III.

Because of magnetic tape cost effectivity, a number of manufacturers are attempting to create a low cost system for minicomputers. The Phillips Cassette is the basis of several systems, some others are based upon their own individual proprietary tape cartridges.

Separation of Input from Output equipment for discussion is somewhat redundant because of their generally complimentary function. In category I, paper tape systems are popular because of cost effectivity and the media format is universal or standardized. Low cost card readers, both hole and mark sense, are available; but card punches are seldom available in category I. Communication equipment is common in all categories, although complexity varies widely. Simple bit-banging, line buffering, low speed, high speed, asynchronous,

Reprinted from *1970 IEEE Int. Conv. Digest*, session 5G, pp. 280–281.

synchronous, multiplexing, automatic call answering, automatic dial - are some of the individual characteristics that make up a multitude of communication devices.

Keyboards and printing mechanisms are used in many applications. In category II and III alphanumeric displays provide a desirable element in applications where there exists realtime information exchange between a system and its user. Much of this information need not be a permanent record. For permanent record or simply for use in category I systems, low cost line printers are becoming common. Graphic displays allow pictorial display of information and are likely to be subject to great effort with the development of systems dedicated to computer-aided design. For permanent recording of pictorial information and for obtaining accuracy in representation, a number of plotting equipments are available.

Optical Character Recognition and Computer Output Microfilm equipment are categories I and III devices. In categories II and III, instrumentation and data acquisition require real-time clocks, A/D and D/A equipment. For some applications, voice response equipment is desirable. To assist the user in the development of his system, a common requirement is to provide computer-buffered output lines and computer-sampled or buffered input lines.

To the user, the computer vendor may seem the logical source of peripheral equipment for a system, yet, with a few exceptions, most minicomputer vendors offer for resale only equipments purchased in whole or in part from manufacturers specializing in those devices. The function of the minicomputer vendor is to supply the interface logic and software for the device and act as a guarantor of performance. Increasingly more common is finding peripheral equipment suppliers looking beyond the OEM market, toward the users. This takes a degree of boldness because competition can become active, especially from the computer vendor. Although of more interest to all concerned could be the results of such an active market development - a competitive requirement to develop and use a standard I/O interface.

The computer industry has long discussed standardization and done little toward implementation. The few existing examples of standardization were not so much based upon agreement as competitive necessity: seven- and nine-track magnetic tape; the common form of EAM card.

Interest is developing within the market for a low cost magnetic tape cassette device. Each manufacturer feels that his system is superior and that he will set the industry standard. This situation is of concern to the computer vendors and the users. No tape of one system is compatible with another. Therefore, a selection once made, could become non-standard, resulting in loss of time to market and development cost to the computer vendor. To the user it would be a matter of inconvenience, and possibly a dollar loss. To the cassette manufacturer it will be a significant loss.

How this stalemate will be resolved and a decision made is currently unknown, but, the market and the need exist. Possibly a group of computer vendors will select one device, or perhaps a major computer vendor will announce his system, thereby creating the standard.

Decisions affecting cassette standardization forecast the difficulties of obtaining agreement on a common interface, but this may happen sooner than anticipated. Standardization is being approached with the advent of integrated circuits, widely divergent voltage and current levels being eliminated in favor of standard ICs. The EIA RS-232 interface has served well for communication systems interfaces. Admittedly far from an optimum computer interface, it is interesting the number and diversity of devices that can be connected to a computer via this approach. Keyboards, printers, plotters, and displays are now common. But, then who knows about tomorrow?

TABLE I - MEMORY DEVICES	TABLE II - INPUT DEVICES	TABLE III - OUTPUT DEVICES
Magnetic Tape	Paper Tape Reader	Paper Tape Punch
Bulk Core	Card Reader	Card Punch
Drum	Communications	Communications
Disc	Keyboard	Line Printer
Magnetic Card	Optical Character Recognition	Display
	Clocks	Plotter
	A/D	Computer Output Microfilm
	Input Interface	D/A
		Voice Response
		Output Interface

DESIGNING MINI COMPUTER HARDWARE/SOFTWARE SYSTEMS--

THE SYSTEMS APPROACH

by David J. Waks, Manager
Control Systems Division
APPLIED DATA RESEARCH, INC.

In designing any hardware/software system, there are a number of crucial questions to which the systems designer must find answers- the nature of information flow to and from the process; the transducers required to convert this information to and from digital form; the interfaces required between the computer and these transducers; the role of the human operator in the operation of the system, and the consequent man-machine interface; the functions to be performed by the computer; etc. The systems approach to system design demands that he find answers to all of these questions, and solve the problems they pose, before firmly specifying any part of the system. These answers, once carefully thought out, determine the over-all systems design, and in turn lead to the detail system specification from which the implementation of hardware and software is done.

It may be thought that the nature of the questions to be asked and the method of arriving at a system design are quite obvious, and that some such formulation as above is self-evident. Indeed, most systems designers do give lip-service to a systems approach. But many fail to use it, often designing and building all the hardware before the computer and operator functions are thought out. And we all know that many hardware/software systems have failed--online too late to be economically justifiable; or costing too much; or never becoming operational at all, frequently by never getting both the hardware and the software working properly together. One effect of this sort of highly-publicized failure is to lead influential people, usually managers, one step removed from the technical people, to be very wary of computer-based systems, in the belief that they invariably cost too much and work too badly, and often never run at all.

In this session, we are discussing the systems approach to the design of systems based upon mini-computers. Such systems are similar in nature to those based on larger computers, but there are lower pressures from above to integrate a large number of unrelated processes into the system. Since the system is usually designed to handle one process, or perhaps a few, it is possible for the designer to concentrate his attention on designing a system which will work-- both technically and economically.

Let us characterize a Measurement System as one in which information flows from a process to a human operator; a Control System as one in which information flows from a human operator to a process; a Computer-Controlled Measurement System as one in which a computer is interposed between the process and the human, typically to convert the process information into a better form for the human; and a Computer-Controlled Control System as one in which a computer is interposed between the human operator and the process, typically to convert the human form of control into that appropriate for the process. A Computer-Controlled Measurement and Control System, of course, is one which involves a loop--from the process, to the computer, to the human, back to the computer, and back to the process. A Closed-Loop system is one in which some degree of feedback from sensors to actuators occurs without the human's explicit control action; in designing Closed-Loop systems, we are prone to forget that the human exists at all, a failing which frequently gets us into trouble.

A more detailed break-down of the information loop would include: the sensors which derive the necessary information from the process; the data input interfaces between these sensors and the computer; the computer program which translates the values and conditions from the sensors into human terms; the operator output interface to the human to present information for his evaluation; the operator input interface from the human to specify his control response; the program required to integrate this response with the input from the process, past history, etc.; the data output interfaces between the computer and the control actuators; and the control actuators which themselves effect control of the process.

In taking a proper approach to the system design, the designer should first determine the necessary information flow to and from the process, and to and from the human operator. The former should in turn suggest the sensors required to derive the necessary information from the process and the actuators necessary to effect control. The latter should in turn suggest the nature of the man-machine interface in the nature of the output transducers--lights, displays, audible signals, teletypewriters, etc.--and the input transducers--switches, keyboards, CRT graphical input, etc. With all the input and output transducers defined, both to the process and to the operator, the designer then faces the major problem--namely, the interfaces between the various transducers

Reprinted with permission from *1970 Joint Automat. Contr. Conf. Amer. Automat. Contr. Council*, paper no. 8-E, pp. 194-195.

and the computer, and the program or programs which tie the entire system together. The jobs of defining the hardware interfaces and the software programs must be done simultaneously if the system design is to be successful, for they are inextricably bound together. It is critical that the systems designer be able to "work both sides of the street" since programming considerations may strongly influence hardware design and vice versa.

In reality, systems design rarely proceeds along the straight-line path described above. Rather, it usually proceeds in the manner of a tightening spiral, in which experience, economics, compromises, perhaps politics, and, finally, the designer's taste all play a role.

It is important to realize that successful systems design depends, not on following a particular path in coming up with the systems design finally exemplified in the detail system specification, but on completing the entire design--information flow, to the human as well as to the process; transducer/computer interfaces; and particularly the program functions--before starting in on any implementation. In this way, the probability of eventually producing a working system, in which the hardware and the software are properly integrated, and in which a human feels comfortable operating, is greatly enhanced.

MINICOMPUTER SENSOR AND INTERFACE SELECTION

A. J. Fanthorp
P/E Development Company
Cincinnati, Ohio

The mini-computer is forcing a subtle yet devastating change in sensors and interface hardware. Anchored in economics, constrained by reliability, these changes threaten to complicate the life of hardware designers.

Computer control system costs dropped abruptly on introduction of the lower cost mini-computers. This in turn increased economic emphasis on the sensor interface area. This now constitutes a greater fraction of the control system cost. Pressure to reduce the cost of this important part of the system continues to increase. Certainly a basic aspect of the control system is the sensor. It is this aspect that is primarily responsible for the basic accuracy of the process control system. In general, it may be stated that the fundamental accuracy of the sensor will not be improved upon throughout the system. Table I shows typical accuracies of various types of process instrument elements. A glance at this table is enough to suggest that the sensor plays a large part in definition of the computer and of the associated equipment in the process control system.

An important parameter in selection of a suitable computer is its word length. Table II provides an indication of accuracy based on the number of bits in the computer word. Referring back to Table I, it may be seen that words in the order of 8 to 12 bits will generally handle most accuracies. There are, although rare, places where 16-bit accuracy is necessary.

While word length is important in selecting a computer, it is not the only criteria. Memory access time can be quite important if it has a major effect on the ability of the system to acquire data. This is particularly true when large quantities of data must be acquired in a short period of time. Cost and machine architecture are also considerations in selection of the computer.

At the same time, the mini-computer is directing more attention toward the need to reduce sensor cost. The improved accuracy of the small computer is forcing the sensor manufacturers to produce more accurate sensors. Thus, the sensor area is under pressure to both reduce cost and increase accuracy. One way of accomplishing these goals is to use the mini-computer as part of the sensor system. Let's consider Fig. 1 as the slide showing basic definitions. We have plotted an output variable as ordinate and an input variable as abscissa.

Two types of general accuracies may be defined. One based on the rated maximum value shown by the lower and upper bands and the other based on the actual value as shown by the same bands. In general, we might say that the sensor is defined as being accurate, based on its deviation on one of these Criteria - the maximum rated value or the actual value.

In the case of a simple non-linearity as shown in Fig. 2, we see that with the definition of accuracy based on the actual value we could have a non-linear function relating output variable to input variable. One way to improve the accuracy of this type of sensor is to store the non-linearity in the computer itself and one such technique is the use of the polynomial fit. This is quite compact in its use of core, and it should be noted that the actual quantity of core occupied for this rectification process is proportioned to the fit desired. It is rather easy to see, however, that by storing the curvature in the computer memory, a sensor having lower cost might actually achieve a greater accuracy since we no longer talk about the band as shown on the slide in Fig. 2, but talk more nearly of the fit of the curve to the actual relationship.

A different type of sensor problem is shown in Fig. 3. This particular problem is one associated with backlash. Shown on the slide are the accuracy limits based on the rated maximum value. Here again, this information may be stored in the computer. It uses about one and a half times the amount of core required for the rectification of a simple non-linearity. Nevertheless, backlash can be handled quite economically in the computer itself. The question of economics, of course, is

Reprinted with permission from *1970 WESCON Technical Papers*, vol. 14, paper C/2.

influenced by how much core is required. It is economically favorable to employ sensor correction in those systems where extra core capacity exists. If this is not the case, then the cost of the additional core must be compared to the cost of more accurate sensors.

A more frequent problem is pictured in Fig. 4. Shown on the slide is a simple two-straight-line type of non-linearity. This might occur in a mechanical system where a second spring is engaged at the point of discontinuity. If this type of function, coming from a sensor, is being used in a system that required an indication of the rate of change of the variable, it may be seen that a rather abrupt change occurs at the point of discontinuity. This function is shown in Fig. 5. As you might expect, a very large change in the rate of change occurs at the point noted. This type of non-linearity can also be easily handled in the computer. It depends on a linear approximation and requires a core utilization very much equivalent to that of the backlash.

The examples shown of non-linearity, backlash, and rate of change suggest one other possible area of improvement. An entirely different kind of benefit in using the computer to improve the input data may be realized in the area of smoothing. For instance, let's take a situation as shown by our Fig. 6 where we would like to have an average value but instead have only the actual values which deviate as shown. It is a relatively simple task for the computer to determine the average value and the averaging process can be employed over any desired interval. Also noteworthy is the fact that the computer can determine the peak reading by taking successive values and indicating and storing the highest value.

One point that should be made here is that the process control system designer has, with these techniques, the ability to change the type of sensing after the system has been installed. This is a particularly powerful tool since in many cases, noise, a change in variable, or process unknowns make selection of the particular sensor prior to the construction of the facility somewhat risky.

Another area where the computer can be particularly valuable as part of the sensor system is in its use for on-line calibration of sensors. In many cases,

sensors tend to change with time. By storing in the computer a known deviation and checking the results from the sensor, a continuous calibration process can actually be programmed in the system.

Handling of long time constants in the sensor-computer set can be accomplished very effectively. This is a particularly useful feature when applied to chemical processes where outputs from sensors may vary only slightly over long periods of time.

Many sensors are not in wide use because of price, accuracy, or lag in output signal. With a computer, it is possible to relate this function to some other variable and thus permit use of a sensor that would not otherwise be considered suitable. An example of this might be specific gravity sensors which are rather expensive and require flow for a time before an accurate signal is produced or some special provision for temperature compensation. A computer can relate specific gravity to a temperature measurement from a curve stored in its memory. Temperature sensors for this type of application are inexpensive and result in a sensor system of excellent accuracy and response without excessive cost.

Another area worth calling to your attention is the possibility of checking the input authenticity. There may be cases where the sensor actually opens or shorts or in some way fails. In this particular situation the computer tied to the sensor has the ability to determine when such open or shorted conditions occur. This could be considered an extreme case of the continuous calibration, but the cause is generally unrelated to calibration problems. This same feature may be utilized for fail-safe operation.

Groups of variables may also be checked to determine if there has been any significant change.

In most processes, the location of the sensor is important. Perhaps we have a situation as shown in Fig. 7. Here the sensors were located as shown by the dots. The curve of output is also shown. The solid black line shows the actual variation along the length; both curves satisfy the data taken. It is possible by modeling to change the effective location of the sensors without physically changing their location.

In the case shown in Fig. 7, we would probably desire a location or an addition of a sensor at point 5. If this is the case, rather than change or add a sensor, it may be more feasible to make a simple model of the relationship of the output variable to length and then adjust the model based on the data received from the sensors already located. In this way we could then calculate in a curve of the output variable as a function of length and base the process control decision on point 5 or any other point we may wish. Note also that this technique may be expanded to determine the average or RMS value if those were essential to the process.

Another interesting point that should be made here is that it is entirely possible to model and thereby obtain measurements at previously inaccessible locations. If a particular process has a significant point at which data should be taken and if that point, because of the temperature or some other condition, is one which makes it difficult, if not impossible, to locate a sensor, the modeling technique could be used. Measuring of secondary variables combined with use of the model and calculated values for the primary variable, perhaps may be the only way that some

systems may be programmed to respond to some particularly important control area where a sensor could not be located.

We have considered the ability of the computer to improve sensors and, at least to some extent, aid in reducing sensor cost. It is even possible that the sensor of the future will have a digital output or at least new sensors will be introduced which will have an output in the form of a pulse train or a frequency. These are not coded outputs, but certainly they suggest that a variation in the number of pulses per unit of time or a change in frequency can represent the input variable. It is particularly easy to handle this in the computer. The computer does, of course, have the ability to time and, therefore, can count pulses or can count cycles if the output tends to be in frequency.

In conclusion, I would note that the mini-computer is forcing sensor interface designers to review their design philosophy. High accuracy is not synonymous with linearity; sophisticated output code is in many cases not warranted; frequently the computer can handle sensor interface problems. Competitive sensor and interface equipment must be designed for the overall system.

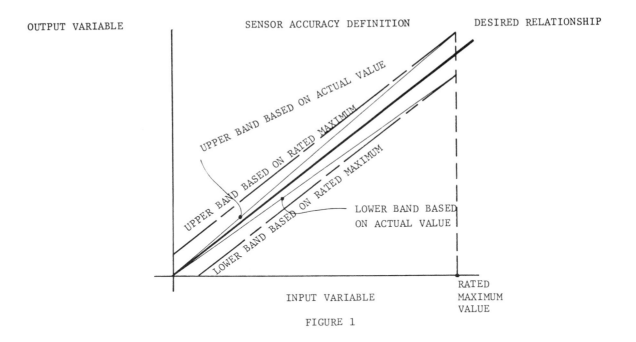

OUTPUT VARIABLE

SENSOR ACCURACY DEFINITION

DESIRED RELATIONSHIP

UPPER BAND BASED ON ACTUAL VALUE

UPPER BAND BASED ON RATED MAXIMUM

LOWER BAND BASED ON RATED MAXIMUM

LOWER BAND BASED ON ACTUAL VALUE

INPUT VARIABLE

RATED MAXIMUM VALUE

FIGURE 1

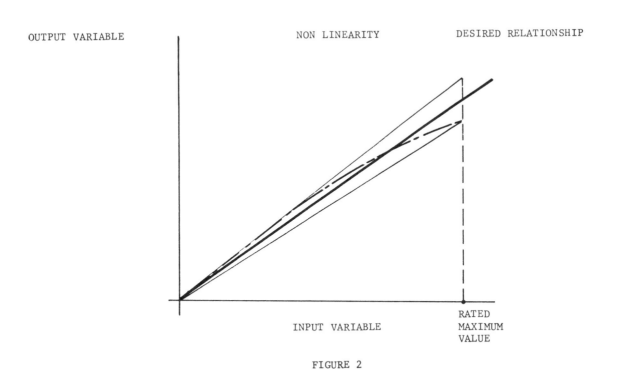

OUTPUT VARIABLE

NON LINEARITY

DESIRED RELATIONSHIP

INPUT VARIABLE

RATED MAXIMUM VALUE

FIGURE 2

64

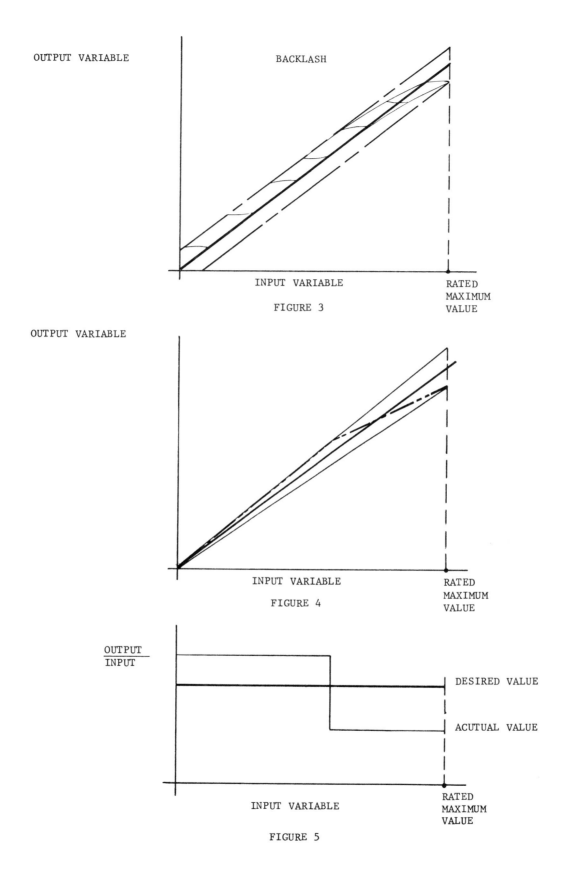

OUTPUT VARIABLE

BACKLASH

INPUT VARIABLE

RATED MAXIMUM VALUE

FIGURE 3

OUTPUT VARIABLE

INPUT VARIABLE

RATED MAXIMUM VALUE

FIGURE 4

OUTPUT / INPUT

DESIRED VALUE

ACUTUAL VALUE

INPUT VARIABLE

RATED MAXIMUM VALUE

FIGURE 5

65

OUTPUT VARIABLE

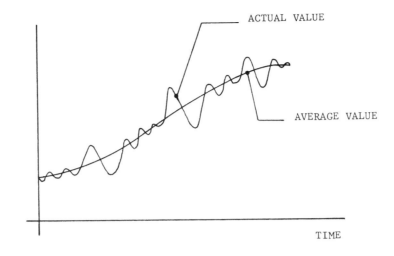

ACTUAL VALUE

AVERAGE VALUE

TIME

FIGURE 6

SENSOR LOCATIONS

OUTPUT
VARIABLE

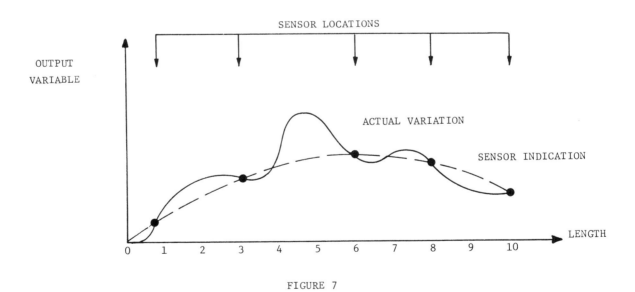

ACTUAL VARIATION

SENSOR INDICATION

LENGTH

0 1 2 3 4 5 6 7 8 9 10

FIGURE 7

66

Part III
Selecting a Minicomputer

This part is an extremely important one. Once the reader has familiarized himself with mini-computer characteristics and jargon, and gained some feeling for programming and interfacing considerations, he is ready to evaluate his problem in terms of minicomputers, and, based on this evaluation, to select a minicomputer to do his job.

In the first paper, Dudley Hartung examines the very basic question: "Should I use a mini-computer or a hard-wired controller?" Next, Bert Forbes discusses what you should be looking for in a computer's architecture to fit your application.

Then to the crux of the matter. Armed with his newfound knowledge of minicomputers, the reader sets forth, money in hand, in search of the "best minicomputer." He is promptly inun-

dated with salesmen, spec sheets, price lists, outrageous claims, model numbers, special features, and jargon he has never heard before. And to top it all off, it seems that each and every manufacturer makes the "best minicomputer."

J. L. Butler comes to the reader's rescue in the next article, "Comparative Criteria for Minicomputers." He provides several useful services. First, he reviews minicomputer architecture, I/O structures, and software, this time with a very critical eye. What do they mean by this spec? What is the real significance of that one? To whom? Why?

He also lists 27 minicomputer manufacturers (with mailing addresses) and tabulates the characteristics of 45 minicomputers. These data are usually found on easily accessible spec sheets and price lists.

Then comes the real contribution. He proposes a list of critical parameters, a set of corresponding weighting factors, and a set of three equations that result in a numerical measure of a given computer's overall price to performance ratio.

The reader should find this article very valuable, particularly if he takes the time to follow the derivation of the equations. This should lead to a much better understanding of how to match a mini to his application. The author then goes on to calculate the price to performance ratio for all 45 computers tabulated, then ranks them in order of ascending ratios (the lower the ratio, the better.)

This tabulation, while not all-inclusive, does provide a rational basis for decision making. There are, however, three things that the reader must consider. First, the data are obsolete. Due to the dynamic nature of the minicomputer industry, new models are introduced, specs are improved upon, and prices (a factor to which his equations are very sensitive) continue to drop. The reader is advised to check the specs and reevaluate the equations before he uses the results.

Second, and equally important, the reader must examine the weighting factors proposed. They are really application-dependent. For example, standard DMA or multiple I/O processors are of no value in applications where only very limited, low-speed I/O capability is used. Similarly, arithmetic capability may be irrelevant in a character-handling operation.

It behooves the reader to evaluate the factors and assigned weights in light of his application if he really intends to base his decisions on the results of this approach.

The third consideration is this. Given the reevaluated parameters and the corresponding table, is the computer with the best price/performance ratio the best one for the reader? The next article by Robin Ollivier attempts to answer this question. Mr. Ollivier proposes his own set of factors and weights, which includes an emphasis on vendor qualifications, then goes on to include "maximum cost" and "minimum performance" criteria.

I think a combination of the last two articles (i.e., Mr. Butler's performance factors plotted on Mr. Ollivier's graph) provides a useful tool in the hands of the reader.

The next article deals with environmental characteristics of small computers. It is valuable not only to those who have severe environmental requirements, but also in the more general applications because of the reliability and maintainability factors that are discussed.

The last article is included because it presents an interesting alternative for some readers who may have decided that minis really are not powerful enough for their application.

An excellent bibliography of articles discussing minicomputer features can be found at the end of Mr. Butler's paper.

The Mini Computer as a Control Element
Dudley B. Hartung
Management Methods, Inc., Waltham, Massachusetts

Mini computers have been used to control a wide variety of processes and functions including machine tools, chemical processes, steel mills, and warehousing systems. Articles in technical journals and talks at seminars have described in some detail many of these individual applications. But what is a good application -- when do you use a hard wired control system and when should you consider a mini computer?

The decision must be based on costs -- dollars per function -- and reliability and maintainability. In general, reliability can be disposed of as being indirectly related to dollars. The simplest or mass-produced system is normally the cheapest system and also the most reliable system. Maintainability can be given a cost value. The decision, therefore, can be directly related to costs. Costs naturally refer to the initial capital cost of the equipment and also to recurring cost of operation, including the aforementioned maintainability cost, operator cost, quality of product value, etc. Some of these costs can only be roughly approximated and may be intuitive guesses. The cost of the equipment, however, should be fairly easy to derive by knowledgeable people during initial planning stages.

A control system -- any control system -- consists of inputs, outputs, and decision makers. In comparing hard wired systems with computer systems, the input and output devices probably stay comparable in cost. Input and output devices consist of operator switches, sensors, solenoids, servo or discrete (on-off) motor controls, etc. The decision maker is the logical system which determines the effect of input changes upon output actions. With a hard wired system, each subdecision or each function of the control system has its own logic. A mini computer time shares its logic to accomplish many functions with a relatively small logical device. The mini computer, therefore, becomes essentially the complete decision maker, even when there are hundreds of inputs and outputs with varying degrees of interrelationship. This is where the cost savings of a computer system come. Many more decisions can be made per dollar with a computer compared to hard-wired logic.

There are some inherently costly aspects of a computer system. Holding functions must be stored externally. All inputs and outputs of data are in high speed serial words which means that switch inputs, for instance, must be held on until polled by the computer. The holding device might be the operator's finger. The outputs must have holding relays or their solid state equivalent. Inputs and outputs to the computer are always the same binary words at low levels, requiring filtering and level conversion at the interface. No power is available for force-type functions, requiring amplifiers and power relays. Of course, some of these restrictions apply to many hard-wired controls. But if the decisions are very simple, the input and output buffering, filtering, and holding may be more expensive than the complete hard-wired control.

The computer itself is limited by speed and by the size of internal memory utilized for storing data and computer program. It may be cheaper even in a computer controlled system to do some complex but frequently used and repetitive functions externally. For example, a servo loop could be performed in a computer but in most cases is done externally. Interpolation for a machine tool, which is the precise control of velocities in two or more axis to draw a straight cut or a circular cut is expensive in computer time in that it takes a large portion of a computer. A single computer can do all interpolation and control one or two high speed, high accuracy machine tools. If the interpolation is done externally, 5-20 machine tools can be similarly controlled.

So how is a decision made to go hard-wired or mini computer? The system costs must be estimated in both ways. This requires some understanding of the end of process and the requirements of both a hard-wired system and the capabilities of computers. In many cases, the computer can supply additional functions at very low cost which have to have some value placed on them to honestly compare systems. In other cases, the function to be performed is so complex that it is immediately obvious the computer is the solution. Labor costs of both of the design and building of a system and the operation must be considered.

Reprinted with permission from *1970 Joint Automat. Contr. Conf. Amer. Automat. Contr. Council*, paper no. 8-B, pp. 191–192.

Costs also include effects of lead time variation, set-up speed, and rejects. All of these costs vary and relate to a particular application.

Rules of thumb are dangerous and can be misleading, but there are some systems where computer control should be looked at very carefully. If many simple decisions -- or many monitoring points, such as those on a transfer line, are required or if very complex relay trees or logical decisions must be made, a computer should be considered. Complicated decisions requiring mathematical functions, particularly if changing either between runs or over a period of time or the requirement for a great deal of stored data for look-up tables or individual parts programs suggest computer control. Finally very specialized problems or machines or processes with only one system or a few systems being built, particularly where modifications between initial concept and final operating equipment are foreseen due to technical unknowns, are particularly good applications for computer control. This is true not only because of the possible savings in hardware costs, but more importantly, because of the normally much lower design cost.

The mini computer can be a panacea for many ills, and should be looked at by the builders and users of any controlled system. It will be found that not all systems justify on an economic basis the utilization of computers, but conversely, it will be found that what seems like an expensive and sophisticated control system can often be easily justified purely on an economic basis.

COMPUTER ARCHITECTURE FOR INSTRUMENTATION

by

Bert Forbes
Hewlett-Packard
Cupertino, California

The term "Computer Architecture" is often used but ill defined. This paper redefines the term
to include the total computer system and elaborates on the concept in a discussion of computer specifications and the user's needs.

To facilitate the discussion of computer specifications, the various types of instrumentation
and other real time computer systems are classified into three categories--1) control computers--
programmed data collectors or device controllers; 2) dedicated single usage systems--predominately
core based and written as a unified whole to operate a particular system; and 3) general purpose
real time executive systems--multiprogramming operating systems designed to allow maximum ease and
protection in designing and implementing a real time system.

At the controller level, hardware specifications such as cycle time, DMA transfer rates and
interrupt response time dominate because the computer is essentially a component. Software and its
interaction with the hardware becomes increasingly more important as the complexity of the system
increases. In a real time executive system, the same specifications--such as interrupt response time
--must be redefined in terms of the different needs of a general hardware-software system. These
specifications are examined in an attempt to clarify real time system definitions.

To date, there has been a lack of communication between the computer designer and the system
user; this paper attempts to bridge this gap and to bring the real world problems of instrumentation
into focus by relating them to specific items in a computer's architecture.

"In the architectural structure," wrote Nietzche, "Man's pride, man's triumph over gravitation,
man's will to power, assume a visible form. Architecture is a sort of oratory of power by means of
form." Although spoken of the architecture of buildings, this quotation perhaps summarizes the
basics of computer architecture, that is, the form into which the power of the computer is shaped.

Although the central processor, the memory and the input-output system are the foundation or
building blocks of a computer system, one cannot meaningfully talk of computer architecture without
including a discussion of the support software available, the systems software needed and the characteristics of the intended application. When discussing real time systems, there are several application categories that usually come to mind--business and commercial time sharing, process control,
data acquisition, and instrumentation. Each has its own characteristics, and in all four, there are
examples of very simple and some very sophisticated computer systems.

Business type real time systems include applications such as information retrieval, time sharing,
and supervisory control of a multiplicity of smaller computer systems. These systems, like those
discussed below, all have the property that they must respond to some stimulus in a fixed amount of
time and/or must complete some set of tasks during a periodic interval. Most business systems are
large and involve a great deal of ordinary data processing work. Their response times are usually
measured in terms of seconds instead of microseconds, since people are often the source of the stimuli.

In process control systems, and in particular, direct digital control, the computer system senses
status conditions and various control parameters of the process being controlled, calculates the response and outputs the necessary control information to keep the process within specified bounds. In
addition, the computer often monitors emergency conditions, performs adaptive control and executes on
line diagnostics of both itself and the system being controlled. The computer system is the feedback
element in the closed loop system. This is a classical systems theory approach, adapted to the quan-
tized discrete nature of digital sampling and control. The actual computation is usually a limited

'set of operations applied repeatedly to many feedback loops. A typical specification for a DDC system is the time spent to calculate control information for a 100 loop process.

Data acquisition systems, on the other hand, have little or no feedback; in their simplest form, they perform only a data logging function, with no processing of the data. More sophisticated systems not only collect the data but also check for errors and out of range readings and compress or format the data before they are recorded. Today, there are data acquisition systems that perform fast Fourier transforms and other correlations on the data as they are received and processed in real time.

Test and instrumentation systems generally have two way data paths, but they are not feedback loops in the same sense as in DDC. In general, some stimulus is applied to the object under observation, and the response is recorded. This control sequencing and data collection can be passive, with the computer issuing predetermined stimuli in a fixed sequence and not making any decisions on the results, or it can take a more active response actuated role. The branch-chain style of questioning is used in many computer aided instruction systems, where the next question asked is a function of the current answer given by the student; an incorrect answer causes the student to receive more drill in that particular area of study, whereas a correct answer will give a different response. Other standard test system actions are fault detection and diagnosis and error condition activated testing and data collection.

All of these systems fall into one of three categories of computer systems--1) control computers--programmed data collectors or device controllers; 2) dedicated single usage systems--predominately core based and written as a unified whole to operate a particular system; and 3) general purpose real time executive systems--multiprogramming operating systems designed to allow maximum ease and protection in designing and implementing a real time system.

Controllers are generally small, fixed program processors designed to handle a specific task or set of tasks. They have a limited amount of read-write memory used for data storage, not programs; they are usually connected either directly or via some data recording media (paper tape, magnetic tape, etc.) to a larger computer. There are two main varieties of controllers--those that are hardwired to perform a device specific action and those that can be programmed in one form or another.

Hardwired controllers are typically found as simple data loggers, as device controllers for magnetic disks, drums and tapes, or as controllers for numerically controlled machines. Today, many programmed controllers are microprogrammed to perform the desired control function. A read-only memory contains the instructions, which pull directly on the control lines of a simple processor designed for easy bit manipulation and data handling. The instruction set is simple and designed to work closely with the hardware. There is minimum "software" overhead at run time, allowing very efficient operation. These microprocessors can be very fast if implemented in a high speed bipolar family of integrated circuits, or they can be slower and less expensive for less demanding applications if implemented in MOS technology. Often, read-write memory is substituted for ROM in cases where the device characteristics are not known ahead of time or where the system is subject to frequent change.

A good example of a microprogrammed controller is the medical history taking unit produced by Predictive Systems, Inc., Palo Alto. They have microprogrammed an MSI 800 to control a 16-mm film strip projector that presents questions with multiple choice answers to the patient, who responds by pressing the appropriate answer buttons. The processor records the answer on a magnetic tape cassette for later printout and selects the next question in the branch chain questionnaire based on the patient's answer to the current question. At the end of the questions, the computer prints out a summary of the patient's medical history in medical terms for the doctor to evaluate. All of the devices on the system are controlled by the 256 word microprogram, which also does the data formatting and branch chaining. This same application could also have been implemented in a software programmed controller, where a general purpose computer is drafted into service as a controller. The program could be stored in an ROM that replaces core and the devices controlled by the standard computer interfaces. In many cases, this is overpowering the situation with the full capabilities of a general purpose computer, of which only a small subset will be used.

A more efficient usage of a general purpose minicomputer is in the dedicated single usage system, which is usually a software programmed, core resident system. Most present day minis fit very well into such a system; they are single user computers. This type of software system is a tightly integrated, unified whole that performs a single function at a time. It is usually written in assembly language in order to obtain maximum code compression and minimum execution time, since fast core memory is one of the major component costs in a system of this type. All functions to be incorporated in the system and their characteristics must be pretty much known when the operating system is written, so that their interactions can be specifically accounted for. This optimization of the program can make it difficult to add additional program functions later. If the user tries to make his operating system general enough to allow for all contingencies, then he has increased his programming task considerably; it soon becomes much more reasonable to use one of the general purpose real time executive (RTE) systems provided by the manufacturer, even if it has to be customized to the particular application.

These RTE systems are disk based multiprogramming systems designed to run on a general purpose computer. The RTE relieves the user from the sometimes tedious and often tricky operating systems programming and allows him to concentrate on his end use of the computer system. Nothing is free, however, and the penalty here is the additional hardware and the general purpose software overhead.

The resident operating system controls all of the computer system's resources, including CPU cycles; it provides protection of one user program from another, both foreground (real time) from background (noninterrupt) and one foreground user from another. The operating system is written to accept modular user programs written in a standard format; these programs are the processes that define the application to which the computer system is directed. The standard interface to the RTE allows maximum ease in designing and implementing a system. In many cases, it is not only desirable but necessary that the user programs be written in a high level language. The loss in efficiency is often not as important in this class of real time system as it is in a controller or dedicated system.

There are numerous long term advantages to be obtained from the use of a compiler language. There is an old rule of thumb that says a good programmer can produce one line of debugged, documented code per hour--independent of the language he is working in. This means that the job will be done much more quickly if that line of code is Fortran statement instead of one assembly language instruction. In addition, higher level languages are to some extent self documenting--it is much easier to understand someone else's Fortran program than it is an assembly language program. Fortran may not be the ideal language for real time systems, but work is underway to produce a systems oriented standard language.[1]

Whether a system is an RTE programmed in a high level language or a microprogrammed controller, the specifications of the system revolve around the specifications of the computer. Some aspects of computer specifications that are traditional criteria of a computer's performance are the interrupt system, the I/O system, the memory, the word size and the instruction set. In order to evaluate these properly in a system, one must first look at them alone.

The interrupt system is specified in terms of the number of levels of priority and the number of devices that may occupy each level. For a real time system, multilevel interrupts are desirable, although the hardware priority should be alterable by software to allow for special situations that arise during execution on a fixed hardware setup. Depending on the type of system, it may be useful to have all interrupts go to a common routine instead of each going to a unique core location, which most minicomputers boast about. The big question is "what is the interrupt response time?" and the sales literature will quote anything under the sun. Most of the numbers given are not defined as to what is actually done in the time specified; the necessary software actions often outweigh the hardware response time.

Some questions to ask about the I/O structure of a computer are: What is the maximum practical programmed data transfer rate? How many channels of direct memory access are available? What is the maximum rate? Are they assignable to any device and are the transfers synchronous with the memory and CPU cycle? (Synchronous data rates will appear to be faster but actually have poor performance for I/O data rates a little slower than the sync rate). How many uniquely addressable devices may be put on the system? Is a party line I/O available? How many standard data processing peripherals and standard electronic instruments have existing interfaces to the computer's I/O system? Is there a universal register interface available for OEM or nonstandard devices?

Both the interrupt system's and the I/O system's performance, as well as the program's running time, are a function of the memory access and cycle time. If the cycle time is tied to the CPU's cycle, then faster memories cannot be easily added to the computer without a major redesign. This could be a big disadvantage, especially with semiconductor memories purporting to become economically feasible in the near future.

Some other relevant areas of concern are the minimum and maximum size of memory and the ease of expansion (programs always seem to take more core than anticipated). Some manufacturers are not even offering a memory parity option; in a real time system, it is highly desirable to know when something as crucial as memory is becoming marginal. All exceptional conditions in a real time computer should provide interrupts so that some attempt may be made to recover and not crash the system with no indication of what went wrong. The ability to split a memory cycle between the read and write portions (assuming a core memory) makes features like direct memory increment, three cycle data break and fast Fourier transforms easy; however, a split cycle has an adverse effect on the interrupt response time and on the maximum burst data rate. (A device could possibly tie up memory for a long time during the split.) Another cogent question is that of memory protection: Is memory protected on physical boundaries by one or two fence registers, or is it protected on logical boundaries that are easily relocated?

The problem of word size has gone on for many years and probably will continue for many more. For real time systems, it doesn't make a lot of difference whether the size is 8, 12 or 16 bits. The tendency is perhaps towards 16, because many state-of-the-art data sources, like 15 bit plus sign A to D converters, can use only single precision for data storage; also, two 8-bit ASCII characters fit nicely into a 16 bit word. However, even 16 bit machines must make some provision for multiple precision arithmetic to allow sufficient accuracy in calculations and to handle high accuracy instruments such as DVMs.

It is important to examine the average number of bits per useful word. For data, this would be determined by the ratio of multiple precision data stored to single precision. For programs, the situation is more complicated. Some 16 bit machines, for example, actually have both 16 and 32 bit instructions, and even those that have only 16 lapse into a 32 bit mode when they branch by doing a "skip on condition, branch unconditionally." Indirect addressing is also a double word operation, but the penalty of the extra bits is spread out over all the instructions that refer to that particular word. When this average number of bits per word begins to approach the next larger size of machine word, then the user is well advised to look carefully at the choice of machine for his job. The advantages and disadvantages of short word lengths have been adequately discussed in the literature.

The biggest problem with short word length machines is trying to pack a powerful instruction set into so few fits. A separate paper would be needed to describe all of the problems and tradeoffs made in designing an instruction set for a minicomputer. Some of the bigger problems are having enough bits to address several registers and still being able to address a reasonable amount of memory with several addressing modes; being able to provide a "Branch on Condition Code" instruction instead of the traditional skip-on-condition type of branching found in so many small computers. Fortunately, most real time applications don't need a very complex or extensive set of instructions. This is especially true of the controller and single usage systems. The power needed is, of course, dependent on the particular application, but most RTE systems that have been implemented on a minicomputer that didn't plan for such a complex system in its instruction set have been programming miracles of the first order. One can program around most any problem, but at a potentially high cost for both manpower and execution efficiency.

The final question to be asked is, "Is the software available sufficient to handle the job at hand?" Nearly every manufacturer offers an assembler, but is it relocating and will it fit into the smallest configuration? What are the higher level languages offered? How efficient are they? What is the minimum system required for their use? There should at least be some kind of basic control system that will handle the drudgery of buffered I/O, equipment tables and the like.[2] Even if it isn't used for the end product, it is certainly convenient if there is a disk operating system or a real time executive available to help the software development effort. The labor cost involved in producing a working system is so large that most any aid that can be given is worth the investment.

With the preceding discussion of computer specifications in mind, let us reexamine the three types of real time systems. Buying a computer for controller use is really like buying a component; the actual hardware specs dominate the decision. One is interested not so much in the software, as it typically will be used only as an aid to microprogramming, but in the processor cycle time, the size of ROM available, the number of registers and the availability of read-write memory. Also of major concern is the number of I/O sense and control lines available, their signal levels and noise immunity, and the ease of connection to other parts of the system. The micro instruction set should be examined to be sure it allows easy bit manipulation and data handling of the type involved in the system under development.

In single usage dedicated systems, the hardware specifications as seen by an assembly language programmer are the important ones to consider. Circuit level descriptions are of concern mainly in reliability and system interconnection problems. The user of this type of system is buffered from the hardware only by an assembler or, hopefully, some basic control system. In looking at the interrupt system, one finds that the hardware response time is only a fraction of the system interrupt response. The remaining portion is the necessary software housekeeping involved in coordinating and saving the various parts of the program. This overhead can easily equal the hardware time, even if only a few critical registers are saved. Another portion of the interrupt system to be considered is the ability to hardware vector to a unique location; this feature can be used to best advantage in a dedicated system where every interrupt routine is written by the user who has knowledge of the rest of the system and can program accordingly. In the I/O area, a limited number of DMA channels will complicate the system to allow for reassigning them and may possibly slow down the system during a critical time.

Another area of concern is what happens to the execution speed and the interrupt response if DMA actually stops the CPU for some period of time. Most interrupt systems are not designed to override DMA, as this would affect the maximum burst rate of the DMA channel. Memory speed also affects interrupt response; the faster the memory, the shorter the time the interrupt housekeeping operations will take. A dedicated system can make use of a small, extra fast memory for just such purposes, since the arrangement of programs and data in memory are determined at system generation time. This allows a certain block of addresses to be used for specific purposes. This cannot be done in a general purpose multiprogramming RTE system without introducing extra overhead to keep track of who is using the special area. It is also possible in a dedicated system to group all of the critical routines into one area of memory and to rely on the good will of the debugged constituent programs not to destroy them, if memory protection is not available on the computer.

Another desirable feature on core resident systems is the ability to add memory in small amounts. The instruction set should be simple, so that the user doesn't pay for features he probably won't use. However, it should be capable of multiple precision arithmetic if much high accuracy computation is to be done--software routines to do those operations can eat up a lot of execution time. Similarly, more minicomputer instruction sets do not contain any operating system aids; this is reasonable, since most user written systems are unique, but it does mean a lot of housekeeping (e.g., saving and restoring registers on interrupts) must be programmed. A valuable asset in developing a real time system is the availability of hardware interfaces and software I/O routines for many of the standard electronic instruments; this saves trying to write software to use an instrument before the interface characteristics are known.

In real time executive systems, on the other hand, it is the software operating system specifications that are important. The performance of the basic system--i.e., the hardware plus the software--should be used in any evaluation, and even this must be considered in light of the particular job to be done. For instance, one is not concerned with how many interrupt devices the hardware will handle, but rather with how many interrupts may be handled in a certain amount of memory under the operating system. How difficult is it for a user to change the basic priority structure of the RTE, if it can be done at all? Even though the hardware interrupt response time may be a few microseconds, the system response time may easily be upwards of 75 microseconds by the time the executive routine has saved the entire status of the current user program, done its own internal bookkeeping, and transferred to the interrupt routine. This is the price paid for generality, where each interrupt program can be written independently of all the others. The hardware could reduce the overhead by automatically saving the user's environment in a portion of memory unique to that user. An alternative would be to provide instructions for saving and restoring the environment.

Extra hardware registers are generally desired to help increase the execution speed of a machine, but they may actually slow down the interrupt response time if they have to be saved. The problem of protecting one user from another is one of the keys to making a general purpose RTE system work smoothly. There can be no reliance on the good will of other programs here, as there could be in a dedicated system. This is especially true where compiling and debugging of programs is to be done in the background while the system is running.

When thinking about the I/O system, one must consider that most or all of the I/O will be done by the operating system. Will it handle the variety of devices needed, and how difficult will it be to write and add special I/O routines to the system? Does the system overhead impair the transfer rate of the hardware? Generally, the user is not allowed to get at the I/O system in an RTE since I/O is a critical resource that is shared among all users--again the problem of protection arises.

Similarly, memory protection among users must be considered. Is it adequate? Does it add time to the basic memory cycle? Is it a hardware or a software function? Associated with this problem is that of virtual memory systems. Does the operating system provide each user with a memory address space that looks as though he is the only program on the machine? If so, how much overhead is added to the system to provide this desirable feature? Memory size then becomes of concern only in that it is big enough to hold the working set of programs.[3] The multiprogramming operating system then handles memory allocation and the swapping of programs, and data are demanded by either an interrupt or the software scheduler.

If the user programs in a high level language, the word size and instruction set are pretty much invisible to him. They may show up indirectly in running time if, for example, too many multiple precision fetches are being made or too many subroutines are called to perform operations that are not in the hardware. The instruction set should contain features designed to help the operating system in order to decrease the overhead. For instance, relative addressing is a must on multiprogramming systems if a large amount of time is not to be spent on every memory swap to relocate the addresses to keep from having to load a program into the same exact location every time. Is the memory protection an integral part of the instruction set, or is it an add-on after thought that may cause additional system overhead? The computer manufacturer's software department has the difficult job of using the instruction set to write the operating system and the compilers. It would seem reasonable that instructions would be included in the initial design to help high level languages have increased code compression and shorter execution times.

The prospective user would be well advised to carefully examine the software provided with an RTE system to see how efficient and easy it is to use. What high level languages interface with the RTE? Can batch jobs be run in the background and tasks added to the foreground while the system is operating? Is there a reasonable library with routines applicable to the job at hand? Can these routines be shared at run time, allowing reduced core requirements? All these questions and many more should be asked, since it is the software specifications that make up a major part of any real time executive system specification.

In summary, one can say that the architecture of a real time system is made up of many facets, including the hardware, the software and all the devices connected to the system in the particular application. The form is not complete and cannot be specified without all of these elements. Each individual specification cannot be set up and examined alone, as though it were the deciding factor in designing or purchasing a real time system, but must be taken as part of the whole. In conclusion, one hopes that both designer and users will go beyond the traditional and parochial evaluation of a potential system, joining me in a plea for sanity in those who conceive the specs, those who write the specs, those who read the specs, and those who analyze the specs in terms of the requirements of the overall system.

References

1. Minutes of Third Workshop on Standardization of Industrial Languages, Part 1, Purdue University, March 2-6, 1970.
2. Basic Control System Reference Manual, Hewlett-Packard, February 1968.
3. Denning, P. J., "The Working Set Model for Program Behavior," Communications ACM, Vol. 11, No. 5, p. 323-333, May 1968.

A review of hardware and software...

Comparative Criteria for Minicomputers

J. L. BUTLER, Fisher Controls Co.

Minicomputers come in many varieties. The author tabulates data for 45 models available from 27 manufacturers. The roundup is not complete, but the minicomputer data presented here is comprehensive and forms the basis for an analysis of "price to performance ratio." The author proposes three equations that permit calculation of a minicomputer's hardware price/performance (P_h), software price/performance (P_s) and overall price/performance (P).

LOW COST IS THE FACTOR that makes "minicomputers," the small computers, so attractive to industry. For less than $10,000, a central processor and 4,096 words (4K) of core memory can be purchased—hardware that approximates the computing power of the top-of-the-line computers available 15 years ago. This economy has been accomplished with medium scale integration (MSI). The large scale integration (LSI) technology which is potentially more economical has yet to be applied in industrial control.

The flood of minicomputers into the marketplace continues because the number of potential applications is almost limitless. In the process industries, these small computers are used in increasing numbers in the laboratory and for process control, as well as in data communications and data acquisition systems.

The dynamic nature of minicomputer technology produces the biggest problem encountered in a minicomputer survey. Computer manufacturers offer and revise new and old models continuously, so keeping up with the minicomputers could be a full time job.

This survey and analysis of minicomputer hardware and software covers 45 models that are made by the 27 manufacturers listed in Table I. Discussion is limited to the manufacturers of computer mainframes; OEMs aren't included. Computers such as the IBM 1130, CDC 1700 and the GE/PAC 4020 were not reviewed because of their price.

Each of the 45 minicomputer models in Table II costs about $25,000 or less; in all cases, the price includes a "standard" processing unit, at least 4,096 words of core memory and sometimes a teletypewriter. Tables III and IV contain data on the IBM 1800, but only so the calculated price/performance ratios for minicomputers could be compared with the ratios for a "big" computer.

The central processor's job

This section presents and analyzes common CPU features, and points out some major design problems encountered by computer manufacturers. Because design trade-offs must be made, users will be better equipped to analyze products if they understand the manufacturers' problems. An "ideal architecture" is not specified in this article—architecture varies with the application. A typical system configuration is shown in Figure 1.

A central processing unit (CPU) contains the circuits to interpret and execute instructions. The CPU performs the following functions:
- Keeps track of the instruction being executed in a "program counter"
- Fetches instructions from memory and interprets or decodes these instructions
- Executes the instructions with the corresponding arithmetic, logic, test, and shift hardware units
- Directs the I/O hardware when I/O instructions are encountered in the program.

The CPU may contain registers for computation, address modification, or other purposes, plus error-detecting circuits to catch certain hardware failures. Obviously, the CPU has a direct effect on the speed with which any program can be executed and determines how easily a computer can be programmed.

Reprinted with permission from *Instrum. Technol.*, vol. 17, pp. 67–82, Oct. 1970.

Table I: Minicomputer makers

Business Information Technology, Inc. 5 Strathmore Road Natick, Mass. 01760	BIT	IRA Systems, Inc. 332 Second Ave. Waltham, Mass. 02154	IRA
Compiler Systems, Inc. P.O. Box 366 Ridgefield, Conn. 06877	CSI	Lockheed Electronics, Inc. Data Products Division 6201 E. Randolph Street Los Angeles, Calif. 90022	LEI
Computer Automation, Inc. 895 W. 16th Street Newport Beach, Calif. 92660	CAI	Micro Systems, Inc. 644 E. Young Street Santa Ana, Calif. 92705	MSI
Data General Corporation Route 9 Southboro, Mass. 01772	DG	Motorola, Inc. Box 5409 Phoenix, Arizona 85010	MOT
Data Technology, Inc. 1050 E. Meadow Circle Palo Alto, Calif. 94303	DT	Philco-Ford, Inc. 3939 Fabian Way Palo Alto, Calif. 94303	PFI
Datamate Computer Systems Box 310 Big Spring, Texas 79720	DCS	Raytheon Computer 2700 S. Fairview Street Santa Ana, Calif. 92704	RAY
Digital Equipment Corporation 146 Main Street Maynard, Mass. 01754	DEC	Redcor Corporation 7800 Deering Ave. P.O. Box 1031 Canoga Park, Calif. 91304	RC
Electronic Associates, Inc. 187 Monmouth Park Hwy. West Long Branch, N.J. 07764	EAI	Scientific Control Corporation Box 96 Carrollton, Texas 75006	SCC
General Automation, Inc. 706 W. Katella Orange, Calif. 92668	GAI	System Engineering Laboratories, Inc. Box 9148 Fort Lauderdale, Florida 33310	SEL
GRI Computer Corporation 76 Howe Street Newton, Mass. 02166	GRI	Tempo Computer, Inc. 340 W. Collins Ave. Orange, Calif. 92667	TEM
Hewlett-Packard Company 1501 Page Mill Road Palo Alto, Calif. 94304	HP	Varian Data Machines, Inc. 2722 Michelson Drive Irvine, Calif. 92664	VDM
Honeywell, Inc. Computer Control Division Old Connecticut Path Framingham, Mass. 01701	HON	Westinghouse Electric Corporation Computer and Instrumentation Div. 1200 West Colonial Drive Orlando, Fla. 32804	WES
Information Technology, Inc. 164 Wolfe Road Sunnyvale, Calif. 94086	ITI	Xerox Data Systems 701 S. Aviation Blvd. El Segundo, Calif. 90245	XDS
Interdata, Inc. 2 Crescent Place Oceanport, N.J. 07757	INT		

Almost all minicomputers now employ a parallel internal processor structure and some form of modified single-address instruction word format; however, there is extreme variation in the number of different address modifications and in the relative "power" of individual hardware instructions for given machines.

A computer's word—From an economic standpoint, the computer manufacturer decides on a standard word length for his computer; consequently, almost all small computers have a fixed word length and this is true of most computers in this article.

The computer word will represent both instructions and data. The determining word-length

Instrumentation Technology

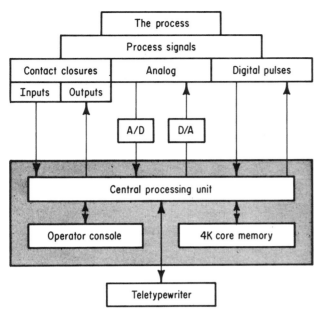

Figure 1. A minicomputer may look small and simple, but its architecture can vary considerably. The configuration of the CPU and the size of the memory, or memories, is determined by the application.

factor for data representation is usually the arithmetic precision needed by the application, but other factors determine the word length needed for the instructions.

The instruction is usually divided into fields, Figure 2, whose size is determined by these factors:

• Address field—size based on the maximum address to be referenced directly in an instruction

• Address-mode field—size based on the number of different address modification and special addressing techniques. (such as indexing)

• Operation-code field—size based on the number of different basic hardware instructions.

Most minicomputers have a 16-bit word length available to provide the capability to indirectly address a maximum 65K of core memory. The largest address that fits into the computer word generally determines the largest core configuration offered for a particular minicomputer. Therefore, word length is directly proportional to the "expandability" of the computer. Experience shows that the 16-bit word is usually of sufficient length to handle the basic single-word fields mentioned previously. Computers with a shorter word length (8 or 12 bits) pay a premium in that many double-word instructions may be needed.

For most process applications, the 16-bit word (15 data bits + sign) provides a precision that is acceptable. The acceptability of shorter lengths is questionable, because it would be necessary in many cases to resort to double precision arithmetic on the 8- and 12-bit computers. On the other hand,

a word length greater than 16 bits is a waste of money for most process applications.

Some computers have an 18-bit word length, but usually these computers are 16-bit machines—with 2 bits for extras like "parity checking" and/or "memory protect." The next word length size is generally 24 bits, a size that usually prices the small computer out of the "minicomputer market."

Kinds of addressing—As mentioned above, the kind of address modification employed determines the size of the address-mode field in the instruction word. The address modifications usually employed in minicomputers are:

• Relative addressing—The address field of the instruction is added to either the program-location register (floating page concept) or a page register (fixed page concept) to arrive at the effective address.

• Indirect addressing—The address field of the instruction holds a "pointer" to the location that contains the address of the operand; this is known as "single-level" indirect addressing. If the indicated location doesn't contain the operand address but does contain another pointer then "multilevel" indirect addressing is in use. Indirect addressing utilizes one extra memory cycle per level of indirectness.

• Indexed addressing—The contents of an index register (implemented as either a flip-flop register or as a word of core memory) are added to the address field to arrive at the effective address. If a core memory location is used for the index register,

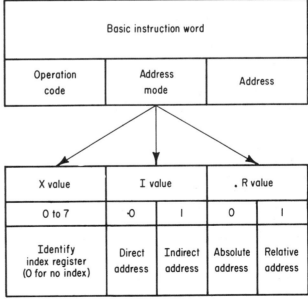

Figure 2. Usually, a basic instruction has three "fields." For a 16-bit word, the address mode's "subfield" can have 3 to 5 bits, then to 11 to 13 bits are available for the other two "fields."

Table IIA: Hardware data for minicomputers

Manufacturer	BIT	CSI	CAI	CAI	DG	DG
Model Number	BIT-483	CSI-16	PDC-208	PDC-216	NOVA	SUPER-NOVA
CPU features						
Instruction word length(s)	Variable	16	8/16	16	16	16
Accumulators	1	3	1	2	4	4
Hardware registers	18	11	8	6	5	5
Index registers	0	1 Hardware	0	1 Hardware	2 Hardware 16 Memory	2 Hardware 16 Memory
Bits for operation code	Variable	4	N/A	N/A	N/A	N/A
Bits for address modes	Variable	2	N/A	N/A	N/A	N/A
Address modes	2	3	4	8	4	4
Bits for address	9	10	9	10	10	10
Words directly addressable	512	1K	512	1K	1K	1K
Words indirectly addressable	512	32K	16K	32K	32K	32K
Indirect addressing (levels)	Single	Single	Multiple	Multiple	Multiple	Multiple
Instruction sets						
Store time (full word), μ sec	4	2	8	5.33	5.5	1.6
Add time (full word), μ sec	Variable	2	8	5.33	5.9	0.8
Fixed point hardware X/÷	No	Standard	No	No	No	Optional
Floating point hardware X/÷	No	Standard	No	No	No	No
Fixed point hardware X time, μ sec	-	8.8	-	-	-	3.8
Fixed point hardware ÷ time, μ sec	-	9.0	-	-	-	6.7
Fixed point software X time, μ sec	N/A	-	370	55	340	68
Fixed point software ÷ time, μ sec	N/A	-	630	95	480	96
Memory						
Memory cycle time, μ sec	1.0	1.0	2.67	2.67	2.6	0.8
Memory word length, bits	8 (multiples)	16	8	16	16	16
Minimum memory size, words	1K	1K	4K	4K	4K	4K
Memory increment size, words	4K	4K	4K	4K	4K	4K
Maximum memory size, words	65K	32K	16K	32K	32K	32K
Parity checking	No	No	No	No	No	No
Memory protect	No	Optional	Optional	Optional	No	Optional
Miscellaneous						
Power failure protect	Standard	Standard	Optional	Optional	Standard	Standard
Automatic restart	Optional	No	Optional	Optional	Standard	Standard
Real-time clock	Optional	Optional	Optional	Optional	Standard	Standard
System cost (CPU + 4K memory)	$7,660	$10,750[1]	$5,990	$7,990	$7,950	$11,700

an additional memory cycle is needed for each indexed instruction. But if a separate flip-flop register is used, there will be no noticable slowdown in instruction execution time.

If all of the above forms of address modification are available in a minicomputer, the order of execution to calculate the "effective address" is generally:

1. Derelativize the address field.
2. Fetch the indirect address (repeat for multilevel).
3. Perform the specified indexing.

A less frequently applied alternative to the above "post-indexing" scheme is one of "pre-indexing." In this latter method, the specified indexing is performed prior to fetching of the indirect address.

Computers which do not have the relative addressing capability are fairly common and this is not an important limitation if the application can be handled with an "all-core" computer. However, lack of relative addressing rules out the possibility of implementing a core-bulk multiprogramming system with dynamic core allocation; programs for such a machine are not relocatable in core.

Figure 2 illustrates the number of bits needed in each instruction word for the above address modification schemes. Subfields in the address-mode field are interpreted as shown in Table II. The relative, indirect, and indexed address modifications can be implemented in 3 to 5 bits (depending on the number of index registers. If only 1 bit is used for the X field shown in Figure 2 the computer can have only one index register. With 3 bits then seven index registers can be identified, which for a small computer in a process application will usually provide sufficient flexibility.

From 11 to 13 bits of a 16-bit word will be available to accommodate both the operation-code field and the address field. This may look like far too few bits to handle both of these fields; however, computer designers often show much ingenuity. One trick reduces the size of the operation-code field by grouping the instructions into two classes: those that reference memory and those that do not. Instead of assigning a unique number in the operation-code field for each instruction, only those that reference the memory are given a unique code.

Instructions that do not reference memory have no need for a memory address, and can be assigned one operation-code number. The address field then codes the specific instructions. Because most instructions are nonmemory reference types, the savings in the size of the operation-code field

DT DT-1600	DCS Datamate-16	DEC PDP 8/I	DEC PDP-8/L	DEC PDP-9/L
8/16	16	12/24	12/24	18
1	1	1	1	1 Std., 1 Opt.
8	6	N/A	N/A	N/A
0	1 Hardware	8 Memory	8 Memory	7 Memory
4	5	3	3	4
2	3	1	1	1
2	8	2	2	2
8	8	8/15	8/13	13
512	256	256	256	4K
16K	32K	32K	8K	16K
Multiple	Multiple	Single	Single	Single
24	2	3	3.2	3
24	2	3	3.2	3
No	Standard	Optional	No	Optional
No	No	No	No	No
-	7	N/A	-	16.5
-	9	N/A	-	18
1,200	-	360	360	421
1,500	-	460	460	528
8.0	1.0	1.5	1.6	1.5
8	16	12	12	18
4K	4K	4K	4K	4K
4K	4K	4K	4K	4K
16K	32K	32K	8K	16K
No	Optional	Optional	Optional	Optional
Optional	Standard	Standard	Standard	Optional
Optional	Standard	Optional	Optional	Optional
Optional	Standard	Optional	Optional	Optional
Optional	Optional	Optional	Optional	Optional
$6,600	$14,900	$12,800	$8,500	$19,900

Notes and symbols:

X/÷   multiply/divide
X   multiply
÷   divide
N/A   not available
K   1,024 words (4K = 4,096 words)

1. Software supplied at extra cost
2. Includes ASR-33 teletypewriter
3. Implied by address
4. 8K core minimum
5. Includes 256 words of ROM
6. Includes 512 words of ROM
7. Monthly rental of $417
8. Minimum 8K core, includes ASR-33
9. Data for P-2000 built in Pittsburgh. Modified P-2000 will eventually be made in Orlando. Refer to Table I.

is dramatic: the field can often be reduced to 4 bits.

If only 4 bits are assigned to the operation-code field, 7 to 9 bits remain for the address field. Assume that only three index registers are specified —limiting the size of the X field to 2 bits; therefore, the address field will be set at 8 bits which can address only 256 words directly. The address modification supplied will usually have enough flexibility to overcome this limitation.

Program execution—The CPU has a significant effect on the speed of program execution. Minicomputers with shorter word lengths (8 or 12 bits) must rely extensively on double-word instructions, an extra word of memory and one extra memory read-write cycle for each double-word instruction that is executed in a program. Even though the minicomputer that uses a shorter word length might have a memory read-write cycle time which is faster than the time for a corresponding 16-bit machine, program execution will probably be faster in the 16-bit machine because it will execute fewer memory read-write cycles for a given program. The CPU in the computer with the shorter word length must work harder to get the same job done.

A trend toward the utilization of multiple, general purpose registers is apparent. These registers in the CPU can be used as accumulators, arithmetic extensions (to multiply, divide, etc.) and index registers to greatly decrease the execution time required for a given program by reducing the number of references made to memory (such as load and store); this innovation is a definite plus in the evaluation of a new computer's features.

Another feature cuts costs and increases flexibility; many new minicomputers have a "microprogramming" capability. A microprogram is "the sequence of elementary steps which permits the computer hardware to carry out a computer instruction." These elementary steps are called microinstructions.

Some minicomputers provide a minimum set of microinstructions and allow the actual machine architecture to be developed from this basic set. This approach could be of great benefit for an OEM in that it results in a very inexpensive mainframe, but it's probably of little value to a company that must apply minicomputers to industrial control problems. The drawbacks for one-of-a-kind applications are:

• Extra programming effort to define and implement the macroinstructions from sequences of microinstructions
• Inherent loss of computer speed (usually 2 to

Table IIB: Hardware data for minicomputers

Manufacturer	DEC	DEC	EAI	GAI	GAI	GAI
Model number	PDP-11/20	PDP-15/10	EAI-640	SPC-12	SPC-16	System 18/30
CPU features						
Instruction word length(s)	16	18	16/32	8/16	16/32	16/32
Accumulators	6	1 Std., 1 Opt.	2	4	16	2
Hardware registers	8	N/A	9	8	19	13
Index registers	6	1 Hardware 8 Memory	1 Hardware	3 Hardware	6	3
Bits for operation code	4	4	4	8	4	5
Bits for address modes	4	2	3	3	4	5
Address modes	12	4	8	6	11	12
Bits for address	16	12	9/15	12	8/16	8/16
Words directly addressable	32K	4K	512	4K	32K	32K
Words indirectly addressable	-	32K	32K	4K	32K	32K
Indirect addressing (levels)	None	Single	Multiple	Single	Single	Single
Instruction sets						
Store time (full word), μ sec	2.3	1.6	3.3	4.2	2	2.4
Add time (full word), μ sec	2.3	1.6	3.3	4.2	3	2.4
Fixed point hardware X/÷	No	Optional	Standard	No	No	Standard
Floating point hardware X/÷	No	No	No	No	No	No
Fixed point hardware X time, μ sec	-	7	18.15	-	-	12
Fixed point hardware ÷time, μ sec	-	7.25	18.98	-	-	13.2
Fixed point software X time, μ sec	N/A	200	-	N/A	N/A	-
Fixed point software ÷time, μ sec	N/A	250	-	N/A	N/A	-
Memory						
Memory cycle time, μ sec	1.2	0.8	1.65	2.0	0.96	0.96
Memory word length, bits	16	18	16	8	16	16 + 2
Minimum memory size, words	4K	4K	4K	4K	4K	4K
Memory increment size, words	4K	4K	4K	4K	4K	4K
Maximum memory size, words	32K	131K	32K	16K	32K	32K
Parity checking	No	Optional	No	Optional	No	Standard
Memory protect	No	Optional	Standard	No	No	Standard
Miscellaneous						
Power failure protect	Standard	Optional	Standard	Optional	Standard	Standard
Automatic restart	Standard	Optional	No	Optional	Standard	Standard
Real-time clock	Optional	Optional	Optional	Standard	Standard	Standard
System cost (CPU + 4K memory)	$10,800[2]	$15,600	$26,500	$5,000	$10,000	$18,000

3 times slower than a computer with a fixed instruction repertoire and a comparable memory read-write cycle time).

Whether the initial savings in purchase price for this kind of machine can offset the added programming expense is debatable.

The problem of evaluating the instruction sets of various computers is very complex. The great majority of new minicomputers are being programmed in assembly language, so the prospective user should take a close look at the instruction sets of machines that are of special interest. The instruction sets in Table II run the full range from very simple microinstructions sets to large, powerful instruction sets.

Because of cost, most small computers are now programmed in assembly languages. The money saved by buying a minicomputer is easily lost if all the extra peripheral hardware needed to compile programs efficiently is added to the system. An economical system that is programmable in a higher-level language has yet to be introduced. As a reasonable alternative to programming in assembly language, programs can be written in a compiler level language (the compilations are run on a large machine). This approach shows promise

and should become more popular in the future. Most manufacturers do not offer this alternative now; therefore, the evaluation of hardware instruction sets is still important.

Particular attributes needed in the instruction set will vary with the application. If many arithmetic calculations are necessary, a hardware multiply/divide package is desirable. If the application is primarily logic-oriented, then an ideal computer would have strong capabilities in this area (such as bit manipulation and bit testing).

Miscellaneous features—It is important to note which features are standard and which are optional. The manufacturer that offers the least expensive mainframe usually does not offer the least expensive system. In real-time applications for example, power failure protection and a real-time clock are highly desirable and are specified for most systems. The manufacturer that offers these features as standard equipment is usually ahead of the game; his price will probably be lower.

Evaluating memories

The magnetic core memory, introduced in the early 1950's, is still today's most common, high speed,

GRI 909	HP 2114A	HP 2115A	HP 2116B	HON H-316	HON DDP-516	ITI 4900	INT Model 3
16	16	16	16	16/32	16/32	16/32	16/32
Variable	2	2	2	2	2	8	16
9	7	7	7	5	5	16	18
32K-Memory	0	0	0	1 Hardware	1 Hardware	6 Hardware	15 Hardware
0[3]	4	4	4	5	5	8	8
2	2	2	2	2	2	2	2
4	4	4	4	4	4	4	3
12	10	10	10	9/14	9/14	6/16	6/16
32K	2K	2K	2K	1K	1K	32K	32K
32K	8K	8K	32K	32K	32K	32K	-
Single	Multiple	Multiple	Multiple	Multiple	Multiple	Multiple	None
3.52	4	4	3.2	3.2	1.92	1.95-3.5	6
1.76-7.03	4	4	3.2	3.2	1.92	1.95-3.5	3.2
Optional	No	Optional	Optional	Optional	Optional	Optional	Optional
No	No	No	No	No	No	No	No
10	-	24	19.2	8.8	5.28	10	23
14	-	26	20.8	17.6	10	25	38
320	187	187	150	258.2	154.6	50	900
600	387	387	310	368.7	220.8	100	1,020
1.76	2.0	2.0	1.6	1.6	0.96	0.98-1.75	1.5
16+2	16	16	16	16	16	16	16
4K	4K	4K	8K	4K	4K	4K	2K
4K	4K	4K	8K	4K	4K	4K	2K
32K	8K	8K	32K	16K	32K	32K	32K
Standard	Optional	Optional	Optional	No	Optional	Optional	Optional
Standard	No	Optional	Optional	No	Optional	Optional	Optional
Standard	Optional	Optional	Standard	Standard	Standard	Optional	Optional
Standard	Optional	Optional	Optional	Optional	Optional	Optional	Optional
Optional	Optional	Optional	Optional	Optional	Optional	Optional	Optional
$9,740	$9,950	$14,500	$24,000[4]	$9,700	$23,800	$9,950	$10,800

random access, read-write memory device. All minicomputers in this survey rely on this kind of memory for primary storage.

Core memories range in size from a few hundred to several million bits, with cycle times from about 0.5 to 10 μsec. The attributes that made the magnetic core memory so popular are reasonably large capacity, high speed, and acceptable cost.

Table II provides comparative specifications on the memory modules with reference to the definitions that follow. The "cycle time" referred to above is the memory read-write cycle time: in other words, the time required to transfer one word of binary data from core memory to the CPU, and to replace the same word in core. "Memory word length" is the number of bits accessed in one memory cycle; this term is usually synonymous with the "fixed word length" described in detail earlier. The "memory size" is given as number of words; consequently, "memory size" must be multiplied by the "memory word length" to obtain the total number of bits contained in the memory. This latter figure is important because it truly represents the storage capacity of a given machine.

Magnetic cores ranging from 100 to 10 mils (thousandths of an inch) in diameter have been made and used. The most common sizes are 50, 30 and 20 mils—in spite of their size, two to four wires are threaded through each core, usually by hand. Wiring of the cores is probably the greatest obstacle to cheaper, faster, and larger memories.

Individual core size is the factor that has the biggest effect on memory cycle time. For example, computers with 50-mil core memories generally have cycle times ranging from 6 to 10 μsec. Similarly, the 30-mil core usually results in cycle times of 2 to 5 μsec, and the 20-mil core performance ranges from 800 ηsec to 2 μsec.

An important point to remember: the sense threshold of the signals (to read from and write into the core memory) will vary in a magnitude that is proportional to the size of the individual cores; if a signal level of 1 unit is necessary to read a 50-mil core, then a 20-mil core will require only about 0.5 units of signal strength. It's obvious that the smaller the core (the faster the memory), the more susceptible the machine will be to noise-induced computer failures such as dropped bits.

Because of the noise sensitivity problem, the industrial user should be wary of a computer that is too fast for the application. Reliability may be lower and cost will probably be higher.

Manufacturer	INT	IRA	LEI	MSI	MSI	MOT
Model number	Model 4	SPIRAS-65	MAC 16	800	810	MDP-1000
CPU features						
Instruction word length(s)	16/32	16/32	16	16	16/24	12
Accumulators	16	2	1	15	2	5
Hardware registers	33	3	6	23	5	9
Index registers	15 Hardware	1 Hardware + Accumulators	4 Memory	0	1 Hardware	3 Hardware
Bits for operation code	8	6	4	4	5	8
Bits for address modes	2	2/3	3	0	3	3
Address modes	3	4	8	1	8	6
Bits for address	6/16	10/16	9	8	8/16	12
Words directly addressable	32K	65K	512	256	32K	4K
Words indirectly addressable	-	16K	65K	-	256	4K
Indirect addressing (levels)	None	Multiple	Multiple	None	Single	Single
Instruction sets						
Store time (full word), μsec	6	3.6	2	1.1 (8-bit)	4.62 (16-bit)	6.48
Add time (full word), μsec	3.2	3.6	2	1.22	5.06	4.32
Fixed point hardware X/÷	Optional	Standard	Optional	No	Standard	No
Floating point hardware X/÷	No	No	No	No	No	No
Fixed point hardware X time, μsec	23	17	9	-	63.36	-
Fixed point hardware ÷ time, μsec	38	30	12	-	90.86	-
Fixed point software X time, μsec	900	-	150	N/A	-	N/A
Fixed point software ÷ time, μsec	1,020	-	300	N/A	-	N/A
Memory						
Memory cycle time, μsec	1.0	1.8	1.0	1.1	1.1	2.0
Memory word length, bits	16	16	16	8,9, or 10	8,9, or 10	8
Minimum memory size, words	2K	4K	4K	256 (ROM)	4K+512 (ROM)	4K
Memory increment size, words	2K	4K	4K	4K	4K	4K
Maximum memory size, words	32K	65K	65K	32K	32K	16K
Parity checking	Optional	No	Optional	Optional	Optional	No
Memory protect	Optional	Optional	Optional	Optional	Optional	No
Miscellaneous						
Power failure protect	Optional	Optional	Standard	Optional	Optional	Optional
Automatic restart	Optional	Optional	Standard	Optional	Optional	Optional
Real-time clock	Optional	Optional	Standard	Optional	Optional	Optional
System cost (CPU + 4K memory)	$13,800	$12,750	$11,950[2]	$5,700[5]	$6,900[6]	$8,500

As previously mentioned, some computers utilize extra bits in each word of core memory for such things as "parity checking" and "memory protect." This feature is usually optional in all but the more expensive small computers. Because of the cost of this feature and the improved reliability of core memories, most computer manufacturers have decided that the extra checking is not warranted. Some manufacturers who feel strongly about this don't offer parity or memory protect as options.

However, some form of parity check is mandatory for a bulk memory device (drum or disc), and memory protect is needed if any form of on-line debugging is anticipated. On-line debugging indicates correction of new programs after the basic system has been installed and debugged. An operational system could be impaired by new programs if it's without a memory protect feature.

If a new minicomputer system is small enough to be implemented on an "all-core" machine, parity and memory protect are not warranted; when talking industrial control applications of minicomputers, this may be the usual case.

The popular ROM

Read only memory has become very popular during the past five years. The ROM is a medium for storing data in permanent (nonerasable) form. Usually a high speed static storage device,—excluding paper tape or other such memories—the ROM provides rapid access to information of a permanent nature. Common square root and exponential routines can be "wired-in" for fast execution from conventional core memory operations. From a programmer's point of view, the result is indistinguishable.

This concept lends itself in a natural way to microprogramming, in which every instruction is a permanent subroutine in a ROM. Microprogramming provides economical realization of complex instruction sets in simple computers, and is the main reason for the rise in popularity of the ROM.

If every instruction is a wired-in subroutine in a ROM, a different set of computer instructions may be obtained by changing the ROM. This notion leads to emulation (executing instructions of one computer on the hardware of another computer), a concept applied extensively in the various IBM 360 and RCA SPECTRA-70 computers.

In the past, ROMs have been wired at the factory to contain programs that were specified previously. After shipment to the field, these ROMs were practically impossible to modify. A new design recently introduced by Digital Scientific Corp.

PFI 1216-F	RAY 703	RAY 706	RC RC-70	SCC 4700	SEL 810A	SEL 810B	TEM TEMPO-1
16	16	16	16/32	16/32	16	16	16/32
1	1	1	1	3	2	2	2
7	6	6	5	10	2	2	7
1 Hardware	1 Hardware	1 Hardware	1 Hardware	1 Hardware	1 Hardware	2 Hardware	1 Hardware
3	4	4	6	4/9	4	4	4
2	1	1	3	2	2	2	3
4	2	2	5	5	4	4	8
11	11	11	7/14	9/16	10	10	9/16
2K	32K	32K	16K	32K	1K	1K	512
32K	-	-	16K	65K	32K	32K	65K
Single	None	None	Single	Single	Multiple	Multiple	Multiple
4	3.5	1.8	1.9	1.84	3.5	1.5	1.8
4	3.5	1.8	1.9	1.84	3.5	1.5	1.8
Optional	Optional	Optional	Standard	Optional	Standard	Standard	Optional
No	No	No	No	No	No	No	No
N/A	17.5	9	6.5	6.44	7	4.5	7
N/A	24	9	12.5	6.90	10.5	8.25	9
N/A	147	75	-	N/A	-	-	N/A
N/A	300	154	-	N/A	-	-	N/A
3.5	1.75	0.9	0.86	0.92	1.75	0.75	0.9
16	16	16	16+1	16	16	16	16
4K	4K	4K	4K	4K	4K	8K	4K
4K	4K	4K	4K	4K	4K	8K	4K
16K	32K	32K	32K	65K	32K	32K	65K
Optional	No	Optional	Standard	Optional	Optional	Standard	Optional
Optional	No	Optional	Standard	Optional	Optional	Optional	Optional
Optonal	Optional	Optional	Standard	Standard	Standard	Standard	Standard
Optional	Standard	Standard	Standard	Optional	Optional	Optional	Optional
Optional	Optional	Optional	Standard	Optional	Optional	Optional	Optional
$11,900	$12,750[2]	$19,000[2]	$13,900[7]	$14,800	$18,000[2]	$33,500[8]	$15,000[2]

(San Diego, Calif.) changes all this; their new ROM allows field programming by plugging "chips" into a ROM board. This ROM can be reprogrammed at any time by the user and forms the base for Digital Scientific's new computer; their META-4 (not in this survey) is unique in that it does not have a fixed instruction set of its own, but it can emulate almost any other computer. This example is cited to emphasize the utility of the ROM.

The ROM provides a very powerful tool for the computer designer. Some strong arguments generally advanced in favor of the ROM are:
• Economy—costs much less than standard read-write core memory
• Speed—typically 5 to 10 times faster than read-write core
• Reliability—the program is protected from overwriting by an errant program.

A number of the small computers employ ROMs in varying degrees; this is an important factor and should be considered for specific applications.

Bulk memories for the mini

The two most popular and economical bulk memory devices of the nonvolatile type are the magnetic disc and the magnetic tape. The magnetic drum is in a class by itself because it's considerably more expensive (per unit of storage) to implement. Small, inexpensive systems are being discussed; therefore, magnetic drums will not be covered.

Magnetic discs—Two general classes are available:
• discs with a single floating read-write head
• and those with a fixed read-write head for each track.

The first disc memories had only one read-write head which (in multiple disc installations) had to "seek" the correct disc surface and then the correct track. Although average access time was very slow, this type of bulk storage proved economical and was popular with many early computer users.

The design was improved by adding a separate read-write head for each recording surface. Popular today, this kind of disc pack cut the average memory access time to about 100 milliseconds; furthermore, bit transfer rates greater than 1 MHz are now common. The cost of disc bulk memory is only about 2 cents per byte (8 bits), and this cost decreases as the size of the bulk memory increases.

Almost all of the 45 minicomputers in Table II can be equipped with a magnetic disc bulk memory system. But many of the manufacturers who will supply a disc do not (as yet) offer a

Table IID: Hardware data for minicomputers

Manufacturer	VDM	VDM	WES[9]	XDS	XDS	XDS
Model number	520/i	620/i	Prodac-2000	CE-16	CF-16	SIGMA-3
CPU features						
Instruction word length(s)	8/16	16/32	16	16	16	16/32
Accumulators	7	2	4 Memory	1	1	2
Hardware registers	7	6	5	6	6	9
Index registers	1 Hardware	2 Hardware	2 Memory	1 Hardware	1 Hardware	2 Hardware
Bits for operation code	3	4	5	5	5	4
Bits for address modes	3	3	3	3	3	4
Address modes	5	4	8	8	8	12
Bits for address	15	9/11	8/16	8/14	8/14	8
Words directly addressable	4K	2K	256	256	256	1K
Words indirectly addressable	32K	32K	65K	16K	16K	65K
Indirect addressing (levels)	Multiple	Multiple	Single	Multiple	Multiple	Single
Instruction sets						
Store time (full word), μ sec	4.5	3.6	7	16	5.34	1.95
Add time (full word), μ sec	4.5	3.6	7	16	5.34	1.95
Fixed point hardware X/÷	No	Optional	Standard	No	No	Optional
Floating point hardware X/÷	No	No	Optional	No	No	No
Fixed point hardware X time, μ sec	-	10	24.5	-	-	7.8
Fixed point hardware ÷ time, μ sec	-	14	32.5	-	-	8.13
Fixed point software X time, μ sec	N/A	200	-	126	42	N/A
Fixed point software ÷ time, μ sec	N/A	200	-	142	47.3	N/A
Memory						
Memory cycle time, μ sec	1.5	1.8	3.0	8.0	2.67	0.98
Memory word length, bits	8	16	16	16	16	16
Minimum memory size, words	4K	4K	4K	4K	4K	8K
Memory increment size, words	4K	4K	4K	4K	4K	8K
Maximum memory size, words	32K	32K	65K	16K	16K	64K
Parity checking	Optional	Optional	Standard	No	No	Standard
Memory protect	Standard	Optional	No	No	No	Optional
Miscellaneous						
Power failure protect	Optional	Optional	Standard	Optional	Optional	Optional
Automatic restart	Optional	Optional	Optional	Optional	Optional	Optional
Real-time clock	Optional	Optional	Standard	Optional	Optional	Optional
System cost (CPU + 4K memory)	$7,500	$9,950	$10,000	$9,980	$7,990	$24,000

disc-operating system with their software package.

The latest innovation in disc packs is the "fixed-head" disc which has one read-write head per track. Using this approach, the only factor that determines access time is the speed of disc rotation. Average access time will be the time required for one-half rotation (an average time of about 15 milliseconds is typical). Data transfer rates vary considerably from model to model, but all are relatively fast transfer devices. A typical fixed-head disc would transfer at least 150K bytes/sec, a bit transfer rate of 1.2 MHz. The XDS model 7211/7212 has an extremely fast bit transfer rate, 24 MHz. The price per byte on these units is typically 3 to 3.5 cents, or about 60 percent above the floating-head units.

The system designer faces a choice between the high speed, high cost, fixed-head disc and the slower but more economical floating-head disc. For most process control and data acquisition installations, the added expense for the fixed-head units probably will not be warranted.

Magnetic tape—If high speed data storage or retrieval is not a major factor, then magnetic tape should be considered. As a bulk storage device, magnetic tape has several strong points. First, there is no upper limit on storage capacity (extra tape reels can be purchased). The capacity of a common 7-track 2,400-ft tape varies from 5M to 20M bytes, which is greater than the capacity of most disc packs. Second, the cost per byte of storage is much lower than for any other bulk storage medium.

Magnetic tape must be read serially, a shortcoming which means the average access time for a piece of information is measured in seconds rather than milliseconds. Of course, if tape must be changed to access the information, then the access time extends to minutes instead of seconds.

Magnetic tape is ideal for a system that faces extensive program development. When combined with a keyboard data entry unit and a crt display, the magnetic tape is a very powerful system development tool. DEC has a good example of this type of system in their LINC-8 and PDP-12 computers. The magnetic tape provides a convenient means for storing programs under development (much more so than cards or paper tape) and the keyboard/crt combination doesn't generate mountains of paper. The program can be written and debugged with a minimum of "hard copy" output.

Another magnetic tape method has become popular recently; the "key-to-tape" unit allows the magnetic tape to replace the punched card without changing drastically the keypunch girl's duties. She still transfers information from the coding sheet to a keyboard, but the information is stored in a tape reel instead of punched cards. Once on tape, the information is of a more permanent nature, less likely to be destroyed, and more convenient to handle; furthermore, it isn't much more expensive than the old keypunch method.

The "cassette" tape housing, physically similar to units designed for stereo tape players, is becoming more popular. The additional ease of handling and storing cassettes is obvious and the tape sees less exposure to atmospheric impurities and dirt particles. The development of cassette tapes for future computer systems will be something to watch.

Interfaces to the mini

The equipment needed for conversation with the minicomputer should satisfy certain requirements:

• Equipment should not be expensive; nobody wants to pay $35,000 for a line printer that will be connected to a $10,000 computer.

• The equipment should be relatively fast, convenient to use, and reliable.

The standard interface of the minicomputer industry is probably the Teletype ASR-33. This versatile machine provides keyboard input, printed output and paper tape I/O—and all at relatively low cost of about $1,500. The disadvantages of this teletypewriter are well known: low speed printed output (about 10 characters/sec), low speed paper tape I/O, and paper tape itself which is unquestionably the least convenient bulk storage medium to work with.

Alternatives to paper tape are punched cards and magnetic tape. Cards are convenient to work with and easier to store than tape but unfortunately the card handling equipment (readers and punchers) is very expensive when compared to paper tape equipment. Historically, magnetic tape has been even more expensive, but it appears that low cost cassette equipment will soon be competitive with paper tape. The added convenience of the magnetic tape more than offsets the added expense.

When magnetic tape is combined with a simple keyboard input device and a crt display, the system is very powerful. We are not far from the day when this kind of system will be much lower in cost; already available is the IRA Systems IRASCOPE, a unique keyboard-input crt peripheral that sells for under $6,000.

The only communication device missing from the above system (keyboard, crt and magnetic tape) is some kind of a printer; of course, the old teletype is always available with its low speed handicap. Current printers include several moderate-to-high speed models. Teletype's INKTRONIC terminal is now available as a receive-only model, a moderately high speed printer without moving parts in its print mechanism. Charged particles of ink shoot toward ordinary teletype paper at a rate of 105 characters/sec, (about 10 times faster than the ARS-33). This rate produces about 80 lines/min.

Also available are several high speed, relatively low-cost printers such as the Clevite 4800 which prints 4,800 (86-character) lines/min, and the Litton Industries DATALOG MC-8800 which prints 6,000 (88-character) lines/min. These small printers appear to be ideal for the small computer system; in addition, they would eliminate the long time required to get hard copy output from a teletypewriter.

Input/output control

Programmed I/O is a term that can describe the type of I/O operation in which the data (input to or output from the computer) must pass through an internal register of the CPU. Usually the accumulator is the register through which the data passes. This means that the computer must be dedicated entirely to the input or output operation throughout its complete cycle—a big drawback.

This method of I/O control requires the least extra hardware; because it's the least expensive to implement, it's in most minicomputers. Programmed I/O is definitely a drawback if the application requires a large amount of I/O. But if the application needs infrequent I/O and only in short "bursts," then programmed I/O is an excellent means of saving money.

Most minicomputers with programmed I/O will provide only one interrupt with the basic system. If more than one peripheral device is to be connected to this computer, the devices must be connected in "party-line" fashion: first come, first served—there is no priority other than the checks by the interrupt handling software to see which device is making the interrupt request.

Minicomputers which provide only this means of I/O control are:

Computer Automation	PDC-208
Hewlett-Packard	2114A
Data Technology	DT-1600
Xerox Data Systems	CE-16; CF-16

These computers offer no option to the programmed I/O method..

Direct memory access—The direct memory access (DMA) channel is a popular alternative to programmed I/O, but DMA requires more hardware so it's more expensive. Most minicomputers with this feature offer it as an option (not included in the basic price). The DMA channel enables an I/O data transfer to be initiated under program control and then carries out the transfer independent of the CPU. The data path is usually to/from the peripheral device directly from/to the core memory.

Completion of the I/O transfer operation is then signaled by a priority interrupt.

Actually, minicomputers don't really carry out the I/O transfers with complete independence from the CPU—it just looks that way. The computers utilize a scheme called "cycle stealing" in which the I/O processor effects the data transfer, usually on a word-by-word basis, while the CPU cycle is delayed. The "cycle stealing" method does not impair a computer's ability to execute other programs while the I/O transfer is proceeding. It only means the program will not be executed at full speed; even this is a vast improvement over programmed I/O in which no programs can be executed during the I/O operation.

Of the computers in this survey, the following offer DMA as standard equipment:

Business Information Technology	BIT-483
Compiler Systems	CSI-16
Data General	NOVA
Datamate Computers	Datamate-16
Digital Equipment	PDP-8/I,-11, and-15/10
General Automation	SYSTEM 18/30 and SPC-16
Lockheed Electronics	MAC 16
Raytheon Computer	703; 706
Xerox Data Systems	SIGMA-3

All other computers may be assumed to have DMA available on an optional basis.

Software for the minicomputer

In general, the software currently offered is minimal. A few manufacturers have fairly comprehensive software packages, but they are definitely in the minority. Perhaps one reason for this situation is that the computer firms simply have not had enough time to develop software packages for their new computers. This condition is certainly plausible because most minicomputers now on the market have been introduced during the past 18 months.

Predictably, the computers with the most software are products of the older computer companies; the companies in this category are: Digital Equipment Corp., EAI, Hewlett-Packard, Honeywell, Raytheon, Systems Engineering Labs and Xerox Data Systems. All of these mini manufacturers offer a basic software package that usually consists of a compiler, assembler, utility routines, math library and an operating system (including I/O driver routines). In addition, most have libraries of application-oriented programs which can generally be adapted to specific applications. DEC appears to have the lead in this field with a library of applications programs that's available through their DECUS organization. Of course, many companies are happy to provide programming assistance to a user, sometimes at not-so-reasonable rates.

Other companies intend to offer a comprehensive software package but do not have their package completed yet. Most of these firms have the same package as those previously mentioned—with the exception of an operating system; this second group includes Business Information Technology, Datamate Computer, General Automation, IRA Systems, Lockheed Electronics, Redcor, Tempo Computer, Westinghouse Electric and Data General.

All other minicomputers in this survey are made by a third category of vendors who can be characterized as offering an assembler, a loader, some utility routines, but not much else. These computers are intended for applications that require a small dedicated machine, one in which the programs are short and easily written in assembly language, and one in which the programs will not be changed. Naturally, the computers in this third group are usually the least expensive.

Several software packages have been developed for industrial data acquisition and process control. In particular, two packages rival the IBM-1800 PROSPRO system in power; the DEC INDAC-8 and the Foxboro CODPAC/BATCH/LAM are both written for the DEC PDP-8 family of computers, and both require considerably more hardware than that found in a "minimum system." Another software system that is in roughly the same class in the SEL COMPAS package.

In general, systems that utilize these software packages will be priced well out of the "minicomputer" class. A minimum configuration to implement any of these packages usually starts at about $50,000 with many configurations priced well above $100,000.

One trend in the computer industry—and the minicomputer field is no exception—is the move toward separate pricing of hardware and software. The following companies now charge separately for software:

Compiler Systems
General Automation
Xerox Data Systems.

Sooner or later, most other manufacturers will probably follow this "unbundling" trend.

Reliability and service

Another point to keep in mind when evaluating minicomputers for a specific application: in many cases, high reliability is more important than high speed. As previously mentioned, usually the faster machines have smaller cores in their memories and are more susceptible to electrical noise than the slower machines with the larger cores. Of utmost importance to the computer user who plans a real-time application is the system's reliability.

The computer manufacturers are all very optimistic about product reliability. Many are so optimistic that they informally quote MTBF figures of

Table III: Parameter values for calculation of price/performance ratios

Mfr.	Model	Cost (K$)	A_h (%)	L_h (%)	I_h (%)	M (Kbits)	E (bits)	W (bits)	R	T (μsec)	N	P_h	D	B	L	A	C	S	P_s	P
BIT	BIT-483	7.66	60	50	50	32	1	8	1	1.0	1	1.49	0	1	1	3	1	25	1.05	1.27
CSI	CSI-16	12.95	100	0	90	64	10	16	3	1.0	1	1.40	1	1	1	1	3	30	1.30	1.35
CAI	PDC-208	5.99	50	50	70	32	1	8	1	2.67	0	1.92	1	1	1	1	0	0	2.39	2.15
CAI	PDC-216	7.99	50	50	70	64	10	16	2	2.67	0	1.21	1	1	1	1	0	0	2.63	1.92
DG	NOVA	7.95	60	65	70	64	10	16	4	2.6	3	1.10	1	1	1	1	0	0	3.18	2.14
DG	SUPER-NOVA	11.7	70	65	70	64	10	16	4	0.8	3	1.04	1	1	1	1	0	0	4.68	2.86
DT	DT-1600	6.6	30	60	50	32	0	8	1	8.0	0	3.30	1	1	1	1	0	0	2.64	2.97
DCS	Datamate-16	14.9	90	50	85	64	8	16	2	1.0	3	1.53	1	1	1	1	1	0	3.31	2.42
DEC	PDP-8/I	12.8	60	65	70	48	8	12	1	1.5	1	1.90	1	1	1	4	5	75	0.66	1.28
DEC	PDP-8/L	8.5	60	65	70	48	8	12	1	1.6	1	1.29	1	1	1	4	5	75	0.44	0.87
DEC	PDP-9/L	19.9	55	65	70	72	13	18	1	1.5	0	2.27	1	1	1	4	5	75	1.03	1.65
DEC	PDP-11/20	9.30	60	90	85	64	0	16	6	1.2	2	1.22	1	1	1	1	0	0	3.72	2.47
DEC	PDP-15/10	15.6	65	65	70	72	12	18	1	0.8	0	1.41	1	1	1	4	5	75	0.81	1.11
EAI	EAI-640	26.5	90	85	85	64	9	16	2	1.65	2	3.14	1	1	1	2	1	90	2.65	2.89
GAI	SPC-12	5.0	50	65	70	32	4	8	4	2.0	1	1.10	1	1	1	1	0	80	0.76	0.98
GAI	SPC-16	10.0	60	90	80	64	8	16	16	0.96	3	0.84	1	1	1	2	1	80	1.05	0.99
GAI	System-18/30	18.0	90	65	70	72	8	18	2	0.96	5	1.72	1	1	1	1	1	90	2.0	1.86
GRI	909	9.74	50	60	70	72	12	18	1	1.76	4	1.15	1	1	1	1	0	0	3.89	2.52
HP	2114A	9.95	60	70	80	64	10	16	2	2.0	0	1.34	1	1	1	1	1	90	1.11	1.22
HP	2115A	14.5	65	70	80	64	10	16	2	2.0	0	1.95	1	1	1	1	1	90	1.61	1.78
HP	2116B	24.0	70	70	80	128	10	16	2	1.6	1	1.80	1	1	1	1	1	90	2.67	2.23
HON	H-316	9.7	65	70	80	64	9	16	2	1.6	1	1.23	1	1	1	2	2	90	0.81	1.02
HON	DDP-516	23.8	70	70	80	64	9	16	2	0.96	1	2.43	1	1	1	2	2	90	1.97	2.20
ITI	4900	9.95	75	70	75	64	6	16	8	1.75	0	1.36	1	1	1	1	0	0	3.18	2.27
INT	Model 3	10.8	60	60	75	64	6	16	16	1.5	0	1.38	1	1	1	1	1	50	1.54	1.46
INT	Model 4	13.8	60	60	75	64	6	16	16	1.0	0	1.52	1	1	1	1	1	50	1.97	1.75
IRA	SPIRAS-65	12.75	90	75	75	64	10	16	2	1.8	0	1.6	1	1	1	1	1	50	1.82	1.71
LEI	MAC 16	11.95	50	65	85	64	9	16	1	1.0	3	1.31	1	1	1	1	1	50	1.71	1.51
MSI	800	5.7	50	50	50	32	0	8	15	1.1	0	1.12	1	0	1	1	0	0	2.85	1.98
MSI	810	6.9	75	60	60	32	0	8	2	1.1	0	1.32	1	1	1	1	0	30	1.73	1.52
MOT	MDP-1000	8.5	50	65	55	32	4	8	5	2.0	0	1.95	1	1	1	1	0	30	2.12	2.03
PFI	1216-F	11.9	50	100	65	64	11	16	1	3.5	0	1.78	1	1	1	1	0	0	4.76	3.27
RAY	703	11.25	50	70	80	64	11	16	1	1.75	1	1.44	1	1	1	2	3	75	0.85	1.14
RAY	706	17.5	55	70	80	64	11	16	1	0.9	1	1.73	1	1	1	2	4	90	1.09	1.41
RC	RC-70	13.9	90	80	80	68	7	17	1	0.86	5	1.25	1	1	1	1	1	50	1.98	1.61
SCC	4700	14.8	75	65	70	64	9	16	3	0.92	1	1.51	1	1	1	1	3	70	1.23	1.37
SEL	810A	18.0	90	80	85	64	10	16	2	1.75	1	2.16	1	1	1	1	1	50	2.57	2.37
SEL	810B	32.0	90	80	85	128	10	16	2	0.75	2	1.83	1	1	1	1	1	90	3.55	2.69
TEM	TEMPO-1	13.5	50	60	65	64	9	16	2	0.9	1	1.49	1	1	1	1	1	50	1.93	1.71
VDM	520/i	7.5	50	60	60	32	0	8	7	1.5	1	1.74	1	1	1	1	0	0	3.0	2.37
VDM	620/i	9.95	65	60	60	64	9	16	2	1.8	0	1.39	1	1	1	1	1	0	2.21	1.80
WES	Prodac-2000	10.0	90	60	65	64	8	16	4	3.0	3	1.49	1	1	1	1	1	60	1.33	1.41
XDS	CE-16	9.98	50	65	70	64	8	16	1	8.0	0	1.88	1	1	1	1	0	0	3.99	2.93
XDS	CF-16	7.99	50	65	75	64	8	16	1	2.67	0	1.27	1	1	1	1	0	0	3.19	2.23
XDS	SIGMA-3	24.0	90	85	90	72	8	16	2	0.98	1	2.0	1	1	1	1	1	95	2.59	2.29
IBM	1800	45.88	90	80	100	72	8	16	5	4.0	5	6.12	1	1	1	2	3	100	3.17	4.64

about 20,000 hours, and most do not offer hardware parity checking because (they say) the memories are so reliable that the extra cost is not warranted. Even if the computer manufacturers are right, one should consider hardware parity checking as a very desirable option when an auxillary rotating memory is to be used with the minicomputer.

When the minicomputer's popularity rose in 1968, the trend was toward selling hardware. The PDP-8/I was introduced with little or no software; the first buyers knew that they would have to develop most of their own software. As the number of minicomputer manufacturers multiplied, the competition grew tougher, and most manufacturers offered more software with their machines. Presentation of other services to minicomputer purchasers followed a similar evolution.

Traditionally, service has been hard to get for small computers. The original approach (of most manufacturers) was to sell the concept of "all you have to do is find the board that is bad and replace it." Only 5 to 10 boards are in most minicomputers, so this doesn't sound unrealistic until one remembers that the minicomputer isn't the only piece of hardware in the system. After the users realized this (which didn't take too long) they demanded and are starting to receive more service.

Several manufacturers (Honeywell, DEC, and Hewlett-Packard) already had extensive service organizations, but most of the others had to develop service groups. Some vendors contracted larger computer companies to service their systems. For example, RCA is servicing General Automation computers, and Control Data furnishes service for Computer Automation.

Most manufacturers have been and still are unwilling to rent or lease their minicomputers; they will consider only an outright purchase or sometimes a third party arrangement. A few exceptions are General Automation, Honeywell, Raytheon, Redcor, and SEL. XDS will rent or lease the SIGMA-3 but not the CE-16 or CF-16 minicomputers.

Criteria for rating minicomputers

A term that is often mentioned but not well defined is "price to performance ratio." This number (if accurate) could tell a user which computer will furnish the most "performance" for his money. A complete and accurate definition of a price/performance ratio for a computer is impossible; however, usable ratios can be calculated. In this section, equations are presented for three criteria:

• P_h—hardware price/performance
• P_s—software price/performance
• P —total price/performance (the average of P_h plus P_s).

Hardware performance—The factors that affect the hardware performance of a computer fall into several categories. First, certain variables are fixed (based on the manufacturer's specifications) for a given computer model. These parameters are constraints:

$M =$ Core memory storage capacity of a basic machine, total bits
$F =$ Number of bits in the address field of single word instructions
$W =$ Word length, bits
$R =$ Number of general purpose registers
$T =$ Core-memory read-write cycle time
$N =$ Number of "extras" in the basic cost of the machine, including:
• Real-time clock
• Power failure protection
• Automatic restart after power failure
• Memory parity checking
• Memory protect.

Other parameters also affect a computer's hardware performance but are not as easy to arrive at as the above. Arithmetic, logic and I/O capabilities must reflect some degree of opinion; to minimize opinion, the following guidelines are suggested:

$A_h =$ A number proportional to the arithmetic capability of the computer—with a range of 0 to 100:
  0 No arithmetic capability
  25 Hardware add and complement
  50 Hardware add and subtract; software multiply and divide (fixed point, slow)
  75 Hardware add and subtract; hardware multiply and divide (fixed point, fast)
  90 Hardware add and subtract; hardware

multiple and divide (fixed point); software floating point arithmetic
  100 Hardware fixed point and floating point arithmetic.
$L_h =$ A number proportional to the logic capability of the computer—range of 0 to 100:
  0 No logic capability
  25 "And" and "or" hardware
  50 "And," "or," and "exclusive or"
  75 All of the above, also word test and conditional branch instructions
  90 All of the above, also bit test and bit manipulation instructions.
  100 All of above, also arithmetic rational test instructions.
$I_h =$ A number proportional to the I/O capability of the computer—range of 0 to 100:
  0 No I/O
  25 Programmed I/O through internal registers only
  75 Same as above, also DMA standard
  100 All of the above, also multiple I/O processors.

The principal factors that affect computer performance can be used in empirical equations for the calculation of "price to performance" ratios. The hardware parameters, M to N and A_h to I_h, are in this equation for calculation of P_h, the hardware-price/performance ratio:

$$P_h = Basic\ system\ cost\ (\$) \div \left\{ 0.1M \left[1 - \left(\frac{W-F}{2W} \right) \right] + \frac{20}{T}(A_h + L_h + I_h) + 100N + 50R \right\}\ (1)$$

The variables are weighted in proportion to their relative importance to system performance. Equation 1 is structured so that a "good" computer will have a P_h value of about unity: the bigger the number, the less performance per dollar. The equation for P_h does not contain factors for operating systems or compilers; however, the value of P_h does give an indication of how easily the machine can be programmed at the assembler level (numbers assigned to A_h and L_h). Calculated values of P_h are in Table III.

The denominator in the above formula is an expression of the basic hardware performance. The first term in the denominator of Equation 1

$$0.1M \left[1 - \left(\frac{W-F}{2W} \right) \right]$$

takes into consideration the effective reduction in core size for machines that need many double-word instructions. It is assumed that the larger the address field in single-word instructions, the fewer double-word instructions will be needed. If $F = 0$ (true for many 8-bit computers), the effective core size will be one-half of the actual size.

The second term in the denominator

$$\frac{20}{T} (A_h + L_h + I_h)$$

provides a measure of arithmetic, logic, and I/O "power" of a computer. The core memory read-write cycle time (T) has an effect on these parameters; therefore, terms A_h, L_h, and I_h are divided by T. The factor of 20 raises this term to roughly the same order of magnitude as the first term in the denominator. The basic effective memory capacity and the basic processing power are considered of about equal importance in determining the computer's "hardware performance" factor.

The third term, $100N$, is added to boost machines with hardware features that are standard, rather than optional.

The last term, $50R$, recognizes the fact that a machine with a larger number of general purpose registers in the CPU is easier to program. This is true because the number of memory references needed in a given program will be reduced.

Software performance—Obviously the hardware price/performance ratio explained above is only half the story, because most computer manufacturers supply software as a part of the basic system package. The software ranges from a simple assembler to a very complex and comprehensive package such as a real-time executive for a system with a bulk memory device and an on-line compiler. In general, the basic price of a machine tends to increase in proportion to the quantity of software supplied with the basic machine.

It isn't possible to evaluate qualitatively the software package of a given machine without the benefit of "hands-on" experience. For this reason, another quantitative (also empirical) equation is proposed. The following variables will be in Equation 2 for software price/performance ratio:

$D =$ Off-line diagnostic routines supplied:
    NO $= 0$ YES $= 1$
$B =$ Debugging routines supplied:
    NO $= 0$ YES $= 1$
$L =$ Loader routines supplied:
    NO $= 0$ YES $= 1$
$A =$ Number of assemblers
$C =$ Number of compilers
$S =$ Power of on-line operating system (range of 0 to 100).

The rating of the on-line operating system (S) only indicates how much the system does—not how

Table IV: Total price/performance of minicomputers

Manufacturer, Model number	P
Digital Equipment Corp., PDP-8/L	0.87
General Automation, Inc., SPC-12	0.98
General Automation, Inc., SPC-16	0.99
Honeywell, Inc., H-316	1.02
Digital Equipment Corp., PDP-15/10	1.11
Raytheon Computer, 703	1.14
Hewlett-Packard Co., 2114A	1.22
Business Information Technology, Inc. BIT-483	1.27
Digital Equipment Corp., PDP-8/I	1.28
Compiler Systems, Inc., CSI-16	1.35
Scientific Control Corp., 4700	1.37
Raytheon Computer, 706	1.41
Westinghouse Electric Corp., Prodac-2000	1.41
Interdata, Inc., Model 3	1.46
Lockheed Electronics, Inc., MAC 16	1.51
Micro Systems, Inc., 810	1.52
Redcor Corp., RC-70	1.61
Digital Equipment Corp., PDP 9/L	1.65
IRA Systems, Inc., SPIRAS-65	1.71
Tempo Computer, Inc., TEMPO-1	1.71
Interdata, Inc., Model 4	1.75
Hewlett-Packard Co., 2115A	1.78
Varian Data Machines, Inc., 620/i	1.80
General Automation, Inc., System 18/30	1.86
Computer Automation, Inc., PDC-216	1.92
Micro Systems, Inc., 800	1.98
Motorola, Inc., MDP-1000	2.03
Data General Corp., NOVA	2.14
Computer Automation, Inc., PDC-208	2.15
Honeywell, Inc., DDP-516	2.20
Hewlett-Packard Co., 2116B	2.23
Xerox Data Systems, CF-16	2.23
Information Technology, Inc., 4900	2.27
Xerox Data Systems, SIGMA-3	2.29
System Engineering Laboratories, Inc., 810A	2.37
Varian Data Machines, Inc., 520/i	2.37
Datamate Computer Systems, Datamate-16	2.42
Digital Equipment Corp., PDP-11/20	2.47
GRI Computer Corp., 909	2.52
System Engineering Laboratories, Inc. 810B	2.69
Data General Corp., SUPER-NOVA	2.86
Electronic Associates, Inc., EAI-640	2.89
Xerox Data Systems, CE-16	2.93
Data Technology, Inc., DT-1600	2.97
Philco-Ford, Inc., 1216-F	3.27
International Business Machines Corp., IBM 1800	4.64

well it does its job. Factors considered for putting an estimated value on S are:

- Will the system handle a bulk memory device?
- Has it interrupt handling capability?
- Are I/O driver routines included?
- Has it memory mapping capability?
- Are miscellaneous routines included?
- Is this a multiprogramming system?

With these variables, Equation 2 can define the software price/performance ratio:

$$P_s = \frac{\text{Basic system cost (\$)}}{500(D+B+L)+1{,}000A+2{,}000C+50S} \quad (2)$$

P_s is calculated for each of the computers in this survey, Table III.

Total price/performance ratio is derived by averaging P_h and P_s:

$$P = \frac{P_h + P_s}{2} \quad (3)$$

Forty-six minicomputers are listed in Table IV by ascending values of P. The data used in calculations of P is tabulated in Table III. The IBM-1800 is included only for general comparison; its P value (4.64) shows how much less expensive the minicomputers are than their larger forerunners.

Who's who in minis

One authority claims 75 manufacturers offer minicomputers; another says that 75 models are available. A third party refers to *about* 100 models and 62 manufacturers. Depending on their definitions of "minicomputer," one or all of the figures may be almost correct.

This article surveys 45 minicomputer systems that cost about $25,000 or considerably less. Admittedly, many more models could have been added if available time and space permitted. Some minicoputer system vendors weren't included because their total basic system cost was too high, others because sufficient data was not available as this issue went to press. This survey includes only those vendors that manufacture mainframes, and does not include system houses that are OEMs.

An attempt was made to get a good up-to-date cross section of the minicomputer industry, a dynamic group of new and established companies that is producing a flood of both new and revised models.

The bibliography contains many articles that discuss minicomputer features. In some cases, details are given for models that aren't in this survey.

Bibliography

Jurgen, R. K., "Minicomputer applications in the seventies," *IEEE spectrum*, Aug. 1970, pp. 37-52.

Young, R. and Svoboda D. E., "Batch Control with a Minicomputer," *Instrumentation Technology*, Aug. 1970.

Sclater, N., "Minicomputers spark new designs of low-cost digital systems," *Product Engineering*, Aug. 3, 1970, pp. 28-33.

Frost, C. R., "Military cpu's, *Datamation*, July 15, 1970, pp. 87-103.

Temple, R. H. and Daniel, R. E., "Status of Minicomputer Software," *Control Engineering*, July 1970, pp. 61-64.

Kilgore, G. L., "Selecting a Mini, *Automation*, May 1970, pp. 102-106.

Rinder, R., "The Input/Output Architecture of Minicomputers," *Datamation*, May 1970, pp. 119-124.

Copeland, J. R. and Jackson, S. P., "Minicomputer Capabilities for Process Control," *Instrumentation Technology*, March 1970, pp. 39-42.

Aronson, R. L., "What's Happening to Peripherals," *Control Engineering*, Feb. 1970, pp. 88-95.

"Instrumentation Forecast For the 70's," *Instrumentation Technology*, Jan. 1970, pp. 41-56.

Ollivier, R. T., "A Technique for Selecting Small Computers," *Datamation*, Jan. 1970, pp. 141-145.

Jordain, P. B., *Condensed Computer Encyclopedia*, McGraw-Hill, 1969.

Lapidus, G., "A Look at Minicomputer Applications," *Control Engineering*, Nov. 1969, pp. 82-91.

Flynn, G., "Forum on Small Computers," *Electronic Products*, Oct. 1969.

Cohen, J. W., "Mini-Computers," *Modern Data*, Aug. 1969.

Staff, "Survey of Small Computers," *Instruments & Control Systems*, Aug. 1969, pp. 69-83.

Lapidus, G., "Minicomputer Update," *Control Engineering*, May 1969, pp. 87-94.

Theis, D. J. and Hobbs, L. C., "Minicomputers for Real-Time Applications," *Datamation*, March 1969.

Lapidus, G., "Minicomputers—A Look at the Breadth of Control Applications," *Control Engineering*, Jan. 1969, pp. 128-132.

Lapidus, G., "Minicomputers Revisited," *Control Engineering*, Nov. 1968, pp. 72-74.

Lapidus, G., "Minicomputers—What All the Noise Is About," *Control Engineering*, Sept. 1968, pp. 73-80.

Knight, K. E., "Evolving Computer Performance 1963-1967," *Datamation*, Jan. 1968, pp. 31-35.

JAMES L. BUTLER is a Research Engineer in New Product Research at the Fisher Controls Company, Marshalltown, Iowa. Article is based on a study prepared when he was a Senior Engineer in the Central Engineering Dept. of the Monsanto Company, St. Louis Mo.

A TECHNIQUE FOR SELECTING SMALL COMPUTERS

by Robin T. Ollivier

 Computer salesmen have multiplied nearly as fast as the machines they sell. The systems engineer selecting a giant number cruncher probably doesn't recall any selection problems—he never drew a sober breath. On the other hand, I've been installing minicomputers. The salesman takes *me* to the automat—I have to contend with dyspepsia, as well as headaches from reading fine print.

The marketing principle implied in this little story demonstrates the necessity of having a quick, analytical method for comparing small computers. It has to be quick. One can't spend $20,000 worth of engineering time to buy a $10,000 computer. It has to be effective. Different applications demand different approaches. As a matter of fact, each of the more than 30 cpu manufacturers thinks his uniquely designed product is the best for most tasks.[1]

terms and conditions

A selection technique is proposed in this paper that has proved both quick and effective. The assumptions on which this technique is based are listed below:

1. Qualified vendors will make competitive proposals.
2. Vendor proposals are factual.
3. The system designer has analyzed the problem to be solved.
4. Evaluators are capable of relating computer characteristics to a detailed task description.

The procedure may be summed up in the following definitions:

Basis. Cpu selection will be based on performance and on effective cost.

Performance. Performance (P) is defined to be the weighted sum of equipment and vendor capability.

Effective cost. Effective cost ($) consists of quoted price plus the software and engineering costs of implementing a given computer.

Equipment capability. The weighted sum of discrete computer characteristics. Each characteristic is evaluated on a 0-4 point basis.

Vendor ability. The weighted sum of discrete vendor performance factors, each rated on a 0-4 point basis.

Quoted price. The number of dollars the buyer sees on the contract.

Software costs. The number of dollars worth of programming service required for this task plus hardware add-ons or deletions to the quoted equipment required by software.

Engineering costs. The number of dollars worth of engineer-

---

1. For a current survey of processors see one of the following:
   D.J. Theis and L.C. Hobbs, "Mini-Computers for Real-Time Applications," Datamation, v. 15, no. 3, 1969.
   R. Ollivier, "Revolt Within the Rack" EDN, v. 14, 1969.
   J. Cohen, "Mini-computers," Modern Data, v. 2, no. 8, 1969.

Mr. Ollivier is vice president of Digital Data Engineering in Pasadena, Cal., a systems and software house specializing in computer-based real-time applications. Mr. Ollivier is widely known for his bonhommie as well as for his data systems designs. He was formerly with the Jet Propulsion Laboratory, MESA, and with Burroughs Corp. He has a BS in engineering physics from the Univ. of Michigan.

Reprinted with permission from *Datamation*®, vol. 16, pp. 141–145, Jan. 1970. Copyright 1970, Technical Publishing Co., Barrington, Ill.

ing services such as design, fabrication, and documentation plus hardware add-ons or deletions to the quoted equipment.

Weighted sum. The relative importance of one factor to another is determined by assigning each factor a multiplier. The score for a given factor is multiplied by its weight and then added to the scores of other factors.

Factor. A discrete, measurable characteristic of some importance to the task at hand.

the method

Computer procurement (of machine, not by machine) proceeds in four distinct stages:

Design. The task is analyzed and one solution (from among many) is chosen. An envelope of constraints is defined. Minimum specs and maximum dollars are established for the computer. Initial hardware/software trade-offs are made. A list of qualified vendors is developed.

Solicitation. A problem description, minimum specs, and approximate job-scope information is supplied to vendors. Proposals are requested. Two to four weeks should be allowed for preparation. (Shorter times restrict competition; longer periods suggest larger systems and more extensive selection procedures.) Prior to receipt of proposals, the evaluators must complete the list of evaluation criteria and assign weights to factors. System design should be reviewed and refined during this period.

Evaluation. Scoring of proposals proceeds quickly. Impartiality is guaranteed by the objective requirements of the weighted factors.

Greater care must be taken in developing effective costs. Software kernel routines for key processes must be flow-charted or otherwise designed to provide a basis for estimating I/O timing, memory requirements, and manpower resources. Engineering and fabrication costs may be highly vendor dependent. The task should be broken down to the cost of each logical function or identifiable module.

The evaluation procedure succeeds in ranking proposed equipments according to their performance and cost. This data may be presented in two ordered lists or plotted as cost vs. performance. This completes the objective evaluation of competitive equipments.

Negotiation. Competing proposals have been analyzed and fairly evaluated. The analytical data forms the basis for final selection. The thought processes that effect this decision are subjective in nature. Only some of the more obvious considerations will be reviewed here.

Guidelines may have been established in the solicitation phase for a maximum effective cost and minimum performance score. Using these guidelines one might choose any of the following:

1. The best performer whose effective cost is less than the maximum.
2. The lowest cost equipment whose performance exceeds the minimum standard.
3. The equipment that satisfies cost and performance standards and has the highest performance/cost ratio.

a sample recipe

The method has been briefly sketched in preceding paragraphs. It is intended that this technique can be applied almost directly from the cookbook. An example of mini-computer selection is given in this section as a means of further defining the technique.

Task Definition. The dynamics of an object falling through a tube will be studied by analyzing time and pressure information. The data is generated by eight pressure ports located along the tube and as many as 16 presence sensors. Enough data will be taken to adequately define the pressure vs. time plot. Event-timing resolution to 5 usec is required. Placement of the pressure sensors, sampling strategy, number and relation of timing events, and extent of postexperiment analysis was (and is) still under discussion. The maximum number of samples for any run should be in the range of 1000 to 2000.

data acquisition

This description by the scientist resulted in the data acquisition system specification shown in Fig. 1. A programmed digital computer provides on-site control and calibration functions. Run data is buffered in core memory. Those runs requiring more analysis than that provided at the site are transferred serially by phone line to a data center computer. System design was undertaken. The ap-

```
1. Digital Inputs
     16 Channels
     Pulse width 1 usec. minimum
     Provision for electrical signal conditioning

2. Digital Outputs (number of bits in parentheses)

     Enable/disable acquisition (1)
     Start/stop A/D scan (1)
     Set end scan channel (3)
     Select sampling rate (3-7)
     Select timer rate (4-9)
     Set submultiplex channel (3)

3. Analog Inputs

     7 primary scan channels
     8 submultiplex channels
     Scan rate to 50 KHZ maximum
     Input impedance > 10 megohms
     Input voltage ± 10 v full scale
     Conversion to 10-bit digital
     All channels single ended

4. Timing Measurements

     Clock increments 8-16-bit register
     Interrupt on overflow
     Parallel read on command
```

Fig. 1 Data acquisition specification.

proach was to develop a multi-application data logger with limited processing and display capabilities. The computer was required to provide for independent calibration runs and to permit rapid modification of sampling strategies. Analog multiplexing schemes were keyed to the occurrence of digital events, bit rates, order of channels. Number of channels, time offsets, etc. are selected by the experimenter. These options are selected by English language commands from a teletypewriter. This method of control provides a hard-copy record of each run.

weighting the factors

Evaluation criteria for the computer were developed and weighted. The same was done for manufacturing aspects of the procurement. The results are shown in Figs. 2 and 3. Note that specifications are firmly tied to objective quantities.

Since we intended to build a single system—or at most two—we felt that the quality of the vendor was relatively important. We therefore assigned an over-all weight of two to the computer and one to the manufacturing criteria. Put another way, the sum of the computer weights was twice as large as vendor weights. No attempt was made to get "neat" numbers for the sum of weights; only to see that the factors be reasonably related to each other. An agreeable way to start is by assigning a weight of one to the least important factor and proceeding comparatively up an intuitively known ladder of significance. Computer characteristics were weighted first. Then half the total of the computer

FACTOR	WEIGHT	SCORING BASES
Word Size	10	4: 16 bits or more; 2: 12 bits 0: 8 bits or less
Cycle time	6	4: 1 usec; 3-1: 1-2 usec 0: 2 usec
Instruction set	5	4,3: Extensive; 2: Adequate; 1-0: Primitive
Arithmetic	2	4: Hardware multiply/divide; double precision and floating point options; good precision 3-1: Adequate capability; hardware mul/div or fast subroutines 0: Very little arithmetic capability
Addressing	4	4-0: Score one for each of the following: indirect, relative, indexed, direct to greater than 4096, or by addressing
Programmable registers	6	4: Many; 3-1: More than one; 0: One
Interrupts	7	4: 3 or more priority, no identification necessary; 3-1: Adequate for 3 devices 0: None quoted
Input/Output	8	4: 2 or more automatic channels at rates to 1.3 megabits/sec; 3-1: At least one 1.0 megabits/sec with good accumulator I/O; 0: Marginal I/O capability
Physical size	1	4-0: Subtract one point for each 5 inches over 11 inches
Console	3	4-0: Sense switches, displays, debugging aids

Fig. 2 Computer criteria.

FACTOR	WEIGHT	SCORING BASES
Delivery time	7	4,3: Less than 45 days ARO; 2,1: 45-75 days ARO 0: Over 75 days ARO
Past performance	4	4-2: Many reports of on-time delivery and good service 1-0: Known for late delivery, poor service
Maintenance	3	4-2: 24-hour turnaround on cpu, on-call maintenance; 2-0: No experience, remote or difficult corporate interface
Location	2	4: Southern California 2: Within 500 miles 0: Distant
Alternative sites	1	4: Same computer installed at JPL 3-1: Locally available 0: No Alternative site
Number installed	4	4: Over 100; 3-1: 10-100 installed 0: Less than 10 in field
Documentation & training	5	4: Excellent hardware and software manuals, or training provided 3-1: Adequate interface and programming manuals 0: Little or no documentation

Fig. 3 Manufacturer criteria.

weights were distributed among the vendor characteristics.

Factors are also rated as to their significance to the project. The following statements illustrate what I mean:

1. Most factors are significant to the project and *must* be scored whether or not the vendor supplies adequate information to do so in his proposal.

2. Some factors are peripheral in nature and need not be scored (changing the basis), or may be given a nominal score if insufficient data exists.

3. A few factors have critical limits. A zero score on any one of these factors would result in disqualification of that proposal.

In this example, three factors—interrupts, i/o capability, and timely delivery—had critical limits. A score of zero on

delivery eliminated two machines, and redefined the model number of a third.

A vendor list of eight was prepared and proposals solicited. In due course the evaluation was completed. The results are summarized in Figs. 4, 5, and 6. The euphemism of numbered rather than named computers was used to spare the editors. However, the discerning eye may distinguish the "made in" Orange County, Framingham, or Maynard features.

For this particular task, characterized by few, but high rate, data sources, some interesting observations result.

1. Eight-bit machines were disappointing. I/o characteristics were not adequate or were relatively expensive.

2. An 8K memory was required for all machines with less

FACTOR/CPU	A	B	C	D	E	F	G	H
Computer								
Word	40	20	0	0	40	40	0	40
Cycle time	6	12	18	6	12	12	0	24
Instruction	15	0	10	10	15	15	15	15
Arithmetic	4	2	0	2	4	4	0	4
Addressing	12	8	16	16	8	12	4	16
Registers	12	0	24	18	18	12	0	18
Interrupts	28	7	21	7	21	14	28	28
Input/output	32	24	8	16	24	24	8	8
Physical size	4	4	4	4	4	3	4	2
Console	6	6	9	6	9	6	6	9
Subtotal	159	83	110	85	155	142	65	164
Vendor								
Delivery time	14	21	28	28	28	0	28	21
Past performance	12	12	8*	8*	16	4	8*	8*
Maintenance	9	6	3	12	9	6	9	9
Location	4	0	8	8	8	0	8	8
Alternative	2	4	2	2	2	4	2	2
Number installed	12	16	4	16	16	8	4	8
Training	20	15	5	10	15	15	10	10
Subtotal	73	74	58	84	94	37	79	76
TOTAL	232	157	168	169	249	179	144	240

*Nominal value; no data

Fig. 4 Evaluation results.

ITEM/CPU	A	B	C	D	E	F	G	H
Quoted	11.9	6.4	8.1	12.7	16.2	11.4	8.8	12.0
Software								
Programming	5.0	5.0	7.5	7.0	6.0	5.5	6.5	5.5
Modifications*	0	4.0	2.5	2.5	0.5	0	3.0	0
Hardware								
Interfacing	1.5	0.5	2.4	0.4	0	0.3	1.6	0.6
Modifications**	4.5	0	2.0	(1.5)	1.7	2.0	0	0
	22.9	15.9	22.5	21.1	24.4	19.2	19.9	18.1

*Modifications are for additional 4096 core memory, except E, additional level of interrupt.

**Addition of I/O channel, except D, deletion of special interface hardware. A represents upgrade to next model computer to get required I/O performance.

Fig. 5 Effective costs.

Cost (1000's $)		Performance	
B	15.9	E	249
H	18.1	H	240
		A	232
F	19.2	F	179
G	19.9	D	169
D	21.1	C	168
		B	157
C	22.5		
A	22.9		
E	24.4	G	144

Cost Maximum

22.0

Performance Minimum

150

Fig. 6 Data summary.

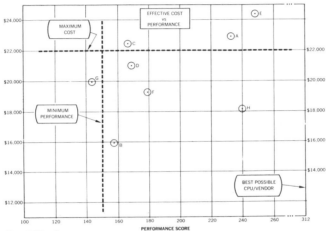

Fig. 7 Performance score.

than 16-bit word length. Shorter words meant longer programs and double length buffers.

3. Programming costs were relatively tightly grouped. The nature of the job and the size of the computer dictated assembly language coding. Better instruction sets required longer learning curves.

4. Interface costs were difficult to estimate unless the vendor provided literature treating this issue in depth.

The cost vs. performance plot in Fig. 7 provides a good visual presentation of analytical results. Processors H and B are the most likely choices. Computer F is a possible but unlikely candidate. Note that the 8-bit computers C, D, and G deliver less bang per buck than the 16-bit cpu's E, A, and F. It is clear from this data that this task is not suitable for

an 8-bit processor.[2]

The results in this case were relatively straightforward. The technical group selected the best performer within the cost envelope. There was a sufficient dollar pad to allow for contingencies. Should some unforeseen fiscal calamity befall the project, management can quickly and reliably shift to a lower-priced computer.[3] ∎

2. A line of constant performance/dollar can be drawn for items C, D, and G and for items E, A, and F. This represents a de facto standard for this particular evaluation. It can be seen that such lines are roughly parallel and that the vertical separation is about $3,200. Thus even a 4K 8-bit machine is found to be a poorer performer per dollar than a 16-bit processor.

3. Several additional 16-bit machines received a cursory evaluation during and after the example procurement. One could quickly determine whether further evaluation was desirable.

Mighty Minis

FRANCIS J. LAVOIE
Senior Editor

Although many minicomputers are housed in air-conditioned comfort, some of them must operate in sub-freezing, dust-laden, corrosive and high-temperature environments. For this kind of service, you need a ruggedized mini, one of a new breed of small, powerful, tough machines.

UNTIL THE MINICOMPUTER made its appearance, the military computer was just about the only option open to the industrial user who needed an extra-tough, reliable machine. Now, minis are regularly designed to withstand environmental and operational conditions that would bring an ordinary computer to a quick halt. And manufacturers of mil-spec machines, realizing that industrial users represent a huge potential market, are designing with this market in mind. The result: a growing choice of machines that differ in price and capabilities, but are alike in being tough, reliable, and designed specifically for harsh duty.

All ruggedized computers are designed to withstand abnormal environmental conditions: High and low temperatures, shock, vibration, high altitude, and contaminated atmospheres.

Not all ruggedized machines can meet rigid military specifications, nor is there any need for them to do so in most industrial applications. But many manufacturers test their machines according to mil-spec procedures, even though their units may not meet specifications for military applications. These procedures are well-standardized and provide a "common language" or reference point among users and manufacturers.

In the final analysis, all ruggedizing boils down to a question of reliability. How much reliability is needed depends on the application. In military applications, high-order reliability is a must. Because of space and weight limitations, redundancy often cannot be achieved, so reliability must be built into the computer. In commercial machines, the question becomes one of tradeoff; if a super-reliable mil-spec machine costs $60,000, two standard $20,000 machines, operating in parallel, may be a better choice. The probability of two computers failing at the same time is so remote that in effect 100% reliability is achieved.

Mean time between failures (MTBF) is the usual

Even being run over can't stop Bunker-Ramo's new micromini computer. A radical new packaging technique accounts for the BR-1018's toughness and small size.

criterion against which reliability is measured. An MTBF of 2,000 hours is not unusual for industrial minis. Some fully ruggedized units have an MTBF in excess of 20,000 hours. Even industrial units are available with MTBF greater than 10,000 hours.

Maintainability is as important as reliability in all but a few exotic applications; for this reason, manufacturers have gone to considerable lengths to simplify servicing. For example, many minis are modular in construction, with each function mounted on a single board. A defective board can

98

A very tough computer is Texas Instruments' CP967/UYK. Built for the military, it must undergo such tests as continuing to operate while a 400-lb hammer drops on it from a height of 5 ft.

Computers designed for industrial control applications needn't be as tough as their military counterparts, but they can't be sissies, either. This shake table ensures that General Automation's SPC-12 automation computers won't fail under rough usage.

be simply slipped out and another put in its place. Test points are normally easily accessible, and special diagnostic routines usually available. Access panels can be easily removed to expose circuit cards and wiring.

Temperature

One of the most important factors in both military and industrial operation is temperature. Generally, a mil-spec machine will operate at temperatures between 0 and 55 C, and will withstand nonoperating (storage) temperatures of −25 to 75 C. One militarized version of a commercial mini can withstand case temperatures ranging from −55 to 95 C; another, −62 to 85 C. These capabilities compare to an operating range of only 20° F for many larger commercial machines.

Most "standard" minis offer relatively wide-range temperature capabilities; it isn't unusual for a standard machine to have a 10 to 50° C operating range. This capability has become commonplace mainly because manufacturers, attempting to make their machines more reliable (thus reducing field failures), regularly subject components to high-temperature testing as a matter of course.

Many ordinary applications subject the computer to wide temperature variations. In one case, for example, the overnight temperature in a gear-grinding shop reaches 30 F. When the shift starts in the morning, heat-treating furnaces are fired up and eventually raise the temperature to about 100 F. Such variations are not rare for small control computers.

From a temperature standpoint, the weak link in a modern computer is the memory. Any read/write memory is an analog device. Thus, component values of associated circuitry are critical, since the circuitry must be designed for the maximum signal/noise ratio. The circuits are normally set up for optimum operating conditions over a given temperature range; for most minis, this represents about a 70-degree range. Beyond this, it's necessary to bring the machine to virtually military specifications, necessitating temperature compensating that may cost as much as the memory itself.

Some manufacturers solve this temperature problem by substituting a read-only memory. Such a memory is quite adequate for control applications where the computer must do a predetermined task repeatedly. Its big advantage, however, is that it doesn't need amplifiers and is thus relatively insensitive to temperature. Sometimes, a small amount of read/write memory is included.

Although almost all ruggedized minis rely on forced-air or liquid cooling, some are available with conductive cooling. But such capabilities cost extra, since heat exchangers must be provided.

In evaluating the temperature capabilities of a mini for industrial application, it must be remembered that the computer is often only part of a larger control system. Other components can add significantly to the operating temperature, especially where all the components, including the mini, are mounted in the same enclosure.

Experts point out that extreme temperature capabilities are not often necessary. For one thing, most computers must operate in an environment that won't destroy a human who ventures into it. For low temperatures, it's often a simple enough matter to keep the temperature reasonably normal with a small heater.

Vibration and Shock

All modern minicomputers are vibration and shock-tested to ensure that parts don't fall off

A computer can handle voltage variations of about ±10%, but beyond this some form of protection is needed. This bank of 43 Ohmite solid-state relays protects the control circuit from high inductive spikes generated by solenoids used in the process being controlled.

Even ordinary minis sometimes find the going rough. This Digital Equipment PDP-8/L, mounted on a preproduction potato picker, monitors and analyzes data during operation.

under normal service conditions. A considerable number can withstand relatively severe shock and vibration. A few can handle shocks that would cause virtually any piece of electronic equipment to fall apart; one just announced micro-mini, for example, can be dropped from a tall building without damage.

Vibration testing varies in intensity, but it is fairly well standardized. Typically, the computer is vibrated by means of sinusoidal mechanical displacement over a range of frequencies along three axes. Vibrations are measured in inches of double amplitude or acceleration. As an example, one fully ruggedized unit is vibrated at 5-15 Hz (0.030 ± 0.006 in.), 16-25 Hz (0.020 ± 0.004 in.), and 26-33 Hz (0.010 ± 0.002 in.).

Shock testing is brutally simple—the machine is hit with a hammer or dropped from a height. One manufacturer fastens his computer to a platform and drops it onto a sand pile. But more common is the hammer test. In one test for a military computer, a 400-lb hammer is dropped onto the machine from 1, 3, and 5 feet. The test is carried out along all three axes, with the computer operating during the entire test.

Manufacturers have adopted a number of vibra-

tion and shock-proofing techniques. Small, low-mass components may be used. Components with a large mass are carefully positioned to avoid long moment arms that might cause fatigue breakage. Shock absorbers and vibration isolators are used. And special shock-resistant component mounting techniques are common. Some manufacturers have reduced the number of components and connectors, and eliminated all processor wires. Those connectors that are used are so reliable that they can be attached hundreds of times without loss of contact efficiency. Special heavy-duty frames are typical.

Contamination

Air-borne contamination can take many forms. Ordinary dust, of course, is most common. But it isn't unusual, in certain applications, to find oily atmospheres. Iron dust is sometimes present and, in some cases, even iron filings. These present a serious problem because they may be attracted to the core memory. In medical applications, the problem is somewhat different: often, the computer must operate in an atmosphere contaminated by

The latest manufacture to enter the tough-computer lists is IBM. The System/7, IBM's lowest-cost model, has monolithic circuitry throughout for high reliability and speed. It is designed for unattended operation in most industrial and laboratory environments, including high-heat, corrosive, and heavy-dust atmospheres.

Two different design philosophies are shown here. Honeywell's HDC-601 avionics computer sits atop the standard DDP-516. Both of these machines have roughly the same capabilities. For applications where mil-spec standards aren't necessary, Honeywell also makes a ruggedized version of the DDP-516.

ether. The machine in any such explosive atmosphere must not emit sparks. This means, for one thing, that all switches must be solid-state; and that any possible spark-emitting components must be sealed.

The simplest way to guard against air-borne contaminants is to put the computer into a special enclosure. Standard NEMA and RETMA enclosures are used for this purpose. To avoid cooling problems, some of these enclosures contain heat sinks that transfer heat to outside cooling fins. But in most cases, forced-air cooling is still necessary, with some kind of built-in air-isolation provision.

Sometimes, no special enclosure is necessary; a relatively crude shield may suffice. In other cases, the easiest solution may be to build a special "room" for the computer. No computer can withstand really bad contaminating atmospheres without special protection.

One approach widely used by manufacturers is to coat sensitive parts with a conformal coating. Such coatings can be used to protect against a wide variety of contaminants, from oil to fungi. Unfortunately, no single coating can protect against all contaminants. Also, the coating can cause heat-transfer problems. And, of course, it isn't possible to simply coat everything, since contacts must be left exposed.

One contaminant that presents a serious problem is moisture. Most ruggedized computers—and many more "ordinary" minis—can accommodate 95% humidity, with some able to handle close to 100%. But manufacturers of these machines warn that this does not include condensating moisture. Resistance to liquids—whether in the form of condensation or spilled coffee—is a more serious problem, one that not all minis can handle. Usually, special protection must be provided if fluids are a problem.

Electromagnetic Interference

One of the more important considerations in choosing a ruggedized computer is its sensitivity to electrical disturbances. These disturbances may take many forms—for example, line-voltage transients, or radiated interference from other equipment. The problem of such interference has become especially severe with the advent of solid-state components. Because these are low-voltage devices, they are very sensitive to noise.

Transients may be especially troublesome. In one typical case, the mains in a plant service directly 500-hp motors, with the motors being turned on and off, and reversed. Such conditions can produce momentary peaks of 4 to 5 kv; this is harsh treatment for a computer built to handle 220 v.

There are many other kinds of noise that the computer must be guarded against if it is to perform reliably in an industrial environment. The machine must be insensitive to both electromagnetic and radio-frequency interference. In addition, it should not emit excessive radio-frequency noise that might affect other instrumentation. In military applications, requirements are particularly stringent, for obvious reasons.

Especially in manufacturing applications, power must be absolutely clean; a dropped bit can cause thousands of parts to be ruined. To reduce the likelihood of this happening, some machines have a built-in tolerance for a certain amount of line-voltage fluctuation. For example, many industrial control computers can handle a ±10% fluctuation, and some as much as ±20%. Where fluctuations may exceed these values, special filtering provisions must be made to "clean" the voltage before it gets to the computer. One way to reduce the EMI problem is to buffer computer i/o through a controller.

Good RFI and EMI characteristics require adequate shielding. For example, circuits are enclosed in metal; RFI stripping is used on enclosure openings; indicator lights are screened.

Altitude

The ability to withstand high altitudes can be important. In aircraft and spacecraft usage, this requirement is obvious. But machinery is not infrequently transported in unpressurized aircraft. If precautions aren't taken, capacitors, for example, could blow open in the reduced pressure at high altitudes.

Commercial ruggedized minis can handle altitudes of about 50,000 feet. Militarized units can go up to 100,000 feet. These are not necessarily operating environments; however. A typical commercial ruggedized machine can operate at up to 10,000 feet. Full-blown military minis can operate at considerably higher altitudes.

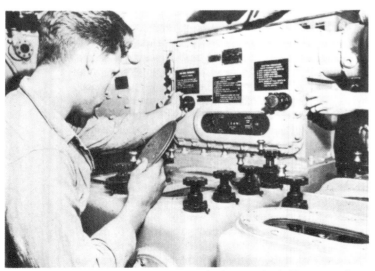

Many military computers don't even look like computers. Here, a sailor cranks target information into a gun computer in a ship's weapons plotting room. There's no room for frills in such applications.

Size

Most ruggedized minis don't differ significantly in size from their ordinary counterparts. Where size and weight are critical, however, micro-minis are available.

Until now, all really small ruggedized computers were developed for military—primarily aerospace —applications. But more and more manufacturers have turned an eye to the industrial market. Perhaps the tiniest example of the breed was introduced very recently. The unit occupies less than 100 cu in., weighs under 10 lb, yet has a capacity of over 8,000 18-bit words.

But extra-small size is expensive; the 10-lb micro-mini, for example, costs $30,000. Manufacturers of military units, realizing this, are making a strong bid for the industrial market, where there is a high-volume potential. The $30,000 unit, for example, is expected to cost only about $5,000 when it goes into mass production.

Size is important wherever space is limited. But compactness offers more advantages than simple conservation of space. Everything else being equal, the smaller the machine, the less power is required to run it; and a small, low-power machine is easier to adapt to severe environmental conditions, since, for example, less heat will be generated. Several ruggedized minis require less than 100 watts of power; most of these are primarily military units. One tiny unit can operate on only 10 w. Still, many ruggedized machines, both industrial and military, require several hundred watts of operating power.

Price

Full ruggedization to military specifications is expensive. The general rule is that a mil-spec version will cost three times as much as its commercial equivalent. Although manufacturers are attempting to bring down prices, such machines are still expensive.

Recent studies indicate that if the ruggedized mini is to find wide acceptance, especially in manufacturing, the price will have to be competitive with standard machines. One large manufacturer surveyed potential users to determine how much they might be willing to pay for a ruggedized machine. The results indicated that a 30% premium was the upper limit. Naturally, such machines won't meet all military specifications for ruggedization. But for most industrial applications, they won't have to.

Prices will come down even for full mil-spec machines. With the Pentagon having its own money problems, the move to ruggedized commercial units for military applications is accelerating. And manufacturers who previously catered strictly to the military are looking to diversify into civilian markets. These and other factors will eventually result in a wide choice of computers in various stages of ruggedization, at relatively attractive prices.

Minicomputer networks—
a challenge to maxicomputers?

Groups of minicomputers, variously interconnected and with special software, can take over certain kinds of large-scale jobs from a big machine—and at less cost

by Wallace B. Riley, *Computers editor*

☐ For many applications, a network of interconnected minicomputers may be as effective as a single large computer—and much less expensive. Today individual minicomputers are available for only a few thousand dollars, yet they execute instructions at respectable speeds and handle 16-bit numbers.

According to one very rough estimate, for instance, eight 16-bit machines with 1-microsecond cycle times and costing $10,000 each might for some purposes give as good a performance, when suitably interconnected, as a machine in the $1 million class, with 64-bit words and a 500-nanosecond cycle time.

Or, to quote a real-life example, one consultant tells of an oil company that approached him to find out how to reduce the oppressive cost of a set of three IBM System 360 model 50s, with which it was processing seismic data. He found that the same job could have been handled by about 10 minicomputers at a much lower cost.

Of course, it's not really that simple. The methods of interconnection range from the straightforward but limited to the complex but flexible, and the software needed can get hairy. Both factors add to the price of a system. But the fact remains that a minicomputer network has great capabilities that are only just beginning to be explored.

One way of building such a network that's just coming into vogue is the modular computer concept [*Electronics*, Oct. 12, 1970, p. 121]. Another is to have the computers transmit data to one another through their input-output channels, so that each computer behaves as if the others were just so many paper-tape readers or card punches. A third way is to group processors around a multiport memory, so that each has access to any part of the memory—though some people would define this as a multiprocessor rather than a network. Naturally, any of these networks would require varying amounts of special software.

A proponent of the minicomputer interconnection idea is Frank Heart, of Bolt, Beranek and Newman Inc., Cambridge, Mass. He is in charge of the interface message producer, or Imp, which BB&N is building for the Advanced Research Projects Agency of the Department of Defense, and which is part of ARPA's vast transcontinental computer network [*Electronics*, Sept. 30, 1968, p. 131]. In that system, which will have many of the advantages of minicomputer networks,

only on a much larger scale, one Imp stands between every computer in the network and the network itself.

Heart says, "Look at the similarities and differences between the large and small computers we have today. The raw speeds of both kinds are limited by the memory bandwidth; and both kinds gain in the same way from advances in memory technology. Both have similar memory access times. So how do they differ? Large machines have more hardware—they have longer words, more instructions, complex input-output controllers, and sophisticated facilities for indexing. If we can get the complexity of the large machine some other way than by adding hardware, we can save money. One way to obtain this complexity is to put it in software; the speed penalty often encountered in software is avoided by executing it in stacked-up minicomputers."

"In this way," he continues, "you can get the power of a very large machine at very low hardware cost. Furthermore, you give the actual user of the system a chance to get his hands on the machine—a chance he rarely gets with large machines, which are surrounded by machine operators, operating system programs, and the like. With this hands-on experience, the user gets a better feel for the computer's handling of his problem—although the computer's efficiency may suffer from his hands-on operation of it."

For calculations involving a large data base, a large processor is most efficient, according to Don Murphy, data communications marketing manager at Digital Equipment Corp., Maynard, Mass. He adds that the larger the number of people who have access to this data base, the less its cost per bit. On the other hand, says Murphy, a small computer is more efficient in control functions, where decision-making can be automatic but where the actual computation is limited. One control function in which a small computer shines is in improving the communication between Man and Large Machine. It can easily handle the trivial tasks that otherwise would tend to load up the big machine with overhead—tasks like data preparation, editing, and format checking.

Murphy proposes extending this concept to several levels. He suggests that a Digital Equipment PDP-11 computer works very well as a front end for a larger machine such as a PDP-10, where it can monitor and consolidate signals arriving from a remote computer such as the PDP-8/E. These in turn can act as "intelligent terminals" that coordinate the communication paths between simple source terminals such as cathode-ray tube displays, with keyboards, data collection devices, and so on. Murphy feels that eventually even the simple alphanumeric CRT unit will be a small computer.

(Murphy, of course, likes to mention his own company's products as typical installations at each of these levels. His concept, however, applies to other hierarchies of computers, including some that are mixtures of several manufacturer's products.)

Eventually, says Murphy, data communication networks will charge their users on the basis of the data transmitted, not on the length of time the connection is maintained. When this kind of network is built, minicomputers will be almost indispensable at the network's nodes to compress the data and revise its format for maximum efficiency.

Other advantages of the network concept, adds Roger Cady, engineering manager for the PDP-11 computer at Digital Equipment Corp., are that it permits the system to be tailored closely to the particular job, and it offers fail-soft operation. Job tailoring is done by equipping each individual processor in the network with the particular hardware features and software packages that adapt it to a specific part of the job to be done. Fail-soft operation means that, if any one processor in the network fails, the network as a whole can continue to operate with a somewhat degraded level of performance, instead of grinding to a complete halt.

As for the number of machines in a network, Heart insists that hooking up three or four wouldn't accomplish much—he'd rather see lots interconnected in a vast network. "If you have many times the memory capacity, many times the bandwidth, with many memory accesses simultaneously, then a whole bunch of problems becomes accessible at a much lower cost than on one large computer."

This view meets with the agreement, in principle at least, of C. Gordon Bell, professor of electrical engineering and computer science at Carnegie-Mellon University, Pittsburgh, Pa. But he warns that the software problems are "fierce." Only when the software task can be broken up to match the individual pieces of hardware does the network approach look attractive, says Bell. Otherwise, in some cases the software costs might exceed the savings in hardware.

Opinions differ about the difficulty of writing the software for a network of minicomputers. Heart claims it wouldn't be an overwhelming job. "Big machines always come with blankets of software," he says. "But people always have to write their own software for little machines. A guy who really wants to try this approach will be able to do it more easily than he suspects."

The main characteristic of software for a network of minicomputers would be its division into segments for the individual computers, as Bell pointed out. Most minicomputer programs aren't segmented because neither the machines nor their problems requires it. But segments occur naturally in software prepared for large machines and, except when actually in use reside on disk files instead of taking up space in the main memory.

Because the big-machine programs already have these segments, incorporating them into a program for a network of minicomputers wouldn't be too difficult, maintains Heart. "Besides," he says, "if the network has one large multiport memory for the use of all the processors—as would be characteristic of one form of network—segmentation won't be necessary, or at least it won't be as severe as it would be otherwise."

However, one of the designers of Data General Corp.'s Supernova computer, Larry Seligman, disagrees with Heart. He says designing the hardware to interconnect the computers is easy, but the real problem is in the software. "Figuring out how to

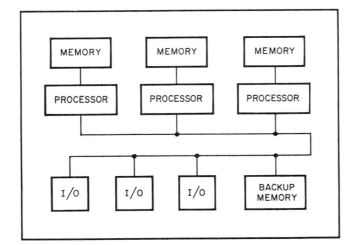

1. Input-output bus. One way of linking minicomputers into a network that boosts their total performance is through the bus along which the individual computer's input-output equipment communicates with the processor.

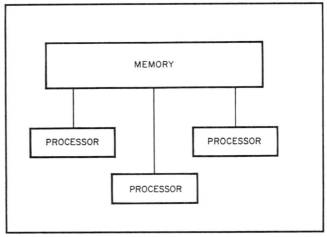

2. Multiport. Another possible interconnection is to permit each processor to have direct access to a large common memory that's independent of the processors, as shown here, or to one another's individual memories.

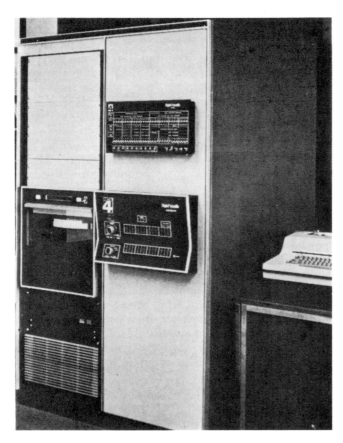

3. Meta 4. This computer, shown here in a configuration that emulates the IBM 1130, has a multiport memory.

break up the job is likely to be pretty tough," he says, but admits that "people are putting things together. Some of our customers are trying it, and we build some stuff on special order for them, as well as offering them our multiprocessor communications adapter, or MCA. I think their interest indicates an important new trend; but that doesn't decrease the difficulty of the job."

Nonetheless, some jobs break up naturally—for example, monitoring a data communication network, which involves input, computation, arranging to a format, and output. In fact, it's hard to handle these jobs on one machine because the machine's time has to be segmented, and that requires a big operating system. "Big operating systems are big headaches," says Seligman.

Cady of DEC believes the day is coming when people will compare a large computer system having "blankets of software" (Frank Heart's term) with a task-oriented network of minicomputers working under special-purpose software—the large system will be found wanting.

"Look at the big operating system that comes with the IBM System 360," says Cady. "Its latest version requires 262,000 bytes of main storage. While that much software can do just about anything for anybody, the fact remains that on many tasks a lot of it is just deadwood, and a smaller computer with simpler software would be a lot more efficient—especially in real-time jobs." While the operating system never actually occupies 262,000 bytes—chunks of it are continually passing back and forth between main

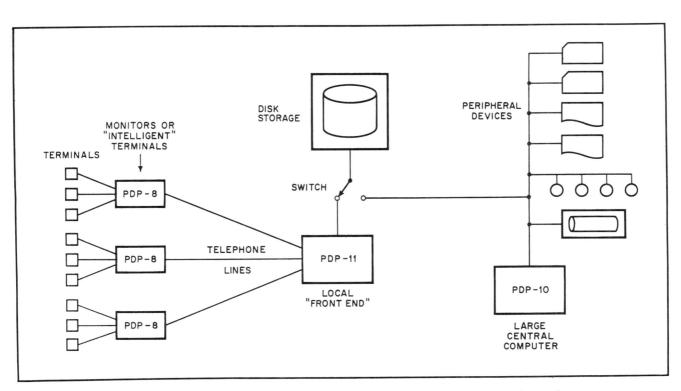

4. Common buffer. A variation on the input-output bus interconnection (Fig. 1), good particularly when the interconnections are measured in miles instead of feet, uses a disk storage unit shared by both a minicomputer and a large central computer.

storage and disk storage—it occasionally would overflow the next smaller standard level of main memory, 131,000 bytes, that IBM offers with its computers.

Some programs written for big computers can be run on smaller ones if the job can be divided up to fit the machine. If it's not easily subdivided, the big number-crunching computer is the only way to tackle it. An example of such a job is processing an extremely large matrix of floating-point numbers—suitable for machines on the scale of Illiac 4.

The actual interconnection in a network of minicomputers can be done in several ways. One is to link several processors, each with its own memory, through their input-output channels to a ring-shaped or open-ended bus, to which one or more backup memory modules and several input-output controllers are also linked (Fig. 1).

BB&N's Heart, however, doesn't think a connection through the input-output channels is adequate for the performance he's considering. It involves too much overhead, he says. First, each of the two minicomputers involved has to use one memory cycle to transfer data from the memory of one to that of the other, and then the second minicomputer needs another cycle to get the data out for its own use. "It would be much better," says Heart, "if every machine had direct access to the appropriate point in one large common memory, independently of access by other machines. Such a multiport memory [see Fig. 2] would be costly, but not nearly as expensive as a Goliath computer."

The memory of the Meta 4 computer, shown in Fig.

3, is similar to what Heart has in mind. The Meta 4, which is built by the Digital Scientific Corp. in San Diego, Calif., has a memory with four ports, which make it accessible by four processors or other units independently.

However, any attempt to discuss the tradeoffs between input-output bus interconnection and multiport interconnection makes Gordon Bell of Carnegie-Mellon University very indignant. In his lexicon, a computer is a processor plus a memory; a multiprocessor is many processors and one memory; and a network is many processors and many memories. Therefore, since the multiport approach effectively makes a system with one big memory, regardless of the number of individual modules, this design, to him, is a multiprocessor.

Is the distinction more than merely semantic? Bell says it is, because there are two different ways of designing an array of minicomputers: as a pipeline, or as a parallel machine. In a pipeline each processor does part of the job and passes its result on to the next. In a parallel system all the components are working simultaneously on some aspect of the problem, while transferring intermediate results, subroutines, and so on between one another. A multiprocessor, Bell says, can easily be organized as a parallel system; but a network, which doesn't have a multiport memory, such an organization is quite difficult.

Nonetheless, Seligman of Data General does compare the input-output bus and the multiport interconnections. Unlike Heart, he feels their relative merits depend on the specific job that the minicom-

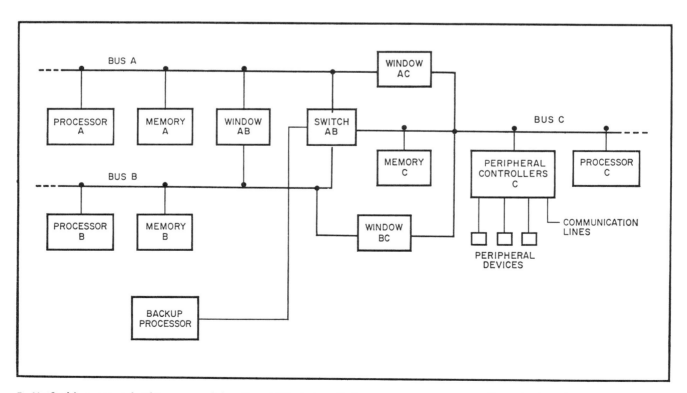

5. Unified-bus network. This approach has the ability to handle input-output operations efficiently. Switches can be set to transmit an unlimited number of words. Protected by "window-shade" logic, windows transmit only one word by cycle-stealing. Other equipment may be attached to any bus.

The irreplaceable maxi

The idea that a network can always equal the performance of a large machine is wrong, says Bell of Carnegie-Mellon University. He has worked out a comparison of various kinds of processors applied to various kinds of tasks, and charted the results, as shown at right.

The costs and relative performance levels in the chart were obtained from a line of reasoning similar to the following simplified example: to buy a CDC 6600 would cost about $3 million, and the machine is capable of adding roughly 3 million pairs of numbers each second, whether they are fixed-point or floating-point numbers. On the other hand, the Digital Equipment Corp. PDP-8, a small machine, costs only $10,000 or so; it can do 300,000 fixed-point additions per second, or 3,000 floating-point additions. Thus it costs two and a half orders of magnitude less than the 6600, but it adds fixed-point numbers only one order of magnitude more slowly. Therefore in an application involving only the addition of fixed-point numbers, a battery of PDP-8s is much more economical than one 6600. But very few applications are that simple. Other applications that require the use of more complex instructions, of which the floating-point addition is an extreme example—it's three orders of magnitude slower—would be rather poorly served by a PDP-8 network.

The black lines in the chart represent costs for typical small computers; the colored lines correspond to big machines. More important than the specific points plotted are the tendencies for the black lines to curve upward to the right, and for the colored lines to curve downward. Thus, as one would suspect, a simple job costs less to do on a simple machine than on a large machine; but a complex problem, such as frequency analysis using the fast Fourier transform, is likely to be more expensive on a small computer than on a machine like the Control Data 6600.

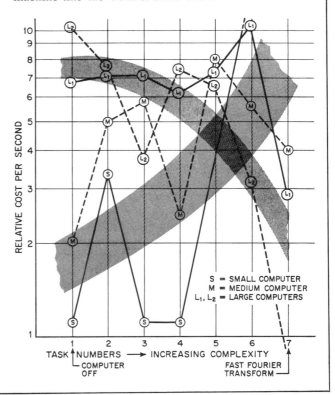

S = SMALL COMPUTER
M = MEDIUM COMPUTER
L₁, L₂ = LARGE COMPUTERS

puter network is expected to perform.

He points out that a large multiport memory requires a crossbar switch or its equivalent between it and the processor connected to it. An equivalent configuration, which also requires a crossbar switch, is an individual memory for each processor with means for each processor to gain access to other processors' memories. This switch may be a stand-alone unit, or it may be built into the individual memories' access circuits; either way, it is expensive, and it affects the speed of access. "It can cost almost as much as a whole additional minicomputer," says Seligman. "But its cost is almost independent of the size of the memories it interconnects, so in large systems it can be, and is, employed economically. In small systems it may not be worth the cost."

And Seligman points out that the crossbar switch also adds an extra hundred nanoseconds or so to the memory's access time. In a machine with a 300-ns computing cycle, like Data General's Supernova, this would be disastrous.

On the other hand, transferring the data through the input-output bus costs time, too—but this time penalty is isolated by the channel structure from the basic machine cycle, which therefore doesn't suffer from it. Obviously, too, it's avoided as long as a given processor can work with data in its own memory.

To compare the two configurations more precisely, the extent of the delays they impose can be calculated in terms of two small computers with 800-ns core memories. If a crossbar switch is interposed between the two processors and their respective memories, the average cycle per processor can vary between 450 and 675 ns; but if the two processors communicate through an input-output bus, the average time varies between 400 and 800 ns.

These estimates take into account the amount of delay, the distribution of data in the two memories, and the probability of interference—and the last factor is crucial. For if the two computers interfere with one another less than about 30% of the time, the input-output bus connection can be shown to result in less lost time. Since in practice the amount of interference in a well designed system is less than 1%, the input-output bus connection is clearly at an advantage.

Cady, however, would qualify this preference for an input-output design. He points out that such a design loses time in interrupt processing as well as in transferring data. Every time a transfer is requested, the processor has to put aside its own program to handle that request. The time lost can be reduced by incorporating additional hardware, and different manufacturers have done this at various levels of sophistication. But adding interrupt-processing hardware to a minicomputer tends to turn it into a maxicomputer.

Transfers along the input-output bus are also complicated when bona fide input-output operations are time-dependent and therefore can't themselves be interrupted. Cady feels that this linkup is best when input-output rates are low and not time-dependent.

Murphy, also of DEC, is more actively in favor of the input-output interconnection. He sees the device that serves as an interface between the network and the computer as a useful buffer that doesn't tie up the main computer. There are alternative ways of handling this buffering process: either by connecting the minicomputer directly to the main computer as a front end, with the transmission lines going out from it; or by using conventional input-output equipment with switching apparatus that makes it accessible to either the central computer or the minicomputer. Murphy predicts the latter is the coming trend.

When the input-output switch is used in the latter kind of system, the minicomputer receives messages from a telephone line, adjusts their format for the central computer, and then sends them through the switch to a disk or drum storage unit, as shown in Fig. 4. When the entire message has been stored, the unit interrupts the central computer, which can respond and pick up the message at its leisure. Its reply goes onto the disk, and is picked up from there by the minicomputer and retransmitted to the remote device.

Despite the extra step of disk or drum storage this approach is flexible and efficient enough to permit real-time use, and it makes better use of the central computer's time. But it doesn't permit direct communication between two remote stations. They must transmit to the central office and let it retransmit. A direct connection would be very expensive, Murphy says, and would also present certain problems in bandwidth and loss of flexibility.

All communications beyond the data concentrator are over telephone lines, using modems connected to the concentrator-computer. This is the best way to set up these networks, even if all the "remote" terminals are in the same building with the central, because hardware and software for the telephone-line connection are standardized.

But all these configurations, Cady points out, ignore input-output. In a system that does a lot of number-crunching, they are all reasonable configurations; but the performance of the great majority of installed systems is limited by the performance of the input-output equipment, which makes fancy ways to interconnect processors and memories only academic.

With the unified bus concept, says Cady, input-output equipment can be added indefinitely. Not surprisingly, the unified bus concept is the principal design feature of DEC's PDP-11 computer [*Electronics*, Dec. 21, 1970, p. 47]. And indeed, Digital Equipment Corp. is building several modular networks on special order, all based on the PDP-11 and all essentially minicomputer networks. Basically each system contains four processors—one master, one task processor, one communications unit, and one backup for use in case one of the others fails at a critical moment (Fig. 5). All the buses in the various individual computers

are interconnected, and every device on every bus has only a single port into that bus. Devices with two or more ports are also possible.

The unified-bus approach to networks is much neater than anything else, Cady thinks. For example, short of using multiport memories, the bus allows a single memory or other unit to be shared by two or more processors, with a switch connected to the unit and to the buses. A comparison of this arrangement and the traditional input-output bus connection is shown in Fig. 6. Obviously the traditional scheme is more complex and troublesome than the unified bus. Furthermore, in the traditional scheme, the switching necessary to add a third memory, shown in the diagram, and to permit an input-output unit to have access to it, not shown, is incredibly messy.

Any job suitable for a large fast computer but too complex for a small one is worth examining to see whether a network of small computer could handle it. The fundamental requirement is for it to be divisible into several parts that the individual computers can handle. Typesetting is divisible in this way—hyphenation and justification for one computer, layout for another, photosetting for a third, and so on.

Because these tasks occur in a well defined order for every paragraph of copy, there is little interference between computers, and the job could be done readily with a network connected through an input-output bus. On the other hand, seismic analysis or other operations that involve a large data base would require a crossbar switch, because the amount of cross-referencing between memories would be very high.

Speech processing is a good example of an application for a pipeline network. At Carnegie-Mellon University, Raj Reddy, a colleague of Gordon Bell, is working on a speech-processing machine using a pipeline of minicomputers. Eventually he hopes to have a computer to which anyone can speak freely, via telephone or similar input device, with few restrictions on vocabulary or syntax. But there are several years of research facing him, with material for many doctoral theses by graduate students at CMU and elsewhere.

Reddy's qualifications for developing such a system are impressive. Before coming to CMU he developed a system at Stanford University using a big computer with a big program. His network at CMU won't be a simple pipeline, which implies a direct hierarchy, but will have complex interconnections between each processor and others in the system, both fore and aft. Both feedback and feedforward would be involved. Reddy visualizes implementing it through what Bell would call a multiprocessor—a big memory containing a common data base used by all processors.

Reddy sees a host of problems to be overcome before his system's physical implementation can begin. For example, ways to interlock the various processors must be developed, the data for each one must be continuously updated, and a protocol must be established for those occasions when two or more processors try to gain access to the same data. No software or programing language exists to tackle these problems, while the hardware that can do the job is expensive. Reddy is thinking in terms of PDP-11s or

108

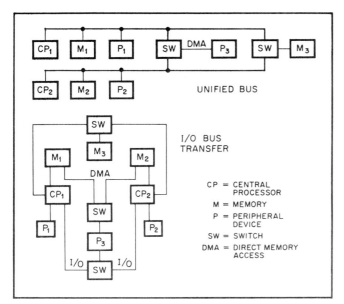

6. **Neatness vs mess.** Proponents of the unified-bus approach to a network point out that it permits new equipment to be added to an existing network much more easily than when the connection is made through the conventional input-output bus.

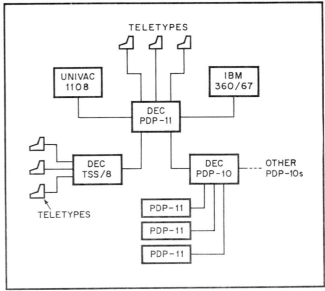

7. **Projected network.** At Carnegie-Mellon University this configuration is envisioned for the eventual use of graduate and undergraduate students. Among other things it will enable research to proceed on the tradeoffs between minis and maxis.

machines of similar size and capability.

Bell agrees that speech processing in one application for minicomputers in a pipeline network. But he thinks the task also requires a big machine somewhere in the mix—for example, a syntax dictionary. Just hanging a big backup memory on the network won't be sufficient for such problems, he feels. Parallel networks of minicomputers can also be useful. Bell points to the management of Control Data's Star computer [*Electronics*, March 30, 1970, p. 52] as an example. The processors in a truly parallel network execute different instruction streams and also process different data banks, their work being correlated by a central supervisory computer. This is different from another kind of network, also sometimes called "parallel," in which all the processors execute the same instructions on different data banks.

Interconnecting small computers without careful designing can lead to trouble, Bell warns. He cites one commercially available product made of three small computers of two different types and a disk storage unit. One minicomputer is a data concentrator, another controls the disk, and the third is the main processor. This particular product, Bell says, contains no provision for failure of one processor, and insufficient computation capability for big problems, and it is quite expensive.

Meanwhile at CMU a network is being constructed that involves several small computers and a few large ones. It represents an expansion of the university's computation center, which students use for course work and research. Already installed are one Univac 1108, one IBM System 360 model 67, one Digital Equipment PDP-10, and one TSS-8—the last a version of DEC's PDP-8 with hardware and software added

for time-sharing. More PDP-10s have been ordered. Eventually the network may have a configuration like that shown in Fig. 7. In that network students will use remote terminals to gain access to the PDP-8; when that computer's capabilities are exceeded, the overflow will go first to the PDP-11 and then to the 360.

In Florida the Data General Corp. is installing a hospital information system comprising three Nova 800 computers with the MCA option. One of the three maintains a large data base containing a variety of hospital records. Each of the other two is connected to 16 interactive remote terminals, preprocessing their inputs before forwarding to the data-base computer. Both updatings and inquiries are processed through the 32 terminals. A wide variety of peripheral equipment is also connected to the data-base computer, which is kept very busy juggling everything. Nevertheless, the whole system is much less expensive than the 360/50 that was originally envisioned for the job.

Data General is also bidding on a reservation system for an international airline. The system would involve six Nova 800 computers connected to an IBM 360. Four of the six would preprocess messages arriving from 64 remote terminals each, a total of 256 terminals. The other two, one of which is redundant, would carry out further processing, and would interface the system with the 360.

At CMU Bell and his colleagues are thinking about building a minicomputer multiprocessor, but without the crossbar switch. He thinks there should be a better way to attain this configuration and level of capability. The details and the corresponding software will keep a lot of doctoral students busy, but Bell feels that once these problems have been overcome, his approach is the way to build really great computers. □

Part IV
General Applications

Papers in this part treat areas of minicomputer applications in a general way. They deal with the nature of the applications and the general characteristics of computers needed to fit the applications. The applications covered are (in order of appearance) automatic test stations, process control, medical, communications, laboratory, and time sharing.

The last article on the "Indirect Measurement of Process Variables" provides insight into the unique power of on-line minicomputers. That is, the computer can carry its own model of the process and calculate values for variables that may be inconvenient or even impossible to measure directly. This principal can be carried over to other application areas as well.

It is hoped that this section will promote the reader's insight into his problem from a computer orientation.

A TIME SHARED COMPUTER DATA SYSTEM FOR AUTOMATED TEST STATIONS

Philip A. Hogan
Averial E. Nelson
Aerospace Division, Honeywell Inc.
Minneapolis, Minnesota

INTRODUCTION

Prodded by the necessity to reduce costs, the electronics industry has turned its attention to the testing function as an ideal candidate for improvements. Test automation through utilization of today's inexpensive small-process computers is being investigated and test techniques developed for all phases of the industry, from component test through complex system test. Honeywell has developed a time-shared Central Data Station which is used to service up to 16 or more computer-controlled satellite test stations. This development multiplies the effectiveness and flexibility of individual computer-controlled test stations, and thereby allows the industry to step into computerized testing within a system evelope which is expandable and cost effective. Individual satellites can be added within the system envelope for specific applications, retaining an autonomous operation, which is augmented by the test program and data storage capability of the central data system.

With this capability, manufacturers can utilize their management initiative and inventiveness in testing new products, controlling their test processes, and supplying quick, reliable data without the limitations of computer memory, punched cards or paper tape. The basic system concept in software and hardware which has been developed has many variations in mechanization that can be applied - depending only upon the needs and test environment of the user.

The following paragraphs describe the problem Honeywell has encountered in applying computerized testing to their production facility. The system concept developed and mechanized to overcome these problems is defined in detail, and a few examples of variations in the application of these basic concepts to meet different test requirements provide an overview of the potential for other applications.

STATEMENT OF THE PROBLEM

There are three areas which pose problems in applying computer-automated test equipment that can be solved with the central data system: storage capacity, program development and flexibility.

Storage Capacity

The relatively high initial cost of computer-automated test equipment makes procurement of this equipment the subject of critical appraisal for cost effectiveness. To obtain the highest return on investment therefore requires that each installation be designed to offer as many automated services as possible, and in most cases be as flexible as possible. Figure 1 shows a chart of accumulative costs for manually testing a device versus automatic testing. It can be seen that the more functions which can be undertaken by the computer the sooner the crossover point is reached for paying off the investment. Assuming testing labor alone, for example, the crossover point is 29 months, whereas adding self-check capability decreases maintenance and calibration costs to a crossover point of 24 months. Adding data accumulation and storage, and quick access to device trouble shooting programs further supports the cost effectiveness analysis. These expansions are all in the software area, and past limitations in software storage have restricted solution of these problems to the capacity of computer core memory, or necessitated agumenting this memory by the use of punched tape, punched cards, or magnetic tape.

Since the goal of all test operations is to make the equipment and operator be continually productive, any delays caused by these auxiliary methods of software access are problems which must be reduced. Thus the ideal computerized test station should: have the required test program immediately available for each unit under test (UUT), have diagnostic programs immediately available for the specific UUT test

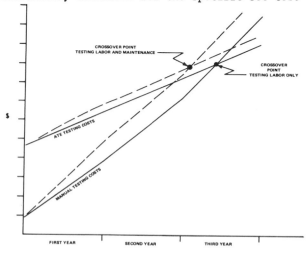

Fig. 1 Automating Additional Tasks
Increases Return On Investment

failures encountered, accumulate test data and make it available in the desired format whenever requested, test itself upon demand, and be capable of easily developing and modifying its various test programs. Each of these characteristics depends upon ready access to large amounts of storage.

Program Development

The development of programs to test or diagnose problems in a UUT is the second problem facing computerized test equipment users. The three phases of program development are initial writing, verification, and periodic modification. The verification and periodic modification costs are the most difficult to justify, since they normally are far more expensive than the initial writing (see Figure 2). Verification, for example, had been 4-6 times the initial writing cost in our past experience. This is because of the difficulty in resolving the problem when a test doesn't work. It could be a human coding error, a misunderstanding of the test station operation, misunderstanding of the UUT operation, or a malfunction. The ease with which a programmer can address this problem is limited not only by his own time, but also by available time on the test system. Modification, or revision, of existing test programs is frequently overlooked, since it is not a part of the initial cost in putting a UUT into production. These may come from several sources such as: UUT revisions, interfacing UUT changes, errors discovered in test methods, reduction of tests after review of field history, and changes to improve test accuracy. If these changes are difficult and time consuming there will be a tendency not to make them and thus allow poor quality or high cost situations to be perpetrated. Knowledge of, and control over, these changes by the user's Quality department is a factor which must be considered in computerized testing.

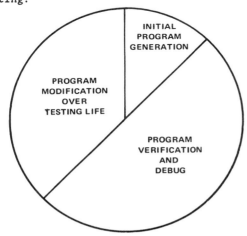

Fig. 2 Content Of Total Test Programming Costs

Flexibility

The need for flexibility in the computerized test system, whether it be a part of the initial requirements or a future consideration, is a necessity in today's cost-conscious environment. This can take the form of additions or subtractions to the initially procured test system, or merely the capability of easy modification of existing equipment for testing a new device. The system concept must be flexible in utilizing major software and hardware elements when expanding to prevent duplication of the complete capability with every addition. The physical proximity of various test system components should not be so restrictive as to dictate production line location. In general, flexibility in the volume of testing, numbers of test stations, locations of test stations, and types of UUT's to be tested is a goal which must be addressed in a computerized test system concept.

TEST SYSTEM DESCRIPTION

The following paragraphs describe the Honeywell Automatic Test Equipment (ATE) system, which was developed to overcome the problems discussed above. There are many possible variations of the system, but the following information describes the specific system in use at the Honeywell Aerospace Division facility in Minneapolis, Minnesota. Other applications are briefly discussed following system description.

ATE is a multiple-station test system designed for general-purpose testing throughout a manufacturing plant or maintenance depot. It is an integrated system with remote satellite test stations connected to a Central Data Station (CDS) as illustrated in Figure 3. The CDS consists of a digital computer and standard computer peripheral devices. It provides centralized data storage and test program control which is accessible to each satellite test station.

Each satellite test station contains a small control computer, the H316, dedicated to that one station. All these control computers communicate with the CDS via a high-speed, party-line data transmission line which operates serially at a 250 kilohertz bit rate. Satellite test stations can be located up to 1000 feet from the CDS, and 16-bit words are transmitted at a rate of 15,000 words per second.

Since each satellite test station has a dedicated computer it operates autonomously by executing test programs from its own core memory. The CDS is used primarily for bulk storage of programs and logged data on a shared disc file which in our specific installation is 3.5 million words. The CDS sends test programs,

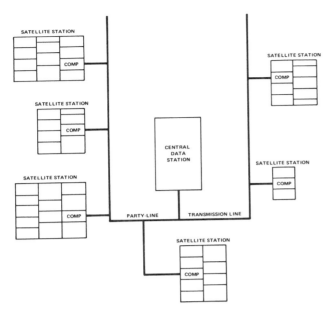

Fig. 3   The ATE System

subroutines, or executive programs to the satellite test stations. The program storage and transmittal system is completely general purpose since the transmitted programs are independent of the specific hardware mechanization at the satellite test stations.

During the testing process, data is taken and accumulated in the satellite computer memory. At the end of a test or when the buffer is full, the data is transmitted back to the CDS for logging on the disc. The data log system is also general purpose in that a data record can be in any format. The CDS merely lays it on the disc exactly as it is received from a satellite. A satellite station can also recover data back from the disc at a later time if desired. Thus, the CDS can also serve as temporary bulk storage for the satellite computers. All disc file bookkeeping functions are performed by the CDS with directories of programs and logged data for all satellite stations.

Communication with the CDS is on an interrupt-request basis. Whenever a satellite computer requires service it raises a common interrupt line. The CDS then polls each station in turn until the requesting station is found. A short message from the satellite specifies the details of the request which is then executed by the CDS. Since there is a computer at each end of a transmission, extensive error checking and error messages are possible with no additional hardware.

The ATE system combines the benefits inherent in a central time-shared computer facility with the functional advantages of autonomous control provided by a dedicated computer in each test station. The CDS provides centralized administrative control over the complete test system since all programs and data are maintained in one central facility. This facility consists of computer equipment that is ideally suited for automatic data control techniques. Each test station is afforded the operational advantages of expensive computer peripheral devices such as a disc file, magnetic tape, line printer and card reader, but at only a fraction of their cost since the peripheral devices are shared among many stations. Since the advent of the modern low-cost minicomputer the cost of the peripheral devices is large in relation to the computer itself. And this cost differential will become even greater with the next generation of minicomputers which will have even lower price tages.

Another very important advantage afforded by the CDS, which will be described later, is an extensive capability for developing new test programs. In a general-purpose test system with application to many devices, this program preparation capability can be the single most important feature of the Central Data Station.

Satellite Test Stations

While it is not the purpose of this paper to describe the individual test stations in detail, a brief description will help to place the role of the CDS in better perspective. Figure 4 shows two of the test stations that are presently operating at the Honeywell Aerospace Division. Their functional similarity to each other is even greater than that indicated by the physical appearance since packaging changes have been made as new stations were added.

The test stations employ building block techniques to be general purpose in their ability to test a broad range of electronic devices - from small modules to complex black boxes. However, there is no attempt to make each station universal in its application. For example, one station has two programmable pressure sources and a programmable oven for testing pressure devices. Another station has more extensive digital test capabilities. A gyro station simultaneously controls several slave substations, each containing its own rate table, since gyro tests are typically quite slow. Conceivably, one satellite could be assembled with all of these features, but its high initial cost would make this level of universality uneconomical.

Fig. 4 Typical Satellite Test Stations

Each station contains the H316 which is a 16-bit computer that occupies only 14 vertical inches of rack mount space. Each computer has 8 K of core memory, but the test system is compatible with core memories from 4 K to 32 K if required for other applications. Each station computer has its own teletype which is a versatile device for presenting status or instructions to the operator, and for accepting inputs from the operator. The teletype is also a very useful tool during test program debug. A control panel is used for displaying test set status and for providing operator control.

The software in the satellite test station computer consists of an executive program and a test program. The executive program, in addition to providing communication with the CDS, consists of a collection of standard subroutines which can be called by the test programs. Test programs are divided into segments which may be called independently to reduce the amount of core memory required in the test station. Checkout of a single device may require the execution if many test program segments. One test program segment automatically calls the next until the device checkout is completed. It can be seen that the test execution software is conceptually very simple. Complicated time-share or background operations are completely eliminated from the test station software.

A third type of program which can be received from the CDS is called "special segments". Special segments are merely standard subroutines similar to those contained in the executive program except that they are less frequently used. However, unlike the executive program which remains in core memory at all times during test execution, special segments are called into core only when needed. Examples of special segments are math subroutines to calculate trigonometric functions, or special hardware control functions such as a subroutine to control a programmable pressure source. After being used, a special segment can be eliminated from core to make room for another. Several special segments can be retained in core at one time, and there is no practical limit to the various different special segments which can be called from the disc. This capability provides an effective unlimited expansion of the executive program -- an absolute necessity for any test system which is to be considered general purpose.

Central Data Station

The CDS unites the satellite test stations into a single integrated test system. The elements of the CDS are shown in Figure 5. It uses the same type of minicomputer provided in each test station. In addition, the CDS includes a 3.5-million word moving-head disc file, a magnetic tape, line printer, and a punched card reader.

The primary purpose of the CDS is to share the disc file between test stations. When a request for a program segment is received from a test station, the CDS immediately retrieves the program from the disc and sends it to the requesting station. The location on the disc of the requested program is first extracted from a directory of the complete program library which is also stored on the disc. In similar fashion, when a request is received from a test station to store logged data, the CDS immediately accepts the data and transfers it to the disc. This process of sending and receiving data, called the foreground mode (illustrated in Figure 6), is both simple and rapid. Each

116

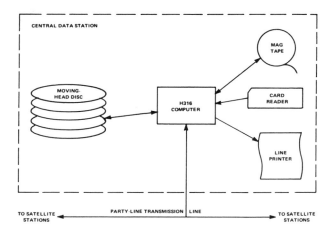

Fig. 5 Elements Of A Central Data Station

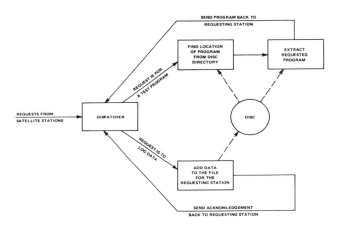

Fig. 6 Foreground Mode

request is immediately completed by the CDS
before it responds to the next request, and is
executed in a fraction of a second since data
is sent down the transmission line at 15,000
words per second.

To perform this foreground task of sending
and receiving data, the CDS computer is acting
as a simple switching computer, and as such is
loafing most of the time. This is fortunate
since there are many other tasks which can best
be performed by the CDS as part of the management
of the complete test system. The most important
of these tasks is the development or modification
of test programs, described in the next section
of this paper. Other tasks are associated with
maintaining control over the programs on the
disc, and with extracting logged data from the
disc. These secondary tasks are all performed
one-at-a-time in a lower priority background
mode. Whenever a foreground request for service

is received from a test station, any background
task being executed is momentarily stalled until
the foreground request is completed. This
operation is illustrated in Figure 7. Each
different background task is performed by a
separate and self-contained program called a
"job program." Job programs are stored on the
disc in the same manner as test programs, but
they differ in that they are executed in the CDS
computer rather than a satellite station computer.

All background jobs can be initiated through
the CDS teletypewriter. In addition, many of
the jobs associated with developing test programs can be initiated through the teletypewriter
at any one of the satellite stations. A "dispatcher" portion of the CDS foreground executive
program is therefore used to queue background
job requests which are received from the satellite stations. When a request is received from
a test station, the CDS also receives a short
message which defines the exact nature of the
request. If it is a foreground request to send
a program segment to the test station or receive
a block of logged data from the test station,
then the request is fulfilled immediately.
However, if the request is for a background job,
it is placed in the background queue. Background
jobs are executed in the same chronological order
in which they were placed in the queue, and each
satellite station has room for three background
jobs in the queue.

The CDS can perform its complete function
with only 8000 words of core memory in a 16-bit
computer. The foreground executive program is
contained in 4000 words, and each background
job program can occupy up to 4000 words since
there is only one job program being executed at
a time.

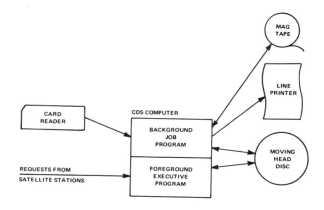

Fig. 7 Background And Foreground Modes

Since the system management tasks can be performed on the CDS simultaneously with normal foreground operation, they can be performed at any time without interfering with operation of the satellite test stations. Testing can be performed on the test stations at any time of day or night since the CDS can be left in the test station service mode of operation continuously. The CDS at the Honeywell Aerospace Division remains in its "on-line" mode of operation 24 hours a day, seven days a week, except for brief periods consigned to system maintenance actions.

The CDS provides both the data storage capacity and flexibility which are needed for a general-purpose test system. Each satellite station can use as much of the 3.5-million word disc capacity as it needs as long as the total of all stations does not exceed that capacity. Test programs or subroutines which are used by more than one satellite station are contained on the disc only once. There is complete flexibility in the number of test programs, standard subroutines, and executive control functions which can be made available to a satellite. The use of a separate control computer in each satellite test station also provides complete flexibility in the hardware which can be included in each satellite station since test program control operates autonomously of the CDS. Finally, there is flexibility in the number of satellite stations which can be added to the system and where they are located as long as they are within 1000 feet of the CDS.

TEST PROGRAM DEVELOPMENT

The ATE system design places major emphasis on facilitating the process of developing and modifying test programs. It was recognized that the high cost of test programming becomes proportionately even higher in a general-purpose test system, since it is able to test a greater variety of devices. Therefore, full use is made of the background job program capability of the CDS for the test program development process. That process, shown in Figure 8, is based on the use of an on-line compiler. Each different step in the process is performed by a separate background job program.

Test programs are divided and developed as individual program segments. Although it may take many segments to test a complete device, each segment is a separate file which is edited and compiled separately. A program segment is first created on the disc in alphanumeric source language from punched cards or magnetic tape. If cards are used they may then be thrown away since all subsequent changes are made directly to the disc file using the satellite station teletypewriters -- thus eliminating cumbersome handling of punched cards or punched tape.

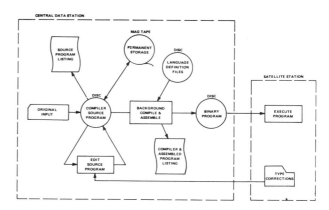

Fig. 8 Test Program Development

A compiler is used to convert test instructions from a high-level compiler source language to the binary machine language which is executed in the satellite station. Figure 9 shows typical source language statements. After compiling, both the source language and the object binary program are retained on the disc. Only the binary test program is transmitted to a test station for execution, but the source language is still available on the disc for editing and rapid disc-to-disc recompiling. After a program segment is completely debugged, the compiler source file, which requires much more disc space since it is an alphanumeric format, can be permanently stored on magnetic tape and erased from the disc. If subsequent program modifications are required the source file can be transferred back onto the disc.

Program editing can be performed from any satellite station teletype as corrections are found necessary during the debug process. Corrections can be referenced to either source language line number or to program tags. Edit instructions are accumulated in the satellite computer. After all instructions have been

```
       NO 1
       SETUP ALTITUDE HOLD
       CONNECT DVM-HI TO 1J6-33
       DELAY 50 MSEC
       MEASURE ACVOLT 10.0
       CALCULATE MEAS = MEAS - NULL / SF
       COMPARE MEAS 15.0 HIFL, -15.0 LOFL
       GO TO N2
HIFL   PRINT MESSAGE, HI LIMIT FAILED
       PRINT RESULT, MEAS
       GO TO N2
LOFL   PRINT MESSAGE, LO LIMIT FAILED
       PRINT RESULT, MEAS
N2     NO 2
```

Fig. 9 Source Language Statements

accumulated they are transmitted to the CDS where the edit takes place as a background job in just a few seconds. Each time a program is edited its revision number is automatically incremented by one to provide positive control over program status. Inadvertent editing of the wrong program is prevented since the edit is rejected if the programmer does not enter the proper revision number of the segment. While editing, it can be requested that compiler source language on the disc be typed on a station teletype for assistance in making corrections. Normally, only the desired secton of a complete source language program is requested for typeout, however, due to the slow speed of the teletype. The test program listing on the high-speed line printer at the CDS is a side-by-side listing of compiler source language, resulting assembly language, and corresponding binary object program.

The request for a recompile and for a program listing on the high-speed line printer can also be made from the satellite stations. Immediately after recompiling, the new program segment can be called into a satellite computer for execution and further debugging, if required.

It can be seen that each satellite station effectively has its own capability for storing alphanumeric compiler source language programs, editing the source language with the satellite teletype, high speed disc-to-disc compiling, and listing on a high-speed line printer. These functions, which normally require expensive computer peripheral devices, are provided at each satellite station at a fraction of the normal cost using the technique of sharing the CDS.

Compiler

Test program compiling either requires a large mass memory in the form of a magnetic disc or tapes, or else necessitates a weak and restrictive programmer's language. For the broad range of electronic equipment encountered in most production and maintenance shops, it is important that the compiler be powerful enough to handle the multiplicity of test functions at minimum programming cost. The higher level programmer's language of a powerful compiler also provides the necessary understandable documentation of the automatic test procedures.

The ATE compiler consists of two separate elements. The first is the basic compiler, which is a character processor that cannot recognize any compiler source language input by itself. It must refer to the second element, which is a Language Defintion File, in order to recognize and interpret the input language. The Language Definition File, which is stored on the disc, is in a form easily understood and easily expanded by test programming personnel to meet expanding compiler requirements. The basic compiler, which never changes even as the programming language expands, is actually a compiler/assembler combination.

As new devices to be tested are programmed for automatic test, it is necessary to expand the programming language of the compiler input. New devices may require new types of measurements or new types of stimuli which must be programmed. It is also necessary to expand the repertoire of descriptive mnemonics, such as connector pin designations, which are recognized by the compiler. To accommodate this requirement for expandability, the language definition files have been made completely modular. At the beginning of each compiler source program, there is a statement which defines the particular set of definition files to be used in compiling that program. The language definition files themselves are merely specially numbered alphanumeric files on the disc that can be modified by editing with the same background job program that is used to edit test program files.

The operating language of test programs in a satellite station is binary machine language. This compiling technique was chosen over the technique of on-line interpretive compiling because it provides significant operational advantages. An on-line interpretive compiler is one which resides in the core of the test station control computer and compiles the test program each time it is executed on the test station. Such a compiler is generally quite restrictive since it must share core memory with the test program and the operating executive program. Even if mass memory is available at the satellite, an interpretive compiler can be restrictive because of the time required to compile the test program each time it is executed. By contrast the ATE programs do not have to be compiled each time they are executed, but the ATE compiler still provides the advantages that test programs are modified in high-level source language and can be immediately recompiled right at the test station without going through a separate off-line compiling facility.

APPLICATIONS

The inherent flexibility of the ATE test system described above provided a hardware/software base from which several different test system configurations have been developed. Different application requirements dictate the need for variations of the basic test system.

Autonomous Tape Programmed Station

Figure 10 illustrates a single autonomous test station with test program input from a paper tape reader or magnetic cartridge tape reader. This configuration is the same as one of the computer-controlled satellite stations of the basic ATE system except that test programs are

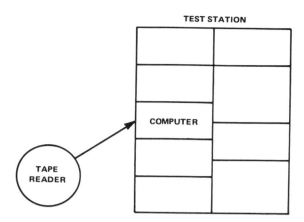

Fig. 10 Single Autonomous Test Station

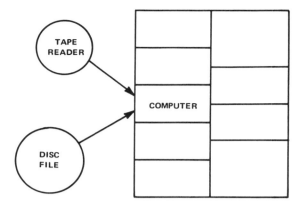

Fig. 11 Autonomous Station Including Disc

derived from the tape rather than a CDS. The test program themselves are the same, but the same facilities for generating the test programs do not exist on the autonomous station. This configuration is used for low-cost remote applications where extensive test program development capability is not required, and where rapid selection of programs from a large program library is not required. Typically, the test programs might be developed on a test system with a CDS, and then transferred from disc to tape for use on the low-cost autonomous stations.

Autonomous Station with Disc

Figure 11 illustrates a single autonomous test station which has its own disc. It essentially integrates the hardware and software features of the CDS plus one satellite station -- combining the functions into a single computer. This configuration is used for applications where extensive test program development must be performed, or where test programs must be extracted quickly from a large program library, or where data logging is required. The configuration is particularly well suited to applications where only a single test station is required initially, but where future growth to a multiple station system is desired. The computer and disc then expand into the CDS with the addition of a high-speed transmission line.

Time Shared Satellite Computer

For some specialized applications the testing requirements are such that a separate control computer is not required in each test station. In these cases it is possible to use a satellite computer on a time-shared basis as shown in Figure 12. The mode of time-sharing can vary from a simple one-station-at-a-time control to a more complicated method requiring time-sharing executive control in the satellite computer.

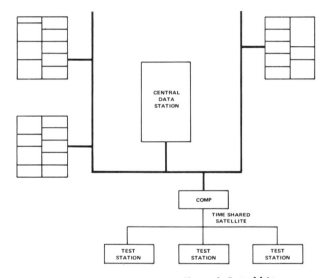

Fig 12 CDS With A Time Shared Satellite

Computer Testing

A prime application of the CDS development, and one which demonstrates the general purpose nature of the concept, is the test system for a computer manufacturing facility shown in Figure 13. It consists of two elements, a CDS in "Building 1", and a secondary data station 4 miles away in "Building 2" connected by a telephone line data link. The stations each have disc storage capability, with the secondary data station having a relatively small disc file (720K words) which enables "Building 2" to operate with normal high speed intercommunication with the satellites. The low-speed telephone line operating in the background mode provides a data link for supplementing the small disc file storage with the 3.58-million word CDS disc file.

120

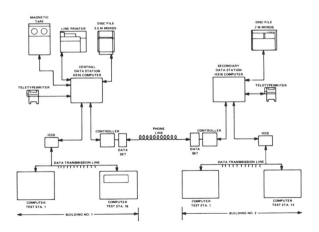

Fig. 13 System For Computer Test

The satellite stations in each building are actually computers, peripheral equipment, or computer systems under test. There are 16 such satellites in "Building 1" and 12 satellites in "Building 2". The test programs requested from the CDS, or secondary data station, are simply computer diagnostic programs. The system provides the same advantages as discussed above of rapid program selection and loading, control of program configuration, data logging, and an extensive capability for program development and modification.

CONCLUSION

The development by Honeywell of a time-shared control of automatic test stations has provided a solution to some of the problems encountered by users, or propsective users, of computerized test equipment. The need for maximum return on the investment of this equipment dictates that each station's function not be restricted by the availability of software storage capacity. The use of a time-shared 3.58-million word moving head disc in a CDS provides this storage capacity. Each satellite test station can utilize this capacity on request which gives the test engineer the opportunity to include multi-UUT test capability, program storage for UUT troubleshooting, data logging capability, satellite self-test programs, and other features which previously required dedicated peripheral equipment.

The industry-wide problem of test program development costs has been eased by the use of the CDS concept. The ability to simply and quickly edit programs from each satellite test station without interrutping operation of other satellites has reduced programmer costs and made schedule conscious management rest easier.

The development has a wide flexibility in its application to testing situations. The number of satellite test stations has varied from one to 32 in particular applications, with each satellite completely independent in its testing capability. For example, digital logic cards, analog devices and pressure devices can be in test simultaneously on individual satellites. The satellites can be separated from each other, and from the CDS, by 1000 feet without sacrificing transmission speed. One application uses a variation involving a telephone line data link without impairing its function. These system characteristics are indicative of the scope of this hardware and software development. They provide another tool in improving the cost effectiveness of the present testing function, while providing a broad systems approach to test facilities of the future.

COMPUTER CONTROL OF VACUUM DEPOSITION PROCESSES

R. M. Centner and R. A. Wilson
Bendix Research Laboratories
Southfield, Michigan

ABSTRACT

With the advent of the low cost minicomputer,
full automatic control of vacuum deposition processes appears both technically feasible and economically attractive. To date, vacuum deposition
processes have been largely controlled manually,
although simple controllers have been available
for controlling portions of the process such as
the vacuum pumpdown and the deposition rate during evaporation. Automatic control promises to
improve process efficiency and performance, and
to improve the uniformity of the resultant products, while freeing personnel from routine
operating tasks. The approach to computer control of vacuum deposition processes (evaporation and sputtering) is discussed, and the conceptual design of an automatic process controller
based on a minicomputer is presented. The
advantages of automating these processes are
reviewed.

INTRODUCTION

This paper discusses the application of a
small digital computer, or minicomputer, to
automatic control of vacuum deposition processes.
Included are the establishment and control of
the vacuum environment, control of the evaporation process, control of the sputtering process,
and control of a number of lesser functions related to these processes. Emphasis is placed on
demonstrating the feasibility of applying a dedicated computer to the control of a single vacuum
deposition system, although of course other
computer/deposition-system relationships may be
preferable under certain circumstances.

In the following sections the control requirements for the vacuum deposition processes
are reviewed, together with the present methods
of control and some of their disadvantages. The
approach to computer automation of these processes is then described and the conceptual design of an automatic controller is presented.
Finally, it is shown that computer automation
leads to improved system efficiency and performance, improved product uniformity, and the freeing
of personnel from routine operating tasks. All
of these are ultimately reflected as economic
advantages.

The following discussion of control requirements and controller design concepts is specifically oriented toward the batch-type vacuum deposition system. Obviously the same general
approach can be also applied to the automation
of an in-line type system, although the specific
control functions will differ somewhat.

VACUUM DEPOSITION PROCESS CONTROL

Control Requirements

The basic vacuum deposition processes
covered in this paper are thermal evaporation
and sputtering. These two basic processes en-
compass quite a number of different operations,
including:

(1) Vacuum cycle control

(2) Pressure control

(3) Substrate conditioning

(4) Evaporation source control

(5) Sputtering control

(6) Glow discharge cleaning

(7) Substrate rotation

(8) Bell jar and base plate cooling

Each of these functions is a somewhat independent operation, although they must be
appropriately grouped and coordinated to yield
the desired process sequence. Each of these
operations requires control functions. In some,
the control is based on the behavior of a sensed
parameter relative to a desired or setpoint value.
Pressure control and base plate and bell jar
cooling are examples of this type of control. In
other cases, control is based on a timed sequence,
as is generally the case for sputtering and glow
discharge cleaning. Evaporation source control
is an example of an operation where both bases
of control are used: the soak power level is
normally maintained for a timed period, whereas
during actual desposition source power is usually
controlled to yield a specific deposition rate
until a specified film thickness is achieved.
During the process control sequence, most of the
items listed require only simple on-off type control of solenoid valves, power supplies in which
the voltage or current levels have been pre-set,
and motors. "Pressure control" involves adjustment of a variable valve, while substrate conditioning and evaporation source control may involve the control of variable power supplies.
Thus, a vacuum deposition process may include a
number of steps or operations, but each operation
by itself constitutes a relatively simple control
requirement which can readily be automated.

Present Control Methods

To date, vacuum deposition processes have
been largely controlled manually, although simple
controllers are presently available for controlling portions of the process. The latter are

Reprinted with permission from *1970 WESCON Technical Papers*, vol. 14, paper 4/4.

hardwired, modular devices or units, each controlling a single operation, and are generally limited to two areas: vacuum cycle control and evaporation source control. Evaporation source control is generally accomplished through the combined efforts of two modules or units. One is a monitor unit which determines film thickness and deposition rate, and provides a signal or contact closure when thickness reaches the set point value. The second unit provides a signal for controlling source power during the soak and deposition portion of the cycle, using signals from the monitor unit as the basis for control during the deposition portion.

These methods of control have a number of distinct disadvantages as follows: Frequent attention by an operator is required during the course of the process cycle or run. Even when the previously cited control modules are used, their operation is normally uncoordinated. When the vacuum cycle controller has established the proper environment, the operator is required to initiate the source control cycle or the actual "process". When the latter is completed, the operator must again manually initiate the return of the chamber to atmospheric conditions. Other auxiliary operations, such as glow discharge cleaning, must also be manually introduced in the cycle as required. Thus personnel who might be performing other tasks are tied up in routine equipment operation.

The high degree of operator involvement can also influence the process in at least two other ways. First, since the steps of the process must each be initiated by the operator, unnecessary delays may be incurred between the completion of one operation and the start of the next, thereby reducing the efficiency of the process and increasing the overall run time. Second, since manual control of the process involves a certain degree of operator judgment in some of the steps, the possibility exists for variations in product quality or uniformity from batch-to-batch. All of these disadvantages are ultimately reflected in cost factors which would be improved by automatic control of the process.

Approach to Computer Automation

Automatic computer control of vacuum deposition processes has been technically feasible for some time. The size and cost of the computers which have been available, however, have generally made such automation impractical and economically unsound. Exceptions to this are cases where the computer can be used to control a number of vacuum deposition systems, or where the computer can be used to control a deposition process in addition to performing other duties. The recent advent of small, low-cost minicomputers has changed the picture dramatically. Now an automatic vacuum deposition process controller based upon the use of a small dedicated computer and designed to serve a single system

appears to be both technically feasible and economically attractive. It is to this approach that we now direct further attention. The next section describes an automatic controller based on this approach. The advantages of such a controller are outlined in a subsequent section.

An Automatic Vacuum Deposition Process Controller

It was noted earlier in this paper that a vacuum deposition process is made up of a number of different operations, each of which constitutes a straightforward control problem. An automatic controller based on the use of a digital computer can serve to organize, coordinate, and control the execution of these operations.

Controller Functions: The automatic vacuum deposition process controller could be capable of performing the following functions:

(1) Automatic vacuum cycle: control of the bell jar; the vent, roughing, foreline, and hi-vac valves; and the ion tube filament. Protection of the diffusion pump from overheating and/or excessive fore pressure.

(2) Automatic pressure control: control damper valve to keep chamber pressure constant at a preset value for part or all of the operating cycle.

(3) Substrate conditioning control: control heating (to bake or conditioning temperature), annealing, and cooling of the substrate.

(4) Thickness-rate functions: using thickness input signal, calculate deposition rate and determine when thickness reaches set point values. These data would be used by the evaporation source control function.

(5) Evaporation source control: control the cycle of one or two sources (power rise, soak, deposition rate, and shutter).

(6) Sputtering control: turn on preset filament, anode, and target power supplies at programmed point in cycle and maintain for timed sequence. Monitor target current while sputtering. Interrupt timed sequence and sound alarm if current drops below a preset value.

(7) Glow discharge cleaning: turn a fixed power supply on for a preset time interval at any of several pre-programmed points in the cycle.

(8) Substrate rotation: turn substrate rotation motor on and off at predetermined points in the cycle. Fixed speed (manually variable via control not provided).

(9) Bell jar and base plate cooling: turn coolant system on and off. Turn on whenever sensed temperature exceeds a set point value.

Controller Description: The automatic vacuum deposition controller would be based on a small digital minicomputer with a read-only memory. Figure 1 is a block diagram showing the relationship of the controller to the vacuum deposition system, while Figure 2 is a simplified block diagram of the automatic controller itself.

etc.) could be introduced via the thumbwheel switch. (Alternative methods of introducing these inputs might include: (1) potentiometers, whose output signals would be sent to the computer via the multiplexer and analog-to-digital converter and (2) a punched card and card-reader arrangement.)

On-off type manual inputs, such as "cycle start", "automatic recycle", and "reset" would be introduced to the computer by means of a status register. On-off signals from the process, such

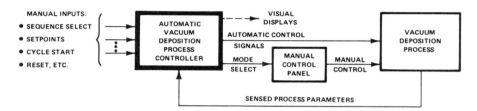

Figure 1 - System Block Diagram

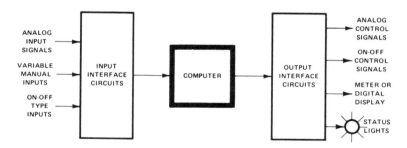

Figure 2 - Simplified Automatic Controller Block Diagram

The automatic controller would be fitted with a front panel typically containing the following: An analog meter and a digital (Nixie tube) readout, each with a function selector switch; a four-digit thumbwheel switch with function selector switch; several toggle and pushbutton switches; and a number of status or indicator lights.

The unit would have connections at the rear for all input signals and for analog and on-off type output (system control) signals. All variable input signals from external sources are assumed to be analog dc voltages. These would include pressure, temperature, and thickness signals. Normalizing amplifiers would be provided to adjust the relative voltage levels of those signals. The normalized signals are fed to the computer by means of a multiplexer and an analog-to-digital converter.

Variable parameters to be displayed could be read out either on the meter or on the digital display. Variable inputs which are introduced manually (set points, soak power, rise times,

as from bell-jar hoist limit switches will be handled in the same way. Two types of control outputs are provided: Digital-to-analog convertors provide analog voltages for functions where variable control signals are required. On-off type control signals or contact closures are provided for the operation of solenoid valves and solenoid-operated shutters, turning preset power supplies on and off, operating bell jar hoist and substrate rotation motors, and in fact most of the system control functions.

The input and output interface circuits would be mounted on plug-in cards and housed in unused space in the computer cabinet. The entire automatic controller could be packaged in a small bench-top cabinet, or as a small rack-mounted unit, occupying less than 24 inches of panel height.

Once the various manual inputs are set, normal operation of the system consists simply of pressing the "cycle start" button. No further attention is required until the automatic cycle has been completed and the bell jar has been raised. Provisions for reset and other controls would be provided, however, for use when manual intervention is felt necessary.

Advantages of Computer Automation

Computer automation of the vacuum deposition processes has significant advantages with respect to either manual control or the use of separate modular units to automate the control of individual operations.

Figure 3 illustrates the cost advantage of computer automation of the vacuum deposition process, as compared with the use of a number of individual hardwired control modules to accomplish the same objective. The diagram shows relative controller cost versus the relative degree of automation. The cost versus features automated for the modular approach will rise at a fairly uniform rate. The cost of computer automation of only a single operation would be rather high, since it would include the cost of the computer itself. Automation of additional features costs relatively little, however, since this mainly involves a revision to the computer program and the addition of appropriate interface circuits. The crossover point at which the cost of computer automation drops below that of the modular controller approach occurs when only a relatively few operations are to be automated. Modular controllers are not known to be available at present for some of the features included within the scope of the automatic vacuum deposition process controller described herein.

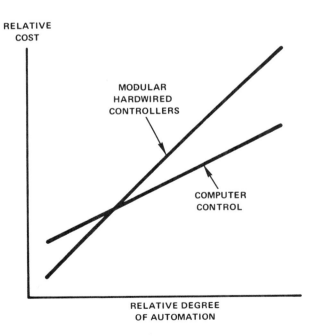

RELATIVE
COST

MODULAR
HARDWIRED
CONTROLLERS

COMPUTER
CONTROL

RELATIVE DEGREE
OF AUTOMATION

Figure 3 - Cost Versus Degree of Automation

The computer automated controller also results in a number of performance or operational advantages:

(1) Flexibility: For the user having varying process requirements it offers flexibility. The operations of the sequence can be quickly added, deleted, and otherwise altered, and set-points can be established by means of switches and other controls on the panel of the automatic controller.

(2) Process Repeatability: For the user making the same product repetitively, it offers a high degree of process repeatability, once a given sequence has been established and set-point values have been set, resulting in uniformity of the resultant product.

(3) Process Efficiency: The automatic controller will provide smooth and rapid transition from one operation or step of the process to the next, completing the cycle or run in a minimum of time and thus enhancing the efficiency of the process.

(4) Personnel Advantages: Once the sequence and set-point values have been established, the operator is only required to press the "start" button and the complete cycle will be executed unattended. Thus personnel are freed from routine operating tasks.

All of these are ultimately reflected in economic advantages of automatic computer control of vacuum deposition process.

CONCLUSIONS

Although vacuum deposition processes require a relatively large number of control functions, each function is reasonably simple and lends itself quite readily to automatic control techniques. The advent of the low-cost minicomputer now appears to make computer automation of vacuum deposition processes both technically feasible and economically attractive. Automated control offers a number of operational advantages over presently used semiautomatic control methods, many of which are ultimately reflected as additional economic advantages. Hence it may be expected that computer automation of the control of vacuum deposition processes will achieve growing importance in the near future.

THE CONSTANT ASSISTANT -
A COMPUTER TERMINAL AT THE INTENSIVE CARE BEDSIDE

Jerome A.G. Russell, Ph.D.
Cedars-Sinai Medical Center

ABSTRACT

With increasing frequency and success, the electronic data processor is being enlisted as an assisting resource to the intensive care unit. In addition to performing the now almost traditional tasks of reducing clerical drudgery, a well founded clinical computer system can provide relentless surveillance of a patient's physiological status and supply the medical staff with timely early warnings of probable disasters, as well as giving rapid and integrated retrospective expositions of the recovery processes.

This paper discusses a computer system whose functional characteristics are supporting a multi-bed cardiovascular intensive care unit. As the usefulness of an on-line, real-time computer patient monitoring system has been established, the exposition will emphasize equipment design and the computer programming to realize the objectives.

INTRODUCTION

At the outset of this exposition, I wish to state the primary objective of our efforts to enlist the power of the modern electronic data processor in the care of the critically ill patient. The computer is but one of the many applications of modern technology which are improving medical care now and during the years to come. Our intent has not necessarily been to make direct advances in the computer sciences or to bring about revolutions in instrumentation technology unless these innovations are required to support the self conscious project of aiding the sick.

We are currently employing the computer to monitor the relevant physiological parameters of our patients. Such continuous multivariate measuring and computation is impossible to achieve manually. The majority of the patient monitoring systems now operating are attempting to measure every heart beat, each breath, and many other parameters at a frequency commensurate with the important time-constants of the physiological processes which the variates represent.[1] The important concept is that of producing early-warning indications of impending physiological deterioration to the medical staff so that measures may be initiated to divert the probably dangerous trend. And in addition, the computer should provide valid and unambiguous indicators of those catastrophic conditions which demand immediate reaction of the medical team. The patient monitoring system must provide those responsible for directing the course of treatment a retrospective exposition of the patient's physiological progress along with the related events of his treatment. The time history of basic variates and the derived parameters are to be presented upon demand at the bedside in a clearly expressed graphical form. While the most useful format for these historical summaries is a volatile television-like display, the computer system can also make permanent records of the time relationships and indicators for subsequent analyses or investigative activities. The life support computer system should avoid producing reams of tabular or graphical data except upon request. A storage and retrieval system gives the clinician or medical investigator just what he needs in the form which best suits his application.

In all the parts of the system - monitoring, computation, filing, display and control - the data processor must exercise effective tests upon the incoming data, be they analogue signals or manually entered discrete data. Also, the results of the computations are to be tested to insure the reliability of that information upon which the doctors and nurses must rely. The exploitation of this self-checking power of a computer assisted patient monitoring system is just beginning.

Those process control techniques, almost commonplace in the chemical, electronic, petroleum and automobile industries, will be applied to bedside monitoring. For example, most of the problems of calibrating analogue information channels have already been solved by computers in the making of paint and other chemical products. Some medical workers are realizing great success in actually using the computer to control certain drug infusion by applying a well tested, multivariate algorithm dependent upon continuous monitoring of the hemodynamic system.[2] While such "closing of the loop" concepts must be realized with cautious conservatism, there is little doubt that a well founded computer system can perform such tasks to maintain fluid balance, titrate a drug such as isoprul, regulate depth of anesthesia or control one of the mechanical cardiac assist devices. The intent of computer control and surveillance should not be misconstrued to imply replacing doctors and nurses but rather that of relieving these medical workers from those almost non-medical tasks which they often perform with a less than satisfactory success.

Reprinted with permission from *1970 WESCON Technical Papers*, vol. 14, paper 12/4.

Other services of the monitoring system include keeping logs, controlling well understood processes, recording information related to a course of treatment and performing all clerical tasks which so often divert the doctor and nurse from their patient.

If one were to divine the objectives of many commercially available electronic patient monitoring systems by looking at the tranquil photographs in the descriptive brochures, he would assume that placing the medical workers in a remote location from the patients and substituting for their direct contacts and observations all sorts of television displays, light-banks and buzzers is the ultimate stage to be achieved. I believe that a major advantage of employing an excellent computer assisted monitoring system is quite the opposite. The equipment and team organization should not separate medical personnel from the patient. The services of medical workers should be augmented but never replaced.

Most modern clinical departments pursue an active research and development program. Even in a small, non-academic unit, one discovers activities designed to find out about some aspect of the clinical practice or the disease processes which are the subject of treatment. The patient monitoring computer system must therefore also be able to assist the clinical or basic investigation by the acquisition of good medical data, a by-product of an effective monitoring system, and by performing those computations necessary for the research itself. It should be possible for a researcher to incorporate his special computer programs into the monitoring operating system without compromising the prime responsibility of care for patients.

THE INGREDIENTS OF A COMPUTER ASSISTED PATIENT MONITORING SYSTEM

It is possible to present the characteristics of a computer assisted patient monitoring system by following the course of information as it originates at the bedside, becomes processed and finally is made available at appropriate locations within the institution.

The Patient Station

The most important element in the physiological monitoring system is the patient. It should not be considered a dehumanizing concept to consider him as a component in his own life-support system. To the patient's body are attached transducers for measuring specific physiological variates. It must be remembered that these transducers provide only indirect indications of those parameters which we really which to know. For example, a blood pressure

electromanometer usually generates an electrical signal whose amplitude is a measure of the displacement of a diaphram. This excursion is brought about by the pressure appearing at the proximal end of a plastic tube which hopefully is directly related to the pressure in a blood vessel beyond the small hole in the distal end of that tube. And even more discouragingly, we probably would not care about the pressure measurement at all if we could actually know the rate of blood flowing through that vessel. The nature of most measurements which we make are defined not by what we really need to know about a patient but rather by what transducers are available. Needless to say, some of these measurements are related to that which we need to know by often complicated models. And, the computer is proving most valuable in solving the relationships between transducer signals and the physiological processes.[3]

Electrical analogue signals such as those representing blood pressure or the depolarization of the myocardium (ECG) are minute in amplitude and power. Usually the signals contain information, or even noise, not usefully related to the process being measured. These minute signals need to be amplified and separated from those components which are unrelated to the basic information. The device which receives the raw transducer signals and effects the waveform processing is often named a preprocessor. Some preprocessors are simply subject the signal to band-pass amplifiers and others may very well effect a sophisticated analysis such as does the Premature Ventricular Contraction Detection Box of Dr. Michael Feezor.[4] Preprocessors are usually located near the patient's bedside so that the weak signals may be amplified before being transmitted to the display, recording or computation apparatus. In some instances, analogue waveforms are converted to a string of digital amplitude representations to realize the improved noise immunity of a binary representation. Whatever the method, preprocessors and their associated transmission systems must possess the following characteristics:

1. Faithful reproduction of the original signal or its desired content derivation.

2. Adequate signal power level to resist aberations from induced electrical noise or the possible reactive characteristics of the transmission lines.

3. A minimum of manually operated controls at the bedside or anywhere else in the system (the best manual control is no manual control).

4. The signal processors should provide several independently isolated output channels so that loading on a channel will not deteriorate the signal fidelity from any other channel.

5. A good electrical decoupling among the locations which receive or originate signals (the computer room ground must be separate from a patient's room ground).

6. Excellent quality of fabrication.

7. Wherever possible, a universal circuit.

8. Modular construction so as to be quickly replaceable in the event of failure or change in measuring requirements.

9. Of increasing importance, the entire system and its components must provide a maximum of safety for the patient and the attending staff. This aspect of patient monitoring design is becoming one of the most important, expensive and difficult challenges to the engineer and the operating personnel.[6]

The safety of any apparatus with which the patient has contact has become paramount because modern medical practices often involve the use of many electrically operated devices at the bedside or in the procedure room. More and more often it is clinically advantageous to establish wires or other conducting pathways directly into a patient's body bringing him greatly improved medical care but exposing him to a potential electrical hazard.[5]

Even though the objective of our work is to engage the computer as a bedside assistant, those of us familiar with the development of such systems know of that exasperating period during which the equipment and programs are being developed when the computer does not process the data successfully. Whatever the system might be doing, the patient must still be effectively monitored so that the clinically guiding information can be displayed to the medical personnel in what is today considered a conventional manner. The preprocessors and their local display devices must operate quite independently of the computer system both to give the medical worker confidence in the project and to avoid compromising medical care to the patient. The computer system accepts the analogue signals from the preprocessors without affecting the usual monitoring facilities.

The Bedside Computer Terminal

A typical bedside computer terminal includes a television display screen, a telephone dial (or touchtone keyboard), four push buttons, four indicator lamps and a set of toggle switches.

The computer must be immediately responsive to commands which a user originates at the bedside, from the results of its own computations (such as a computer physiological alarm) and from time-clock scheduled requests. A doctor or nurse should seek information or assistance by pushing single function buttons on a simple task-oriented keyboard. A typewriter keyboard is not an appropriate bedside terminal but rather, ther terminal user should request action by a direct indication of what he needs. For example, a doctor wanting to review a patient's heart rate for the last eight hours would push a button which specifically causes this time-dependent display to appear on the bedside display screen. Touching another button might superimpose the variance of heart rate on the screen.

Most of the commands, originating at the bedside, direct the computer to display a graph or a set of numerical indicators. Also, operations such as the calibration of transducers or measuring cardiac output by one of the indicator techniques involves an interactive dialogue between the system and the operator. Plain language messages appearing on the television screen supply the communication from the computer to the bedside. The operator returns commands and data by using the touchtone keyboard (or telephone dial) and manipulating the appropriate measuring equipment. As an example of such a dialogue, let us follow the steps by which a doctor might measure the cardiac output of a patient. He has available to him one of the newly perfected thermistor catheters for measuring the initial and downstream temperature of blood. He will alert the computer system of his intention to make the measurement by dialing-in the appropriate command. The program responds by displaying a message which asks the doctor to enter the catheter number. As the characteristics of each thermistor vary from one to another, the computer program needs to identify the specific catheter being used so as to select the related calibration expression. The message response also implies that the executive program has successfully retrieved the Thermo-Dilution Cardiac Output Program from the mass storage device and the measurement may proceed. The display then directs the physician to inject the contrast media (in this instance, a bolus of ice-water) into the catheter. A microswitch on the water injector signals the program that injection has occurred. The program samples the thermistor temperature analogue channels. If the thermistors detect the passage of the ice-water bolus within a prescribed time interval and if the magnitude and duration of the signals are reasonable, the program computes the cardiac output, cardiac index, stroke volume and a host of other derived parameters from a combination of the thermistor data, heart rate and body surface area. To insure that the process has proceeded normally, the temperature analogue-time relationships are displayed along with the computed values. If the data are accepted by the physician, he commands the program to enter the values into the patient's history file. If

128

either the physician or the diagnostic portions of the computer program reject the measurements or the subsequent calculations, appropriate messages are conveyed to the bedside and posted to the activity log. At every step in this example, the program can exercise measurement quality criteria for acceptance or rejection. For example, if the physician has identified a catheter for which no calibration relationship exists, that fact will be presented to the physician. Or, if the thermistor signal magnitudes measured during the electrical calibration fall outside of the anticipated ranges, the operator will also be informed. If the computed cardiac output falls without the range expected for that patient, a message will assist the physician in questioning the value. And so on.

The toggle switches, a weak point in the operational scheme of the terminal, inform the data acquisition programs that certain channels of analogue information are active. The purpose of these indicators is to divert the application programs from monitoring data channels which are not supplying useful information so as to minimize the generation of false alarms and avoid the complex computer programming which might detect whether a channel were passing useful data or not. Unfortunately, setting and resetting these switches places a non-medical burden on the medical staff. Identifying active data channels remains, to this author, an only partially solved problem.

The lamp indicators on the terminal and the separate buttons will become useful for control of special research activities not requiring the graphics-telephone keyboard communication programming.

The terminals should be small, inexpensive and contain few components. This television and telephone keyboard terminal has proved effective for the bedside to computer communication and costs less than $2000 per site including the interfacing electronics. One is reluctant to throw away an obsolete terminal if it originally cost $20,000. But these terminals or their parts may be replaced as more economical and effective apparatus become available.

Information Central -
The Recording and Analysis Room

It is important to establish a Recording and Analysis Room adjacent to each patient care area. This room is not a computer room and it houses only the personnel and equipment immediately involved with the data acquisition and analysis aspects of patient care and clinical research. All signals - analogue, control, display and communication - arrive at a control patching and routing panel in this room. Channels can be routed to specific receivers within and without the medical institution. For example,

the analogue signal representing a patient's arterial pressure can be routed to a pen recorder in the Recording Room, returned to the bedside analogue display, sent to the computer center and attached to an experimental analogue preprocessor in a remote laboratory. Or contact closures within the computer can be made to activate a valve controlling a circulatory assistance device in a treatment room by suitable cross connection. Signals being sent to remote areas are buffered by line driving isolation amplifiers. The patch panel also offers an excellent facility for trouble-shooting signals and information channels without requiring non-medical personnel to work in the patient care areas.

Also in the Recording and Analysis Room are facilities to assist the clinician and researcher in data review. There are several analogue magnetic tape recorders, polygraphs, an editing oscilloscope and a battery powered master clock to serve the entire patient care and computer areas.

For more complicated interaction with the computer facilities, there is a more general terminal in this room that that which is possible at the bedside terminal. In addition to the television screen, the doctor-user will find a general purpose keyboard and a lite-pen for actual graphics interaction and for more flexible communication. It is expected that doctors and nurses will introduce detailed patient data and conduct extensive review of a patient's progress using this terminal. From here, researchers can activate their real-time or off-line computer programs enabling them to interact with information files or previously recorded analogue data.

Spare signal preprocessing modules and limited selection of electronic test equipment will also reside in the Recording and Analysis Room. While this is not an equipment repair depot, the resident technician can effect minor repairs, adjustments and module substitutions.

The Computer Room

The computer and its associated equipments and personnel should be located outside the immediate patient care area but within an easy walking distance to facilitate delivery of computer produced documents to the ward.

All of the signals from the patient care Recording and Analysis Room as well as information channels from diagnostic and research laboratories will be connected on a patch panel similar to that found in the Recording and Analysis Room. The actual connection of lines to the analogue input channels of the computer is currently a manual operation but one can anticipate these connections being effected by a computer controlled cross-bar system when the magnitude of the measuring problem expands. Analogue signals are received at the patch panel through isolating high common-mode rejection amplifiers. By delivering the analogue signals to the Computer Room on double ended, twisted pair, individual shielded leads, the problem of induced noise and ground looping are minimized. Perhaps this much care is not necessary, but the specifications had to be made before the noise problems of an unfinished building could be assessed.

At this time, most intensive care unit computer systems utilize commercially available analog-to-digital converters with their associated sample-and-hold amplifiers feeding the channel multiplexers. Unfortunately, most of these systems do not provide a differential input and must rely on the buffer amplifiers to provide common-mode variation immunity. The analogue multiplexers, while able to suppor dynamic amplitude ranges of perhaps plus and minus 40 volts, are especially vulnerable to damage from high voltage transients. Each input channel must be protected by a zener diode network to minimize the danger of these hazards. Many clinical monitoring systems begin operation with a single analog-to-digital converter, but initial provisions must be made to support a second device. Even though the signals produced by most medical transducers are not precise to better than 1%, it is helpful if the analogue-to-digital converter produces ten or eleven bit integer numbers at each conversion. Having this precision, one can still realize a suitable significance for a measurement while maintaining a wide amplitude window. For example, an electrocardiogram amplitude window of plus and minus 6 millivolts about zero volts represented by an eleven bit conversion will give ample resolution to the usual 1.5 millivolt QRS complex and still allow for baseline drifts associated with respiration, patient movement or possible amplifier instabilities without off-scale cupping of the signal. The objective here is to avoid manual adjustments of sensitivity and baseline offset. Unfortunately, many computer manufacturers only provide fifteen bit converters whose cost, speed and complexity are not matched to the economics of a medical unit. And many of these converter systems are tacked-on to the computer and require and inordinate amount of computer time for their operation. The analogue measuring sub-system should certainly operate on a direct-memory-access port of the central processor if such is available. When the number of analogue channels being measured exceeds perhaps 50, it is not unreasonable to make a sub-system in which one of the many available little general purpose computers is dedicated to the tasks of acquiring and formatting signal samples into a memory bank which is shared with the main processor.

The Computer

Typically, most institutions select a single medium sized (whatever that is) single data processing system for their automatized patient monitoring project. Usually the computer operates under some sort of multi-programming Executive System. If there is but one computer available, it should operate under an interrupt-responsive foreground executive with a background monitor service so that off-line computation may proceed without degrading patient monitoring. Popular computers and their manufacturer supplied programming packages are the Digital Equipment Corporation, PDP-15; the Xerox Data Systems, Sigma 3; and the IBM, 1800.

The computer must be equipped with sufficient high speed magnetic core storage to support the usually complicated and voluminous real-time monitor, the patient care executive and the many medical applications programs. The core storage should be augmented by a disk or drum unit to store copies of all systems and applications programs, data, patient files and temporary working storage. At least one IBM compatible digital magnetic tape transport provides long term storage and permits communication with other computer centers. We are building an information library of all patient data from our practice which can become a data base for retrospective studies of heart disease and its responses to various treatments.

I believe that it is essential to include a high speed line-printer, card equipment, an incremental plotter and a console typewriter in the peripheral inventory. Program development without these aids is inefficient and costly.

But perhaps the most important special device which should appear in the computer inventory is the display generator. Computer generated graphical displays should appear at each bedside, in all surgical and treatment areas, in the doctors management room and in the computer room itself. There is no substitute for the well designed graphical facility. The generator equipment itself may consist simply of a computer driven two-channel digital-to-analogue converter connected to a two axis oscilloscope or it can take the form of one of the more sophisticated devices. At this time, I prefer the video storage disk system from which conventional television monitors are driven by composite video signal to any other design. The disk-stored television information is generated by the computer without an intermediate optical image. The pictures can be line drawings, alpha-numerics or a combination of both. The computing load can be greatly reduced if the display generator includes a character generator so that the program need only transmit a binary character code such as

ASCII along with positioning information to produce text. Our recent device comparison indicates that such a system becomes economical for driving three or more graphical display devices. Also, one may choose a screen size to suit the particular location as the television monitors are standard commercial units.

In a large computer system, supporting many beds, surgical units and, perhaps, laboratories, it may be advantageous to dedicate a separate data processor to the management of displays. This processor modularization becomes particularly attractive when one considers using graphical interactions such as the light pen or a "mouse cursor". At this time, the disk storage display system made by Data Disc, Incorporated in Palo Alto, California, seems to provide the best cost and performance characteristics of the available multi-terminal apparatus.

Computer Programming

Most usually, a medical institution engaged in developing a computer assisted patient monitoring system will build its Executive System to operate in the general environment of a manufacturer-provided programming package. Examples of such commercial systems are the Multi-Program-Executive (MPX) of IBM and the Real-Time Batch Monitor supplied by XDS for the Sigma 3. It must be remembered that these are supposed to be universally applicable programs, designed to support many types of processing activities. They are not necessarily tailored for biomedical applications but hopefully will give adequate services to a medical Executive. So long as system designers employ the single central processor time-sharing system concept, such systems probably provide medical institutions with the best means of making an effective system with a modest programming effort. Whatever the system, it should support a foreground-background operation so that the computer may perform off-line data processing and new program development without compromising the actual patient monitoring.

The majority of system and medical applications programs should be written in FORTRAN. This language, however inadequate for specific applications, is universally understood and well supported in this country. And, programs must be well documented. I prefer some variety of the Single Unit Documentation Format in which the source program constitutes the sole and sufficient information for operating, maintaining and modifying a program.[5] The applications and systems programs are written in separable subroutines. The job of calling into action the appropriate subroutines to perform a task falls on the Executive System Program. In a well designed system, no User Application Program may ever take control away from this Executive Pro-

gram but should issue requests to it for such services as printing, creating displays and calling into action other subroutines. The Executive is responsive to internal and external interrupts and is the sole administrator for the medical applications programs.

There may be some advantage realized by writing the application subroutines in a re-entrant form but that decision is dependent upon the response-time demands of the system, the nature and size of the computer equipment and even the preference of the Executive System programmer. I am not convinced that the added complexity which might be introduced in writing re-entrant subroutines is really warranted in improved system performance.

An essential service of any real-time Executive program is its ability to recover from a power or equipment failure. It should also also be able to establish some kind of diagnostic operation following a catastrophic system program failure. A clever Executive program permits the computer system to fail gently, continuing to give some kind of service even with the loss of one or more system components. During the act of failing, or preparation for a power failure, the Executive must try to capture the states of those volatile registers whose restoration is necessary to successful restarting of the system.

Another very useful feature which can be built into the Executive is the system transaction log. The identities of subroutines or major programs in operation at any instant are determined by the particular set of interruptions which have occurred. Interrupts are set by the demands upon the system for service - a usually random phenomena.

Almost any of the programs stored in the system library may be in operation at any instant depending upon the origin of the recent interrupts. When a program error causes a system failure, it becomes essential to know which programs were operating at the moment of catastrophe. The Executive System Log keeps an instant-by-instant record of the subroutines, interrupts and other system conditions to assist the programmer in locating the offense. Of course, keeping the Log requires system time. When there is confidence in the system's stability, the Log activity can be suppressed. It can be reactivated at any time there has been system or application program alterations which might have introduced potentially system-damaging errors.

The Executive System Programs also allow a terminal oriented system start-up procedure to be initiated by a simple boot-strapping routine. The intent here is that any one of the intensive care unit technicians can initiate the entire system after a failure without the assistance of a programmer. A programmer should always attempt to write himself out of the operations.

Variates, Parameters and Processes

To conclude this exposition of the patient care computer assisted monitoring system, let us present several typical analogue physiological signal (variates) and propose examples of what the computer system might do with these variates to create derived, and hopefully more significant, indicators (parameters) for the medical staff. For the cardiac patient, the most meaningful, easily obtained signal is the electrocardiogram. There is some arrangement of surface electrodes attached to every patient. In some instances, this system is a simple single-lead, but a vector arrangement is considerably more revealing. And for a few patients, their treatment requires establishment of an intra-cardiac lead opening the possibility of monitoring atrial electrical phenomena with an improved signal-to-noise ratio compared to the surface lead measurements.

The electrocardiogram signals, after analogue preprocessing, are sampled by the computer system at rates usually not greater than 1,000 samples per second for each channel. The computer will process the electrocardiogram waveforms on a continuous basis, not necessarily for diagnostic purposes but rather to detect and anticipate the life threatening electrical arrhythmias. It has been mainly through the suppression of the electrical arrhythmias that care of the heart attack victim has been so increasingly successful. The computer programs initiate plain language and flashing lamp alarms to the medical staff.[7] The text identifies the patient and presents a terse description of the findings. The computer program is designed not to give obscure alarming messages. For example, if the program finds that no electrocardiogram (ECG) appears on any of the leads, it will contact one of the Blood Pressure Monitoring subroutines (if blood pressure is being measured). If the blood pressures and pulsations are within safe limits, the ECG program warns of a failure in the ECG equipment. But, if the ECG arrhythmia program finds that the parameters computed by the blood pressure program are also out of range, it creates a message to summon immediate medical aid to the bedside. In addition to arrhythmia surveillance, the ECG processor also computes such waveform analyses as heart rate, timing among the several components of the ECG waveform and vector angles time relationships when the lead system is appropriate. All of these measured and computer parameters along with the nature of any detected arrhythmias are recorded as incidents in the continuous Patient History Log.

Another set of clinically important physiological analogue signals are derived from blood pressure measuring catheters placed in the patient's vessels or within the chambers of his heart. Measurements of aortic blood pressure reveal important information about the performance of the heart and the state of the circulatory system. An Aortic Pressure Processor analyzes the pressure transducer waveform so as to calculate such parameters as peak and effective systolic pressures, peak and effective diastolic pressures, the time during which blood is being ejected from the heart, a stroke volume index, pulse rate and its variance, the magnitudes of the positive first derivative of pressure and countless other parameters. The intent here is not to deluge the physician with a myriad of derived data but rather to make such parameters available to him at his request. These derived parameters often are utilized by other more sophisticated programs such as simulations of hemodynamic sub-systems.

Pressure measurements from the pulmonary artery, chambers of the heart and several other locations in the circulatory system are processed by their own specific application subroutines.

The bedside operator, nurse or doctor, can also call into action specific service routines such as the thermo-dilution cardiac output program (discussed as an example of interactive terminal use). The application programs include subroutines to monitor respiratory mechanics, respiratory and blood gas analyses, fluid balance and the always changing research oriented programs. The Executive system has responsibility for calling these routines into action and supplying them with data input and output services.

WHAT LIES AHEAD

I believe that those of us who have been instrumental in building several existing computer assisted patient care units will unanimously agree on the improvement in patient care which seems to accompany the successful operation of the computer monitor. These systems are currently valuable even without any subsequent innovations in transducer design, computing equipment, their programs and operating strategy. But the questions to be posed lie in whether these installations can ever be economically justifiable under the current health economics of the United States. And a related question is how the application of such techniques can be expanded to serve more and more patients with a greater variety of effective monitoring algorithms.[8]

I do not believe that more patients can be given better care by an extrapolation of the currently popular single central processor time-sharing concepts. The next step in bringing computer power to the bedside is that of building decentralized computer networks comprising small, task-dedicated, general purpose computers. It is not unfeasible to dedicate one of the new, inexpensive, small processors to each patient or to a single task or to a small unit of beds. In this concept, the system terminals would be little, stand-alone computers acting as terminals to a communication network. The terminal computer would manage all local data acquisition, provide alarming capabilities and handle the man-machine terminal interactions.

When the little terminal computer needs historical information or other previously stored data for a patient, it can make its request to a central file management computer. This central computer would not operation under a real time-sharing system but rather under some simpler batch monitoring program. After interpretation of the file request, data would flow to or from the file facility in standardized rigidly formatted information blocks. The terminal computer can also call upon the file facility for core images of programs it wishes to run itself. A manually initiated bootstrapping routine can summon the appropriate core image programs from the central file to start the terminal. Among the several advantages of this organization are the stand-alone capability of each element, the simplicity of the overall system programs, the ability to begin a computer assisted unit with only a modest investment in machinery and programming, freedom from equipment obsolescence and greater overall system reliability in the event of elemental failure. And of great importance, the functional characteristics of the patient care unit can be fashioned by members of the medical staff rather than by computer system programmers.

Another facet of the patient monitoring system needs a re-evaluation. It is doubtful that one can extend monitoring to many beds by merely buying additional units of the currently available electronic signal preprocessors. These ECG amplifiers, electromanometers, temperature measuring bridges and the like are too expensive, too large, lack sufficient long term stability and, most important, are usually designed for an old fashioned monitoring system devoid of a high speed computation elements. This equipment is just not designed for automation. Medical sciences should begin to adopt techniques already commonplace in industrial process-control and space sciences for making multi-channel real-time measurements. One of the responsibilities of the currently operating computer systems is to define the characteristics of preprocessors for the automated system.

I believe that the potential power of applying modern automatic data processing methods

and equipment to medicine has only begun. There lies before us the ability (perhaps even a responsibility) to create accurate models of physiological systems which, after having been adjusted to depict individual patients, can be operated as a prognosticator, physiological system helping to select and evaluate the treatment plan before and during its actual application. Within this decade the bedside terminal will present the clinician and medical researcher with a continuously operating monitoring and physiological subsystem simulation to enhance and augment his own diagnostic and therapy management abilities.

Through these systems we are beginning to extend our understanding of health and disease. Through the application of the computer sciences, we will acquire the tools, within a realistic economy, to extend excellent medical care to a society who recognizes such service as a right rather than a priviledge.

BIBLIOGRAPHY

[1] Osborn, J.J., Beaumont, J.O., Raison, J.C.A., Russell, J.A.G., and Gerbode, F.: Measurement and Monitoring of Acutely Ill Patients by Digital Computer. Surgery. Vol. 64:6, 1057-1070, December, 1968.

[2] Sheppard, L.C., Kouchoukos, N.T., Kurtts, M.A., and Kirklin, J.W.: Automated Treatment of Critically Ill Patients Following Operation. Annals of Surgery. Vol. 168:4, 596-604, October, 1968.

[3] Osborn, J.J. and Russell, J.A.G.: The Measurement of Relative Stroke Volume. Journal of Vascular Diseases. Vol. 5, 1968.

[4] Feezor, M.D.: Analogue Preprocessing of Electrocardiograms in a Computer Monitored System. Proceedings of the San Diego Biomedical Symposium. Page 129, 1970.

[5] Wattenburg, W.: The Single Unit Documentation Approach to Computer Programming. Internal publication, Belcomp. 1966.

[6] Walters, C.W.: Safe Electric Environment in the Hospital. Bulletin of the American College of Surgeons. Vol. 54:4, July-August, 1969.

[7] Raison, J.C.A., Beaumont, J.O., Russell, J.A.G., Osborn, J.J., and Gerbode, F.: Alarms in an Intensive Care Unit; An Interim Compromise. Computers and Biomedical Research. Vol. 1:6, June, 1968.

[8] Miller, A., Russell, J., and Harris, P.: A Modular Approach to an Intensive Care Patient Monitoring System. DECUS Conference, Dallas, Texas, October, 1969.

THE USE OF A SMALL COMPUTER AS A COMMUNICATIONS CONTROLLER OF MULTI-USER ON-LINE SYSTEMS*

Joan Felberbaum and D. Gerd Dimmler
Brookhaven National Laboratory
Upton, New York

Summary

A programmed communications controller (PCC) has been designed using a small digital computer. The PCC is connected to a multi-user on-line system which controls nine experiments at the Brookhaven High Flux Beam Reactor. The purpose of the PCC is to process and switch all messages between sixteen teletypewriter terminals and the time-sharing system. The PCC serves "local" terminals at each experiment and "remote" terminals at distances up to one mile from the reactor. The PCC also controls message transfers between local and remote terminals. Arguments are given why a digital computer has been chosen rather than a hardwired device.

Introduction

This paper describes the programmed communications controller (PCC) which has been connected to the multiple spectrometer control system (MSCS) at the Brookhaven High Flux Beam Reactor. The MSCS operates, controls and monitors eight neutron spectrometers and one X-ray spectrometer in a time-shared mode.[1]

The PCC serves a "local" terminal at each experiment and several "remote" terminals at distances up to one mile from the reactor. Figure 1 shows the equipment configuration of the MSCS as of May 1969, including the connection of the PCC.

General Description

The decreased cost of small computers and their increased reliability and flexibility have made them a feasible and sometimes less expensive alternative to the hardwired "black box." With this in mind, we designed a communications controller for sixteen teletypewriters using a small computer[2] as a satellite to the time-sharing system.[3] The satellite computer handles all inputs from and outputs to the terminals. It assembles, edits, converts and prepares the messages with its own stored programs so that the main computer can be used more efficiently for data processing programs. Reprogramming of the time-sharing operating system has therefore been kept at a minimum. In addition to handling messages between the time-sharing computer and the terminals, the small computer can relay messages between terminals as well as initiate its own messages for transmission to the terminals. These and other control features would have been very difficult, if not impossible, to implement on a hardwired device. Since the PCC is programmable, its procedures can be modified and expanded as conditions warrant. At this time only 3000 of the 4096 words of core memory are used.

The overall flow of data in the PCC and its connection to the time-sharing system is shown in Fig. 2.

Information is transmitted from the teletypewriter terminal a bit at a time. In order to reduce the effects of noise, we sample the bit eight times at equal time intervals. In this way, up to three-eights of the bit may be distorted without producing an error. The bits are assembled into characters and the characters are assembled into messages. Some editing is done as the message is being assembled. An individual character or an entire message can be deleted. The message is

*This work was performed under the auspices of the U.S. Atomic Energy Commission.

Reprinted from *IEEE Trans. Nucl. Sci.*, vol. NS-17, pp. 419–422, Feb. 1970.

134

complete when the terminating character (carriage return) or eighty characters have been assembled. The message is then checked to see if it is a valid control message for the time-sharing computer. If so, the message is then converted from ASCII to the internal code of the time-sharing computer. The edited, converted message, tagged with the appropriate experiment number, is then delivered to the main computer ready for processing. No further input is allowed for that terminal until a response to that control message is received.

Output messages from the time-sharing computer must similarly be processed for transmission to the appropriate terminal. Output from the time-sharing computer can be the response to a control message previously entered, or a message from the user's stored program in the time-sharing computer, or an error message which is monitored in the time-sharing computer. Output from the time-sharing computer consists of the message, the number of words in the message, and an indication of the terminal for which it is destined. The PCC converts the character code to ASCII, the transmission code on the communication lines. As the message is broken down to the character level, special control characters may be added. For example, a line feed is inserted after each carriage return, and a "TAB" is simulated with the appropriate number of spaces. The characters are broken down into bits which are transmitted to the proper terminal.

The discussion thus far has centered on the PCC as a handler of messages between a terminal and the time-sharing computer. In the following paragraphs we shall show that the small computer can also relay messages between terminals and initiate its own messages for transmission to the terminals. Figure 3 shows the various message transfer paths. It should be noted that the box marked "Input Message Handler" includes message assembly, editing, validity, and switching programs. Similarly, the box marked

"Output Message Handler" includes message disassembly, editing, switching, and composition programs.

Remote Control Terminals

A novel feature of this system is the introduction and implementation of the remote teletype terminal. Each of the nine experiments has one "local" teletypewriter permanently assigned to it and physically located at the experiment. This teletypewriter functions as a control device, accepting control messages related to the experiment, and as an output device, maintaining an experiment log. Referring to Fig. 3, the data transfer from the local terminal to the time-sharing computer is via paths 1, 2 and 3, and from the time-sharing computer to the local terminal via paths 4, 5 and 6.

In addition, there are seven "remote" teletypewriters located in different buildings at varying distances (of up to one mile) from the experiments at the reactor. Each remote teletypewriter can be connected to any of the nine experiments (one at a time). If a user wishes to control an experiment from a remote terminal he must first "log in" with the PCC. The "log in" procedure consists of a number of tests to determine the validity and feasibility of the request. The user must first identify himself and the experiment with an identification code. (This code is overprinted on the hard copy at the terminal for security reasons.) If (a), no other remote is controlling the experiment, and (b), the local terminal at the experiment is not currently transmitting or receiving information, control is transferred to the remote terminal. In addition, a message is sent to the local terminal indicating the identification number of the remote terminal which is in control of the experiment. If condition (a) is not met, a "busy" message is sent to the remote terminal. If condition (b) is not met, the remote terminal must wait until notified that the current transaction is complete and that it can "go on." The "log in" procedure uses data paths 7 and 8 shown in Fig. 3. Output to the local terminal is switched to path 6; the conversation with the remote terminal uses path 9.

When control is transferred to the remote terminal, the local terminal functions as an output-only device. This mode of operation can be followed with reference to Fig. 3. Data is entered from the remote terminal via path 7. If the message is valid, it is sent via paths 2 and 3 to the time-sharing system and via paths 8 and 6 to the local terminal. The response from the time-sharing system is sent via paths 4, 5 and 9 to the remote terminal and 6 to the local terminal.

A user at a remote terminal retains control of the experiment until he voluntarily gives it up or a user at the local terminal "decontrols" it. If for any reason an experimenter at the experiment wants to take over control, he can do so by using the "ESCape" key. A message is sent to the remote terminal informing the user that he is "off."

Provision is made for the remote terminal to send a message to the local terminal. This type of message could be used to give instructions to someone at the experiment regarding some piece of apparatus. The data transfer here is by way of paths 7, 8 and 6 in Fig. 3. As yet, there is no provision for sending a message from the local terminal to the remote terminal, but this can be easily added.

Acknowledgements

It is a pleasure to thank D. Ophir for valuable discussions regarding the overall design of the PCC. For the design, construction and implementation of the computer interface, we wish to thank S. Rankowitz, N. Greenlaw and G. Perry.

References

1. D. R. Beaucage, et al., Nucl. Instr. & Meth. 40, 26 (1966)

2. Varian 620i Documentation. Varian Data Machines, Irvine, Calif.

3. SDS-920 Documentation. Scientific Data Systems, El Segundo, Calif.

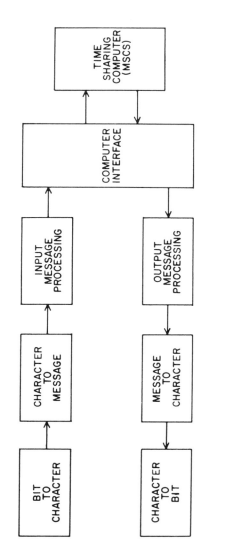

2. Overall flow of data in PCC.

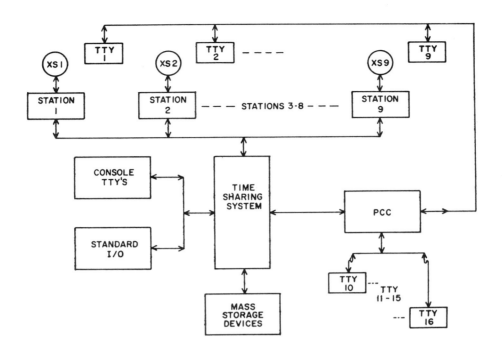

1. MSCS configuration including PCC.

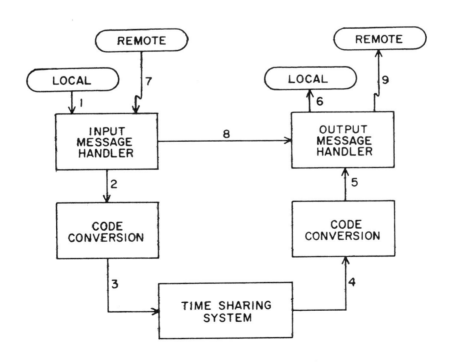

3. Various message transfer paths.

137

Kenneth B. Wiberg
Yale University
New Haven, Connecticut 06520

The Small Computer in the Laboratory

For many years, computers have normally been large general purpose instruments designed to handle the needs of a major body of users. However, in recent years, a group of small computers have become available in the $8000–20,000 price range. Even the least expensive of these has a memory which can store 4096 twelve bit words. Each word corresponds to one instruction or one datum. In addition, they have a teletype with paper tape punching and reading facilities for input to and output from the computer, a moderately large group of instructions, and the possibility of adding a variety of external devices which may be operated by the computer.

These computers have great potential in both undergraduate instruction and in graduate research in chemistry. The following will indicate some of the more useful applications.

It is generally agreed that some experience with computers is desirable for undergraduates. Three approaches are possible. A large computer may be used in a "batch" mode in which the student prepares his program on cards, leaves them with the computer operator, and returns later to obtain his results. Second, a large computer may be used in an "interactive" mode. Here, many teletypes are attached to the computer, and each person types his program using the teletype. The amount of actual interaction varies —some systems check each statement as it is typed and immediately supply error messages whereas others check for errors only after the entire program has been typed. The third approach is to use a small computer, again operating from the teletype.

The first approach is usually the least efficient for undergraduate students since errors can be corrected only by changing cards and resubmitting the program— a time consuming process. The second two approaches are, for short programs, essentially equivalent. However, for smaller schools a large computer may be too expensive to be supported, whereas one or more of the small computers might be within reason. Also, it is relatively expensive to provide television type output facilities (for data plotting, rapid output, etc.) with a large computer, whereas it is relatively inexpensive with a small computer. As will be indicated later, a computer is very useful for data collection and control. In many cases, it is still difficult to collect data directly from an instrument using a time shared large computer. The small computers can do this easily. Thus, in many cases, the small computers have real advantages over the larger instruments. A final consideration is that

This work was supported by a grant from the National Science Foundation.

students have much more of an opportunity to learn about computers when using a small computer themselves than when tied in to a large computer.

What are the advantages in using computers in undergraduate chemistry courses? In the general chemistry, analytical chemistry, and physical chemistry courses, a major component of the instructional process is solving problems. These have generally been of a relatively simple type which could easily be solved using a slide rule because more complex and valuable problems have required an impractical amount of the students' time.

The small computers may be used in a "desk calculator" mode in which one types the equation to be evaluated, and the computer performs the evaluation including the calculation of trignometric, exponential, and logarithmic functions. This will suffice to handle a wide variety of problems and ensures that the arithmetic will be done correctly. For more complex problems, programs may easily be written using BASIC, FOCAL, or similar languages which are learned with no more than a few hours instruction. Since the numerical answers are obtained, the students have a better opportunity to check whether or not their method of setting up the problem is correct.

A more important task is that of data reduction, as in fitting a set of experimental data to an analytical expression by a method such as that of least squares. Here, the student has a possibility of treating his data in a really careful fashion and to critically examine the errors in his data and in the derived quantities. The relatively long and tedious calculations which are required for such calculations normally discourage both the instructor and the student from carrying them out. The student now has an opportunity to make a careful analysis of the data he obtains in laboratory experiments, particularly in the physical chemistry laboratory.

The main restriction in the use of small computers is that the amount of data storage must be kept to a minimum because of the small memory. If the problem involves only a relatively small amount of data, the program may be written in Fortran, or in the simpler Fortran like languages such as BASIC and FOCAL. Here, the arithmetic operations may be written in essentially the normal algebraic form, and the computer, with the aid of a program known as a compiler, will work out the sequence of individual steps needed to evaluate the algebraic expressions. These languages are easily learned and after a few hours of study students are able to write simple computer programs.

Common calculations of the type referred to above include the calculations of rate constants, of activation parameters, of dipole moments, and of nmr spectra (for simple cases). These calculations are often needed in

Reprinted with permission from *J. Chem. Educ.*, vol. 47, pp. 113–116, Feb. 1970.

```
C;        ACTIVATION PARAMETERS
          DIMENSION RATE(10),T(10),CALC(10),F(10),DIF(10),Y(10)
          CONST = 2.083E+10
          C1 = LOGF(CONST)
1;        TYPE 2
2;        FORMAT (/,"THIS PROGRAM CALCULATES ACTIVATION ENERGIES")
          TYPE 3
3;        FORMAT (/,"N IS THE NUMBER OF DATA POINTS",/,"N= ")
          ACCEPT 4, N
4;        FORMAT (I3)
          TYPE 6
6;        FORMAT (/,"NOW TYPE RATE CONSTANTS AND TEMPERATURES")
          TYPE 7
7;        FORMAT (/,"THE RATE CONSTANTS ARE IN SEC-1",/)
          DO 10 J = 1,N
          ACCEPT 11, RATE(J), T(J)
          T(J) = T(J) + 273.16
          Y(J) = LOGF(RATE(J)/T(J))
10;       CONTINUE
11;       FORMAT (E,E,/)
          SUMX=SUMY=SMXX=SMXY=0.0
          DO 15 J = 1,N
          RT = 1.0/T(J)
          SUMX = SUMX + RT
          SUMY = SUMY + Y(J)
          SMXX = SMXX + RT*RT
          SMXY = SMXY + RT*Y(J)
15;       CONTINUE
          G = N
          DEN = SUMX*SUMX - G*SMXX
          SL = (SUMX*SUMY - G*SMXY)/DEN
          B = (SUMX*SMXY - SUMY*SMXX)/DEN
          H = -SL*1.987
          S = (B - C1)*1.987
          TYPE 16,H,S
16;       FORMAT (/,"DELTA H = ",E,/,"DELTA S =",E,/)
          DO 20 J = 1,N
          CALC(J) = CONST*EXPF((-H/T(J) + S)/1.987)*T(J)
          F(J) = -(Y(J) - C1)*1.987*T(J)
20;       CONTINUE
          TYPE 21
21;       FORMAT(/,"    K          T          CALC K        F")
          DO 24 J = 1,N
          TYPE 25, RATE(J), T(J), CALC(J), F(J)
25;       FORMAT (/,E,E,E,E)
24;       CONTINUE
23;       TYPE 26
26;       FORMAT (/,"T = ")
          ACCEPT 27, TT
27;       FORMAT (E)
          IF (TT) 1,28,28
28;       TT = TT + 273.16
          R = CONST*EXPF((-H/TT + S)/1.987)*TT
          TYPE 29, R
29;       FORMAT ("   K = ",E)
          GO TO 23
          END
```

Figure 1. Fortran program for calculating activation parameters.

physical chemistry laboratory experiments and in graduate research problems. In order to indicate the simplicity of the Fortran language for these cases, Figure 1 shows a program which may be used for activation parameter calculations, and for extrapolation of rate constants to other temperatures. The Fortran language is that used with the standard PDP-8 computers. The TYPE statements cause the teletype to type the specified information using the FORMAT statement with the corresponding number (see Fig. 2). The ACCEPT statement allows the computer to accept the specified quantities (such as N = number of data points) from the teletype keyboard. The DO statement causes the following statements through the one having the corresponding number (10 in the first case) to be performed the specified number of times (N in this case). The central part of the program contains the expressions necessary to obtain the slope and intercept for

$$\ln\left(\frac{k}{T}\right) = m\left(\frac{1}{T}\right) + b$$

where SL = m and B = b. The quantities are converted to $\Delta H\ddagger$ and $\Delta S\ddagger$ and are typed on the teletype using the TYPE statement.

```
THIS PROGRAM CALCULATES ACTIVATION ENERGIES
N IS THE NUMBER OF DATA POINTS
N= 4
NOW TYPE RATE CONSTANTS AND TEMPERATURES
THE RATE CONSTANTS ARE IN SEC-1

4.87E-4  15.0
1.13E-3  25.0
3.09E-3  35.0
7.92E-3  45.0

DELTA H = +0.17449 5E+5
DELTA S =-0.134596E+2

    K               T              CALC K
+0.486999E-3    +0.288160E+3    +0.399104E-3    +0.213168E+5
+0.113000E-2    +0.298160E+3    +0.114763E-2    +0.214718E+5
+0.309000E-2    +0.308160E+3    +0.306468E-2    +0.215962E+5
+0.792000E-2    +0.318160E+3    +0.779992E-2    +0.217221E+5
T = 5       K = +0.789714E-4
T = 50      K = +0.121431E-1
T = 100     K = +0.534766E+0
T = -1
```

Figure 2. Output from the activation energy program. The underlined quantities were typed by the user; the rest was typed by the computer under program control. The values of F are the free energies of activation. The final T's are requests for temperatures at which rate constants are to be calculated. When a negative temperature is given, the program returns to the first statement and is prepared to accept further data.

The rate constants are then calculated for each temperature and are typed. Finally, a "T =" is typed. If a positive number is entered, the rate constant corresponding to that temperature is typed. If a negative value is typed, the program is restarted for the entry of a new set of data.

The output resulting from the program is shown in Figure 2. Here, only the underlined quantities were typed by the user, and the rest were typed by the computer under program control. It should be noted that the program is written so that it is used in an interactive mode. The computer asks questions or gives instructions, and the user responds. In this way one need not remember exactly how or in what order data should be introduced.

Rate constant calculations with up to 20 data points as well as many other calculations may be programmed for use with these computers using Fortran. A wider variety of problems may be examined if a larger memory is attached to the computer. A second 4096-word memory would permit the use of a more sophisticated Fortran compiler and would greatly increase the storage available for data. The cost of these memory units has decreased considerably in recent years, and it is now reasonably possible to go to 8192 words.

However, even without an expanded memory, an increase in program sophistication is possible if one writes the program in a form which is closely related to the language actually used by the computer. Here, each individual step is coded separately, and with efficient organization, a relatively large program may be written. For example, using 4096 words of 12 bit storage, we have written a first-order kinetics program which will accept up to 42 data points, which will accept the observed quantities as absorbance, percent transmission, or as volume of titrant, and will calculate the rate constant, the intercept, the rms deviation, the correlation coefficient, and an estimate of the percent error in the rate constant. The latter is particularly important in that the correlation coefficient is not a good measure of the degree to which the slope is determined by the experimental data.

In addition, the program permits the deviations between observed and calculated values to be plotted on

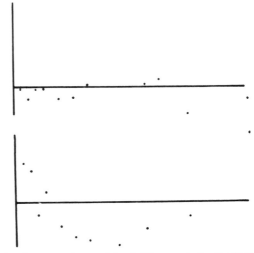

Figure 3. Computer drawn plots of difference between observed and calculated quantities for a first-order reaction. The upper plot corresponds to the data in Figure 4 and shows a normal scatter. The lower plot is for data which are not well represented as a first-order process.

Figure 4. Output from first-order kinetics program. The underlined quantities are input data. The iteration part is not included in order to conserve space.

an oscilloscope. Good first-order data will be associated with an even scattering of points on both sides of zero, whereas data which do not fit well will generally lead to some obvious curvature (Fig. 3). Finally, if desired, the computer will adjust the infinity value to give the best fit to a first-order plot. Typical output from the program is shown in Figure 4. The underlined quantities were typed by the operator; the rest was typed by the computer. It may again be seen that considerable interaction is possible between the computer and the operator.

As another example, in many problems in which one wishes to perform sigma molecular orbital calculations, estimate nmr chemical shifts and coupling constants or calculate conformational energies, one needs a reasonable starting geometry for the molecule. This, of course, can be done by hand but it is generally slow and tedious. However, a computer may be programmed to do the necessary calculations. For example, using a computer with a 4096-word memory, we have written a program which will allow us to do the following.

1) Set up the framework of the molecule by specifying for each new atom the distance from the atom to which it is attached, the bond angle involving the new atom and the torsional angle involving the new atom.

2) Change or delete any of the coordinates, and add new coordinates.

3) Calculate bond lengths, bond angles or torsional angles by specifying the numbers of the atoms involved.

4) Add secondary or tertiary hydrogens to any carbon atom by specifying the CH bond length, and in the case of secondary hydrogens, the HCH bond angle.

5) Translate, transpose, or rotate coordinates.

6) Examine, change, add to or delete entries in the bond register (which contains the numbers of the atoms which are bonded to each other).

7) Print or punch the coordinates of all or any of the atoms.

8) Display a projection of the molecule on an oscilloscope screen, and to rotate the coordinate system while viewing the projection.

A sample output sheet from this program is shown in Figure 5. Here again, the underlined quantities are those typed by the user, the other items are typed by the computer under the control of the program. The letters following the > sign indicate which calculation or operation the computer is to do next. A asks for the bond angle formed by the three atoms whose numbers

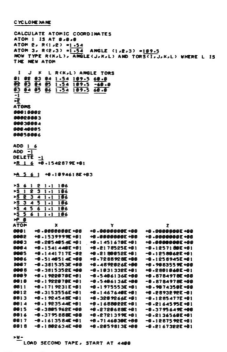

Figure 5. Output from atomic coordinates program. The underlined quantities are input data; the rest is output from the computer.

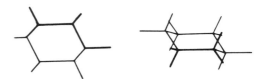

Figure 6. Computer drawn projections for cyclohexane. The left projection corresponds to the coordinates given in Figure 5, and the one on the right is the result after the computer has rotated the coordinates.

follow; R asks for the distance between the atoms whose numbers follow; T asks for the torsional angle formed by the four atoms whose numbers follow; P asks for a printout; S asks for secondary hydrogens to be added to the carbon whose number follows (the next numbers are the desired C-H bond length and H-C-H bond angle); V asks that the coordinates of the atoms be translated by the x, y, and z amounts which follow; and U asks that the molecule be rotated about the $x(1)$, $y(2)$, or $z(3)$ axis by the angle given. A number of other commands are available.

In the example shown in Figure 5, the bond lengths and angles associated with atoms, 1, 2, and 3 are introduced as answers to the computer typeout. Then the coordinates of atoms 4, 5, and 6 are introduced by specifying the bond lengths, angles, and torsional angles with respect to the previously defined atoms. The E command leads to a listing of the bond table—the missing bond is that between atoms 1 and 6, and this is added. The -1 is a terminating character. As a check, the 1,6 bond length and the 5,6,1 bond angle are requested and are found to be correct.

Secondary hydrogens are now added to all carbons using 1.1 Å C-H bond lengths and 106° HCH bond angles. The P command leads to a listing of the coordinates which have been generated. The W command instructs the operator how to obtain a perspective drawing of the molecule on the attached oscilloscope. The oscilloscope output for the final coordinates is shown in Figure 6. Using this program, the coordinates

140

of fairly complex molecules may fairly quickly be obtained.

The above uses are not unique to these small computers, and the calculations could have been carried out using a large general purpose computer—but often with less convenience. The interactive feature of these small computers is only slowly being implemented with the larger machines. In the case of the coordinate program, operation with a large computer in the batch mode would be most inconvenient since one has to be able to follow the development of the coordinates in order to know what to do next.

There is one area in which small computers are uniquely useful—data collection and control of laboratory experiments. Many analytical instruments such as X-ray diffractometers, mass spectrometers, and nmr spectrometers are now available in models which have small computers attached for these purposes. There are many other cases in which these computers may be used.

A major problem in our laboratory has been that of collecting spectrometric data as a function of time in order to examine the kinetics of reactions. The time scale of these experiments varies widely—from a few milliseconds to several hours. In any case, one wishes to collect a relatively large amount of data with the best possible precision in order to precisely define the course of the reaction. This is particularly the case when intermediates are involved, giving relatively complex kinetic behavior.

The computer is ideal for this purpose since by the addition of an analog to digital converter, it is able to accept the output of the phototube amplifier and convert it to digital form with 0.1% precision in a short period of time (~50 μsec.). The precision of the measurements is much better than could be obtained by using an oscilloscope (±3%) and is directly in digital form, avoiding the necessity of manually digitizing the data. The numbers may be stored in the memory unit. With the addition of a digital clock, the computer may sample the amplifier output at specific times and thus assemble a table of spectrometer output as a function of time. This may then be printed or punched out, displayed on an oscilloscope, or operated upon to give the desired rate constant(s). The computer may be used to process the data, thus permitting the derived results, such as rate constants, to be available immediately after the completion of the experiment. Also, the raw experimental data may quickly be examined via the oscilloscope display.

With slower reactions, one must take into account drifts in the light source output, and in the amplifier. We have done this by moving the cell compartment in a Beckman DU spectrometer using a pneumatic solenoid under computer control. Then, the computer may obtain readings on both the reaction cell and the reference cell at appropriate times determined by the digital clock. With these data, the correct absorbance may be calculated for each observation time.

Many other laboratory experiments may be profitably monitored by a small computer. For example, heats of reaction are now particularly conveniently studied in this fashion. A quartz thermometer is able to measure temperatures to ±0.001°C (or better) and give as one output the temperature in a binary form which may be accepted by a computer. Thus, a computer may measure the temperature changes which occur during the fore period, the reaction period, and the after period, and may calculate the heat of reaction after making all of the appropriate corrections.

In other cases, the computer could sample two or more signals and implement proper adjustment in the case of a drift in one of the signals. The adjustment may be made arithmetically by correcting the input data, or the computer may exercise control over the experiment in order to restore the fixed quantities to their normal values. This may be done via relays, solenoids, stepping motors, etc. A wide variety of devices may be controlled by the computer using relatively inexpensive and easily set up external circuitry.

The computer is able to accept data from many types of sources—any data which may be converted to an electrical signal (via a strain gauge, etc.) or a digital signal (such as the output of electronic counters, quartz thermometers, shaft position encoders, etc.) may be sampled. The remarkable versatility of small computers suggest that they should play an important role in many future experiments.

Appendix

An important question in considering a small computer is how much additional equipment is needed in order to make a genuinely useful system. The answer will vary from one computer to another, but may be illustrated by considering one of the more common of the small computers, the PDP-8L. The basic computer ($8500) is supplied with a Teletype and a variety of programs (Fortran, FOCAL, an editor, two assemblers, several debugging programs, and a variety of arithmetic and input-output subroutines). As such, it is a complete system and may be used without the purchase of additional items.

However, the user will quickly find the time required to read in programs such as the Fortran compiler is excessive (10–15 min). Thus, it is almost essential to add a high speed reader (30× as fast as the Teletype) at a cost of $2000. A high speed punch would be a convenience but is not essential. This would add $1300 to the cost.

Other additional equipment may be needed for certain types of applications. These include

1) An additional 4K of memory ($3500). This would permit the use of the more sophisticated 8K Fortran compiler and would greatly increase the amount of data which could be handled.

2) A disk storage unit ($6000). A disk can store 32K words (i.e., eight complete core loads). This may be used to store commonly used programs, intermediate data in calculations, and the text version of programs which are to be operated on using the Fortran compiler or an assembly program. A disk will minimize the need for tape handling and is particularly convenient in the development of new programs in which the text versions frequently need to be corrected. It is not of as great a value to those who principally use the 4K Fortran system.

3) An oscilloscope output ($3600). An oscilloscope output will permit visual examination of data which is often very helpful (see Figs. 3 and 6).

4) Data input facilities. If one wishes to collect data from an instrument, one needs an analog to digital converter. If the data are to be collected as a function of time, one needs a digital clock and some method for synchronizing the clock with the start of the experiment. These functions are available on a unit called a laboratory peripheral ($4600), which also includes an oscilloscope control.

A variety of other equipment also are available. This includes magnetic tape units, card readers, incremental plotters, etc. However, for most purposes these items are not needed although they may be convenient. It should also be clear that items 1–4 above are not required for many uses of the computer but rather extend the capability of the instrument in important ways. Other equipment may be added—and the hardware is designed so that the user may construct his own interface units by suitably connecting plug-in modules which will perform specific functions (i.e. flip-flops, gates, inverters, delays, etc.).

FRANCIS J. LAVOIE
Senior Editor

MINI TIME-SHARING

Time-sharing has always presupposed a large, relatively expensive central processor. For this reason, only a handful of big companies could afford their own in-house system. But the minicomputer has changed this. Now, you can buy a remarkably sophisticated time-sharing system, complete with terminals, for as little as $15,000.

Minicomputers can be time-shared in the classic sense, through time-slicing, just as the larger machines are. The basic difference is that most minis do the job with software. This is admittedly not always satisfactory, and a number of manufacturers will undoubtedly eventually offer minis with wired-in time-sharing capabilities. Some already do.

There are two approaches to designing a mini time-sharing system. The first is to design the system to do only part of the job a large-scale machine can do—for example, restrict the user to only a single language. The second is to design a system which does everything the larger system can do, but on a smaller scale. The first approach is much more common at present. But as the use of mini time-sharing grows, more manufacturers can be expected to adopt the second approach, primarily because of the added flexibility. At present, the first approach has the advantage of being simpler and less expensive; and it's quite adequate for many applications, especially where only a small number of terminals must be accommodated.

Many minicomputers, time-shared themselves, are also serving as "terminals" to larger time-shared computers. Several such hierarchical systems already exist, and industry observers feel that they'll become much more common. Such systems have wide application possibilities—for example, control, communications—in addition to conventional time-sharing.

Some mini time-sharing systems can accommodate a considerable number of users. The Digital Equipment Corp. TSS-8 system (top) accommodates 16 users, and can be expanded to handle many more. Hewlett Packard's HP 2000A (right) can also handle 16 users.

Reprinted with permission from *Mach. Des.*, pp. 138–141, Mar. 19, 1970.

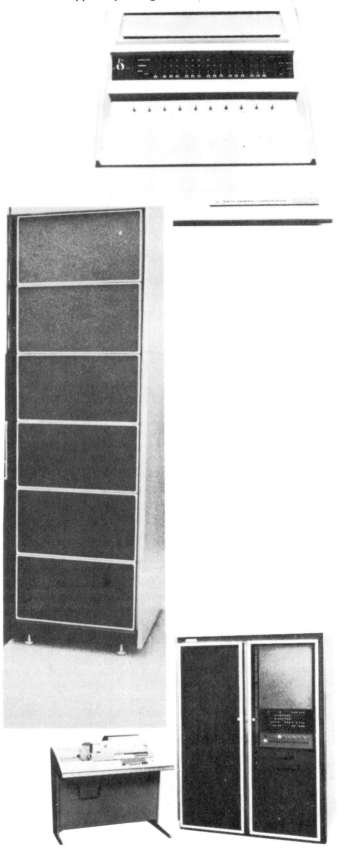

Billed as the fastest minicomputer available today, the Supernova, made by Data General Corp., is one of several minis which can now be time-shared. The system can support up to eight users, costs about $35,000.

From an operating standpoint, the minicomputer isn't particularly well suited to time-sharing. But its advantages far outweigh its disadvantages in many applications.

The most important advantage of the mini t-s system is its low cost. Where only a limited number of users must be serviced, and where the problems don't require a great deal of calculation ("number crunching"), it's hard to beat, even by large commercial systems. One observer points out that the vast majority of statistical and engineering problems can easily be handled by a small time-sharing system.

Is the mini time-sharing system always a better buy than, say, renting time from a commercial time-sharing bureau? It depends on the specific case. Quite often the cost per month will be significantly lower. (As a rough guide, tying into a large-scale commercial system will average about $200 per user per month—plus, in some cases, communications costs.) But of course, this price buys a great deal more capability, both in computing power and available memory. For large programs, there is no comparison: the large system is almost a necessity. The small system can do the job, but it has to do it in small pieces—an inefficient procedure.

There are other advantages to the time-shared mini. Like any time-sharing system, the mini system often makes much fuller and more efficient use of a computer, since the machine is less apt to be standing idle. In addition, programs—and the hardware associated with storing and retrieving them—can also be shared.

Of course, the mini system has its limitations. Most obvious is its unsuitability for number-crunching operations and for running large programs. Also, the minicomputer's instruction set is far less powerful than that of a larger-scale machine, so the user is restricted in what he can do with the computer.

The mini system has the big advantage of expandability. It's possible to start with a basic system handling only four people and add terminals—and, eventually, CPUs—to handle just about any number of users. This eliminates buying a larger machine that won't be used to its full capacity right away.

Who's Interested

There seems to be a considerable diversity of opinion as to where mini time-sharing will have the greatest impact. Some of the established manufacturers have made a strong push into the educational field. Others feel that the engineering field promises a lucrative potential. Still others are looking at control applications.

At present, only a few manufacturers are making a strong pitch to the engineer. But conversations with company representatives reveal a definite feeling that a vast potential for in-house mini time-sharing systems exists in the engineering field, and that this field is about to be invaded by the manufacturers.

Mini time-sharing has proved eminently successful in control applications, usually in hierarchical systems. In such applications, a number of minis "report" to a larger computer. Each mini is in turn time-shared by several machines and, perhaps, an operator. Such systems can include peripherals—for example, graphic displays.

Communications have made good use of the mini's time-sharing capabilities. One typical mini, designed specifically for this purpose, can interface up to 96 low-speed, and 32 medium-speed, lines. Processor logic is time-shared under microprogram control. The system can handle a variety of different communications devices at the same time.

Even commercial time-sharing service bureaus are discovering the advantages of the mini T-S system. Several firms are offering time on such systems, reportedly at lower rates than those for the larger, conventional commercial systems. One typical service bureau uses Digital Equipment Corp.'s TSS-8 mini system, which can handle several languages, and can accommodate up to 32 users simultaneously. The service bureau (Strategic Time-Sharing Inc., New York) lists the following prices: Terminal connect time, $6.50/hr; CPU usage, $0.03/unit; storage, $1.75/2048 characters. Unlimited use is available at $1,000/mo.

How Many Terminals

Single time-shared minicomputers normally accommodate up to sixteen terminals. The smaller machines usually can handle a maximum of eight users. Beyond this point, the hardware becomes overloaded. (This isn't always true, however; for example, the TSS-8 can accommodate up to 32 users, and the MiniComp system can handle 48 users. But these are extraordinarily sophisticated systems.)

To get around this restriction on numbers of users, several manufacturers have turned to multi-mini systems incorporating several minicomputers as central processors. In such a system, one mini acts as controller, giving the mini-system an important capability missing in the simple single-processor system; core transfer. This permits data to be transferred from one computer core memory to another.

Some observers feel that the multi-mini system will grow significantly in use during the next few years. They point out that even for a large number of terminals, the mini system will still be the most economical approach to time-sharing for many engineering applications. And for this, the multi-mini system is the only practical approach.

How many users can such a system handle? No one knows for certain; theoretically, there is no limit. But there are practical limits. One observer feels that, for example, a 32-terminal, 4-CPU mini system might have some cost advantage over a single medium-scale system. But whether on balance the system would prove more practical would depend in great measure on the specific case.

Said to be the first time-shared mini to combine both BASIC language programming and sophisticated computer-supported calculator functions in one desktop terminal, Interplex Corp.'s System I rents for about $1800/mo. for a 16 terminal system.

Latest of the minis designed specifically for low-cost time-sharing is Wang Laboratories' Model 3300. This system sells for only $15,250 in a two-terminal configuration, and can be expanded to 16 terminals.

Languages

As a general rule, the more sophisticated (and expensive) the system, the greater the number of languages it can accommodate. Many of the simpler systems offer only a single language, usually BASIC.

In many cases, BASIC may be wholly adequate. Although not as flexible or as powerful as some other languages, it has one big advantage—it's easy to learn and to use. This is particularly useful in time-sharing applications, where the user

Remote Batch Processing on a Mini

Time-sharing provides immediate and simultaneous access to a computer from several remote terminals. But there's a price to pay for this conversational capability; for one thing, some of the computer's memory capacity must be given over to the executive programs that control the time-sharing mode of operation. And there are other tradeoffs.

In many engineering applications, this immediate response may not be necessary. In this case, the central computer can operate on a remote-batch basis; that is, it will finish one job before going on to the next. The CPU can still service a number of users located at remote terminals.

Several manufacturers offer minis capable of remote batch processing; in fact, some minis can operate in either a remote-batch or a time-sharing mode.

Control computers are often time-shared. This General Automation 18/30 supervisory computer controls a number of smaller "worker" computers tied directly to the machine or process. The "workers" themselves are often time-shared.

Communications and time-sharing have long been associated. The time-shared mini has been put to use in interfacing communications devices. The Micro 812, with a basic price of $10,000, can interface up to 96 low-speed lines and 32 medium-speed lines. It was designed specifically for communications applications.

often isn't too interested in spending a great deal of time learning to be a programmer. And, as is the case in all well-established languages, a considerable body of application software already exists, ready for use.

Some manufacturers have developed their own simple languages. Typical is FOCAL, developed by Digital Equipment Corp. for use in its TSS-8 mini system. This "mathematically oriented" language is similar to the well-known JOSS language and is claimed to be one of the most powerful conversational languages ever developed. According to DEC spokesmen, FOCAL, like BASIC, can be mastered in just a couple of hours.

The more sophisticated mini-system offers a number of languages. DEC's TSS-8, for example, can accommodate FORTRAN, BASIC, and FOCAL.

Price

Since minicomputers offer low price as a prime inducement, it stands to reason that the same would hold true for time-shared systems based on these machines.

This isn't to imply that all mini time-sharing systems are inexpensive. Depending on how sophisticated the system is, it can cost from about $15,000 to well over $100,000. And it can be expanded to cost several times that much.

A typical "simple" time-sharing system might consist of, say, a minicomputer with 8,096 words of memory and 8 ASR-33 Teletypewriters. Such a

simple configuration could be bought outright for about $35,000. One actual system, which includes a 12K central processor, concentrator, and four terminals, sells outright for about $47,000. The system can accommodate an additional 12 terminals, at a cost of about $1,500 each.

But prices may be coming down. Recently, one manufacturer introduced an 8-bit system with a 4K memory (expandable to 65K) and two Teletypewriters for $15,250. For four users, the price is $21,250. The system can accommodate up to 16 users. Accessories are available. Such systems, designed for low-cost time-sharing from the ground up, will undoubtedly be appearing on the market with increasing regularity.

Some systems can be leased. One company offers its $47,000 system for about $2,350/mo. on a two-year basis and $1,300/mo. for four years. Additional terminals are $76 or $42 each.

Like any in-house t-s system, mini time-sharing eliminates one costly adjunct of most large time-sharing systems—communications. If the mini system is otherwise adequate, this factor alone can swing the decision in its favor.

In some cases, it may pay to shop around. For example, there is no requirement that the Teletypewriters be bought from the same source as the CPU—or, for that matter, that they be bought at all. And some manufacturers offer discounts in certain cases, so that the same capabilities might be available at significantly different prices from several sources.

INDIRECT MEASUREMENT OF PROCESS VARIABLES BY MINICOMPUTER

A. Ben Clymer, P.E.
Consulting Analytical Engineer
Columbus, Ohio 43221

Summary

Mathematical methods and computer techniques for indirect measurement of process variables and parameters are described.

Digital minicomputers are nicely applicable to most tasks of indirect measurement which are too complicated for solution with instrumentation alone. Indirect measurement by computer is desirable and usually feasible when sensors for direct measurement are not available.

The opportunities for such indirect measurements in the service of process control, production accounting, and R&D, are not widely enough appreciated.

The relative advantages of minicomputers (compared with analog or hybrid computers) for indirect measurement are discussed briefly.

The general problem of "indirect identification" of parameters in differential equations is posed, and an approach to the linear case is presented.

Introduction

The purpose of this paper is the stimulation of wider application of minicomputers[1] in process industries for indirect measurement of process variables and parameters by any of a variety of methods.

The paper is aimed at the thousands of engineers in process industries and process control firms whose work requires numerical determination of terms and coefficients in the equations which describe the processes and the equipment in which they take place. The paper is primarily tutorial, pointing out basic mathematical approaches and some of their typical applications in industry. However, the body of the paper does not go into the mathematics at all; it merely refers the reader to helpful treatments in the literature.

The key idea in this paper is that it is often desirable to determine numerical values for dependent variables, forcing functions, or parameters of processes indirectly by use of a computer operating upon other measurements. This possibility is most favorable when the usual practice of direct measurement is impractical. For example, in many situations the required sensor has yet to be developed, and the development effort would be too costly.

Indirect measurement by computer requires the knowledge of some mathematical relationship which holds among the measured quantities and the unknown quantity. This relationship might be a function, an algebraic equation, or a differential equation. The methods differ in detail with the type of relationship, but the indirect measurement principle remains the same.

Indirect measurement is a very common experimental strategy. It is most often implemented with sensors and transducers, which convert measured quantities into the desired quantities. In fact, much of the art of measurement is indirect measurement. Few instruments measure directly the desired quantity. In none of these applications of indirect measurement is a computer necessary, because of the simplicity of the mathematical relationship involved (usually merely a direct proportionality).

The type of indirect measurement which is of concern in this paper is that in which the relationship is sufficiently complicated to render infeasible any hardware short of a small computer. There have been already many isolated applications of this idea, each a clever idea independently conceived. However, there is no standard doctrine or art which an engineer can follow and exploit. The spread of the idea has been haphazard. Thus, although indirect measurement by computer is by no means novel, it deserves wider appreciation as an available approach, a greater degree of formalization of methods, and intensified universal application.

The chief industrial areas of application of the approach are process control, production accounting, and R&D. Indirect measurement by computer is a necessary preliminary to automation of the control of most processes. Many engineers in the management of process industries have made remarks such as the following: "Process control automation is well and good in some industries, but in our unique processes we don't know how to measure some of the chief variables, so why should we think seriously about computer control of our processes?". They do not realize that indirect measurement by computer is a technique which is probably applicable to their problems. Similarly, accountants faced with determination of process inventories and throughputs are not yet accustomed to thinking in terms of indirect measurement by computer as a possible solution to their problems. Likewise, engineers and scientists in an R&D laboratory are more likely to think of Rube Goldberg devices than of computers for measurement, unless their laboratory is well stocked with small computers for just such purposes. Thus, most potential applications lie unimagined.

The organization of the subject which seems most appropriate to this paper is a treatment by

Reprinted from *IEEE Trans. Ind. Electron. Contr. Instrum.*, vol. IECI-17, pp. 358–362, June 1970.

considering one type of mathematical relationship at a time. Each type of relationship gives rise to its own set of mathematical methods of calculation of the desired quantities. Moreover, each set of methods is best suited to particular types of computer hardware (analog, digital, or hybrid).

Function Evaluation

The simplest type of mathematical relationship which is relevant to indirect measurement by computer is an algebraic function. Given some measurements of a variable at certain points and times, one is required to determine the variable at other points or times. The general class of methods which is applicable to this problem is function determination and evaluation. Usually the most suitable function to use is a series, such as a power series (Taylor series) or Fourier series.

One class of methods consists of two steps: (1) determination of the coefficients of the series, (2) evaluation of the function at a particular point or time. The first step is accomplished by application of numerical methods of curve fitting, such as "least squares" (minimization of the sum of the squares of the errors), or Fourier series determination. The second step is accomplished by substitution of coordinates and times into the series formula in order to calculate a specific value of the function.

Another class of methods proceeds in one step. In these methods there is derived a direct formula for interpolation or extrapolation of the given measurements. The type of function used is implicit in the formula, having been assumed in the derivation.

There are many situations in process industries in which function evaluation lends itself to indirect measurement by computer. One category of common situations is a one-dimensional grid of sensors continually giving spatial samples of a variable, such as temperature, from which one is to measure indirectly the temperature at some point which might or might not be a grid point where there is a sensor. For example, one could save the cost of additional sensors by interpolating among readings from a smaller number of sensors than would otherwise be necessary. Also, one could monitor the integrity of all sensor readings by comparing each with the local function value obtained from all of the other sensors, so that malfunctions of sensors or signal lines could be detected promptly and so that synthesized signals could be used in the time during which repairs are being made. In fact, if individual sensors have a significant uncertainty in their readings, none of the readings need to be used directly; instead one can work with only synthesized signals in which individual sensor errors have been washed out to some extent by least squares, thereby increasing the precision of measurement. Another purpose might be to get synthesized measurements at points which are inaccessible.

Similarly, one can interpolate or extrapolate along the time dimension, such as for prediction of a future value of a variable. Thus one can monitor trends, such as slow drifts, in order to take corrective action well in advance of critical need.

More generally, one can determine indirectly a variable in two or three dimensions and time from a grid of sensor readings.

All applications of function evaluation can be implemented with any kind of computer hardware. However, hybrid hardware would never be necessary, so the choice lies between analog and digital. In many cases a digital minicomputer would be most satisfactory and economical, but it would not be prudent to make categorical assertions of universal superiority, disregarding particular conditions surrounding a specific application.

Algebraic Equation Solving

A more complicated type of mathematical relationship which can underlie indirect measurement by computer is one or more algebraic equations. In general, one is dealing with measurements of several different variables, rather than with measurements of the same variable at different points or times.

One classification of methods is in terms of explicit and implicit methods. Explicit methods enable direct calculation; implicit methods are indirect or iterative. Usually direct methods are preferred when the equations are linear, whereas implicit methods might be necessary for nonlinear equations. The most common explicit method for a system of linear equations is matrix inversion, for which many algorithms exist. Even nonlinear systems are often treated in a two-stage process ("quasilinearization"), in which an iterative loop contains a local linearization in the forward path.

A simple example of algebraic equation solving would be the use of the gas law for calculation of the density of a gas at known temperature and pressure in a vessel of known volume. Another example would be the calculation of the weight of a gob of glass, knowing its density, given a few measurements of dimensions in two orthogonal profiles, and making a few assumptions about the shape in three dimensions. Another example would be calculation of the steady-state temperature of an object at an interior point, given sufficient boundary measurements and a formula for the temperature profile. Similarly, one can use algebraic equation solving to find a material property parameter, such as thermal conductivity, given an appropriate formula and given sufficient temperatures, or such as viscosity from velocity or flow measurements. A frequently occurring example of matrix inversion is determining chemical composition of a mixture from a set of readings of spectral peak responses from some instrument. Similarly, one can identify something in a field of view by processing with matrix inversion the outputs from parallel measurements through different filters in a "remote sensing" system.

The hardware appropriate to algebraic equation solving applications could be either digital or analog; hybrid hardware is not necessary. Digital computers are better suited than analog for solution of large sets of linear algebraic equations or for sets of equations in which the matrices are ill-conditioned. Digital computers can be used satisfactorily also for most sets of nonlinear algebraic equations. Analog computers are especially powerful and convenient in cases in which nonlinear equations are to be solved by implicit methods, since control of the gains of the forcing loops is best designed by thinking like that of a control engineer seated at the console of a general-purpose analog computer. In contrast, reliance upon standard algorithms in a digital computer is likely to be risky for solution of nonlinear equations, since one can encounter phenomena such as failure to converge or jumping to a wrong root. On the other hand, the limited dynamic range and precision of analog computers can be a severe handicap in dealing with an ill-conditioned system or a system in which the variables range over several decades of magnitude[2].

Differential Equation Solving

Another general class of methods of indirect measurement by computer is differential equation solving. A differential equation is the appropriate relationship to use when a system's behavior involves the rate of change of the dependent variable. Examples are chemical kinetics and transient temperature distribution. A differential equation arises also if a nonlinear algebraic equation is deliberately converted to an initial value problem for solution, as in the case of the method of steepest descent[3]. If there is only one independent variable (usually time), one has an ordinary differential equation, but if there are two or more independent variables (usually time and one or more space variables) then one has a partial differential equation. In this paper only ordinary differential equations will be considered, since a partial differential equation can readily be converted to a set of ordinary differential equations (such as by property lumping, finite differencing, or by use of normal or assumed mode amplitudes as generalized coordinates).

There are two general problems associated with differential equations: (1) the parameters and forcing function are known, but the dependent variable is to be determined at some particular value of the independent variable, and (2) the dependent variable and forcing function are known as continuous functions of the independent variable, but one or more of the parameter values are unknown. The second problem could be construed to contain also the problem of determining a forcing function, knowing the parameters and the dependent variable. The first problem is merely conventional "solution" of the differential equation; the second problem is the "identification" or "parameter determination" problem. A differential equation can be solved by integration and algebraic operations. Identification, however, is a more complicated procedure, for which many methods are known.

If there is only one unknown parameter (or sometimes even if there are two), the method of "implicit synthesis"[4] can be used. A popular method for any number of unknown parameters is the method of steepest descent[3]. There are also other methods which make use of the local gradient of the error in parameter space. Also there are methods of systematic and/or random search[5].

A more difficult task is identification of a function appearing as a coefficient in a differential equation. Methods for dealing with this problem have been developed[4,5,6,7]. One approach is to represent the function as a series expansion in which the constant coefficients can be found by parameter determination methods. Another approach is to treat the function as if it were a constant, then plot its value continuously against the variable upon which it is presumed to depend, thus revealing the function as a curve[4].

A still more complicated problem is parameter determination in a situation in which the dependent variables cannot feasibly be measured. Since there seems to be no prior art for this problem, a preliminary treatment of it is appended to this paper.

A common class of applications of the identification of forcing functions arises in the case of ambient disturbances of a process. For example, a thermal control system might need to determine the net effect of ambient fluctuations of temperature or convection velocity in order to correct for them.

It is more frequently necessary to determine parameter values. The classic problem of this type is determination of constant coefficients in a linear differential equation. Simple examples are afforded by the equations of motion of an airframe[7,8], whose aerodynamic coefficients might be unknown; the transfer function of a human operator[7,9]; the force coefficients of a tire[7]; the dynamic properties of an artery[10]; and the parameters of an ecosystem[11] or physiological system[12].

All kinds of computer hardware have been applied to problems of identification and solution of differential equations. Hybrid computers are either necessary or economically desirable for very large problems of identification, such as determination of the coefficients (rate constants) in the differential equations for chemical kinetics. This type of problem is so widespread in the process industry that special hybrid and digital software is available (e.g., Electronic Associates Inc.'s OPTRAN[13]). Analog computers are especially valuable as tools during development of new applications of identification, but they can be used also for on-line identification in most cases. Digital computers are less commonly used, but they too are widely applicable. If the set of differential equations is not too large, a minicomputer can do the job nicely.

Conclusions

In summary, there are many points to be made in favor of the use of minicomputers in the process industries for indirect measurement:

1. A minicomputer is nearly always applicable.

2. A minicomputer requires less investment than the smallest available general-purpose hybrid computer, so it is preferable when applicable.

3. Any digital computer has more precision than an analog computer, a fact which is sometimes important.

4. A digital computer has a much greater dynamic range than an analog computer, enabling it to handle easily process problems involving a wide range of values of the variables (such as in start-up of a nuclear reactor).

5. A minicomputer is preferable to a larger digital computer for many purposes and in several respects, such as feasibility of full-time commitment, quick computer reassignment, programming flexibility, and avoidance of conflict among users.

6. If a selection of minicomputers is available, one can be chosen which accommodates the job most nicely and economically.

7. Often the same minicomputer which is used in process control development for indirect measurements can be used also later for automatic control.

8. If a multiplicity of minicomputers are used in the bottom echelon of an automatic control system, it is fairly simple later to put them all under the supervision of a single higher-echelon digital computer; this step would be more difficult if the lower-echelon control and indirect measurement computers were analog.

Appendix

One occasionally encounters a problem of parameter identification in which it is not practical to measure some or all of the dependent variables, although it is possible to measure their sum or weighted sum or some other function of them. This might be called a problem of "indirect identification", in which name the word

"indirect" refers to the fact that the differential equations for the dependent variables cannot be used directly in the identification algorithm.

One example of such a problem would be in the chemical decomposition or radioactive decay of particles which cannot readily be distinguished from one another, whereas one is able to count the total number easily. The task is to determine the values of the decay rate constants or half lives. A closely related problem is determination of the coefficients in differential equations for competition among species, when it is not desirable or feasible to make separate population counts for each species.

One approach to such a problem, which is possible when the differential equations are linear, is to use Laplace transforms[14] to derive a differential equation for the sum of the variables, the coefficients of which, when identified, determine the desired parameters. (The same procedure is applicable to the basic and crucial problem of deriving a differential equation for an aggregated dependent variable for use in an upper-echelon model in a hierarchy of models[15,16].)

Consider, for example, a system represented by two uncoupled differential equations of first order:

$$\begin{cases} \dfrac{dP_1}{dt} = \lambda_1 P_1 + \mu_1 \\ \dfrac{dP_2}{dt} = \lambda_2 P_2 + \mu_2 \end{cases}$$

Here the dependent variables P_1 and P_2 cannot conveniently be measured individually, it will be assumed, whereas it is feasible to measure their sum, say P. The four parameters λ_i and μ_i are to be determined, knowing the time histories of P and its derivatives. The Laplace transform procedure gives:

$$\mathcal{L}(P) = \mathcal{L}(P_1) + \mathcal{L}(P_2)$$

$$= \frac{\mathcal{L}(\mu_1)}{s - \lambda_1} + \frac{\mathcal{L}(\mu_2)}{s - \lambda_2}$$

$$= \frac{(s - \lambda_2)\,\mathcal{L}(\mu_1) + (s - \lambda_1)\,\mathcal{L}(\mu_2)}{(s - \lambda_1)(s - \lambda_2)}$$

Then the desired differential equation is:

$$\frac{d^2P}{dt^2} - (\lambda_1 + \lambda_2)\frac{dP}{dt} + \lambda_1 \lambda_2 P$$

$$= \frac{d\mu_1}{dt} - \lambda_2 \mu_1 + \frac{d\mu_2}{dt} - \lambda_1 \mu_2$$

This differential equation can then be used as the basis for identification of the sum and product of λ_1 and λ_2, hence the values of λ_1 and λ_2 individually, and hence the sum of μ_1 and μ_2. In this case it does not seem possible to separate $\mathcal{M}_1$ and $\mathcal{M}_2$, however, unless either P_1 or P_2 can be measured.

A similar procedure applies to a case in which any number of differential equations are coupled or in which a weighted sum of the dependent variables can be measured. However, the Laplace transform procedure cannot be applied to nonlinear differential equations. New methods are needed for such problems, which could arise in chemical kinetics, ecology[17], physiology, etc. The writer does not know of any work done on these problems.

References

1. Bartik, J. J., "Minicomputers Turn Classic", Data Processing, Jan. 1970, pp. 42-50.

2. Davidson, R. S., and Clymer, A. B., "The Desirability and Applicability of Simulating Ecosystems", Annals of the New York Academy of Sciences, vol. 128, art. 3, Jan. 31, 1966, pp. 790-794.

3. Rogers and Connolly, "Analog Computation in Engineering Design", McGraw-Hill, New York, 1960, Chap. 6.

4. Clymer, A. B., "Direct System Synthesis by Means of Computers", Communication and Electronics (Trans. AIEE), Jan. 1959, pp. 798-806.

5. IEEE Transactions on Automatic Control have contained the greatest concentration of new methods of identification.

6. Kohr, R. H., "On the Identification of Linear and Nonlinear Systems", Simulation, vol. 8, no. 3, March 1967, pp. 165-174.

7. Potts, T. F., Ornstein, G. N., and Clymer, A. B., "The Automatic Determination of Human and Other System Parameters", Proc. of the Western Joint Computer Conference, May 1961, pp. 645-660.

8. Rubin, A. I., "Continuous Regression Techniques Using Analog Computers", IRE Trans. on Electronic Computers, Oct. 1962, pp. 691-699, vol. EC-11, no. 5.

9. Ornstein, G. N., "Applications of a Technique for the Automatic Analog Determination of Human Response Equation Parameters", Ph.D. dissertation, Dept. of Psychology, The Ohio State Univ., 1960.

10. Stacy, R. W., "Diagnosis of Arterial Disease with Analog Computers", IRE Trans. on Medical Electronics, vol. ME-7, no. 4, Oct. 1960, pp. 269-273.

11. Bledsoe, L. J., and Van Dyne, G. M., "Evaluation of a Digital Computer Method for Analysis of Compartmental Models of Ecological Systems", Oak Ridge National Laboratory, ORNL-TM-2414, Feb. 1969.

12. Clymer, A. B., and Graber, G. F., "Trends in the Development and Applications of Analog Simulations in Biomedical Systems", Simulation, April 1964, pp. 41-60.

13. Carlson, A. M., "A Hybrid/Digital Software Package for the Solution of Chemical Kinetic Parameter Identification Problems", Proc. of the Fall Joint Computer Conference, 1969, pp. 733-750.

14. Gardner and Barnes, "Transients in Linear Systems", John Wiley & Sons, New York, 1942.

15. Clymer, A. B., "The Modeling and Simulation of Big Systems", Proc. of the Simulation and Modeling Conference, Pittsburgh, Pa., April 21-22, 1969, pp. 107-118.

16. Clymer, A. B., "The Modeling of Hierarchical Systems", keynote address for the Conference on Applications of Continuous System Simulation Languages, San Francisco, Cal., June 30, 1969, Proceedings pp. 1-16.

17. Clymer, A. B., and Bledsoe, L. J., "A Guide to the Mathematical Modeling of an Ecosystem", Ford Foundation Workshop on Ecological Effects of Weather Modification, Albuquerque, New Mexico, June 1969 (available from authors).

Part V
Specific Applications

This part contains a series of specific examples of problems solved by minicomputers over a wide range of areas. It is included to give the reader something with which to compare and contrast his problem, and to offer helpful hints toward its solution.

The first two articles are surveys of several applications. The remaining articles include examples from the fields of (in order of appearance) chemical process control, education, automatic drafting, analog data acquisition, nuclear instrumentation, and data communication.

Hopefully, the reader will find some information that might apply, or point the way, to the solution of his problem.

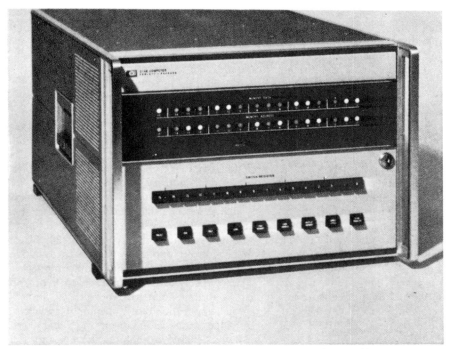

HEWLETT-PACKARD'S 2114B minicomputer is a 16-bit machine.

An IEEE SPECTRUM applications report

Minicomputer applications in the seventies

*Small, programmable digital computers
are taking over many of the tasks that have been handled
in the past by hard-wired logic systems or by large,
expensive computers. The strength of the minicomputer is
in the fact that it is the cheapest form of digital
logic system that you can buy today*

Ronald K. Jurgen   Managing Editor

The purpose of this report is to give the reader, by means of specific application examples, an overview of the extreme versatility of the minicomputer. The basic system configurations that will be described may be adapted, by analogy, to many other tasks. In this manner we hope to stimulate the reader to think about ways in which a minicomputer might be able to do a job for him at less cost, in less time, in a more thorough manner, or more reliably than that job could be done—if it could be done at all—without the minicomputer.

It is beyond the intended scope of this report to discuss minicomputer architecture, to describe in detail commercially available minicomputers, or to attempt to offer detailed guidelines for the selection of a specific minicomputer model for a system.

Reprinted from *IEEE Spectrum*, vol. 7, pp. 37–52, Aug. 1970.

Using as an indicator the publicity given to the mini-computer, one would think that it is a revolutionary new device. It is not. It is the result of engineering know-how in using commercially available integrated circuits to package a physically small computer at low cost.

The term "minicomputer" is catchy but misleading. The "mini" portion of the term is generally appropriate when referring to physical size and cost—and possibly word length and memory size—but not when one is considering computer power. Today's small computers outperform many of yesterday's large computers.

Setting limits on the definition of a minicomputer is an elusive task. A minicomputer is often defined, for example, as a general-purpose, programmable digital computer, small in size, that sells in its basic form for under $20 000. At the low end of the price range (under $7500), however, the minicomputer is apt to be a dedicated or single-purpose computer—a process controller, for example—rather than a general-purpose device. At the upper price limit, the $20 000 selling price is subject to debate. Perhaps the figure should be $25 000, $30 000, or even $40 000. Or should it be less than $10 000? It depends on your point of view.

For purposes of this report we have not attempted to apply strict limits to the cost of a minicomputer. The significant fact is that there are available commercially small digital computers, relatively low in cost, that can do a remarkable variety of jobs extremely well.

FIGURE 1. **A block diagram showing how a digital computer interfaces with man and the real world.**

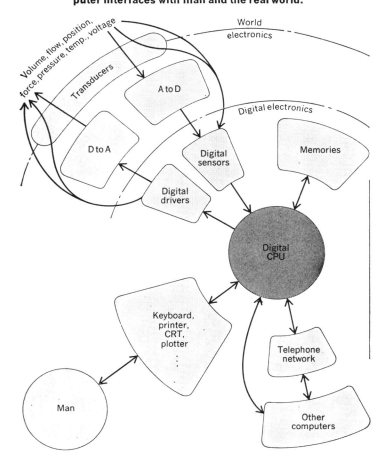

The actual cost of the basic computer is not nearly as important as the cost of the total system in which that computer will be used. Most important of all is whether or not that total minicomputer system cost can be justified for the job that is to be accomplished.

The minicomputer industry is a fast-growing one. The first minicomputer was introduced only about five years ago. Since then—according to Reg A. Kaenel of Bell Telephone Laboratories who chaired a minicomputer session at the recent Spring Joint Computer Conference—more than 10 000 minicomputer installations have been made. The industry has grown, he says, to the point where there are about 100 different minicomputer models available from 62 different manufacturers. For example, at Bell Telephone Laboratories there are 120 mini-computers in use; they consist of 34 different models that have been supplied by 12 different manufacturers.

The proliferation of minicomputer models with varying characteristics can be confusing to a prospective user. An important point to remember, however, is that the specific application of a minicomputer is what determines the value to the user of any one of its characteristics.

Before taking a look at what comprises a typical minicomputer, let us first see how any computer interfaces with man and the real world. Professor Thomas F. Piatkowski of the Thayer School of Engineering at Dartmouth College introduced a recent minicomputer seminar at that college by stating that one can view the computer as a component in the hierarchy of information-transfer devices, as indicated in Fig. 1. He described the illustration as follows: The keypunches, keyboards, printers, plotters, Teletypes, and telephone networks that operate with digital computers are essentially digital in nature. This digital communication is interactive with man typically through printed characters. The central processing unit (CPU), or mainframe, does all of the logical and arithmetical processing associated with the computer. Ordinarily, it comes with a collection of memories—from very fast core memories to slow magnetic and paper tapes. Here, too, all of the devices are essentially digital.

In order to use the computer as a system component to interact with an outside world that is typically nondigital, one must convert the external parameters into equivalent digital signals and also convert digital signals into variables usable in the outside world. In practice, these conversions are accomplished in a number of ways.

Moving from the outside world toward the computer, it might be that the input to the digital sensor can be obtained directly in the outside world. Typically, however, one is dealing with parameters such as volume, flow, position, and force, which are not even electrical in nature. These parameters may be converted to electric analog signals by using analog transducers and then be converted to digital signals. Thus, one can go step-wise through conversion from, say, flow rate to proportional analog voltage to proportional digital signal to digital sensor to computer input. Going in the reverse direction, the computer can influence the outside world by generating digital data that are sent to a driver that has the digital signal converted to analog through a digital-to-analog converter. The analog signal may then go through a transducer and be converted into force or temperature, and so on.

Figure 2 is a block diagram of a simple minicomputer.

154

It was used by Eric M. Aupperle of the University of Michigan in his role as one of the faculty at the recent excellent seminar on minicomputers sponsored by the National Electronics Conference as part of its continuing series of Professional Growth in Electronics Seminars. Mr. Aupperle explained the system components in this manner: The computer control unit (CCU) in Fig. 2 coordinates all of the other parts of the computer to insure that the logical sequence of operations will be carried out correctly and at exactly the right time. The CCU receives its instructions (the stored program provided by the programmer) from memory via the memory control unit. These instructions are interpreted to produce the specific logical sequence required by each program.

The memory modules usually consist of thousands of ferromagnetic cores. For each core one bit or binary digit can be obtained. It is common to deal with a small collection of bits referred to as the computer's memory word. Usually one or more memory modules are purchased for any given minicomputer application. Slower-speed mass-storage devices such as magnetic tape, disk, or drum may also be used. They are not included in Fig. 2 since they are peripherals rather than part of the minicomputer mainframe. Read-only memories are sometimes included as part of the computer main memory or as an addition to or a substitute for the computer's read/write memory.

The memory control unit serves as the master index for the insertion and retrieval of information from the memory modules. Under direction of the CCU it is able to route memory words to and from all of the other units at very high speeds. The time it takes the memory words to go through the memory control unit is called the memory cycle time. The memory control unit is also able to function independently of the CCU when data are transferred at high speed through the direct memory access unit or when several minicomputers share a common memory.

The arithmetic unit accepts data previously stored in the memory or newly provided and performs various algorithmic operations on these data. Results of these arithmetic operations either may be returned to the computer memory or transferred elsewhere, perhaps to the input/output (I/O) unit. The arithmetic unit contains mainly flip-flop registers and gating circuits to provide both temporary storage and complex logical switching.

Most peripheral devices are connected to the I/O bus, an extension of the I/O unit. Through this bus and unit flow commands or output data from the minicomputer to its attached devices (not shown in Fig. 2). In the other direction flows device status information or input data. This combined information flow may be controlled either by the CCU or by individual devices via the minicomputer's interrupt structure.

When data must be transferred quickly, the direct memory access unit is used. This unit, once set in operation by the CCU, is able to pass data directly between memory and a device without intervention of the program that is being executed.

Now that we have seen how a computer interfaces with man and the real world and what a basic minicomputer looks like, let us next consider a generalized minicomputer system such as might be used in a typical application. Again the writer is indebted to Mr. Aupperle for the illustration in Fig. 3 and its explanation. Figure 3

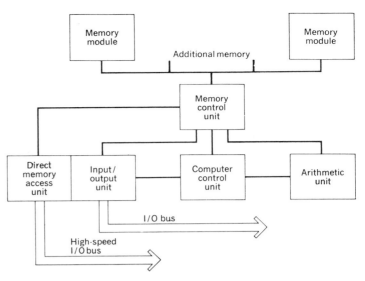

FIGURE 2. Block diagram of a basic minicomputer.

FIGURE 3. A generalized minicomputer system.

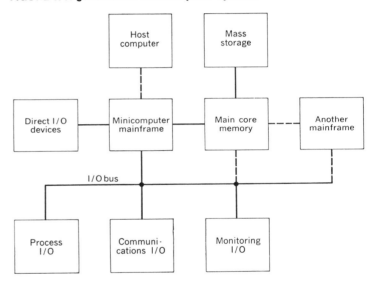

shows a simplified, basic block diagram for a generalized minicomputer system. Excluded from the illustration for the sake of clarity are direct memory access channels, device controllers, interrupt systems, etc. The host computer shown as one of the blocks in Fig. 3 is usually a large computer to which a minicomputer may be tied in certain applications. Variations of this basic block diagram will be used throughout this report as specific categories of applications are discussed.

In order to impart some sense of order, the applications that comprise the major part of this report have been grouped in four categories: original equipment manufacturer (OEM) applications; stand-alone computing, laboratory, and monitoring applications; process control applications; and communications applications. These categories were selected by Mr. Aupperle, except that we have combined stand-alone computing applications with laboratory and monitoring applications. For each category, the basic description quoted and the basic block diagram are Mr. Aupperle's.

It is often difficult to categorize a particular application clearly. In such cases the decision whether to place the application in one category or another has been an arbitrary one. In the OEM category, any one of the application examples could conceivably appear under one or more of the other categories. The distinction here, however, is that the end user is purchasing a system in which the minicomputer is only a component rather than buying the minicomputer as such to incorporate in a system of his own design.

OEM applications

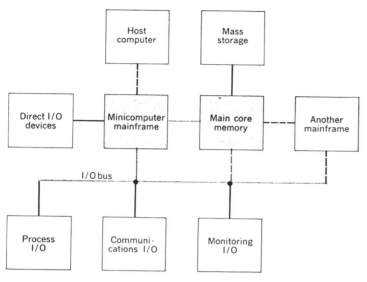

FIGURE 4. Shown in color are those portions of the generalized minicomputer system that pertain to original equipment manufacturer applications.

Those portions of the generalized minicomputer system of Fig. 3 that are relevant to OEM applications are indicated in color in Fig. 4. It is assumed, for purposes of Fig. 4, that a program has been put into the computer.

The following specific applications of minicomputers are typical of those that are in the OEM category.

Performance monitoring system

Control Data Corporation's new CDC 5100 minicomputer is designed to be used in environments that preclude the use of standard commercial computers. Typical of such systems is the Ocean Data Equipment Corporation Model CPMS-216 computerized performance monitoring system. It is designed to be carried on ships for test and monitoring purposes.

One specific application for the CPMS-216 is active sonar testing. The application of a computerized system in testing sonar transducers has significant advantages over the manual methods previously used.

Manual testing involved the use of an oscilloscope to test for signal characteristics of amplitude, current, and phase. The time involved in testing a transducer was five to ten minutes. Typical large systems have several hundred transducer elements active simultaneously and manual methods require several days to collect data.

In contrast, the computerized performance-monitoring system can test several hundred elements in a single

"*Several small computer manufacturers are specializing in the sale of their products as original equipment for other manufacturers to use as components in larger, more complex systems. Clearly, most minicomputers can be used in this way, e.g., as component testers, numerical control machines, automatic weighing systems, and transfer machines. Frequently, this type of application will require only the mainframe and some memory, perhaps even without an input keyboard equipment. In this most basic configuration, minicomputers are extremely inexpensive but the user must be able to develop the necessary interfacing required by his application.*"

"ping" of the system. The full acquisition and correlation of real-time data take about 200 milliseconds. Printing the results takes another 5 seconds. In addition to the time saved, the computerized system also provides higher-quality data and a hard-copy record of the results.

Aside from collecting and recording data that had previously been collected manually, the computerized system provides other information such as signal frequency, circuit impedance, and a real-time analysis of collected data.

The CDC 5100 used in this application is a general-purpose 16-bit minicomputer with 4K to 64K memory (K = 1024 words).

Stored-logic numerical control

A programmable all-stored-logic numerical control that is capable of both contouring and multifunction point-to-point control of machine tools incorporates the mainframe of the Westinghouse Prodac 2000 minicomputer as its logic element. In this instance, Westinghouse, the minicomputer manufacturer, is supplying a minicomputer to Westinghouse, the OEM. The new control operates on instructions from any punched paper tape system or from a general-purpose computer as part of a direct numerical control system.

Typical applications for the control are machining centers, multiaxis vertical turret lathes, horizontal boring mills, multiturret chuckers, and engine lathes.

Figure 5 is a block diagram showing activation of a machine tool by conventional contouring control. The motion interpolator activates the servo system that moves the machine members. Auxiliary functions operate on the machine through the external machine interface magnetics. The machine response to the auxiliary functions is fed back through the interface to the control. The components in the first through third columns—input logic, input control, buffers, and motion interpolator—and the auxiliary functions active store in the fourth column are hard-wired functional programs.

The portion of Fig. 5 that is indicated in color is what is replaced by the minicomputer in the new stored-logic numerical control system. All the hard-wired programs of the conventional contouring control are implemented as software in the minicomputer.

The Westinghouse Prodac 2000 minicomputer is a 16-bit model with 4K of core memory expandable to 32K.

Component test system

The Birtcher Corporation's Model 8000 automatic test system can be used to test discrete components, integrated circuits, logic cards, complete logic assemblies, and many other devices and circuits. The system may be used, for example, for production testing, incoming and final inspection, process control, and engineering evaluation.

The test system has two basic parts: the control section and the measurement section. The control section transmits digital control information to the system's measurement section, which then performs its operational functions as instructed by the control section.

Two different control systems are available with the Model 8000—tape or computer control. The tape-controlled version gives economical, medium-speed, automatic testing with a capability of basic go/no-go testing. When a minicomputer is used for the computer-controlled version the test system becomes extremely versatile, operates at high speeds, and is capable of performing a wide range of sophisticated test programs, including data analyses. The computerized version uses a Lockheed Electronics Company MAC 16 minicomputer. A block diagram of the computer-controlled system is shown in Fig. 6.

The MAC 16 is a 16-bit device with 4K to 64K plug-in core memory and a one-microsecond cycle time.

Remote monitoring system

Integrated Systems, Inc., designs and builds "Duo-Scan" remote control, alarm, and telemetering systems.

The basic block diagram of the system is shown in Fig. 7. Time division multiplex is used on all inputs. Each input is sequentially examined by the remote encoder and inputs are transmitted repeatedly, one after the other, over a narrow-band communications channel to the master station decoder. The status of all inputs at the remote station is received at the master station and reconverted to parallel information by the decoder. In the Duo-Scan system, this procedure is repeated once, thereby requiring two identical pulse frames before the information received is considered valid.

To provide increased flexibility in the system, Integrated Systems is now using a GRI-909 minicomputer manufactured by GRI Computer Corporation. The computer permits the system to be adapted to changing scan rate requirements and numbers of inputs. It provides logged alarms in special formats and makes calculations and decisions on digitally telemetered quantities to determine if a given reading is out of limits or exceeds a certain rate of change. On-line system analysis can be performed based upon point status and telemetered quantities. The computer can issue control commands when initiated by an operator or automatically in emergency conditions.

The computer interfaces with the system by replacing the Duo-Scan decoder and performs all the manipulations of the code word that the normal decoder would accomplish.

The basic computer master system can handle up to 100 remote substations, each with up to 254 points of control, or, in a data logging system, at each of 100 re-

FIGURE 6. Component test system.

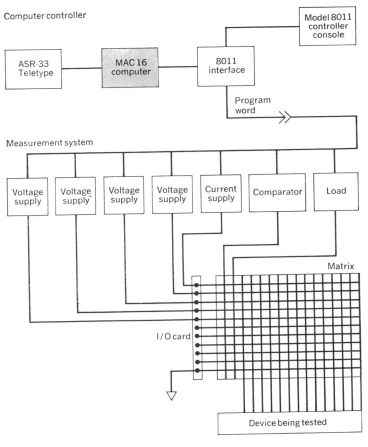

FIGURE 5. Block diagram showing activation of a machine tool by conventional contouring control. Area in color has been replaced by a minicomputer.

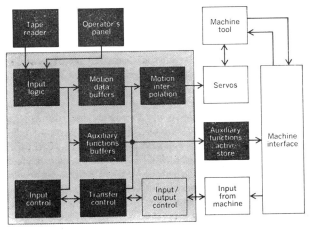

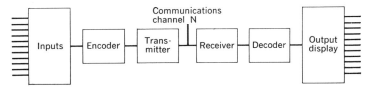

FIGURE 7. Duo-Scan alarm or telemetering system for handling up to 100 remote substations.

mote substations it can continuously monitor and update up to 256 points every 16 seconds.

The GRI-909 computer has a 16-bit parallel-word format, 4K to 32K memory, and 1.76-μs cycle time.

Data-handling system

A good example of a multicomputer hierarchy—a complex system in which smaller computers are subordinated to larger computers in order to save costs and facilitate communication—is the System Seventy designed by Mark Computer Systems and scheduled for installation this fall by the Uni-Card Division of the Chase Manhattan Bank. Based on Data General Corporation's Supernova minicomputer, Mark's System Seventy will be used by Uni-Card for on-line data entry and file inquiry into Uni-Card's IBM 360/50. The availability of the

minicomputer-based system will not only facilitate data handling but may also eliminate the need for a second system 360 as a backup. This type of business data processing is common for large computers but has not usually incorporated minicomputers.

In the initial installation, each of the two Supernovas will control 20 DD-70 CRT terminals, also designed by Mark, and each of the minicomputers will be responsible for the entry of individual sales transactions and a variety of system housekeeping tasks such as account status changes and credit authorization. The installation will pave the way for eventual entry of Uni-Card sales from remote terminals located in merchant stores.

In performing all its functions, the System Seventy is designed to look to the 360/50 like a magnetic tape drive. This reduces the user's interface problems substantially and also relieves the larger computer of additional housekeeping tasks.

If the 360 should go out, an exception file of accounts to which credit should not be extended can be transferred from magnetic tape to the Supernova disk. The Supernova can then answer credit authorization inquiries on a yes or no basis while, at the same time, temporarily storing the transaction information until it can be transferred to the 360.

The Supernova is a 16-bit minicomputer with 4K-32K of core memory, read-only memory, and an 800-nanosecond cycle time.

Stand-alone computing, laboratory, and monitoring applications

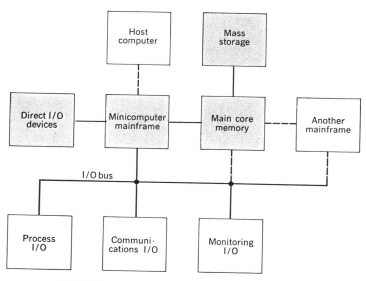

FIGURE 8. Stand-alone computing applications use those portions of the generalized minicomputer system of Fig. 3 that are shown in color.

"Stand-alone computing applications occur typically in university and research laboratories or in industrial engineering departments where real-time (as distinct from batch programming) analysis and computation are required.... Laboratory and monitoring applications represent an extension of stand-alone computing applications where usually a variety of transducers, sensors, multiplexers, and analog-to-digital converters are connected to the basic stand-alone system. Included in this category are systems configured for data acquisition, spectrum analysis, fast Fourier transformations, biological studies, medical research, oceanographic analysis, experimental physics, and many others."

Those portions of the generalized minicomputer system of Fig. 3 that are relevant to stand-alone computing applications are shown in color in Fig. 8. The direct I/O devices usually are Teletypes but paper-tape readers and punches or card readers and line printers might be

added as I/O devices. The mass storage facility can be magnetic tape, disk, or drum storage devices—or, possibly, tape cassettes.

Those portions of the generalized minicomputer system of Fig. 3 that are relevant to laboratory and monitoring applications are shown in color in Fig. 9. These applications require a lot of individual tailoring of hardware. In the monitoring I/O block one would find such devices and converters as operational amplifiers, sample and hold circuits, analog-to-digital converters, digital-to-analog converters, digital voltmeters, counters, multiplexers, oscilloscope displays, plotters, programmable signal generators and power supplies, and special-purpose transducers and sensors.

The following selected applications are typical of those in the stand-alone computing, laboratory, and monitoring category.

Test of a new propulsion system

A 250-mi/h (400 km/h) linear induction motor test vehicle, Fig. 10, is being low-speed-tested with the help of a minicomputer by the Garrett Corporation under a contract from the U.S. Department of Transportation.

The heart of the electric-propulsion research is a Varian Data Machines 620/i general-purpose minicomputer located in a nearby instrumentation and telemetry trailer.

The goal of the testing program is to develop practicality studies for the new propulsion method. A vehicle propelled by a linear induction motor is theoretically capable of high speeds because thrust isn't limited by rail-wheel contact. The linear induction motor is a rotary motor that is cut along a radius, unrolled, and laid out flat. This technique gives an air gap between the primary and secondary windings, allowing linear motion between the two. One of the members is lengthened along the path of travel so that motion can be continuous.

In collecting data to evaluate the system, the Varian minicomputer accepts telemetered data into two buffers at the rate of 32 000 readings—i.e., data words—per second. The computer actually serves as a speed regulator for the data coming in from the vehicle. Incoming data are filling up one buffer as the other is feeding data to a magnetic tape. When the first buffer is filled, it starts feeding data to the tape while the second buffer starts accepting incoming data from the sensors on board the vehicle.

This procedure saves test time, according to Garrett engineers, and enables them to record accumulated data on the tapes in the correct format. One reel of magnetic tape covers a 10-minute run and contains more than 20 million data words.

Tapes filled with data from the minicomputer are calibrated and converted to engineering terms by another program fed into the minicomputer that uses an additional 32K of disk storage. The results from later data analysis will enable investigators to determine performance characteristics of the linear induction motors.

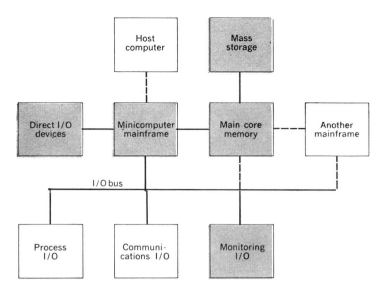

FIGURE 9. Laboratory and monitoring applications use those portions of Fig. 3 shown in color.

The Varian 620/i is a 16-bit machine equipped with an 8K core memory.

Multiprocessing approach to engine testing

Small computers have come into widespread use in all types of development and testing laboratories for combustion engines. The computers are used to increase testing efficiency, which can mean either to enable more tests to be performed per test stand or to get the results of a given test to the engineer sooner.

The functions performed by the computer can be divided into two broad categories—test measurement and control, and generation of test reports. Parameters measured in almost all reciprocating-engine tests include torque, speed, fuel consumption, and a variety of temperatures and pressures. In many test stands, the control consists of throttle and dynamometer load control, which enables programmed performance testing to be done automatically.

A multiprocessing computer system, the MODCOMP III/70 by Modular Computer Systems, is shown in Fig. 11.

FIGURE 10. Linear induction motor test vehicle that is being low-speed-tested with the aid of a minicomputer.

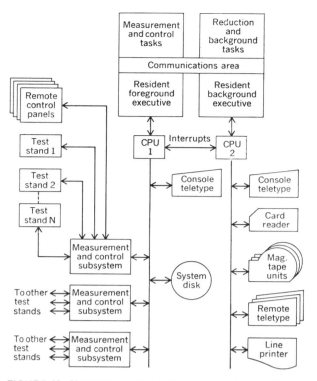

FIGURE 11. Multiprocessing system for engine testing.

A principal advantage of the multiprocessor approach to foreground/background applications is the degree of security provided between the foreground and background functions. For example, CPU 2, Fig. 11, cannot affect the measurement and control subsystem or the memory, interrupts, or any machine states associated with CPU 1. It can only interrupt CPU 1 at a preassigned level and communicate through the common memory area addressable by both computers.

A second advantage of the multiprocessor approach is system backup capability. If CPU 1 or its private memory becomes inoperable, CPU 2 and associated memory can be connected to take over the foreground tasks, including recording data on magnetic tape if required. Thus, testing can continue. Test backlog buildup and idling of test personnel because of computer failure also can be avoided.

The flexibility of the multiprocessor system can be made as great as desired. New test cells and new test programs can be brought on line without requiring system shutdown. Each CPU can have access to the peripherals connected to the other CPU by I/O service requests through the interrupt and common communications facility.

Medical research

The Cardiovascular-Renal Research Laboratory at Howard University monitors cardiac dimensions and pressures in conscious dogs and derives dynamic ventricular performance data with a Hewlett-Packard general-purpose 2116B minicomputer with a 16K memory.

Figure 12 shows the measured variables, conditioned and derived signal paths, and the elements of the data acquisition and processing system used at Howard. With a variety of implanted sensors, the investigators measure, monitor, and record the primary cardiac variables of physical dimensions, pressures, flow rate, ECG, and heart rate of conscious dogs, acquiring the data under computer control. After a selection is made of the segment of data that is of particular interest, the data are used as source information for rapid calculation by the computer of the parameters descriptive of dynamic cardiac performance such as cardiac output, flow, power, wall stresses, and other information.

The minicomputer permits the on-line computation, printout, and display of the measured and derived quantities. It also permits the simultaneous measurement, in-

It consists of two 16-bit computers that have shared core memory as well as private core memory. Each is capable of interrupting the other and communicating via shared memory. In engine testing, the system is applied as follows:

One CPU is assigned the measurement and control functions for all test stands. Test stand measurements are collected and stored. The second processor is then called to store the test data on magnetic tape for subsequent processing. This second processor produces test reports from the data stored on magnetic tape for archiving. In addition, it is capable of performing independent functions such as program assemblies, compilations, or executions.

FIGURE 12. Basic elements of a minicomputer system for testing ventricular performance in conscious dogs.

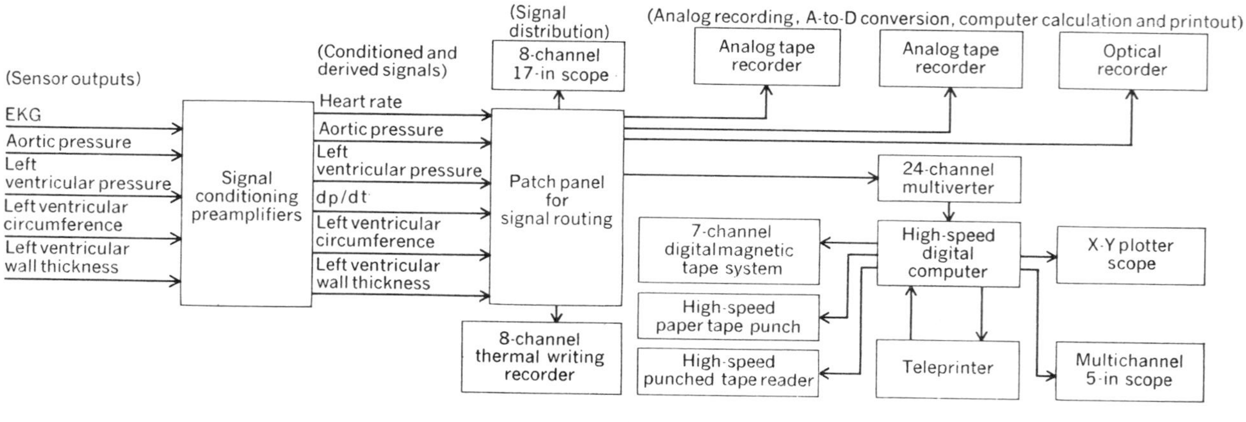

IEEE spectrum AUGUST 1970

the intact animal, of the variables for a moment-to-moment assessment of ventricular performance.

IC logic card testing

A minicomputer that can accommodate a specially built 160-line buffer to expand its basic 16-line I/O bus capability is making as many as 650 tests of 60-circuit IC logic cards in only milliseconds whereas it previously took a highly skilled operator several hours.

Computer Entry Systems, Inc., a manufacturer of time-shared, multistation key-to-disk systems, is using a Varian 620/i minicomputer to cut costs and personnel training expenses while at the same time guaranteeing that the logic cards used in its systems are 100 percent free of logic circuitry flaws. The minicomputer determines whether various logic circuits are go or no-go and also determines where the failure is when one is detected.

When the minicomputer was introduced into the testing process, Computer Entry Systems built its own 160-pin buffer to expand the minicomputer's output capability and also constructed a low-cost tape transport to interface with it. This tape stores programs developed by the company, retains the assembler for the minicomputer, and also stores a look-up table in memory which holds the addresses for instituting various test procedures and programs.

In a sense, the Varian computer programs itself when it receives the signals that tell it which part of the preformatted tape to read. An untrained, inexperienced operator can then sit down at the test console, enter through Teletype various accounting routines such as item part number, date, etc., and then tell the minicomputer to start the test.

The machine goes to the appropriate portion of the tape, reads the program required, and looks up the appropriate procedure in the look-up table. It then executes all the required tests for the logic card in question and signals go or no-go. If a part has not tested properly, the minicomputer pinpoints the circuit at fault.

Before the minicomputer system was installed, the firm was hiring trained test operators to test the logic cards on a pin-to-pin basis. After training and setting operational procedures and inspection routines, the test operation took several hours.

Process control applications

"This class of applications usually places a minicomputer system in charge of an industrial manufacturing, treating, assemblying, etc., operation. The range of applications also is broad. At one extreme are systems designed largely for monitoring,* next comes systems with progressively more control sophistication in addition to their monitoring functions, and, at the other extreme, are systems using adaptive control concepts. While most process control applications occur in continuous operations (e.g., chemical, glass, steel plants), there are considerable interest and activity by discrete part manufacturers in incorporating small computers in their plants. Finally, it should be clarified how this class of applications differs from OEM applications. Truthfully, the distinction is largely one of degree rather than of fundamental differences. In the former case only the mainframe is imbedded in the equipment it controls. Here the mainframe, usually augmented by several peripherals, is viewed more as a separate element in the system. In many cases it is added to already existing equipment and/or shared among several pieces of equipment."

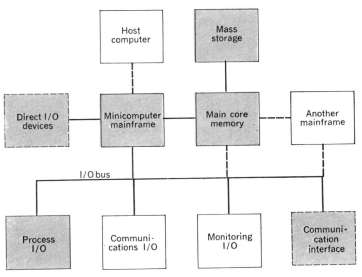

FIGURE 13. Process control applications use the portions of Fig. 3 that are shown in color.

The portions of Fig. 3 that are relevant to a typical process control application are shown in color in Fig. 13. The process control I/O block will contain both analog and digital output devices. Analog output signals cover a broad range of voltage and current levels; digital outputs can be in the form of logic levels, pulsed signals, or contact closures provided by relays. The signals are used to

---

* These systems might alternatively be considered with laboratory and monitoring applications and the distinction, if any, is application rather than functional.

drive and control the actuators of the process equipment.

The following applications are typical of those in this category.

Nuclear-fuel-handling system

The precision of a Digital Equipment Corporation PDP-8/S process minicomputer will control refueling operations at the 330-MW (e) Fort St. Vrain Nuclear Generating Station near Denver, Col. Gulf General Atomic developed the automated refueling system for

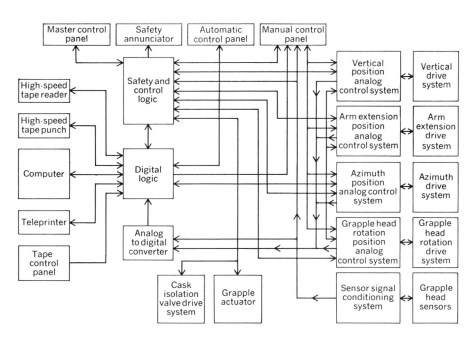

FIGURE 14. Computerized nuclear-fuel-handling system.

the advanced nuclear plant, which is under construction by GCA for Public Service Company of Colorado.

The reactor core contains nearly 3000 uranium/thorium-loaded graphite blocks located inside a prestressed concrete containment vessel. The hex-shaped blocks, about 80 cm tall, are arranged in vertical stacks some six meters high.

In order to accomplish the transfer of fuel, a large fuel-handling machine is used. (It is 14 meters high and weighs 160 tonnes.) The heart of the machine is the manipulator mechanism and its control system. A block diagram of the system is shown in Fig. 14. There are four controlled freedoms of motion. Automatic control is initiated from the automatic control panel. Included are the digital computer, its I/O interface hardware, and peripheral equipment consisting of paper-tape reader and punch and a teleprinter.

The tape-control panel allows the operator to input information to the computer by means of paper tape without actually using the more complex controls on the computer itself. A multiplexed analog-to-digital converter brings analog signals to the computer from position potentiometers, grappling head translations, and tachometers.

The safety and control logic contains hardware interlocks and failure protection devices. A prime consideration in the design of this system was to maintain a failsafe condition at all times and to prevent inadvertent operator error. Connecting to the positioning mechanisms are the control interfaces, which are basically analog servo systems.

The computer-controlled system has been completed, mated with the fuel-handling machine, and is now being used to test the machine operation.

Minimization of the time involved in refueling is desirable because no electric power is being produced by the plant during the refueling period. Initial studies indicated that a manually controlled fuel-handling machine would be too time consuming to operate, would be

subject to operator error because of the numerous steps involved, and would create a problem in fuel inventory. A number of automated control types were then investigated. Numeric control by paper tape was studied but ruled out due to requirements for decision making during the fuel-handling process and the desirability for a flexible control that could be modified easily as the system was developed and put into operation. A digital-computer-based control system was finally selected. Tests have shown that fuel movement under computer control is three times faster than under manual control, which is provided as a backup mode of operation.

The minicomputer used in this application is a PDP-8/S with 4K memory. It was selected for the application some time ago during the initial design of the system, and can be replaced by either the PDP-8/L or PDP-8/I in future applications.

Glass batch weighing

At the Dartmouth College seminar on minicomputers, T. H. Finger of Owens-Illinois presented a paper on an automated glass batch plant computer system. The description of the system that follows was excerpted from his paper.

Glass batching is that portion of the glass-making process in which various raw materials are stored, weighed, mixed, and delivered to the glass furnace for melting. The glass batch plant that was described in the paper was one that was modernized from a manual weigh system to a process control computer system.

The batch plant is designed to weigh and deliver 1800 tonnes of mixed raw material per day in 4-tonne batches. A typical glass batch is made up of 2540 kg of sand, 815 kg of soda ash, 725 kg of lime, and various minor material. The weigh tolerance on 2540 kg of sand is ±4.5 kg and on the smaller minor ingredients is ±0.05 kg.

The batch house is divided into two weigh lines, each of which can operate independently of the other. The raw

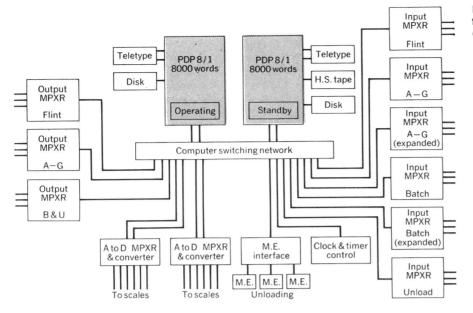

materials are weighed into the scales from silo bins and after complete weighing are delivered to a high-speed gathering conveyor that directs them to the check scales. The actual weight from each scale is totaled and compared with the check scale weight to verify that all material was delivered to the check scale. The materials are then delivered to a mixer and, after mixing, are delivered to the furnace requiring the batch. In the plant, there are nine furnaces in the system, two batch bins each, for a total of 18 batch bins to schedule.

The plant modernization will include a total of 22 new scales, new conveyors, new mixers, and a new batch conveying system. The computer system will schedule the furnaces and weigh the raw materials.

The Owens-Illinois approach has been to size the computer system to do the task, as would be done in purchasing any other type of equipment, rather than defining a computer system and then developing enough tasks to justify the expenditure.

The first function of the computer is for direct control of the turning on and off of equipment. Material flowing into the 22 scales will be controlled, as will the control of the weighed raw material and its flow to the nine furnaces, with various printed outputs as records.

To accomplish these controls various interfaces were designed for process monitoring or reading of process information into the computer—mainly, are switches open or closed? There are six input multiplexers (switch selectors) in the system of 84 points each for a total of 504 contact sense points. Three output multiplexers of 72 points each for a total of 216 relay closures are used. Also included are two analog-to-digital converters and multiplexers of 24 points each for a total of 48 voltage readings.

The process monitoring or checking of various conditions will cover 54 bin level sensors, 120 equipment positions (is a gate open or closed?, is a mixer on or off?), 35 equipment service switches (is the equipment in or out of service, or is a diverter in a correct position?),

35 manual entry decades, and 85 scale unit weights (beam counterbalance weights).

Process control in the system will add and subtract unit weights to the scales as the weighing is performed. In all, there are 42 scale unit weighs, 31 scale gates, 65 raw material gates, 4 conveyors, 18 equipment on–offs, and 18 furnace schedules under process control. Process analog, or the measurement of voltage and the reading of

FIGURE 16. Minicomputer control of a remote electric power substation is accomplished with the system shown.

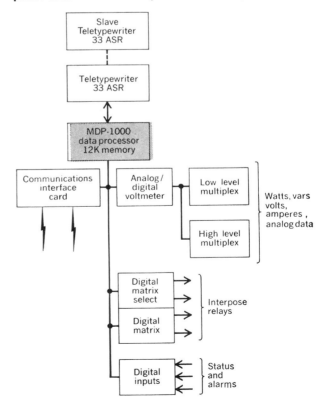

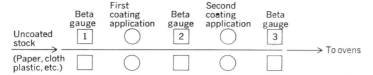

FIGURE 17. Basic components of a system for applying various coatings to uncoated stock.

FIGURE 18. Computer-based system that permits non-destructive testing of coating thickness.

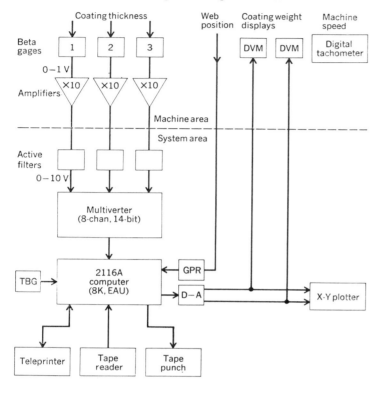

the raw material scales, covers 42 scale weight potentiometers, two power supply voltages, and four test voltages.

A block diagram of the complete computer system is shown in Fig. 15. Two Digital Equipment Corporation PDP-8/I minicomputers, each with 8K core memory and 32K disk storage, are used. One is the operating computer and the other is a standby computer. If the operating computer fails, a computer switching network turns over the process to the standby computer, which is also used for off-line programming for the system.

The interfaces are divided into subgroups so that a failure of one subsystem will not stop the whole process. At the right in Fig. 15 are the input multiplexers for the reading of information from the process into the computer. Six small input multiplexers are used instead of one large one so that failure of one would not affect the other parts of the process. Two analog-to-digital converters and multiplexers are on the left in Fig. 15. Again, two are used for redundancy. At the bottom right are the unloading manual entry stations and the clock and timer control.

A standard electromagnetic weigh system was originally proposed for the modernization. The proposed equipment specifications, the material flow timing layout, point

list, and hardware specifications were determined. Next, the hardware and software programming was done. The computer system economics was based upon the replacement of the electromechanical weighing equipment.

A general rule was used that the interface and sensors should cost about the same as the basic computer system and that the software programming should cost about the same as the computer system.

The total process control computer system and software programming is about one half the cost of the standard electromechanical equipment—but that does not include the extra computer. The extra computer system was purchased in lieu of a three-shift service computer maintenance contract.

Control of a remote power substation

Supervisory control of a remote, unattended power station with a Motorola minicomputer has been accomplished by Wisconsin Electric Power for its new Granville Substation. Increasing power demands required system expansion and the need arose for a substation at Granville with a new set of requirements for control, indication, and event recording that exceeded the functional capability of the existing Telememory remote.

The Motorola Control Systems Division MDP-1000 minicomputer is used at Granville to perform the following functions:

1. It receives control commands from a central station and operates the circuit breakers.

2. It stores data, and upon request of the central station, converts the data to binary coded decimal form and transmits it to the central station for display.

3. It scans ampere quantities every two minutes and performs high-limit checks for out-of-limit alarming.

4. It performs logging functions by logging data on the hour and listing all out-of-limit alarms still existing at that time and logging circuit breaker status changes in the order in which they occur and alarming the dispatcher in the event of abnormal operation.

A block diagram of the system is shown in Fig. 16. Changes are reported to the central station as soon as they occur. When the central station issues a control command, the MDP-1000 accepts the command, checks it for validity by performing multiple security checks, and decodes it. The computer then sends a signal via the appropriate digital command module in the I/O module network to operate the correct interpose relay of the two provided for each circuit breaker. One relay closes the circuit breaker, the other trips it. When the command has been carried out, a signal is returned through the correct I/O module to this effect. The computer challenges this signal and requires that its correctness be verified. When correctness is confirmed, the computer initiates a change-of-status signal to the central station, which changes the status display at the central. Status indications also are logged locally. Time of occurrence is added automatically as part of the logging routine.

Status indications are logged in the order of occurrence. The status of 65 points is monitored every 4 ms so that any changes in control positions or measured values will be detected within that time. In order to detect status changes with 4-ms resolution, the 65 points are scanned continuously. The computer checks eight points each of eight digital input cards in the I/O card cage.

164

In addition to cycling through the 65 points at 4-ms intervals, the MDP-1000 collects quantitative data, does data logging, and reports alarms. Scanning for ampere quantities that exceed the high limit is initiated every two minutes. The computer also stores watts, vars, and voltage levels. At hourly intervals it signals the ASR 33 Teletype through the appropriate I/O module and logs about 35 quantitative data readings indicative of plant operation. These include 15 ampere readings, eight voltage readings, six megawatt readings, and six megavar readings.

The MDP-1000 has 4K to 16K core memory with an access time of 2.16 μs.

Coating thickness detection

Measurement and control of coating weights is of major production concern to the Norton Company. Destructive sampling wastes money in terms of material destroyed and requires production stoppages. Material is also wasted if more than the optimum amount is applied. Conversely, the product will not give satisfaction if coating thicknesses are below specification or vary too much.

A minicomputer-based system permits the nondestructive testing of coating thickness. In this method, coating thicknesses are measured by beta gages that provide an electrical output related to the mass of material in the gage measuring gap. Gages are placed before and after each coating station. The process block diagram is shown in Fig. 17.

The complete system diagram is shown in Fig. 18. The system is under control of a Hewlett-Packard 2116A minicomputer with 8K memory. Web speed (up to 1 meter/second) is measured through a switch closure occurring for every 6 cm of web passing through the machine, which acts as an interrupt to the general-purpose register. This allows 66 ms for measurement, computation, and output, but only 12 ms were required in practice. Since the speed of the web and the web length between reading heads were known, an appropriate delay was inserted between samples of successive beta gage outputs so that the same portion of the web was measured.

Computed digital displays of the two coating weights are provided for the machine operator, using the two outputs of the digital-to-analog converter to drive two three-digit digital voltmeters. A digital tachometer can be switched by the operator to read web speed, coating material supply speed, etc.

In operation, the system measures, computes, and outputs the actual net coating weights to the process operator about five times per second. At the completion of each run (up to 915 meters) the system outputs a run data summary, listing average weights and standard deviations for the backing material and each of the coatings.

Communications applications

"Minicomputers are and will continue to serve many vital communications applications. One example is data concentrating systems where a number of low-speed input devices such as Teletypes and other human input/output terminals are connected to the minicomputer. The minicomputer then concentrates all of this data to transmit it efficiently to some other device, usually a larger computer. Another example is the use of minicomputers to facilitate intercomputer (large CPU systems) data transmission. Still another is the addition of a card reader, line printer, and a communication interface to a minicomputer to build a remote batch terminal for a large central processor. Minicomputer time-sharing systems may be included here too. Such applications have been known for a long time, but have been seriously considered only in the last few years. Considerable activity in data communications will be generated in the future."

The portions of Fig. 3 that are relevant to communications applications are shown in color in Fig. 19. Mass storage devices are not always included but most systems include one or more direct I/O devices in addition to the communications hardware. Some kind of interface to a host computer is common. The communications I/O block may contain data set controllers to service various common carrier data sets.

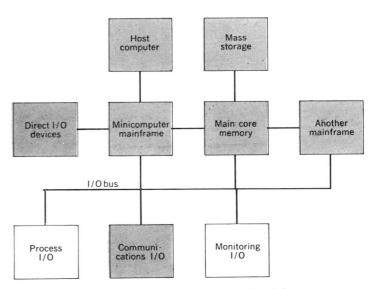

FIGURE 19. The portions of the generalized minicomputer system of Fig. 3 that are used for communications applications are shown in color.

The selected applications that follow are typical of communications applications.

Warehouse data handling

A major reason behind the proliferation of minicomputers has been their application in new and frequently never-before-computerized jobs. The chief advantage of the minicomputer in such applications is its ability to provide an improvement in price/performance over the way a job has been done before.

Newly developed uses of minicomputers in noncontrol applications such as warehousing and retailing point up both the versatility of the small computer and the advantages it can provide to the user. One system, developed for warehouse applications around Data General Corporation's Nova minicomputers, consists essentially of a series of free-standing minicomputer systems, each of which may be used as a terminal for a larger computer. Each of the remote minicomputers in the system is tailored to a specific warehousing situation and each is designed for use by unsophisticated warehouse personnel.

The small computer is programmed to operate in a question-and-answer mode. The computer presents the series of questions and warehouse personnel check off the correct answers. Use of the minicomputers on site at the warehouse eliminates the need for more expensive data communication facilities. The small computers may also perform certain data processing on site, including inventory control, payroll, and other duties related to the specific warehouse.

As the on-site computation is completed, the minicomputers, now acting as terminals, condense the data and forward relevant parts over telephone lines to the central computer facility for further data processing and management information on the corporate level.

Small computers acting as terminals also may be used to save communication costs. One such system has been designed for a major retail operation to allow the retailer to take advantage of a party line telephone cost and reduce the number of telephone lines required. In this instance, it proved possible to cut the telephone bill from a potential $10 000 per month to $1200 per month. Equally important was the fact that the retail warehouse network system was designed around existing production facility procedures, thus enabling each computer in the system also to act as a translator between the individual warehouse departments and the machine's central processor.

Supermarket control

The Food Fair Store in Baldwin Hills, Calif., is the scene of a wedding between a cash register and a minicomputer to produce a totally new control system.

The shopper gradually notices that each item in a department has the same color label but its own code number and that odd-weight packages of meats and produce are stamped simply with a price per pound. At the checkout station, the checker taps the code color, code number, and quantity into a counter terminal whose display flashes the correct price for each purchase. Since 60 percent of all products sold are groceries, the system is programmed to assume that a grocery sale of one item has been made unless otherwise indicated.

The checker is completely relieved from concern with such factors as prices, coupons, and sales taxes. Meats and produce are weighed and priced automatically. The computer even notifies the checker of any invalid entry and waits for a correction before the next entry can be punched. The customer is provided an accurate, detailed record as shown in Fig. 20. Officials of Inventory Management Systems, who designed the system for Food Fair, believe it can be improved by having the checker hold a portable electronic scanner before the coded label on an item. The scanner will read the code into the computer system, which will print out, via the terminal, the correct information on the customer's receipt tape.

A block diagram of the system is shown in Fig. 21. It uses a Honeywell DDP-516 in the prototype system or a Honeywell H316 in the standard version. When the checker enters an item code, a multiplexer identifies the particular check-stand number, adds an address, forwards data with the address attached, and converts the data into EIA-compatible signals. The multiplexer shifts levels to convert data from digital and logical numbers to frequency changes that can be handled by the telephone data set. It scans all terminals for information, which is forwarded over a single telephone line to a remotely located data center where another data set converts the frequency back to EIA levels. A communication-line controller then converts the signals into logical levels for computer input.

The computer accepts the data, identifies the source terminal, stores the new data, and performs arithmetic or erasing functions. The computer then sends return messages via the controller and data set, telephone line, data set, and multiplexer back to the specific terminal. Backup provisions include two telephone lines between the store and the data center and an H316 computer on the store premises.

In the standard system, the H316 is the primary computer in a central data center. The Honeywell H112 is

FIGURE 20. Customer's record of marketing transactions at minicomputer-controlled supermarket.

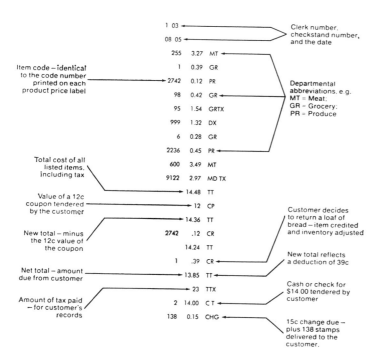

used as a controller for a Librascope disk in the store for backup purposes. This backup eliminates the need for more than one lease line per store.

The system's most valuable asset is probably its real-time capability for updating inventory records at the store, warehouse, and within a total retailing network. This approach permits accurate electronic ordering. When the checker records an item purchased (or returned) the inventory of the item at each level is corrected.

System benefits are extensive. Automatic recording is possible, each store's ideal product mix can be determined, capital investment (e.g., cash registers) can be reduced or eliminated, and daily and weekly sales reports by department, as well as weekly reports of low turnover items, are available.

The H316 is a minicomputer with 4K to 16K memory, disk storage option, and 1.6-μs cycle time. The H112 is a 12-bit stored-program controller with 4K to 8K memory and 1.69-μs cycle time.

Telephone trouble reporting

A Motorola MDP-1000 minicomputer in combination with a MDR-1000 electronic document reader is making more efficient the handling of customer telephone troubles for a western telephone company. The system being used for reporting trouble to the proper service center and initiating corrective action has reduced both costs and reaction time substantially.

When trouble is reported, a clerk checks the appropriate boxes on a printed form. At frequent intervals the forms are collected and placed in the document reader, which reads the cards automatically and transfers the information they contain via dataphone data set to the computer.

In the system, the computer performs the function of separating and classifying the trouble information, then routing it to the proper service center. It also performs an accounting function. In this role, it classifies and summarizes the trouble information by type and source of trouble.

The statewide system consists of nine terminals that originate trouble reports and 16 terminals to which trouble information is routed for action. The computer polls the readers in sequence and transmits the sorted trouble information in a format suitable for Teletype readout.

In-house time-sharing system

The Wang Laboratories Model 3300 Basic is a low-cost, easily operated minicomputer time-sharing system. It accommodates any number of terminals up to 16. With the Wang Model 1103A acoustic coupler, the user may operate from remote locations using a Teletype terminal and standard telephone lines.

The central processor is an 8-bit minicomputer called the 3300. It has 4K memory expandable to 64K and 1.6-μs cycle time.

Since the Wang system uses an extended version of the Basic language developed at Dartmouth College as a problem-solving tool, it is easily used for solving mathematical problems. The steps involved in solving a quadratic equation for its real roots are as follows:

Given the equation

$$2x^2 + 9x + 3 = 0$$

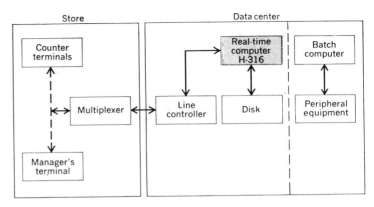

FIGURE 21. Block diagram of a supermarket system controlled by a minicomputer.

when

$$x = \frac{-B \pm \sqrt{B^2 - 4AC}}{2A}$$

Turn on the terminal-press ATTENTION key
BASIC READY. (The system is ready to go.)
:10 REM THIS SOLVES THE QUADRATIC
:20 LET B = 9, LET A = 2, LET C = 3
:30 LET S = SQR (B ↑ 2 − 4 * A * C)
:40 PRINT "X1 =", (−B + S)/2*A, "X2 =", (B−S)/2*A
:Run—
X1 = −0.36254134 X2 = −4.1374586

Conclusion

This report has concentrated on presenting specific minicomputer applications to give the reader an insight into the wide range of minicomputer capabilities. As was stated earlier, it is beyond the scope here to discuss in detail how systems are configured or how minicomputers are selected. But one grossly simplified example of a system configuration may serve as an indicator of just how involved the configuration of a complex system may be.

Hewlett-Packard tells the potential user of one of its HP 9500 Series Automatic Test Systems how to configure a system of his own. It involves making a block diagram with the computer in the center, leaving room above for computer input and output devices, with stimulus instruments on the left, measuring instruments on the right, and switching devices on the bottom. After particular instruments and interfaces are selected from information supplied by Hewlett-Packard, the next step is to totalize the I/O channel and memory requirements from the information given about the various instruments.

For memory requirements, you add the expected number of words that would be required for applications test programs to the total required for instrumentation. A minimum of 1500 to 2000 words for test programs is recommended.

The choice of computer and appropriate options must be made last since the computer requirements are not known until all the automatic test system requirements have been fulfilled. Then you make a choice of computer and extended options to satisfy the requirements of total memory and I/O channels. Next you select computer

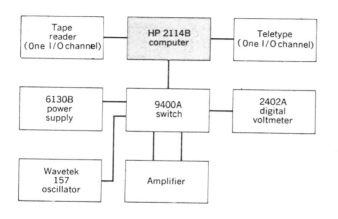

Model number	Option or accessory number	Description	Words of memory	I/O channels
6130B	J20	Digital voltage source (first one)	(207)	(1)
157	S-134	Waveform synthesizer (Wavetek)	(168)	(1)
9400A	003	Distribution switch (3 relay trees)	(33)	(1)
2402A		Integrating digital voltmeter	(106)	(2)
		Total	514	5

2114B		Computer	2649	7

FIGURE 22. Simplified system for testing an amplifier showing number of memory words and input/output channels required for specific devices.

mainframe options and also power fail interrupt and parity error check, if desired, and cabinet requirements.

The elementary system shown in Fig. 22 might be used for testing an amplifier. This system uses a computer with tape reader and Teletype, a dc power supply, an oscillator, a digital voltmeter, and a switching device. In Fig. 22 are also shown those portions of the tabular information supplied by Hewlett-Packard that apply to the particular instruments and devices used in the block diagram.

The number of words in memory that are required for the instruments totals 514. If the HP2114B minicomputer, for example, is considered for the system, it has available 2649 words of memory and 7 I/O channels.

Subtracting the 514 words of memory from the 2649 available leaves 2135 words for the applications test programs. The number of I/O channels available is sufficient without need for I/O channel extenders.

The Hewlett-Packard configuration example works easily because the HP 9500 system was designed to be modular. The amount of core memory used for the computer reflects the fact that it uses a resident interpreter to greatly simplify programming.

Designing a system of your own is not the only alternative, of course. Ronald H. Temple of the NEC minicomputer seminar faculty stressed the fact that the end user of a minicomputer has four avenues open to him: do it himself, get it all from a computer vendor, have a systems house do it, or buy the whole system from an OEM. Doing it yourself is the riskiest, he said, and buying from an OEM is probably the safest.

The prime requisite is to find someone who understands *your* problem. Such a person is the best investment you can make toward your goal of a workable computer system that is not a financial disaster.

The writer wishes to thank all those people who contributed their time and knowledge to make this report possible and, especially, Eric M. Aupperle and the National Electronics Conference for allowing use of some of their minicomputer seminar material.

A Look at Minicomputer Applications

GERALD LAPIDUS,
Control Engineering

With about 5,000 minicomputers now in the field and another 4,000 on the way in 1970, there can be no doubt about the impact of the minicomputer, nor that the breadth of its applications is indeed wide. Yet, despite its simplicity and low cost, many engineers do not realize that the answer to many of their digital-control and data-acquisition problems might truly lie in a minicomputer. Whether used as a digital controller, satellite data terminal, preprocessor of data for a large-scale computer, data-monitoring system, or low-cost logic device, the minicomputer is proving to be a versatile block in a system block diagram—free of the aura and hoopla accorded large-scale machines.

To determine how minicomputers are used and the specific functions they are being called on to perform, Control Engineering examined some representative applications. This article might be considered a sequel to "Minicomputers for the Control System" (Aug. '69, p. 90), which dealt with the feasibility of using minicomputers. Information on what's available in these machines appeared in Sept. '68, p. 73; Nov. '68, p. 72; and May '69, p. 87. The latter three articles are now available in reprint form. See p. 179 of this issue for details.

automated inspection . . .

Allis-Chalmers Manufacturing Co. has developed a high-speed inspection station for sheet metal, using a Data General Corp. NOVA computer as a data-acquisition device. Thin sheet metal traveling at 4,200 ft per min is inspected for pin holes, large holes, and cracked edges. An X-ray gage also evaluates the thickness of the sheet—determining whether it is prime, heavy, extra heavy, light, or extra light. All these parameters are fed to the NOVA for every foot of product, and the data is stored.

When a predetermined length of sheet (up to 199,-000 ft, at a maximum width of 40 in.) has passed the sensors and has been rolled into a coil, the computer commands the system to stop and cut the sheet. The operator then pushes a button, and the computer prints out a summary of all the measured characteristics of the completed coil of sheet metal, i.e., so many feet of prime gauge, heavy gauge, etc., and so many feet of sheet having a particular density of defects of each sort. This summary is attached to the coil of sheet metal and serves as a quality control document throughout the manufacturing process.

The inspection station operator can obtain a subtotal for the sheet already inspected at any time in the process. He also has on-line visual displays for each of the parameters being measured. If the density of defects exceeds a predetermined level, he can stop the coil immediately and the computer can tell him where, for example, the five most recent pinholes occurred in the sheet.

If the defects are unacceptably close together, the operator can reverse the movement of the coil and rewind past the area of high defects until he has rewound past the unacceptable area. Then he may command the system to shear out the bad area and weld the sheet together again. In such a case, the NOVA automatically recalculates its subtotal figures—subtracting the statistics for the area spliced out—and also recalculates the new length of the coil.

Allis-Chalmers is now offering this system for use in all types of sheet-metal mills. Its chief application so far, however, has been in the production of thin sheet steel for food containers, which must have almost no porosity. The system has been implemented on a NOVA with 4,096 16-bit words of alterable core memory for storage of variables and 3,072 words of fixed (read-only) memory for the operating program. The system also includes an ASR-35 Teletypewriter for communication with the computer, a Victor printer for producing summary reports, and interfaces with the various sensors. Allis-Chalmer's Digital Systems Group developed the software for the system.

Reprinted with permission from *Contr. Eng.*, pp. 82–91, Nov. 1969.

concentrating data for transmission . . .

A rapidly expanding use of minicomputers is controlling communications between multiple low-speed remote computer terminals and a large central computer. Redcor Corp., Canoga Park, Calif., is offering a communications concentrator software package (CCSP) for its RC 70 to provide line control, code conversion, error control, and buffering of bidirectional message transmission between low-speed terminals and the central computer.

Under control of CCSP, the terminal transmits data to the RC 70 in serial fashion. Characters are buffered and read into the appropriate terminal buffer area under program control. When the end of a message segment is received, the message is queued for transmission to the central computer over the synchronous line. At this point, the RC 70 may wait for a response from the central computer before continuing communications with the terminal, or it may optionally continue communications immediately. Similarly, when the central computer has a message to transmit to a terminal, the message is first sent to the RC 70, one segment at a time, and then is transmitted to the terminal under control of the CCSP.

Communications between the remote terminals and the central computer is via units of information called messages, which are bounded by a start-of-message symbol and an end-of-message symbol. A message is subdivided into units called segments. A segment is terminated by a carrier return character from the IBM 2741, by line-feed carriage-return

symbols for the ASR-33 or -35 Teletypewriters—or by other characters or character combinations for other types of terminals. A message segment is essentially a line of input or output for a typewriter-like terminal.

The buffer provided in the RC 70 holds message segments. A message segment received from a terminal may be blocked with other segments for transmission to the central computer. Conversely, a block received from the central computer is deblocked by the RC 70 into separate message segments for transmission to the terminals.

Communication with the large computer is over a high-speed line in a synchronous, duplex mode. As soon as a message segment is ready for transmission to the central computer, it is queued for the output buffer in the CCSP. Message segments received from the central computer are read into the input buffer. Each segment received from a terminal has the terminal's ID code appended to it so that it can be properly processed. Conversely, the central computer must append the terminal ID code to any segment that it transmits to assure reception by the correct terminal.

If the central computer is transmitting to a terminal which is not currently on-line, the call-up number for that terminal must initiate the message. Central-computer communications may also send status-request messages to the CCSP. These information requests tell the central computer when it can transmit to or expect inputs from specific terminals.

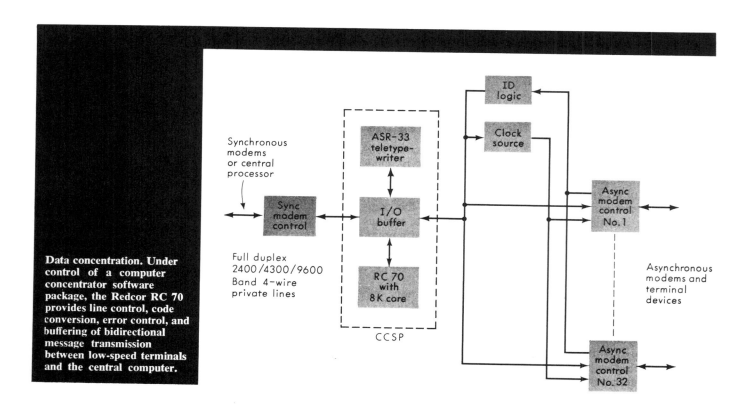

Data concentration. Under control of a computer concentrator software package, the Redcor RC 70 provides line control, code conversion, error control, and buffering of bidirectional message transmission between low-speed terminals and the central computer.

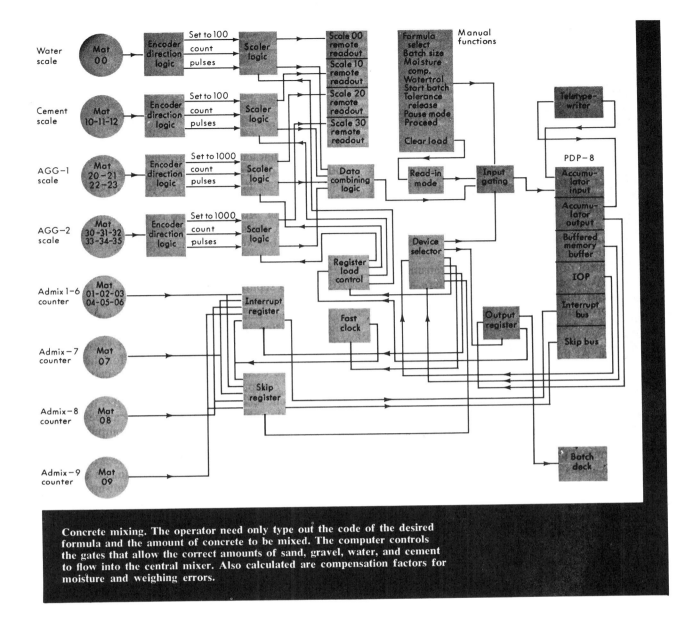

Concrete mixing. The operator need only type out the code of the desired formula and the amount of concrete to be mixed. The computer controls the gates that allow the correct amounts of sand, gravel, water, and cement to flow into the central mixer. Also calculated are compensation factors for moisture and weighing errors.

batching control for concrete results . . .

A Digital Equipment PDP-8 is helping concrete contractors to precisely obtain required blends of sand, gravel, water, and cement. Incorporated in a batching control system call Mark II Selectron—manufactured by American Hoist Co., Oakland, Calif.—the computer specifies and controls the quantities of various grades of solid materials and adds the proper amount of water. The ingredients are either mixed at a central location or loaded into a cement truck and mixed enroute to destinations.

The concrete formulas are stored in memory and the operator need only type out the code of the desired formula and the amount of concrete to be mixed. The computer controls the gates that allow the material to flow into the central mixer and monitors the weighing scales. In order to pour the correct amount of material, the computer must calculate an early cut-off, compensating for material still on its way down. Also to be adjusted is the reading of the weight of the material on the scale, which tends to be high during loading because of the impact of falling material.

Additional compensation calculated by the computer assures correct moisture content. For example, a moisture content of, say, 10 percent in the sand must be taken into account in adding the water, to assure that the final formulation contains the correct amount of water. Still another calculation adjusts the error tolerances of the mix to specified amounts.

The operator can call for a printout of the running totals of material used during a specific period of time, determine the amounts on hand, compute the demand for various formulas, and calculate truck utilization. A paper tape of the day's activities is also available for further processing.

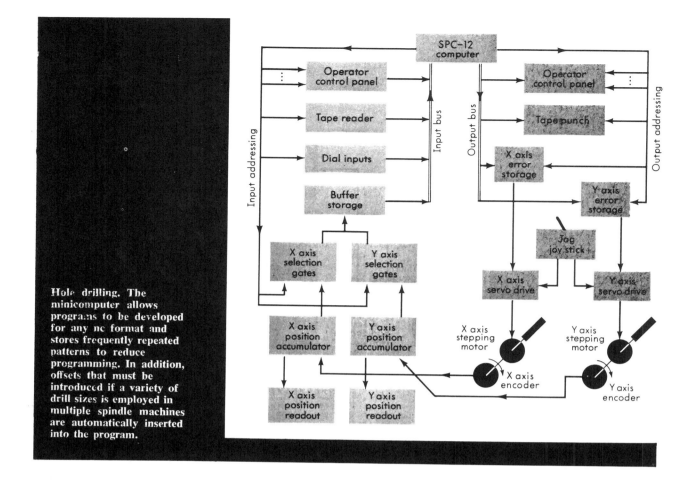

Hole drilling. The minicomputer allows programs to be developed for any nc format and stores frequently repeated patterns to reduce programming. In addition, offsets that must be introduced if a variety of drill sizes is employed in multiple spindle machines are automatically inserted into the program.

numerically controlled hole drilling . . .

A General Automation SPC-12 minicomputer adds versatility to circuit-board hole drilling machines built by Digital Systems, Inc., of Covina, Calif. With about a half-dozen circuit-board drilling-machine manufacturers on the market, there are many different instruction formats available. For example, one machine might use an absolute coordinate positioning system, while another may use incremental positioning.

To illustrate the problem, suppose the first instruction is $X = 3$, $Y = 4$. The first hole for either format is drilled in the indicated position. However, if the next instruction is $X = 1$, $Y = 6$, the second hole will be one unit from the X axis and six units from the Y axis in the absolute coordinate system, but four units from the X axis and ten from Y in the incremental format. To interchange formats, the logic must be rewired at considerable expense.

Digital Systems has employed the SPC-12 to allow for any desired format in a new stand-alone programmer designated Model 3060-C. To convert from one format to another, the user need only load the computer with the appropriate set of instructions. The format can be switched back and forth with no hardwired changes. If production demands should suddenly increase for a specific circuit board, new instruction sets can be developed on the computer to accommodate drilling machines not compatible with the previous format.

Another advantage of the computer is that it can store frequently repeated patterns in core memory,

reducing the programming task. For example, assume an operator has a series of 24 dual in-line packs, each having 14 leads. Normally, this would require him to program 346 hole positions. Also, boards with heavy packing densities are not easily adapted to step-and-repeat drilling operations because warping, shrinkage, and stretch cause intolerable deviations. With the computer, the 14-lead pattern can be stored in memory and the operator need only position the number one and seven holes of each pack, for reference. The computer will automatically position the remaining holes. Thus, the 346 locations require only 48 moves on the part of the operator. The 4K words of memory for the SPC-12 for this system can accommodate about 400 hole positions.

Further use of the computer is found in automatically providing offsets in the program. In multiple-spindle machines with different drill sizes, the table coordinates have to be offset slightly each time the drill size is changed in order to bring the hole position under the proper spindle. The computer can be programmed to do this each time it recognizes the code for a specific drill size.

Looking into the future of this application, computers may be used to optimize the sequence of a program while the programmer is copying an existing tape. Some sequencing patterns presently in use are so inefficient that they cost a drilling machine up to 30 percent of its productive time. One user already reports that the computer has reduced hole cost to about two cents from seven to eight cents per hole.

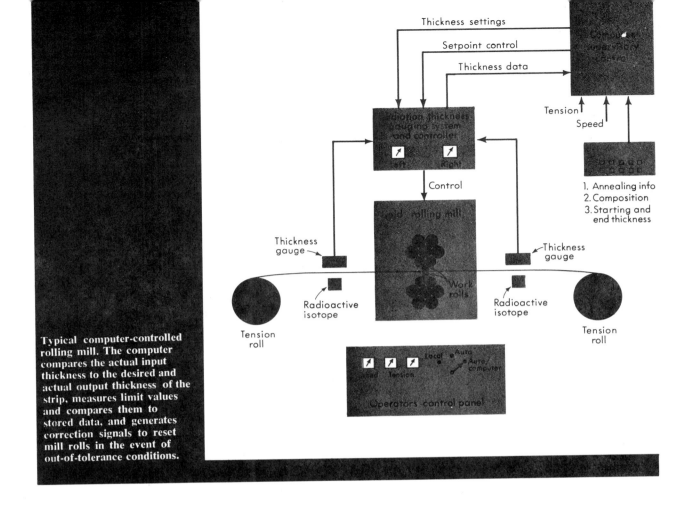

Thickness settings

Setpoint control

Thickness data

Tension

Speed

1. Annealing info
2. Composition
3. Starting and end thickness

Control

Thickness gauge

Thickness gauge

Radioactive isotope

Radioactive isotope

Work rolls

Tension roll

Tension roll

Local · Auto

· Auto/ computer

Tension

Operators control panel

Typical computer-controlled rolling mill. The computer compares the actual input thickness to the desired and actual output thickness of the strip, measures limit values and compares them to stored data, and generates correction signals to reset mill rolls in the event of out-of-tolerance conditions.

computer-controlled rolling mill . . .

Carpenter Technology Corp. Reading, Pa., one of the first manufacturers to put third-generation cold-strip milling equipment in service, has an installation controlled by a Digital Equipment Corp. PDP-8/I.

Incorporating an 8⅝-in. Sendzimer reversing cold-strip mill designed and built for Carpenter by Waterbury Farrel of Cheshire, Conn., the installation is capable of rolling alloy or stainless-steel strip up to 0.080 in. thick at production speeds of up to 500 ft per min. Strip of this thickness can be reduced in several passes to any desired thickness, down to approximately 0.001 in.

The PDP-8/I provides continous monitoring and control of the strip rolling mill to hold output size within specified limits. At both the input and output of the mill, strip thickness is monitored by gages.

Operating on a constant volume principle, the computer generates correction commands that raise or lower the bite of the mill. The PDP-8/I compares the absolute input thickness to the desired output and the actual output thickness of the strip; limit values are measured and compared to stored data. When the measured value falls outside the limit values, a correction signal is generated to adjust the mill rolls to correct out-of-tolerance conditions.

A secondary correction loop in the computer monitors the output gage over 16 calculation cycles and a correction signal modifies the corrections of the first loop to compensate for minor variations of second-order variables, such as material width, placement and location of gages, and thermal expansion of pulse generator wheels.

Within a 25-millisec span, the computer receives, compares, generates, and modifies control signals. This alone makes possible the production rate of 500 ft per min. Working with beta-ray gages, the automated control system maintains strip output thickness to within 0.10001, 0.00005, or 0.00001 in. Final tolerances on a finished length of strip can be held to plus or minus 50 millionths of an inch.

A continuous visual record of the number of feet passed through the mill and all of the deviations from the desired output is made by a strip-chart recorder. The profile of a pass can be supplied by merely typing in a question mark at the end of each pass.

When requested, the computer system prints out the total number of feet, the number of feet that are within tolerance limits, and the number of feet outside tolerance limits. These deviations are grouped by increments.

gas chromatography for process monitoring . . .

One of the largest minicomputer markets is in gas-chromatograph control. Typical is a process-monitoring system employed by Mobil Oil at its Midland, Tex., natural gas facility. Developed by Mobil Oil and Unitech Corp. of Austin, Tex., the system utilizes a Data General Corp. NOVA computer to control the switching of five chromatographs between 12 different sampling points located in the plant's input, process, and output streams.

Raw natural gas is piped into the Midland plant from nearby oil fields. The input-stream chromatographs evaluate the variations in composition of the raw gas as it comes from the field. The natural gas is dehydrated and stripped of its liquid elements in the process stream, and chromatographic samples taken at several points in this stream are analyzed in real-time to determine the efficiency of the process and to detect any problem areas. At the output stream there is another chromatographic analysis for a final check.

The minicomputer is programmed to direct the chromatograph to draw gas from the various sampling streams at appropriate times. It also analyzes the data taken from the chromatographs, and prints out results on-site on a typewriter terminal. Results are also available to an IBM 1800 computer located 25 miles away from the plant. The 1800, which is essentially a on-line control computer, interrogates the NOVA periodically and uses the data in optimization studies of the gas stripping process. Thus, the role of this system is to serve as a local loop in a large-scale system.

In the chromatograph, the sample gas in liquid form is heated to over 170 deg for 20-min, inside a pressurized chamber. As the elements are vaporized one by one, a hot-wire thermal conductivity detector monitors the conductivity of each of nine possible elements and the data is read out on a chart recorder and fed into the computer via an A-to-D converter. The computer integrates the area under the curve to calculate the mol percentage of the element in the gas. Data is printed out for each sample, and summary information is also transmitted to the IBM 1800.

The complete installation consists of the NOVA, an IBM 2713 typewriter terminal for local output, an ASR-33 Teletypewriter, the converters interfacing the gas chromatographs with the minicomputer, and the interface between the NOVA and a Dresser electronic-control and data-acquisition system used by Mobil to interconnect all facilities in the area. The Dresser system interfaces in turn with the IBM 1800.

The NOVA selected for this application has 8K × 16 bit words of memory, power fail-restart, and real-time clock options.

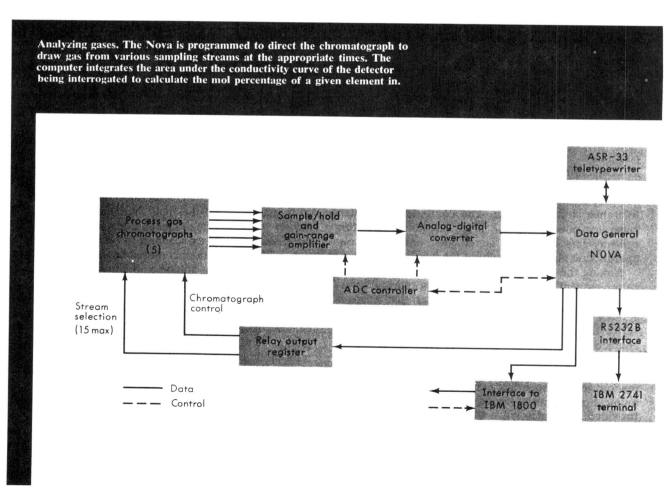

Analyzing gases. The Nova is programmed to direct the chromatograph to draw gas from various sampling streams at the appropriate times. The computer integrates the area under the conductivity curve of the detector being interrogated to calculate the mol percentage of a given element in.

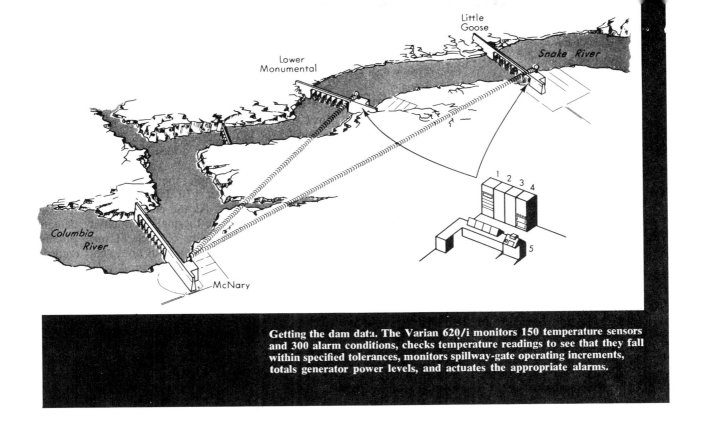

Getting the dam data. The Varian 620/i monitors 150 temperature sensors and 300 alarm conditions, checks temperature readings to see that they fall within specified tolerances, monitors spillway-gate operating increments, totals generator power levels, and actuates the appropriate alarms.

dam site better with automated data acquisition . . .

Progress Electronics Co. of Portland, Ore., has developed a data-acquisition system to monitor 400 conditions in a section of a supervisory control system for a three-dam complex. The system, developed for the U.S. Army Corps of Engineers, is located on the Snake River in Eastern Washington in a complex consisting of Little Goose, Lower Monumental, and McNary dams. Using a Varian 620/i with 16-bit word size and 12K words of memory, the system monitors 150 temperature sensors and 300 alarm conditions.

Temperature readings are checked to see that they fall within specified limits, and alarm indicators are actuated if any temperature problems or other out-of-tolerance situations arise. The computer also totals generator power levels in megawatt-hours, monitors spillway-gate operating increments, and prints out malfunction alarms throughout the whole complex.

Among the peripheral devices are an A-to-D converter-sequential scanner that digitizes and multiplexes the inputs, a pulse data converter that changes contact pulses to digital words, an annunciator-converter that monitors the steady-state status of relay contacts, and a water-level converter that converts analog water-levels signals to digital words. An output from the pulse data converter produces a digital readout in the supervisory control system. Data communication channels among sites in the complex are provided by a microwave frequency diversity system operating through the existing microwave link.

The system's location presented some interesting and perplexing design problems. Inherent switching transients in excess of 1.5 kilovolts, when combined with stringent reliability and accuracy requirements, made existing digital scanners impractical. An economical solution was achieved by combining integrated circuits with an interface of mercury wetted relays. The combination was packaged on plug-in pc boards to permit the logical separation of 96 high-priority channels and 204 secondary-priority channels, with expansion capability for each.

The 150 resistance temperature sources produced other problems which could not be readily solved with standard off-the-shelf hardware. Preliminary studies suggested the design and development of a true differential-input FET scanner, to be used in conjunction with a modified commercial digital voltmeter functioning as an analog-to-digital converter. The combination produces a double-ended input A-to-D subsystem expandable to 1,000 channels in increments of ten channels, to satisfy the required 0.1 percent accuracy in the 0 to 50-millivolt range. Noise rejection at 60 Hz is 80 dB with minus 120 dB common-mode rejection.

The first such system has been installed in Lower Monumental and a second is being readied for Little Goose. An existing system incorporating the supervisory control is already in operation at McNary.

replacing hardwired logic for micropositioning . . .

Engineers at Electroglas, Inc., of Menlo Park, Calif., feel the small computer is the most expedient controller for flexible programming of high-speed micropositioning equipment. They have connected a minicomputer to Electroglas' Model 1100 programmed digital actuator and Model 1200 master control to provide X-Y table control for translating rotational direction of stepping motors into linear motion via direct-coupled lead screws.

Systems such as this are finding favor with semiconductor manufacturers in processes such as scribing, probing and classification. It is possible to expand the system by having a third motor driving the Z axis and a fourth rotating the table.

While it is true that the system can be controlled by a program derived directly from tape, the computer offers more flexibility for this purpose. It monitors speed and senses limits, sequences operations, senses direction of motion, and controls braking conditions. In addition, control by computer is accomplished on a selective, time-shared basis.

Commands to the master controller are in machine language and the program—internally stored—can be read in by any peripheral device. Manual access from the control panel is also available.

The master control unit translates the computer output into the digital actuator format and drives an Electroglas E98 display showing the position of the stepping motor under control of the particular actuator. The loop is closed by returning position signals through the master control to the computer.

For Electroglas' applications the computer is considered to be a logic element rather than a general-purpose machine, and as such serves to reduce the need for high-priced, special-purpose logic.

Two computers have been applied by Electroglas for this application. One, the Computer Automation Model 808, has an eight-bit data format. Because the digital actuator working with the 808 operates on a 16-bit format, the master controller used with this version of the positioning system converts the computer output into 16-bit words. For more elaborate systems, the company has employed the Digital Equipment Corp. PDP-8. Here, the master controller converts the 12-bit output of this computer to the required 16-bit format.

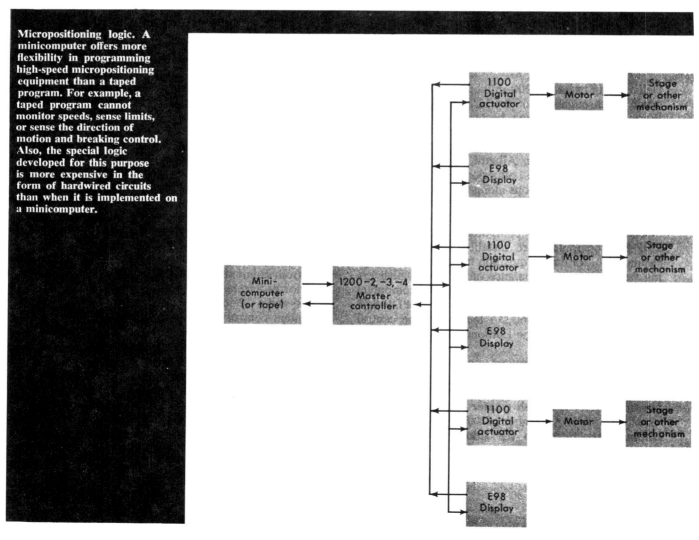

Micropositioning logic. A minicomputer offers more flexibility in programming high-speed micropositioning equipment than a taped program. For example, a taped program cannot monitor speeds, sense limits, or sense the direction of motion and breaking control. Also, the special logic developed for this purpose is more expensive in the form of hardwired circuits than when it is implemented on a minicomputer.

testing fibers for quality control . . .

Datatype Corp. of Miami, Fla., has installed a tensile-strength measuring system at the Research Triangle Park (North Carolina) facility of Beaunit Corp., a producer of nylon, rayon, and polyester fibers. The Computer Data Div. of Datatype designed a system in which a Data General Corp. NOVA computer processes data from an Instron tester. The basic function of the tester is to stretch a fiber until it ruptures, and to output analog data on the load, elongation, stress, etc., experienced by the fiber prior to rupture.

This is essentially a quality-control test to determine whether or not the fiber meets production specifications. Automobile-tire manufacturers evaluate incoming nylon cord this way.

The standard output of an Instron tester is a strip chart recording which, with manual data reduction, yields results in about three days. This is too slow for critical situations. Before designing the NOVA-based system, Datatype and Beaunit developed an off-line computer system that took data from the Instron tester, digitized it, and punched out a paper tape. The data was then reduced off-line on an IBM 1130, and

results were obtained 16 hours later on second-shift computer time.

The current on-line system gives immediate results. Before the operator can complete the next set of tests, results for the previous test are printed out. The parameters include breaking strength (load applied at time of fiber break), elongation at break, tenacity in grams per denier, toughness (area under the curve of load vs displacement), load at a specified elongation, modulus at a specified elongation, and elongation at a specified load.

The Datatype on-line system consists of an operator's console through which the operator loads the test environment specifications, the NOVA computer with 4,096 words of 16-bit core memory, and a Teletypewriter for input. The interface between the Instron tester and the NOVA consists primarily of analog-to-digital conversion. The system is housed in a typist's desk, with the computer completely concealed inside.

The software package is being developed for Datatype by Beaunit Corp. Datatype will sell the hardware and software to customers as a package.

keeping it coming down the pipe . . .

Deliveries in excess of 200-million barrels per year of crude oil through one of the largest pipelines in the Western Hemisphere have become more economical and efficient with minicomputers providing distributed control of the line, owned by the Interprovincial Pipe Line Co. of Edmonton, Alberta, and its subsidiary, Lakehead Pipe Line Co., Superior, Wisc.

All 32 pumping stations along an 1,100-mile route (Edmonton to Superior) of the 2,000-mile line have been placed under the control of 20 Digital Equipment Corp. PDP-8/S computers. Two additional PDP-8/S computers are installed in Superior and Sarnia, Ont., for data acquisition from 30 more pumping stations along the balance of the line, which extends to Port Credit, Ont. The two remote computers are in turn connected on-line to two more PDP-8/S systems and an IBM-360/40 located in the central computer complex at the Edmonton headquarters of Interprovincial.

The 22 remote computers automatically monitor and control the pumping stations—performing data acquisition, interpretation, and transmission control functions faster and with greater accuracy than previously possible. A number of safety checks are also computer-generated. In the Edmonton center, the PDP-8/S computers control communications, and the

IBM-360/40 stores and processes the data.

The purpose in automating was to centralize control without sacrificing safety, while achieving economy of operation. Prior to the installation of computers, some sections of the line were monitored by banks of fixed-display, hardwired devices that required an operator to interpret and transmit data to a central information center. Design of the computerized control system began in 1965 when, according to a company report, it had become evident that a conventional fixed-display system in a rapidly growing pipeline system could become quickly obsolete.

The computer-monitored network consists of three lines from Edmonton to Superior, a 30-in. line from Superior to Sarnia, a 20-in. line from Sarnia to Port Credit, and a 12-in. spur line to Buffalo. The remote computers control both diesel and electric pumping stations, in some cases without an operator on the premises. Each computer must handle three separate pipelines through each pumping location, where there are up to 13 pumping units. The computers scan the pumping locations on a continuous basis and transmit to the central system such information as suction pressures, discharge pressures, case and holding pressures (where applicable), station electrical load, gravitometer and interface detector readings, and

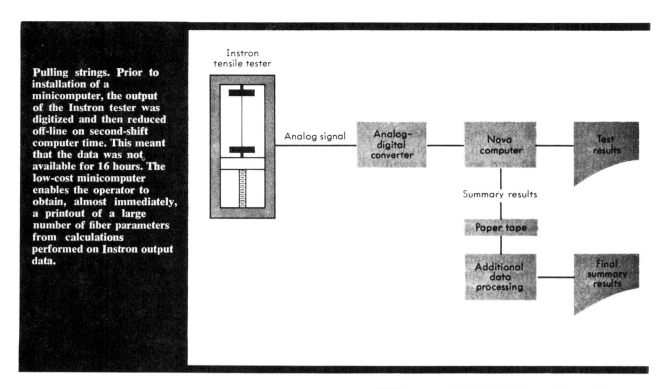

Pulling strings. Prior to installation of a minicomputer, the output of the Instron tester was digitized and then reduced off-line on second-shift computer time. This meant that the data was not available for 16 hours. The low-cost minicomputer enables the operator to obtain, almost immediately, a printout of a large number of fiber parameters from calculations performed on Instron output data.

Instron tensile tester

Analog signal

Analog-digital converter

Nova computer

Test results

Summary results

Paper tape

Additional data processing

Final summary results

tank gages (where practical). In addition to scanning the locations, the remote PDP-8/S computers compare all readings to those last reported to central control, and if these are beyond predefined limits, or if there has been a change in contact sense, they originate a transmission of the discrepancies.

The computerized control functions consist of starting and stopping main pumping units—one at a time—on command from the central computer, opening and closing main breakers on command, sounding alarms, and changing predefined limits for reporting functions.

All commands from the central control system in Edmonton are subjected to two passes before being executed. On the first pass an operational command is checked to determine whether it is valid and whether it is reasonable. If valid and reasonable, the command is executed on the second pass. □

Acknowledgment

The author wishes to thank CE correspondent Bill Wallace for gathering information for this article in the Los Angeles area.

CONTROL ENGINEERING

Pipeline control. A network of 22 remote minicomputers monitors and controls pumping stations. The computers scan the pumping locations on a continuous basis and transmit to the central computer information such as suction pressures, discharge pressures, case and holding pressures, station electrical load, gravitometer and interface detector readings, and tank-gage readings. In the area of control, the computers start and stop main pumping units on command from the central computer, open and close main breakers, sound alarms, and change predefined limits for reporting functions.

Batch Control with a Minicomputer

R. YOUNG, Emery Industries, Inc. and
D. E. SVOBODA, Jackson Associates

At Emery Industries, a minicomputer controls batch production of chemicals, consisting of esterification reactions of fatty acids with alcohols. Functions of the mini-system range from simple alarm-point monitoring to ddc. The authors describe the hardware and software for a system that demonstrates the minicomputer's value as an economical, flexible, sophisticated production tool.

FOR PROCESS APPLICATIONS, it's often more economical to design the control system around a digital computer rather than hardware logic components and analog setpoint controllers. Prices of minicomputers start at $3,000 to $4,000 without core memory; therefore, for all but the simplest systems, the cost of the computer will be less than the cost of the hardware it replaces.

In addition, the overall effort required to design computer software (even with assembly-language programming) is less than that required for equivalent hardware, and the computer programs are easier to modify. Sophisticated control algorithms that can reduce operating costs—but which are difficult to implement with hardware—can usually be programmed for a computer with little difficulty.

The process control system described in this article performs a variety of functions typical of computer-based systems. These functions include "contact-closure" input and output, analog input and output, direct digital control (ddc) of analog process variables, timing and sequencing of process events, and logging of process variables and events. The computer hardware is discussed first, followed by an explanation of programming techniques.

Hardware for the mini

The computer control system (shown in the figure) is built around Digital Equipment's PDP-8L computer and Peripheral Equipment's 7820-9 magnetic tape unit. Additional equipment consists of analog-to-digital (A/D) and digital-to-analog (D/A) converters, contact closure inputs and outputs, a time-of-day clock for event logging, a 60-Hz interval timer which provides the time base for the entire system, a stall alarm, and a teletypewriter for logging. Operator messages are presented through an annunciator panel.

The computer memory holds the control program and the parameters associated with each product that will be manufactured. The magnetic-core memory consists of 4,096 12-bit words, and has a 1.6-microsecond cycle time.

Computer I/O facilities consist of 12-input and 12-output data lines. Data can be selected and placed on the output lines or accepted from the input lines at appropriate times, under control of the program. In addition, six address lines are used by the external logic to route input or output data to or from external equipment such as contact-closure sensors and D/A converters. Control lines that can be pulsed or tested by the program synchronize the external logic with the control program.

Contact-closure inputs are arranged and addressed in groups of 12 that correspond to the 12-output data lines of the computer. DC input circuits consist of RC filters (to take out contact-bounce noise) followed by Schmitt triggers (to convert inputs to logic levels). AC inputs pass through isolation transformers and diodes for conversion to dc. Contact-closure inputs include signals from the annunciator panel, operator pushbuttons, valve-position limit switches, and level detectors.

Contact-closure output hardware consists mostly of solid-state devices: triacs for ac output and transistor switches for dc output. A few relays, driven

Reprinted with permission from *Instrum. Technol.*, vol. 17, pp. 72–74, Aug. 1970.

179

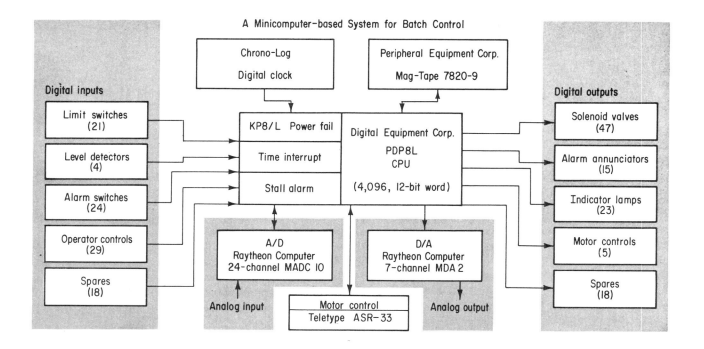

A Minicomputer-based System for Batch Control

by transistors, are used where continuity is desirable in case of a logic power supply failure. The contact-closure outputs are also arranged in groups of 12.

Each contact-closure output has a storage flip-flop which receives and holds the data from one of the output lines. Groups of contact-closure outputs are selected to receive data by codes provided on the six address lines. The outputs include signals to the annunciator panel, motor start/stop signals, and signals to solenoid-operated pilot valves that supply air to the process valves.

Analog voltage inputs are multiplexed to an A/D converter, changed to binary numbers, and put into the input data lines of the computer. Process variables such as temperature, pressure, and flow are entered into the computer via the A/D converter. Manual setpoints (operator-adjusted potentiometers) also pass through the A/D converter.

The D/A converters accept binary output data and produce coresponding analog voltages. A separate converter is used for each analog output, with a range of ± 10 volts; each D/A converter has a separate six-bit address. Analog output voltages go to panel meters which display process variables, and to electric-to-pneumatic (E/P) converters which provide air to throttling control valves.

The interval timer generates a time-interrupt signal for the computer every $\frac{1}{60}$ of a second, the basic timing for sequencing of the process. The timer also provides a reference for integral and derivative control in the ddc loops.

The stall alarm consist of two 10-millisecond timers that can be reset by the program. The timers must be reset so that at least one is always running; otherwise, an alarm signal is produced. If a program error or hardware malfunction alters the normal sequence of the program, the timers will not be reset often enough, thereby actuating a stall alarm.

The teletypewriter and clock are used in a conventional manner for event logging. Time in hours, minutes, and seconds can be read from the clock and printed by the teletypewriter with a typical message: 08:16:57 THERMINOL FROM ESTERIFIER LOW FLOW.

Software for the mini

The computer programming, or software, regulates the operation of a computer-controlled process, and constitutes a major part of the design and development effort of such a system. Some of the general tasks for Emery Industries' computer can be mentioned; they are typical for a control computer that is applied to a batch process.

Depending on the product's requirements, the software sequences the valves, provides timing, and monitors the status functions that determine when steps should be taken. The computer checks six variable and 14 logical (yes or no) "endpoints," any combination of which can control the duration of a step or the branching to one of several possible next steps. Computer software must also check a total of 50 temperatures, manual valve positions, and other status signals that show the system is operating normally. Critical status errors can stop the chemical process.

The annunciation function of the software puts out printed messages (on the teletypewriter) concerning the status indicators and program flow. A self-checking function detects and annunciates computer malfunctions.

It's impressive that the minicomputer has sufficient capacity for all of these functions. The key to fitting them in was the careful organization of the software into subroutines. Besides the normal advantages of easier troubleshooting and simplified program changes, an important feature of subroutines for this application is that a subroutine can be called many times during a program sequence, which minimizes the total required number of program statements. For a program of routine operations but unique sequence and duration of the operations, this approach greatly shortens its length.

A general principle of the software organization: every function which is routine is a subprogram, and only those functions unique to the particular chemical product remain in the main program.

One operation illustrates the application of this principal. Changing the combination of the 47 on-off valves of the process system can happen as many as 30 times during the batch process. A change takes two program statements, a valve-change subroutine call followed by an encoded combination. The valve-change subroutine decodes the combination, selects the valves to be opened or closed, and produces a valve-change message which gets printed by the annunciator subprogram. Finally, the proper valves are actuated by the update subprogram which does all I/O functions.

Time-sharing is another familiar tool that has been applied in this system. Simultaneous operation of functions such as output printing, system error detecting, endpoint detection, and ddc was deemed necessary; therefore, a time-interrupt system for time-sharing was devised. The executive control program is divided into 15 equal time slots, each of which contains parts of the programming. Four passes per second through the 15 slots are required for the execution of all statements. At the end of the first $\frac{1}{60}$-second interval within each slot, the contents of the accumulator and the address of the next statement to be executed (in that particular time slot) are saved by the executive before going on to the next slot, and on to the 15th.

At the start of the corresponding time slot during the next ¼ second pass, the accumulator is restored by the executive and the program proceeds as if the interruption had not taken place.

An executive "fork control" subroutine (an un-

conditional jump) permits programming in one slot to alter the flow of that in another slot. Parameter values in one time slot can be read or modified from another slot.

The ddc loops go into a single time slot. These loops are the digital-computer equivalent of analog control loops that operate valves. Five valves control nine process variables. Each loop has setpoint inputs from the main program and process variable inputs from the update program. The control algorithm resembles that of a normal analog loop, except that summation replaces analog intergration and digital differentiation replaces analog.

A "tune-up" control panel permits rapid optimization of various constants for these loops. Considering the computer speed and the time constants of this application, the ddc control is indistinguishable from analog control but it is much easier to tune and modify.

Because of possible failures, safeguard procedures have been included in the software design. Manual takeover of any valve or any ddc-loop setpoint is possible; these options are designed so that automatic control can be reestablished smoothly.

For safety as well as convenience, all of the above software is stored on magnetic tape which is read into the computer by a simple loader program. Normally, all subprograms remain in the computer core and only the main program is read in at the beginning of each chemical process. Provision for updating the magnetic tape is also part of the software.

In Emery Industries' system, every phase of real-time computer usage is represented—from simple alarm-point monitoring to unattended direct digital control with self-checking features. The system has been designed so that the operator can interact with the control system to alter setpoints if necessary, or adjust the control system to handle process upsets manually if the need arises.

Some of the software concepts borrowed from computer time-sharing technology (which permit many subroutines to be activated simultaneously), contributed to the flexibility of the system. This organization permits a new main program to be written for an entirely new product with a minimum of effort, inasmuch as the main programs consist primarily of a sequence of calls to the various utility subroutines, along with their required endpoints and setpoints.

Dr. Robert Young is Director of Engineering at Emery Industries, Inc., Cincinnati, Ohio; Dr. Dean E. Svoboda is a consultant with Jackson Associates, Columbus, Ohio. Article is based on paper presented at the Conference on Solid-State Devices for Industrial Applications, sponsored by IEEE with ISA as a cooperating society, Cleveland, 1970.

THE COMPUTER IN THE HIGH SCHOOL PHYSICS LABORATORY

Clifford C. Little
The Hill School
Pottstown, Pennsylvania

ABSTRACT

The use of a PDP-8/I computer to increase the efficiency of a weekly laboratory period is discussed. Examples from PSSC experiments demonstrate how time can be saved by pre-written programs and computer-aided calculations, in addition to the training of students in computer procedures.

The use of the computer provides more opportunity for discussion of experimental results. Written programs use the FOCAL language and are written in both 8K and the 4K dual user version.

INTRODUCTION

Since many colleges are now using small computers either as a curricular subject or as a tool in science and related courses we, at The Hill, thought that a well prepared student about to enter college should be familiar with the use, application and limitations of computers in general. For example, 60% of the incoming freshman class last year at Harvard had some "hands on" experience with computers.

Our initial effort was a trial of the G. E. time-sharing system. This procedure was so popular that students had to sign up for terminal time (three per hour) three days in advance. Giving students unlimited access to the terminal also resulted in a bill for telephone lines, terminal time, and CPU time in access of $1,000 per month. The conclusion was that we should have our own educational computer system where in the long run we could keep the cost down, and also give the student more "hands on" experience. With Trustee approval, we purchased a PDP 8/I system consisting of an 8K memory, 32K disc and two ARS 33 terminals, one located in the computer center and the other remotely in the physics laboratory.

TRAINING THE STUDENTS

As only one-third of our student body had "on line" experience with the time-sharing system of the year before using BASIC, we set up a series of six lectures, over a three week period. These lectures were voluntary and were attended by approximately 100 students. The FOCAL language was used as our means of conversing with the computer since we were planning the dual user version with out two terminals in a time-sharing mode. The students used the FOCAL manuals prepared by DEC as a text and the lecture topics were expanded along the lines of the KEMENY book on BASIC[1]. The following topics were covered:

1. Mechanics of Operation-Simple Commands.
2. Output Format.
3. Simple Programming.
4. Loops.
5. Lists, Tables and Functions.
6. Debugging - Modify and Trace Rountines.

Upon conclusion of the series, the students were given free access to the computer on a first come, first served basis. They were permitted to experiment with programming using problems of their own choice. They worked with games, golf handicapping, horse race predictions, stock market trends, homework problems in math and physics. In the meantime, our math and science departments were planning how to integrate the use of the computer into our already scheduled math and science classes.

USE IN PHYSICS LABORATORY

There are three main areas where we put the computer to use in our physics laboratory program:

1. Short calculations.
2. Pre-written programs.
3. Computer-aided or simulated laboratory experiments.

The following are examples of some of the material developed.

Short Calculations: Here the computer replaces the slide rule as a calculator. The FOCAL simple type commands save considerable time. One excellent feature of FOCAL is that these short calculations can be made without affecting the program that may be residing in core. A student interrupts the user, quickly uses the type command to average numbers, solves simple equations, takes square roots, or makes estimates of experimental results.

Pre-Written Program: In a double forty-five minute laboratory period, a student has difficulty performing and writing up this laboratory experiment in a single session. By preparing programs ahead of time he only has to feed his data into the computer to obtain his results. Two examples of this type of program and the results are shown in Figure 1 and Figure 2.

One is a simple refraction experiment where the student measures the angle of incidence and its

Reprinted with permission from *Proc. Digital Equip. Comput. Users Soc.*, pp. 61–67, May 1969.

corresponding angle of refraction. This information is then given to the computer, where the sine of the angles of incidence and refraction are recorded along with their ratio (N), the index of refraction of the material used. Besides giving a mean value for the index, a print-out of standard deviation, probable error and percentage error is also given.

The second example uses a very simple apparatus (diffraction grating and meter stick)for measuring the wavelength of the lines in the hydrogen spectrum. From these results Planck's constant is calculated. The Planck's constant calculation is a messy one, and here the pre-written programs save the student many hours of hard work.

Computer-aided Laboratory Experiments: There are a number of experiments where the student is to find a functional relationship between a number of variables. Sometimes the data taken by the student is marginal in determining the functional relationship and very time consuming shifting variables while holding others constant. In the inertial and gravitational mass experiment (Figure 3 and 4), the student first observes its behavior in the laboratory, trying different mass and observing what happens. Then he goes to the computer which asks a series of questions to check his laboratory observations and if all goes well will give him a table of masses with their corresponding period. Then the student is direct-

ed to return to the laboratory and complete his report.

The centripetal force experiment asks the student to find the relationship between force, mass, period and radius of revolution. The simple equipment used works well, but is limited in the degree in which the variables may be varied. Once the student sees how the experiment works and decides on what range his variables should take, he goes to the computer for his data and then returns to the laboratory for graph plotting, results and conclusions of the experiment (Figure 5).

CONCLUSIONS

The use of the computer has stimulated more interest in the laboratory work. The drudgery is now gone. Students find it exciting. Having more time available, they begin to ask more questions about the experiment and try other methods of attack. A good number are now writing their own programs and with open-ended laboratory experiments are continually trying new ideas. I would say that the use of the computer has been highly successful.

REFERENCES

1   Basic Programming - J. Kemeny and T. Kurtz - Wiley and Sons.

```
C-FOCAL , 8/68

01.05 ERASE
01.10 T  "  INCIDENCE      REFRACTION          SIN I      SIN R          N",!,!
01.20 SET P = 3.14159
01.30 ASK A,B; IF (A-B) 1.4,2.50,1.4
01.40 SET R = FSIN(A*P/180)/FSIN(B*P/180)
01.50 SET N=N+1; S S=S+R; S S2 =S2 +R*R
01.60 T A,B,       FSIN(A*P/180),   FSIN(B*P/180),R,!
01.70 GOTO  1.30

02.50 SET M= S/N; SET  V =(N*S2-S*S)/N/(N-1)
02.60 SET D=FSQT(V); SET P=.6745*D;SET E=FSQT(V/N)
02.70 S Y=100*(M-1.3333)/1.3333
02.80 TYPE "MEAN VALUE    STD.DEV.   PROB ERR   PERCENT ERROR",!,!
02.90 TYPE M, D,P,Y
*


        GO
```

INCIDENCE	REFRACTION		SIN I	SIN R	N
:10 : 8 =	10.0000=	8.0000=	0.1737=	0.1392=	1.2477
:20 :16 =	20.0000=	16.0000=	0.3420=	0.2756=	1.2408
:30 :23 =	30.0000=	23.0000=	0.5000=	0.3907=	1.2797
:40 :30 =	40.0000=	30.0000=	0.6428=	0.5000=	1.2856
:50 :36 =	50.0000=	36.0000=	0.7661=	0.5878=	1.3033
:60 :41 =	60.0000=	41.0000=	0.8660=	0.6561=	1.3201
:80 :48 =	80.0000=	48.0000=	0.9848=	0.7432=	1.3252
:3 :3					

```
MEAN VALUE      STD.DEV.   PROB ERR   PERCENT ERROR

=    1.2860=     0.0330=    0.0223=-    3.5446*
```

Figure 1
Refraction Experiment

GO
THIS PROGRAM DETERMINES THE WAVELENGTH OF THE SPECTRAL
LINES IN HYDROGEN USING A DIFFRACTION GRATING AND USES
THE RESULTS TO DETERMINE PLANCK'S CONSTANT

GIVE DATA IN THE FOLLOWING ORDER*X,A,B,WAVELENGTH

X	A	B	WAVELENGTH	EXP. VALUE	PERCENT ERROR
:50	:69.5	:31.2	:6562	= 0.678012E+04	= 0.321701E+01
:50	:64.0	:36.5	:4861	= 0.502656E+04	= 0.329368E+01
:50	:62.5	:38.1	:4340	= 0.449362E+04	= 0.341852E+01

PLANCK'S CONSTANT
= 0.668318E-33
= 0.668502E-33
= 0.668799E-33

AVERAGE VALUE = 0.668540E-33*

```
@@@@@@@@@@@@
C-FOCAL , 8/68

01.01 T "THIS PROGRAM DETERMINES THE WAVELENGTH OF THE SPECTRAL"
01.02 T !"LINES IN HYDROGEN USING A DIFFRACTION GRATING AND USES"
01.03 T ! "THE RESULTS TO DETERMINE PLANCK'S CONSTANT"
01.10 T !!"GIVE DATA IN THE FOLLOWING ORDER*X,A,B,WAVELENGTH"
01.15 S N=0
01.20 T !!"  X ","  A ","  B ","  WAVELENGTH ","  EXP. VALUE  "
01.21 T "          PERCENT ERROR"
01.22 A !X,A,B,W
01.40 S A1=FABS(A-50); S A2=FABS(B-50)
01.50 S R= FATN(A1/X); S S=FATN(A2/X)
01.60 S N=N+1
01.70 S L(N) = FSIN((R+S)/2)/5275E-8
01.80 S P1=100*FABS(W-L(N))/L(N)
01.90 T "       ",%,L(N), "          ",P1
01.91 IF (N-3)1.22,2.1,2.1

02.10 S N=0
02.11 T !!"PLANCK'S CONSTANT"
02.13 S N=N+1
02.20 S M1=L(N)*(1.6E-19)↑4*9.1E-41/(8*(8.854E-12)↑2*3E8)
02.30 S M2= (1/4-1/(N+2)↑2)
02.40 S H= M1*M2
02.50 S Y=FLOG(H)/3
02.60 S Z=FEXP(Y)
02.70 S V= V+Z
02.80 T !Z
02.90 IF (N-3)2.13,3.1,3.1

03.10 S W=V/N
03.20 T !!"AVERAGE VALUE ",W
03.30 QUIT

04
```

Figure 2
The Spectrum of Hydrogen and Planck's Constant

C- 8K FOCAL

```
01.10 T "INERTIAL AND GRAVITATIONAL MASS EXPERIMENT"!!
01.20 T "ANSWER EACH QUESTION BY TYPING THE FIRST LETTER"!
01.21 T "OF THE WORD WHICH BEST ANSWERS THE QUESTION"!
01.30 T "THE INERTIAL BALANCE IS A DEVICE FOR MEASURING"!
01.40 T "THE INERTIAL MASS OF DIFFERENT OBJECTS."!
01.41 A "FROM YOUR OBSERVATIONS IN THE LABORATORY IS THE "!
01.42 A "PERIOD GREATER OR SMALLER FOR SMALLER MASSES?"D
01.43 S R=D-10
01.50 IF (R) 4.1;
01.60 A ! "GOOD! HOW DO THE ACCELERATIONS OF DIFFERENT MASSES COMPARE "!
01.61 A "WHEN THE PLATFORM IS PULLED ASIDE ABOUT 2 CM AND "!
01.62 A "RELEASED? SELECT:(A) LARGER MASS, LARGER ACCELERATION"!
01.63 A "(B) LARGER MASS, SMALLER ACCELERATION"E
01.64 S G=E-2
01.70 IF (G) 4.1;
01.75 T "YOU ARE DOING FINE"!
01.80 A ! "DOES THIS SEEM TO BE IN ACCORD WITH NEWTON'S LAW OF MOTION?"L
01.81 S W=L-20
01.82 IF (W) 5.2;GOTO 6.1

04.10 T "YOU SHOULD RETURN TO THE LAB AND TRY AGAIN";QUIT

05.20 T "NEWTON'SECOND LAW SAYA:   F=MA"!
05.30 T "IN THE INERTIAL BALANCE, THE RESTORING FORCE"!
05.31 T " IS PROPORTIONAL TO ITS DISPLACEMENT FROM "!
05.42 T "THE EQUILIBRIUM POSITION. FOR A CONSTANT DISPLACEMENT"!
05.43 T "F IS CONSTANT"!
05.50 A "IF M INCREASES, WHAT HAPPENS TO A?"Q
05.60 S I=Q-6
05.70 IF (I)6.1;GOTO 5.2

06.10 T "NOW YOU ARE TO DETERMINE  HOW THE PERIOD OF THE BALANCE"!
06.11 T "VARIES WITH MASS."!
06.20 A "WHAT SHALL I USE FOR MY RANGES OF MASS IN GRAMS,LOWER AND"!
06.21 A "UPPER LIMIT?"X,Z
06.30 T ! "MASS              ","PERIOD"!
06.40 FOR M=X,100,Z-100; DO 7.0

07.10 S T=2*3.1416*FSQT((M+50)'(9.25+4))
07.20 T ! M,T

08.20 T ! "NOW USING LOG-LOG PAPER, PLOT A GRAPH OF THE PERIOD AS"!
08.21 T "AS A FUNCTION OF MASS AND ANSWER THE FOLLOWING QUESTIONS:"!!
08.30 T "WHAT IS THE SLOPE OF THE GRAPH?"!
08.40 T "WHAT IS THE RELATIONSHIP BETWEEN THE PERIOD AND THE MASS?"!
08.50 T "WHAT IS THE VALUE OF PERIOD WHEN THE MASS IS ZERO?"!
08.60 T "WHAT DOES THIS REPRESENT?"!
08.70 T "CHECK IN THE LABORATORY TO SEE IF GRAVITY PLAYS A PART IN THE"!
08.71 T "OPERATION OF THE INERTIAL BALANCE."!!
08.80 T "WHAT DO YOU CONCLUDE ABOUT GRAVITATIONAL AND INERTIAL MASS?"!
*
```

Figure 3
Inertial and Gravitational Mass Program

INERTIAL AND GRAVITATIONAL MASS EXPERIMENT

ANSWER EACH QUESTION BY TYPING THE FIRST LETTER
OF THE WORD WHICH BEST ANSWERS THE QUESTION
THE INERTIAL BALANCE IS A DEVICE FOR MEASURING
THE INERTIAL MASS OF DIFFERENT OBJECTS.
FROM YOUR OBSERVATIONS IN THE LABORATORY IS THE
PERIOD GREATER OR SMALLER FOR SMALLER MASSES?:S

GOOD! HOW DO THE ACCELERATIONS OF DIFFERENT MASSES COMPARE
WHEN THE PLATFORM IS PULLED ASIDE ABOUT 2 CM AND
RELEASED? SELECT:(A) LARGER MASS, LARGER ACCELERATION
(B) LARGER MASS, SMALLER ACCELERATION:B
YOU ARE DOING FINE

DOES THIS SEEM TO BE IN ACCORD WITH NEWTON'S LAW OF MOTION?:Y
NOW YOU ARE TO DETERMINE HOW THE PERIOD OF THE BALANCE
VARIES WITH MASS.
WHAT SHALL I USE FOR MY RANGES OF MASS IN GRAMS,LOWER AND
UPPER LIMIT?:50 :800
MASS   PERIOD

=   50.0000=   0.7344
=   150.0000=   1.0385
=   250.0000=   1.2719
=   350.0000=   1.4687
=   450.0000=   1.6420
=   550.0000=   1.7988
=   650.0000=   1.9429
=   750.0000=   2.0770
NOW USING LOG-LOG PAPER, PLOT A GRAPH OF THE PERIOD AS
AS A FUNCTION OF MASS AND ANSWER THE FOLLOWING QUESTIONS:

WHAT IS THE SLOPE OF THE GRAPH?
W
 HAT IS THE RELATIONSHIP BETWEEN THE PERIOD AND THE MASS?
WHAT IS THE VALUE OF PERIOD WHEN THE MASS IS ZERO?
WHAT DOES THIS REPRESENT?
CHECK IN THE LABORATORY TO SEE IF GRAVITY PLAYS A PART IN THE
OPERATION OF THE INERTIAL BALANCE.

WHAT DO YOU CONCLUDE ABOUT GRAVITATIONAL AND INERTIAL MASS?
*

Figure 4
Inertial and Gravitational Mass Experiment

```
C-FOCAL , 8/68

01.10 A "R IN METERS =", R
01.20 A " M IN KILOGRAMS =",M,!
01.30 A "RANGE OF FORCE IN 10-2 NEW"S1,"TO",S2,"IN STEPS OF ",S,!
01.40 T ! "        FORCE "," PERIOD   (M AND R CONST)",!
01.50 FOR A=S1,S,S2, DO 2.0
01.60 GOTO 3.1

02.10 S T=6.26*FSQT(100*M*R/A)
02.20 T ! A,    T,

03.10 A !!"R CONST =",R," T CONST="T,!
03.15 A "RANGE OF MASS-",G1," TO ",G2," IN STEPS OF",Q,!
03.20 T ! "        FORCE ","        MASS (T AND R CONST)",!
03.30 FOR M= G1,Q,G2, DO 4.0
03.40 GOTO 5.1

04.10 S G=M*R*4*3.1416*3.1416/T↑2
04.20 T !   G, M

05.10 A !! "WHAT IS T",W,"WHAT IS M",Z,!
05.20 A "RANGE OF R, FROM", R1," TO ",R2, " IN STEPS OF ",P,!
05.30 T ! "        FORCE ", "     RADIUS (T AND M CONST)",!
05.40 FOR R = R1,P,R2, DO 6.0
05.50 QUIT

06.10 S V= Z*R*(2*3.1416/W)↑2
06.20 T ! V,R
*
R IN METERS =:1.0
 M IN KILOGRAMS =:.115

RANGE OF FORCE IN 10-2 NEW:40 TO:76.5 IN STEPS OF :7.3

        FORCE         PERIOD   (M AND R CONST)

=    40.0000=     3.3566
=    47.3000=     3.0867
=    54.6000=     2.8730
=    61.9000=     2.6982
=    69.2000=     2.5519
=    76.5000=     2.4271

R CONST =:.5    T CONST=:1.5

RANGE OF MASS-:.113  TO :.67  IN STEPS OF:.113


        FORCE       MASS (T AND R CONST)

=    0.9914=     0.1130
=    1.9827=     0.2260
=    2.9741=     0.3390
=    3.9654=     0.4520
=    4.9568=     0.5650

WHAT IS T:1.5 WHAT IS M:.115

RANGE OF R, FROM:.50  TO :1.10  IN STEPS OF :.1


        FORCE      RADIUS (T AND M CONST)

=    1.0089=     0.5000
=    1.2107=     0.6000
=    1.4125=     0.7000
=    1.6142=     0.8000
=    1.8160=     0.9000          Figure 5
=    2.0178=     1.0000    Centripetal Force Experiment
=    2.2196=     1.1000*
```

BIG APPLICATIONS FOR SMALL COMPUTERS

Kenneth D. Mackenzie

Optical Digital Systems Corporation
St. Paul, Minnesota

I. INTRODUCTION

Computers which cost more than an automobile but less than a house are becoming commonplace, yet their capabilities are not fully appreciated. These small machines, often referred to as minicomputers, are generally less expensive than the people who use them, yet perform many functions as adequately as most large expensive computers.

For illustration, a relatively large minicomputer-based system currently under development will be described. This system produces conventional engineering drawings on an array of incremental plotters, with input from a dozen interactive display consoles.

II. MINICOMPUTER CAPABILITIES

The strengths and weaknesses of minicomputers are best appreciated by making the distinction between computational power and processing agility. Power refers to the computer's ability to perform complex arithmetic and logical operations on data, many of which are accomplished by single commands in large computers. The speed with which a floating point addition or a conversion from binary to decimal can be performed is a useful index of processor power. Agility, on the other hand, refers to the ability of the computer to cope with a variety of dissimilar but routine demands placed on it by external events. The speed with which interrupts are handled and conditional transfers of control are decided is a useful index of processor agility. In these terms, minicomputers are quite agile, though not very powerful.

PROS

While the ratio of power/price tends to go up somewhat as computers increase in size and expense the ratio of agility/price tends to fall off rapidly. In fact, the most expensive computers are only a few times as agile as the typical minicomputer although they may cost hundreds of times as much. This disparity makes minicomputers extremely good real-time and input/output processors for their size.

A moderate level of computational power is required if the minicomputer is to perform any useful function beyond the most primitive level of device control or testing. The small computers currently on the market vary widely in this respect. Until recently, all were drastically deficient in computational power, word length, memory size and speed. Now, however, a number of models are available which are powerful enough to be considered as general purpose computers in the usual sense. It is this recent increase in power which makes the minicomputer suddenly suitable for many special purpose applications.

CONS

In addition to moderate computational power, other deficiencies common to small computers tend to restrict their usefulness. The absence of memory banking or memory phasing and the presence of a single multiplexed data channel prohibit the high data rates associated with certain peripheral devices. Small memory sizes limit the complexity of the programs which may be executed. The absence of relocation and protection logic implies that the processor will be dedicated to a single fixed group of application programs at a time.

The most important practical disadvantage of minicomputers is that they are expensive to program. Programs must be relatively efficient to yield acceptable performance, and no adequate compilors are available. This problem is offset somewhat by the fact that equipment cost is a negligible factor in program development.

III. MINICOMPUTER APPLICATIONS

From an applications standpoint, the most important impact of the minicomputer is that the dedication of a processor to a specific function becomes much less expensive. Some applications heretofore performed inefficiently on a bigger machine through time-sharing, can now afford to be performed separately on a dedicated minicomputer at some savings in cost or increase in performance.

Other applications, by their nature, have always required more or less continuous computer surveillance. Some applications in this category are now economically feasible for the first time. For instance, rather than thinking of an information retrieval system as a computer with some data storage, it makes more sense to view it as a data storage device with an attached computer for its interface to the outside world. Rather than thinking of a classic-type interactive

Reprinted with permission from *Proc. Nat. Electron. Conf.*, 1969, vol. 25, pp. 707–710.

graphic display as a computer system with an attached display terminal, it makes more sense to regard it as a display screen with its associated minicomputer picture control.

A second major area for the use of minicomputers consists of the rather mundane data processing applications which require little computation and power. Even the least powerful processor will spend most of its time waiting for the next payroll card to be read, or previous paycheck to finish printing.

IV. AUTOMATED DRAFTING SYSTEM

An illustration of minicomputer capability is provided by one of the automated drafting systems currently under development at Optical Digital Systems Corporation. The increasing shortage of draftsmen prompted the design of this ODS system to produce inked drawings for the electronics industry. Typical of the drawing types to be handled are logic diagrams, schematics, flow charts, PERT charts, and block diagrams. The design objectives for the system require that the service provide the quality of conventional manual drafting, but at a lower cost. The choice of a minicomputer was the primary answer to the cost consideration, while incremental plotters provided the requisite quality.

The system is designed for easy input specification and output plotting of most graphic symbols in common useage. Procedures for specification and drafting of additional special symbols are added to the application program from time to time as needed.

INPUT PROCEDURE

Diagrams to be drafted by the ODS system are supplied in the form of rough sketches on grid paper by the client engineer. An excerpt from such a sketch is reproduced in Figure 1. The only restriction on drawing size is that the shortest dimension may not exceed 30 inches, the width of the plotter drum. Standard drawing sizes A through D are usually requested.

Each data input operator works at an online display console composed of a keyboard and television screen. Reading from the client's sketch, the operator scans one grid square at a time. For each square the correct combination of keys are struck which specify the symbols observed in that square. As the coded specifications are input to the system, the corresponding graphic symbol is portrayed on the screen of the console for immediate verification of each input step. The television screen is not large enough to display an entire drawing. However, as the operator proceeds from square to square on the sketch, the display shifts to provide a visual "window" portraying the contents of several

squares to the left and above the current position on the sketch. Figure 2 represents this "window" display which enables the operator to verify the interconnection and alignment of symbols in the neighborhood of her current coding position on the sketch. The on-line display console feedback will provide an input mechanism with significant advantages in accuracy, reliability and cost over off-line data preparation methods.

When the input specification of a drawing is complete, the operator gives the recorded drawing a cursory audit by causing the display "window" of her console to portray a moving scan of the drawing. Errors in input may be corrected during this phase before the drawing is released to be plotted.

OTHER PROCESSING

Drawings which have been released for plotting are transferred from disk storage to a cassette magnetic tape. The tape serves as intermediate storage while the drawing awaits plotting and eventually becomes the permanent record for the drawing. Drawings are indexed and may be readily retrieved for revision and re-drafting should the client desire.

When a drawing is selected for plotting, blocks of specification records are read from magnetic tape into storage. For each specification, a table look-up is performed to obtain the parameters necessary to recreate the specified symbol on the plotter. In this way the plotters produce finished drawings with liquid ink on vellum paper. An excerpt is shown in Figure 3.

In the background, the minicomputer can handle accounting functions associated with individual clients, keeping a current status log on each drawing by recording such items as expended operator time per drawing and drawing completion status. It can also monitor operator status as she enters or leaves her work station.

SYSTEM CONFIGURATION

The hardware configuration of the ODS drafting system (pictured in Figure 4) centers around the Data General NOVA computer. This model was judged to be one of the most powerful minicomputers available as well as one of the least expensive. A teletypewriter, six incremental plotters, six cassette magnetic tape drives and the keyboard portions of twelve display consoles are driven directly through simple interfaces, since their data rates are extremely low. The television portions of the twelve display consoles are refreshed from a buffer external to main storage. A small head-per-track disk file buffers data in and out of main storage through a more elaborate peripheral controller.

Although the system is highly input/output

oriented, all peripherals except the television display are of sufficiently slow speeds so as to permit a high degree of simultaneous operation. There is very little demand on the system for computational power; the bulk of the processor's time is consumed in servicing the various peripherals.

SYSTEM CAPACITY

The throughput and economic advantage of the ODS system can be judged by comparison with manual drafting methods. It is anticipated that when the system is run on a three-shift schedule, it will produce high-quality drawings at a rate to match a 120 man drafting pool. Operating costs will permit the system to be run profitably and yet provide the service to industry at prices unavailable with conventional drafting methods.

V. CONCLUSIONS

A sharp decline in the minimum cost of computing is being caused by the commercial availability of remote access time sharing and by the advent of minicomputers. This cost decline is engendering many new specialized computing applications because of low startup and fixed equipment costs. Where these applications require short bursts of computational power, they will continue to employ remote terminals to a large shared computer. However, free-standing minicomputers will be employed increasingly often where the specific application requires relatively more agility, more real-time responsiveness, or more low-speed device control than time sharing services can provide. Indeed, the strengths (and weaknesses) of remote computing and minicomputing complement each other so well that any function inappropriate to one is probably a candidate for the other.

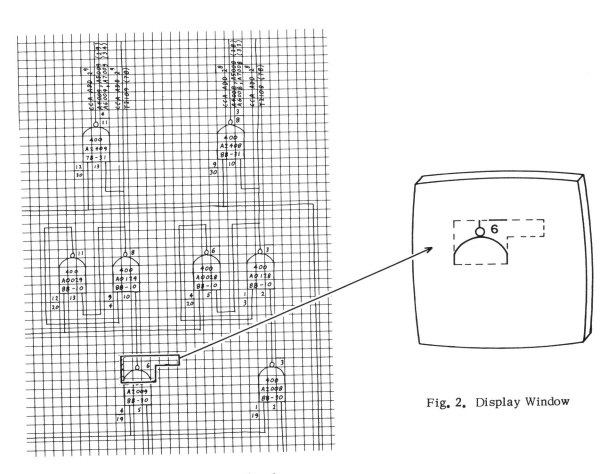

Fig. 1. Excerpt From Clients Sketch

Fig. 2. Display Window

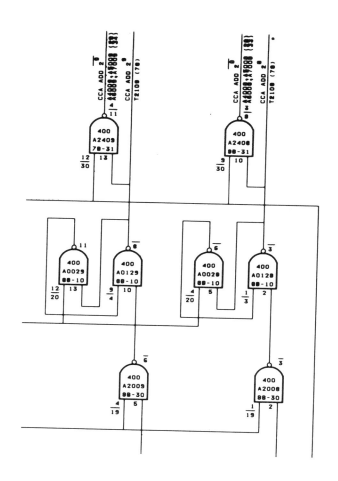

Fig. 3. Excerpt From Finished Drawing

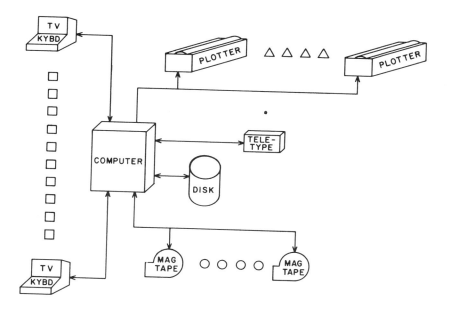

Fig. 4. Hardware Configuration

The digital computer with an A-to-D converter is beginning to replace multichannel analog recording methods and slide-rule data analysis much in the same manner as the latter supplanted the meter-and-clipboard approach of the past. Bell Telephone Labs found that the minicomputer is a rapid and economical approach to the problem of acquiring and analyzing large quantities of test data to aid in the design of prototype gas-turbine generator systems. Out of this project emerged Digital Equipment Corp.'s INDAC language, developed to facilitate data acquisition by minicomputers. Here is a description of Bell Labs' data collection system, along with Bell's reasons for taking the computer route.

Minicomputerizing
Analog Data Collection

P. J. TORPEY, Bell Telephone Labs

During the development of prototype systems, it is usually necessary to acquire large quantities of data to measure the performance of a prototype before it is committed to production. Where new systems are being developed on a continuing basis, the efficiency, versatility, and dependability of an R&D data-taking facility should be matters of prime importance. Thus, the high initial cost of computerized testing may well be worthwhile.

Computer-controlled data acquisition has become more attractive than manual methods for the following reasons:

■ Large amounts of information are obtainable at greater speed and with improved accuracy. Multichannel inputs may be rapidly scanned and both A-to-D conversion and conversion of the digital signals to engineering units may be performed with great precision.

■ Recent innovations in software development, such as those discussed later in this article, have made programming so straightforward that the engineer can communicate with the system on an English-language basis.

■ High-speed acquisition rates that effectively "stop the clock" can extend the technical capability of the data system. Furthermore, the digital computer can be programmed to initiate new action just as easily as it may be made to analyze old action. Thus the loop may be closed and one may control, as well as monitor.

■ Data may be formatted, arranged and grouped to suit the user. Also, it can be outputted in a form that facilitates further processing.

To make sure its communication network can meet emergency conditions, the Bell System provides standby power-generating systems in telephone offices across the country. These standby units consist primarily of gas-turbine and diesel-generator systems that can be called upon in the event of a power failure. Since various sizes (0.5 to 2,500 kilowatts) of these standby power systems are needed, and since they are constantly being updated to reflect state-of-the-art improvements, it was felt that the efficiency of prototype development could be improved through modern methods of data acquisition and processing. Previously the necessary data was read out on multichannel analog recorders and had to be sifted laboriously in order to be evaluated.

Defining the system

The mechanical response characteristics of gas-turbine and diesel engines are usually measurable in seconds, since important parameters such as compressor discharge pressure, fuel delivery pressure, fuel flow rate, rotational speed change, and exhaust gas temperature, normally change fairly slowly. A number of transducers such as strain gages (for pressure measurements), turbine-type flow sensors, and thermocouples do the measuring, and then convert the parameters they measure into low-level dc voltages or frequency signals. To make it possible to monitor a large number of transducers simultaneously, an A-to-D converter with multichannel input capability is tied into the computer. The effects of electrical noise on low-level transducer-output signals—particularly in a power-generating environment—dictate

Reprinted with permission from *Contr. Eng.*, pp. 69–74, June 1970.

"To minimize interfacing and compatibility problems, and to avoid having to design and maintain the computer system, it was decided to procure the system instead from a single source."

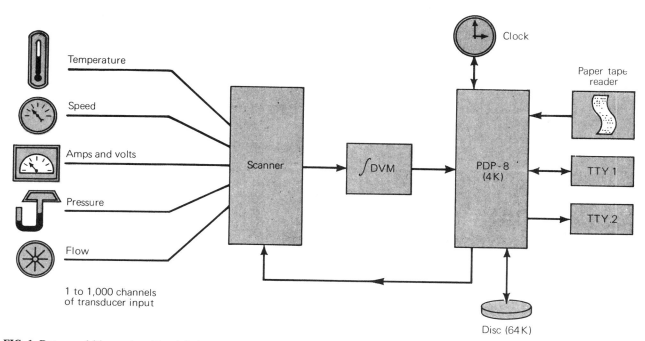

FIG. 1. Data acquisition system. To minimize noise, the A-to-D conversion (performed in the IDVM) is accomplished by the relatively slow procedure of integration rather than by the faster successive approximation method, because the noise rejection properties of the former are far superior to those of the latter.

a converter with superior noise rejection capability.

To further minimize noise, the analog to digital conversion is accomplished by the relatively slow procedure of integration rather than by the faster successive-approximation method. The noise-rejection properties of the former method are far superior to those of the latter. And slowness of the integration method is not a hindrance in this case because the need for speed in monitoring essentially low-frequency mechanical signals is not critical. In fact, wherever power system testing under noisy conditions is necessary, this type of A-to-D conversion is ideal.

Since one of the more obvious characteristics of any engineering development is change, it is essential that the data-acquisition system lend itself to frequent programming modifications. In addition, it is desirable that the programming language be sufficiently user-oriented to permit programming by the engineer in charge of development. After considering all available software for the PDP-8, the computer selected for the project, Bell Labs decided

to work with the PDP-8's manufacturer, Digital Equipment Corp., to develop a high-level data-acquisition language subsequently called INDAC (Industrial Data Acquisition and Control). Bell Labs submitted its requirements to DEC, and after eight months of debugging, the language was ready.

For hard-copy output at reasonable cost, a teletypewriter with a tape punch capability was the logical choice. Further, the keyboard of the teletypewriter permits user interaction with the system. Since information was to be acquired at a faster rate than it could be printed out, some added storage (magnetic tape or disc) was required as a buffer. Disc was selected over tape because it served the additional purpose of being usable as "virtual memory" (to be described later) in conjunction with the system software. To speed up the input of software, a high-speed photoelectric reader replaced the mechanical paper-tape reader on the teletypewriter. To speed up the output and to segregate transient data from steady state, a second teletypewriter was acquired.

"Recent innovations in software . . . . have made programming so straightforward that the engineer can communicate with the system on an English-language basis."

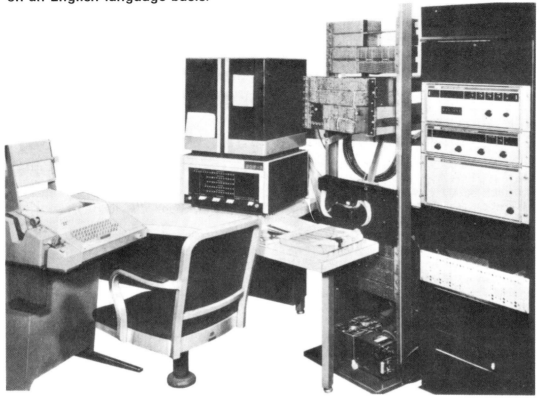

FIG. 2. Realization of the hardware. Shown here is the system as it appeared prior to the arrival of the second 32K disc unit and the ASR 35 teletypewriter. The PDP-8 is shown in the center. To its right is a rack housing the first disc unit (partially disassembled) and the high-speed paper tape reader. The rack at the extreme right houses the scanner, IDVM, and coupler in the upper half and a number of transducer power supplies at the bottom.

The timing requirements were that actual acquisition tasks should be under automatic clock control, clock interrupts should be programmable, and the system should be able to keep track of several timed sequences simultaneously. Another desired capability which was subsequently added was "foreground-background" swapping. This feature allowed the computer to be programmed to perform a nonreal-time or background function during the deadtime existing between one clock-controlled real-time task and the next one.

To illustrate how background-foreground swapping works, in one project trial runs were made on a 1.5-kw turbine and eight channels of data were sampled and stored on disc every second (for 90 secs) during the startup or initial foreground phase. The disc was used for storage to avoid the time delay inherent in typewriter output devices. Within 5 min after startup, steady-state (normal turbine operation) data was acquired and processed, and typed out during a second foreground phase. The second phase was activated every 5 min until manual interruption.

Meanwhile the background phase was executed between successive 5-min steady-state acquisition periods to retrieve, process, and output the data collected during the initial startup phase. To avoid mixing startup data with steady-state outputs, the background data was sent to the auxiliary teletypewriter.

Making the selection

To minimize interfacing and compatibility problems, and to avoid having to design and maintain the computer system, it was decided to procure the system from a single source. In addition to the computer, other Digital Equipment Corp. components included were a low-level scanner, an integrating digital voltmeter, two teletypewriters, two discs, an elapsed-time clock, and a photoelectric tape reader.

Figure 1 depicts the resulting system. Up to 200 transducer signals may be handled by the reed relay scanner. The channels may be switched in sequential or random fashion either manually or under program

Sampling Rate, Resolution, and Noise Rejection
For Various Integration Intervals

Integration time (period of 60-cps wave)	Sampling rate (channels/second)	Resolution (10-millivolt range)	Common mode rejection (dB)
0.1	50	10 microvolts	100
1.0	25	1 microvolt	120
10	5	0.1 microvolt	140

control. Input channels may be activated in groups of ten up to 200, and slave scanners may be added to increase capacity to 1,000 channels. Not shown in Figure 1 are the auxiliary power supplies and converters that are required to energize various transducers.

The dc signals from the scanner are sent one at a time to the integrating digital voltmeter (IDVM), where they are integrated for either 0.1, 1.0, or 10 periods of a 60-cps waveform. The longer the integration period, the greater the common-mode noise rejection and the slower the analog-to-digital conversion process. The lengths of integration periods as well as ranges of inputs may be set for each channel under program control. The available sampling rates, resolution, and noise rejection for various values of integration time for this equipment are listed in the table above.

Frequency and period measurements may also be made by the IDVM—a capability useful for pulse count devices such as some types of flowmeters and speed pickups.

The digitized signals in bcd format (three words per channel) are received by the computer, where they are converted to pure binary form and held along with channel identification information until further instructions are given. When the data processing portion of the program is called out, the computer automatically retrieves from the disc, the particular sections of the executive and user programs that are needed to activate successive operating sequences. This interplay between disc and core, which has the effect of making core appear much larger than it is, is referred to as "virtual memory."

The main computer memory is the basic 4,096-word configuration offered for the PDP-8. Two disc surfaces operated by a single controller add 64K of auxiliary storage for retaining the system software and the collected data.

A 12-bit digital clock, deriving its 60 cps frequency (16.67-millisec pulses) from commercial power, provided system timing. The timing functions normally include determining when data is to be taken from each transducer, determining how long the data is to be acquired, and sequencing data processing and printout. This version of the system software restricted timing operations to integral multiples of a second, though it would have been more desirable to be able to operate in fractions of a second.

The peripheral bottleneck

The two teletypewriters consisted of an ASR-35, which served as both an input and output device, and an ASR-33 (subsequently replaced by a more rugged RO 35), which was used only as an output device. The 10-character-per-sec typing speed of these units was tolerable for the real-time testing of most standby power systems, and with both teletypewriters operating in parallel, the effective data output rate was nearly 20 characters per sec. Such a rate is probably close to the maximum assimilation rate of the typical observer viewing instrument readings.

However, the adequacy of a ten-character-per-sec speed for loading system software and user-generated programs is quite another matter. The process of reading in the monitor system, compiler, and the executive (operating) system would have taken literally hours at this rate—loading of a typical user program alone takes upwards of 15 min. For this reason, a high-speed photoelectric reader with a read-in rate of 300 characters per sec was added to the system at the outset. Since the system software had FORTRAN-like computational capabilities, there was little need to take the data to a larger computer for further analysis. If this had been a consideration, a high-speed punch would have been added as well.

Digital inputs from sensing relays connected directly to the computer, and contact closure outputs from the computer to other devices, were not required for this system. Also absent was digital to analog conversion at the computer output. But hardware for these features can easily be added, and provision for implementing them is included in the system software. Future projects might require these capabilities for synchronization and remote signaling.

Figure 2 depicts the computer system prior to the arrival of the second 32,000-word disc unit and the ASR 35 teletypewriter unit. The scanner, integrating digital voltmeter and coupler are grouped on the upper half of the equipment cabinet at the right. At the bottom of this cabinet are a number of regulated dc power supplies to activate strain gage pressure transducers.

An essential feature—user-oriented software

To make proper use of such a system, it was essential that a software package be created which would allow the programs to be modified easily as the development progressed, and that the programing language be as simple as possible. To meet the second requirement, DEC and Bell Labs' Power Sources Development Group cooperated to produce English-language-based INDAC in mid-1969.

INDAC is a high-level computer language syntactically similar to FORTRAN. It retains the more commonly used arithmetic functions found in FORTRAN and possesses FORTRAN's versatility of output formatting. In addition, INDAC permits clock interrupts to initiate data acquisition and facilitates the conversion and processing of data during lull periods. The basic elements comprising the software package are the system builder, the compiler, the executive, and the library. In working with INDAC, the system builder requests information about hardware configuration and then structures the compiler and the executive to handle that configuration. The result is a conservation of core and disc space due to the elimination of handlers and subroutines, which are not needed in a specific situation.

Programs to assist in debugging, editing, and dumping are loaded along with the compiler. The compiler converts the user source program into object code that is executable by the operating system. The compiler also outputs the amount of core space required by each element of the user program. Altogether, 166 numerically coded, detailed diagnostic statements are available during compilation, for output on the teletypewriter as required. The executive program, following a compiler-generated object code, allocates disc and core space, detects clock interrupts, schedules program phases, handles data flow, and monitors the keyboard for user interaction during run time.

The library holds subroutines for arithmetic and trigonometric operations. It may also contain conversion routines for the more common thermocouple types. Additional routines for specific devices can be either added to the library, or incorporated into each user program as external subroutines.

The entire software system as presently used for power system development testing is contained on a single paper tape. This tape is loaded once through the high-speed reader and then stored on a portion of the disc. Program segments are transferred from disc to core as needed.

Some of the more useful features of the system software include:

■ Foreground-background swapping to allow data processing and output between the acquisition tasks.

"An informal, but cooperative effort between DEC and Bell Lab's Power Sources Development Group resulted in the emergence of INDAC in mid-1969."

```
        .EQUIPMENT *AF04
        CHAN(57,60)PRES
↑#10    DC,10MV,.01
↑       *CLOCK
        .STORAGE ICLK(1,3)


#1      .PHASE
        .ACTION
#101    DO SNAP #100 EVERY 10 MIN
        TIMER(RESET)
        TIMER(START,#101)


#100    .SNAP
#20     .FORMAT
        XX"HR"   XX"MIN"   XX"SEC"
#30     .FORMAT
        "PRES"X"=" XX.XX "INCHES OF H2O"
        .PROCESS
        GET(CLOCK)ICLK
        GET(AF04,#10)PRES
        DO PCON(PRES)
        SEND(TTY,#20)ICLK
        FOR I=1 TO 4
        SEND(TTY,#30)I,PRES(I)
        NEXT I
        EXIT




        .SUBROUTINE PCON(X)
        .STORAGE M(1,4)/348.0,375.0,355.0,355.0/,
↑       B(1,4)/-0.35,-0.1,0.0,0.0/
        .PROCESS
        FOR I=1 TO 4
        LET X(I)=M(I)*X(I)+B(I)
        NEXT I
        RETURN PCON
        .END

*
```

FIG. 3. Sample INDAC program. This segment of the program reads the dc voltages with 0.01 percent resolution from channels 57 through 60 (pressure transducers) once every 10 min. The transducer outputs are next processed by subroutine "PCON," which converts them to engineering units (inches of water). The four pressures together with time are then sent to the teletypewriter.

> "Since one of the more obvious characteristics of any engineering development is change, it is essential that the data-acquisition system lend itself to frequent programming modifications."

```
ØHR  IØMIN   ØSEC
PRES1=  0.86  INCHES OF H2O
PRES2=  0.10  INCHES OF H2O
PRES3=  0.08  INCHES OF H2O
PRES4=  0.08  INCHES OF H2O




ØHR  2ØMIN   ØSEC
PRES1=  0.86  INCHES OF H2O
PRES2=  0.10  INCHES OF H2O
PRES3=  0.08  INCHES OF H2O
PRES4=  0.08  INCHES OF H2O




ØHR  3ØMIN   ØSEC
PRES1=  0.85  INCHES OF H2O
PRES2=  0.10  INCHES OF H2O
PRES3=  0.07  INCHES OF H2O
PRES4=  0.08  INCHES OF H2O




ØHR  4ØMIN   ØSEC
PRES1=  0.86  INCHES OF H2O
PRES2=  0.10  INCHES OF H2O
PRES3=  0.07  INCHES OF H2O
PRES4=  0.08  INCHES OF H2O
```

FIG. 4. Data printout. The data acquired from running the program segment presented in Figure 3 is printed out on the teletypewriter, as shown. The four pressure transducers being monitored were checked every 10 min, and the data acquired over four successive scans is presented here.

This feature also allows certain channels to be periodically monitored for limit checks while other channels are monitoring data.

■ User selection of floating point or integer variable designation.

■ Multiple teletypewriter output to facilitate data flow and to segregate different types of data at the discretion of the user.

■ Variable preset to permit the user to set certain constants in his program prior to startup and to change these values while the program is running.

■ User-dedicated disc storage space designated as "file" to hold raw or processed data prior to output. Approximately 20,000 words are available for this purpose.

■ Segregation of the user program into free standing elements called "snaps," only one of which is resident in core at a time. This allows the user to execute a much larger program than would otherwise be possible.

■ Provision for logic decision in conjunction with digital pulse (on-off) input and output capability.

A sample user program

The program listed in Figure 3 is a small segment of a much larger program for power systems development testing. The computer first reads the dc output voltages in the 10-millivot range and with 0.01 percent resolution of four strain-gage differential-pressure transducers (channels 57 to 60 on the scanner), along with elapsed time.

The output signals from the transducers are processed by subroutine "PCON," which converts the signals (a linear slope-intercept conversion) to engineering units, in this case inches of water. The four pressures, together with time, are then printed out on the teletypewriter.

The system will repeat this operation every 10 min until halted by the operator. Although Figure 3 does not demonstrate the use of foreground-background swapping, multiple teletypewriter output, variable preset or user generated "file," it does illustrate the inherent simplicity of the language and its similarity to FORTRAN. The output which resulted from running this program appears in Figure 4.

The sequence of operations required to start the system after all the transducers have been connected and calibrated is as follows: A paper tape of the user program, prepared on- or off-line, is loaded via the high-speed reader and then compiled, the compiler being called from the disc by typed instructions. If the program must be debugged, it is corrected at the keyboard under control of the editor program. Once compilation has been completed, the executive is called into operation and it, together with the object version of the user program, provides all the instructions needed to begin running. Execution is initiated when the user types a special character at the keyboard console. □

ON-LINE SMALL COMPUTER DATA HANDLING IN PULSE HEIGHT ANALYSIS AND TWO PARAMETER MULTICHANNEL COINCIDENCE DATA STORAGE*

E. DER MATEOSIAN

Brookhaven National Laboratory, Upton, New York, U.S.A.

Received 5 May 1969

The role which small "on-line" computers may play in nuclear spectroscopy is reviewed and a computer-analyser combination at Brookhaven National Laboratory is described. The data handling capabilities of this combination for "singles" spectra and plans for its use for storing two parameter 1000 × 1000 channel coincidence data on tape are reviewed. A system for two parameter 1000 × 1000 coincidence data storage on a disc is proposed and advantages and disadvantages of the system are discussed.

1. Introduction

The introduction of better resolution into α-, β- and γ-spectroscopy through the use of solid state detectors has had an accompanying effect of increasing to the dismaying point the amount of data confronting experimentalists engaged in these studies. It is no longer satisfactory to run an experiment for a period of time, to print out a few hundred numbers, to go to a desk calculator and to compute by hand the desired results of the experiment. With data being stored frequently in 2000 to 4000 "channels", a common method of handling data has become to record on paper or magnetic tape and to carry the data to a large central computer for reduction. When the data may contain from thirty to several hundred "peaks", as often happens, it is no longer just convenient, but almost mandatory, to adopt mass methods of data handling.

The large computer, however, has not been the final answer to the problem of data reduction for the nuclear radiations spectroscopist. The advent of computerization has confronted the experimentalist with the need for programming computers to do a variety of tasks. Large computers, centrally located and shared with other users, impose new conditions upon the experimentalist. There is a waiting period between the time the data are taken to the computer complex and the time of delivery of the results, and programs tend to become more complex as the computer undertakes more of the functions once performed by the experimentalist. For example, in the analysis of spectra, the program is written to not only determine the position and area of peaks, but it is asked to find them as well[1]. As a result, the researcher often experiences a feeling of isolation from the data and computations.

In the past several years another alternative has presented itself to the problem, mainly due to the availability of small computers at considerably reduced costs. This has opened up the on-line use of small computers for the dual purposes of pulse height analysis and data reduction[2]. Two basic systems are possible: 1. a small computer interfaced to a wired pulse height analyser for control of the analyser during data accumulation and for data reduction and computations following completion of data accumulation; 2. a small computer (perhaps with augmented memory) interfaced to analog to digital converter (ADC) input units and programmed to do data accumulation and pulse height analysis as well as subsequent data reduction.

2. Analyser-computer combination

The author has had a two parameter, 4 k memory pulse height analyser with 4000 channel ADC's interfaced to a Digital Equipment Co., PDP8/I computer[3]. The interface is so constructed as to allow the computer to perform the following functions:

1) Control of the mode of operation of the analyser, i.e., "accumulate", "display", "print", "plot", etc.;

2) Transfer of data from analyser memory into computer memory through the computer accumulator under program control;

3) Control of ADC's-ability to inhibit or to allow storage of data in the analyser under program control and to transfer data from the ADC's into the accumulator of the computer either directly or through the program interrupt feature of the computer.

An advantage of this system over the second kind to be described is that the analyser and computer may be isolated one from the other and may be used independently. Thus, while data are being accumulated

* Work performed under the auspices of the U.S. Atomic Energy Commission.

in the analyser, the computer may be used for other tasks. New programs may be debugged without fear that a programming mistake might obliterate the results of an experiment.

Data may be accumulated either through computer control or through the analyser control system. Similarly, the other functions of the analyser are under this dual control. Complex sequences of data acquisition, print out, etc. may be initiated and executed through suitable programming of the computer.

3. Pulse height analysis programmed computer

The alternative approach to a system for pulse height analysis is to program a small computer to accumulate, store, and display data. A typical system would contain one or two ADC's interfaced to the computer, some sort of display unit and teletype keyboard, punch and tape reader for input and output of data. This system suffers from several disadvantages: some of the memory necessarily must be set aside for program storage, programs must be written for all functions of the system and there does not exist the option of using the computer "off-line" while accumulating data. On the other hand, this system is economical, since one does not invest in an analyser, and it offers some distinctly interesting opportunities to improve on the capabilities for data storage and display offered by the conventional analyser. In a wired analyser, the maximum number which may be stored in a given storage location is decided upon at the time of construction. If this maximum is exceeded, the number is reset to zero and is incremented from that value. These "spill overs" are a problem in conventional counting and some method must be devised to keep count of them in order to reconstruct the value of the number stored in that location. With a computer "analyser", one is free to arrange the method of storage to either minimize or to eliminate spillover. For example, if one knows that the capacity of an adress is going to be exceeded, one can assign two adresses for the storage of the number ("double precision"). In a computer with a 12 bit word storage capacity this now assigns 24 bits to a number, giving a maximum capacity of about 16 million. Furthermore, this decision may be made by the computer while accumulating data.

Again, if the analyser is accumulating pulses from a device whose efficiency varies with energy (this is the usual situation with Si or Ge detectors), the computer may be given the efficiency-energy relationship for the particular detector used and it can be asked to increment not one count at each address for each event, but a number which is inversely related to the efficiency, so that the resulting spectrum stored (or displayed) will be "corrected" for efficiency. The cost of this kind of analyser is very attractive. Small computers have become very inexpensive; for example, a 4 k 12 bit memory computer may be obtained for under $ 9 000, including the cost of a teletype unit[4]). A 4 000 or 8 000 channel ADC may be obtained for about $ 2 500 which may be interfaced to the computer for a few thousand dollars more. A scope and display may be added for about $ 3 500 so that a basic analyser unit could be assembled for about $ 17 000. For about $ 3 500 an additional 4 k memory could be added, so that for about $ 21 000 a basic unit could be acquired that could be used for pulse height analysis.

4. Data handling

The philosophy adopted in developing the data handling software for the computer-analyser combination described above is that interaction between the experimentalist and the computations is desirable. The data display is frequently consulted for decision making. Programs are so written that the teletype is often used by the computer to ask for the input during computations of such quantities as efficiencies, fluorescent yields, and absorption corrections. The experimentalist inputs these quantities through use of the teletype keyboard, which is used also to call for various computing routines. Programs have been written to enable the computer to perform the following functions:

1) Stored data relocation — N channels of data stored in addresses starting at analyser address A1 are reproduced in N channels starting at address A2. This is accomplished by typing the initial address of the program (where upon the program asks for the input of data) and typing the two addresses and the number of channels. This program is useful when it is desired to compare two spectra taken under identical conditions, or when data manipulation is desired without loss of the original data.

2) Least squares fit of parabola to background — When it is desired to obtain the area under a peak, often one must subtract contributions from backgrounds upon which the peaks stand. This program extrapolates the background under a peak by fitting a parabola to a portion of the background chosen by the experimentalist. After calling for the extrapolation program, the operator types five channel numbers, or addresses, in a segment of the spectrum extending to both sides of a peak. By observing the spectrum in

the display, he may choose addresses of representative points of the background which fall outside of peaks or local fluctuations. The computer then constructs the extrapolated curve in another quarter of the memory which may be superimposed in display on the original data. The operator may decide whether he is satisfied with the fit or wishes to modify it further before using it in computations.

3) Subtraction of spectra — The difference of two spectra stored in two separate locations in memory is stored in a third location.

4) Sum under peaks — This routine asks for two addresses to be typed on the keyboard, then types the sum of the contents of all channels between and including the two addresses given. The sum so obtained may be retained in memory for further computations.

5) Least squares Gaussian fit to peaks — This is really an approximate Gaussian fit. A least squares fit is made of the first three terms in the series expansion of the Gaussian function. The program asks for five channel numbers which are judiciously chosen so that the third address given is the peak position, and the first and last two are symmetrically spaced above

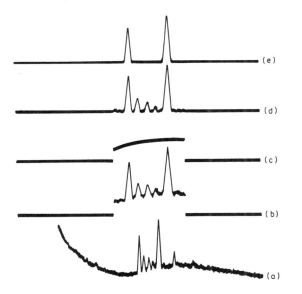

Fig. 1. Manipulation of spectra for computational purposes. A typical spectrum (X-rays) is shown in fig. (a) containing several peaks on a varying background. A portion of this spectrum was transferred to another section of the memory and is displayed in (b) in a slightly expanded scale. A least squares fit of a parabola [fig. (c)] was made to the background under the peaks and was stored in a third portion of memory. The difference of spectra (b) and (c) was stored in another section of memory and is shown in (d). A least squares fit of "Gaussians" to two of the peaks is shown in (e).

and below the peak position. This is accomplished in the following manner: The program calls for five numbers, then a channel number, or address. For example, if it is desired to fit a peak 11 channels wide, the following series of numbers −10, −5, 0, 5, 10 may be given the computer via the teletype keyboard, followed by the channel number of the peak position. The computer then constructs a Gaussian peak in another section of memory. In spite of the approximation these fits are remarkably good. In most cases, when the sum under a peak was compared to the area of the "Gaussian", the agreement was better than to a few parts per thousand.

6) Further calculations — The above programs have been written in a language called "Focal", which is a compiler language developed by Digital Equipment Company and which is extremely suited to the calculations which normally accompany the reduction of data encountered in pulse height analysis. Thus, it is extremely easy to write programs in this language to utilize the results of the above described manipulations. An example of a series of operations one might employ in the handling of a typical spectrum is shown in fig. 1. Fig. 1a shows a spectrum which contains K X-ray lines of Cd and In. A portion of this spectrum is shown in fig. 1b after it was transferred to another part of memory. A least squares fit to the background under the peaks is shown in fig. 1c and the difference of figs. 1b and 1c is shown in fig. 1d. Finally, in 1e, one sees "Gaussian" peaks which were least squares fitted to two of the peaks in the spectrum. If it were desired to know the ratio of Cd to In X-rays, the computer could be programmed to sum under both peaks and to type out the ratio. If absolute intensities were desired, a program could be written to ask for the input of fluorescent yields, efficiencies, and absorption corrections and the corrected intensities of the X-rays could be typed out.

The versatility offered the operator by the Focal language may be illustrated with an example. Assume that after the series of operations pictured in fig. 1 it were desired to obtain the area under one of the peaks and to correct this area for fluorescent yield and the efficiency of the detector. Let it also be assumed that the program to do this has not been written as yet. The operator would write a three step program, the first step of which would ask for the input of addresses to locate the peak in memory, the second would instruct the computer to calculate the sum under the peak and the third step would ask for the input of the fluorescent yield and efficiency corrections and print out the corrected area. This program would be written in less than five minutes and would look like the following:

4.1. Ask A1, A2; Set S = 0
4.2. For I = A1, A2; Set A = FGet(I); Set S = S + A
4.3. Ask "fl. yd", Y; Ask "eff. corr."E; Type S/Y*E,!
4.4. Quit.

Now the operator would type "GOTO 4.1", the computer would ask for the peak location and then the fluorescent yield and efficiency correction. The operator would type these values on the teletype keyboard and immediately the corrected area would be typed out by the computer. It is a tremendous advantage to be able to program in a compiler language because the use of this language allows one to program as the need arises. In machine language, this would be impractical and all programs would have to be anticipated and prepared beforehand.

5. Two parameter, multichannel coincidence data storage

When a pulse height analyser is to be used to store two-parameter multichannel coincidence data, a commonly used scheme is to "arrange" its memory into a matrix of m rows and n columns, where m corresponds to the number of channels of input 1 and n to the number of channels of input 2. Then a coincidence between a particular channel i of input 1 and a particular channel j of input 2 may be stored in location l_{ij} of the matrix. To use this scheme with 1000 channel inputs, however, would require a million storage sites and the cost of such an array would be prohibitive. Alternative storage schemes[5]) have been devised to overcome this difficulty, the most useful and interesting of which has been the idea of storing on magnetic tape. A coincidence of events in channel i of input 1 and channel j of input 2 may be recorded by writing this pair of "addresses" on magnetic tape at the time of occurrence of the event. A better scheme, from the point of view of efficient utilization of the computer, is to set aside a block of addresses in the core of the computer as a buffer for the storage of events, the data stored being the two addresses of the inputs. When the buffer is filled, accumulation is stopped, the buffer contents are "dumped" onto magnetic tape, and accumulation is resumed[6]). In many applications the interruption of accumulation is not a serious problem. However, there is a (now standard) way of avoiding the necessity to interrupt the accumulation which has been adopted in a program written for the 4000 channel analyser — PDP8/I combination at Brookhaven. The computer has been programmed to

reserve two buffer storage areas. The main program (and "idle" program) of the computer is to wait until one buffer has been filled. It then switches to the second buffer for storage and prints out the first buffer contents onto tape. When the second buffer memory is filled it again switches back to the first buffer for storage and prints out the contents of the second buffer. If an event occurs which should be stored, the computer "interrupts" its main program and proceeds with storing the event in the proper place. The accumulation of data may be ended by the experimentalist by touching any key on the teletype keyboard. The use of two buffer storage areas and the interrupt mode of data storage allows one to avoid the necessity for periodically stopping the accumulation of data in order to print.

The final product of this procedure is a tape containing a large number of pairs of addresses, each pair associated with one event, and appearing on the tape in the order in which they occurred. Before this data can be useful, it must be assembled into m spectra of n channels each. A program to do this has been written which sets aside n locations in the computer for the assembly of one spectrum and which asks the operator to give the computer one address i of input 1 whose corresponding coincidence spectrum it is wished to assemble. The computer then scans through the tape and each time it finds an event i, j where i corresponds to the "search" address of input 1 it increments by one the count in location j in the n channels set aside in the computer for the assembly of the spectrum. When the search is completed, the spectrum is transferred to the analyser memory for display, and data reduction and handling. If one were to do 1000×1000 channel coincidences 1000 such searches would be required. To reduce this number, several devices are available. While the computer is storing the coincidence data on tape the analyser is programmed to store all coincidence events in input 1 in 1000 channels of memory set aside for it, and to store all coincidence events in input 2 in another 1000 channels of memory. These, in a sense, are the projections of the "$m \times n$ matrix" on its x and y axes. An inspection of these projection spectra tells the operator which channels contain relevant information and which are empty. Thus empty channels may be eliminated from the search routine. Another device which may be adopted shows the flexibility of the system. If the data collected by the analyser were typically pulses from lithium drifted germanium counters detecting gamma rays, a photoelectric peak associated with one gamma ray might be 3 to 10 channels wide depending on the conditions of the experimental set up. In assembling spectra for subsequent use for obtaining quantitative numbers related to the intensities of the photons present, one might wish to add all spectra in coincidence with the channels which make up the peak of the selected gamma ray in input 1. In the example above this would be equivalent to taking a 3 to 10 channel wide cut in the $m \times n$ matrix and adding the 3 to 10 channels point by point along the n axis. This task is easily accomplished by supplying the computer the addresses of all the channels in the cut (i.e. the "3 to 10" channels) and assembling these spectra in the same n locations in memory reserved for one spectrum previously. Thus, ten channels may be scanned and added together in the time of roughly one scan. If enough core memory is available, two sets of n channels may be set aside to assemble two spectra in one scan. Thus a cut containing the spectra in coincidence with a peak and an adjacent cut to be used as a background could be assembled in one scan.

With the expenditure of a modest amount of money (\$ 3 500 for each additional 4 k of memory in the case of the PDP8/I computer) one could expand this capability by an impressive amount. If, for example, an additional 16 k of memory were to be added to the PDP8, one would have available 4 k of memory for program storage and 16 k of memory for spectrum assemblage. One could assemble 16 spectra in one pass; each spectrum could be, if so desired, an addition spectrum composed of as many adjacent spectra as there are channels in a peak in the "Y" direction (input 1). If this number happened to be five channels, one would be capable of "scanning" 80 channels at a time. When this capability is combined with the ability to detect and reject empty channels through inspection of the sum spectra stored by the analyser, it becomes apparent that the burden of scanning tape to assemble spectra can be reduced to a remarkable degree.

Recently the price of storage discs has come down to levels which make them acceptable as an alternative device for the storage of a large number of data. An inexpensive disc capable of storing roughly a quarter of a million 12 bit words is available from Digital Equipment Company for use with the PDP8/I. The disc may be expanded to a capacity of a million word storage with the addition of up to three more discs. This now opens up the possibility of storing assembled spectra as accumulation proceeds — a decided improvement over the tape storage since the scanning time is eliminated and there is offered the opportunity to display during accumulation. The disc, however, is slow if one asks for random access for storage of

experimental data and counting rates of the order of 60 to 100 a second would seem to be the maximum counting rate which would be tolerated. If one does some coarse sorting prior to storage and devises programs to offset the wait dependent upon the mechanical motion of the device, one may increase the rate of storage. Several schemes immediately present themselves. For example, instead of storing events on the disc in chronological order, the incoming data could be stored in a buffer and then as each address of the disc appeared one could search the buffer to see if there were an event to be recorded. Since not much time would be available for searching, the buffer memory could be divided into sections, each corresponding to a sector of the disk. The incoming data could than be subjected to a coarse selection to choose the appropriate buffer section for storage and then, as each sector of disk approached the recording heads, a data search could be started in but limited to the section of buffer reserved for it[7]). Through such presorting of data, one may achieve several hundred counts per second. For some applications, this is a sufficiently large rate to make this idea attractive, but it is hoped that with a few more innovations in the use and design of discs the storage rate may be increased to from 2000 to 4000 counts per second. With a million storage locations and the need for 5% statistics or less, it might on occassion be necessary to collect 10^9 counts in one run. At 1000 counts per second, it would require of the order of ten days to collect this amount of data. Hence the need for count rates in the thousands per second. At the moment, existing limits to the capacity of amplifiers to handle count rates larger than 40 000 counts per second and the recognition that 10% efficiencies in detectors may be the best one may have available in a general experiment allows one to predict that coincidence count rates larger than 4000 counts per second will not often be attained. These considerations lead to the conclusion that 4000 counts/sec may be an upper limit to the counting rate requirement one should impose on a coincidence system, and that 1000 counts per second need be achieved before the system could be considered to be of general use and worth the cost of the storage device.

The program for two parameter, multichannel coincidence storage on tape described above was written for and tested with a fast paper tape punch while the decision as to which storage system (magnetic tape or disc) to use is being considered. This has allowed "debugging" and testing of the storage and assembling programs to proceed during this interim period. The final system will contain a Dectape unit with two tape transports if the tape storage system is decided upon, so that programs and data may be stored at the same time. If a disc system is decided upon, a disc will be acquired for program and data storage and one tape unit, not necessarily a Dectape unit, will be acquired for permanent storage of data at the end of the data accumulation and reduction period.

The author wishes to acknowledge helpful discussions on various aspects of nuclear spectroscopy with W. Gelletly, M. Mariscotti and A. Sunyar. E. Willen and members of the Applied Mathematics Department at Brookhaven National Laboratory were exceedingly helpful and encouraging with advice on decisions related to the kind of computer and system which was assembled by the author. Finally, L. Elekman and E. Glazer of the Digital Equipment Company were generous with many suggestions and with programming help.

References

[1] M. A. Mariscotti, Nucl. Instr. and Meth. **50** (1967) 309.
[2] A description of a program called *Strip, a data display and analysis program* may be obtained from J. C. Alderman, Georgia Institute of Technology, Nuclear Research Center, 900 Atlantic Drive, Atlantic, Georgia, U.S.A.
[3] The interface was constructed by Geoscience Nuclear, a division of Geoscience Instruments Corp., Hamden, Connecticut 06518, U.S.A.
[4] Digital Equipment Corp., Maynard, Massachusetts 01754, U.S.A.
[5] For more complete references to the field of pulse height analysis with computers consult articles in IEEE Trans. Nucl. Sci.
[6] R. A. McNaught and J. W. Bowman, Chalk River Report ELI-99.
[7] These ideas were developed through discussions with L. Elekman and E. Glazer of Digital Equipment Co.

MATURING MINI-COMPUTERS*

by Christopher B. Newport

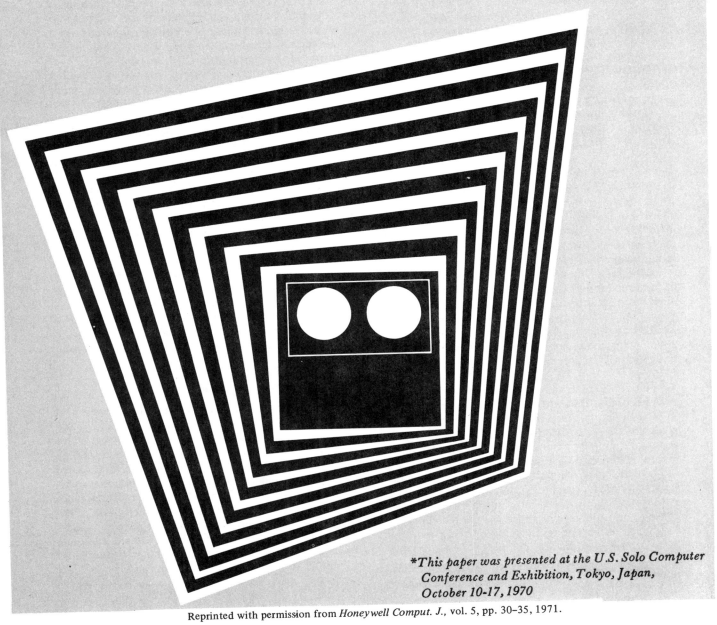

*This paper was presented at the U.S. Solo Computer
Conference and Exhibition, Tokyo, Japan,
October 10-17, 1970

Reprinted with permission from *Honeywell Comput. J.*, vol. 5, pp. 30–35, 1971.

A mammoth central computer has traditionally been the heart of most large real-time systems in government and industry. Because of increasing demands for service, users have upgraded to larger systems, only to find that increasing usage of their systems necessitates another upgrade in a few years. This type of growth cannot go on indefinitely, and one option is being developed through the medium of networks of mini-computers. By segmenting the application problem, a network of smaller computers can handle a distributed processing load, and can provide more processing power than could possibly be built into one central site super computer. A system of mini-computers has the ability to grow fairly easily as increasing demands are made upon it; minor variations for specific parts of the network can be handled conveniently, and software development is significantly facilitated. Through applications such as these, mini-computers are beginning to mature into sophisticated computing modules, and are being accepted as full-fledged members of the computer family.

INTRODUCTION

The most elaborate computer systems in use today are the large real-time systems which have been built up at great expense by the government and major industrial corporations. They cover applications such as military command and control, airline reservations, time-sharing, on-line banking, stock brokerage, and so on. Many of these systems have taken thousands of man years of effort to bring to completion, and sometimes the results have not lived up to expectations. To achieve the desired throughput, users have frequently had to substitute larger and larger computers as the complexity of software pushed up the overhead. In addition, successful systems, particularly those for airlines, have found that the increasing demand for service has outstripped the rate at which hardware and software can be expanded. For instance, the American Airlines SABRE System was initially implemented on IBM 7094 computers, then upgraded to include IBM System/360 machines, and now, because of the increasing load, consideration has been given to changing to 360/195's.

This type of growth cannot go on indefinitely, and it is now becoming apparent that the only practical solution is segmenting the problem through networks of smaller computers to handle a distributed processing load. In the airlines case, instead of providing more powerful centralized facilities, a better solution would be to provide small computers to handle all the reservation traffic over specific routes. For instance, one small system might handle all traffic between Boston and New York, and another might handle the Chicago-Los Angeles route. For reservations covering multiple legs, a central coordinating computer (of reasonable size) could be used. A more sophisticated implementation would allow the small single-route systems to

interact with each other in obtaining multiple-route reservations. Thus, an interconnected set of small computers could be organized to provide more processing power than could possibly be built into one central site super computer.

An analogy might be drawn with a democratic society in which each individual acting freely (but within certain guidelines) brings about a far more prosperous community than can be achieved by a single super dictator attempting to control every action.

ADVANTAGES OF MINI-COMPUTER SYSTEMS

The distributed computing network brings additional advantages which should make it very attractive once the basic operating principles have been established. The system can be made very tolerant to failures since the failure of one part of the network can be made to have limited, or even zero, effect on the total network operation. It is also fundamentally simpler to develop such a system since it can be built, tested, and put into service one leg at a time. It is not necessary to have a huge central software complex running correctly before any service can be provided.

An interconnected computing system, therefore, has the ability to grow fairly easily as additional demands are placed on it. It can accept local modifications and enhancements as special needs become apparent without impacting other parts of the network, provided the fundamental intercommunication rules are obeyed.

I believe that the development, in recent years, of economical mini-computers which have both significant computing power and the ability to handle communications very efficiently will lead to the growth of sophisticated computing networks. Different types of computers will be interconnected both locally and remotely to provide more power, easier development, and greater failure protection. Because of the high performance/cost ratio of mini-computers, more of these systems will be implemented with machines that have previously been considered incapable of sophisticated computing. The mini-computer will become a vital member of the computing family, and be shown to be capable of taking over major real-time computing tasks.

IMPLEMENTED SYSTEMS

There are a limited number of examples at present of multiple mini-computers undertaking jobs previously assigned to large machines, but a major trend in this direction is the off loading of processing from central computers to preprocessing mini-computers. It is becoming fairly widely accepted, for example, that mini-computers can handle the data communication functions required for real-time systems much more effectively than the main data processor. Manufacturers such as Honeywell, Comcet, Tempo, Varian, Interdata, and many others all offer mini-machines as front end communication processors to IBM and other data processing machines. An example of such a system is

206

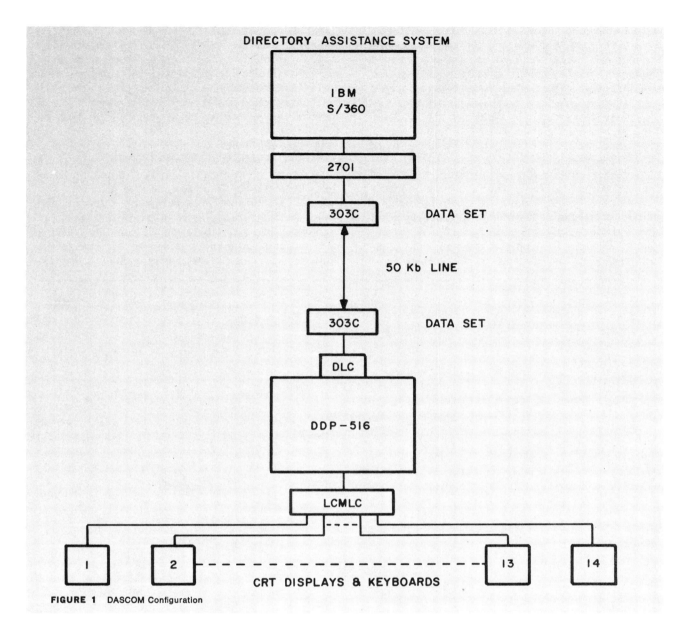

DIRECTORY ASSISTANCE SYSTEM

IBM S/360

2701

303C — DATA SET

50 Kb LINE

303C — DATA SET

DLC

DDP-516

LCMLC

1 2 — — — 13 14

CRT DISPLAYS & KEYBOARDS

FIGURE 1 DASCOM Configuration

shown in Figure 1, where a Honeywell DDP-516 computer is used as a sophisticated control computer for 14 display consoles each accessing data held in an IBM 360 machine. The system is used to provide directory assistance information in the Bell Telephone Network. The telephone operators sit at the display consoles and use keyboards to communicate with the computer system. When they receive a call requesting directory assistance, they key in the partial name, address, and possible other information identifying the person whose phone number is required. The DDP-516 validates that the information has been entered correctly, and if it has, it formats the information for transmission to the 360. At the same time, the DDP-516 opens a record of transaction information from which statistics can be deduced giving the performance of the system and of the operators. This information includes the operator number, call connect time, acknowledge time, key data timings, display time, and call disconnect time.

The 360 responds to the information request by replying with that portion of the telephone directory which contains the information most nearly matching the request. This is then checked and routed by the 516 to the display making the request. It can be seen that the display control computer is off loading the 360 from handling up to 14 separate displays with their individual control procedures, and from maintaining statistics on the operation of these units. There is only one communication line into the 360, and only valid data is sent over this line. In addition, neatly packaged statistical data is provided by the 516, making it much simpler for the 360 to accumulate overall records of the system performance.

Another good example of small computers being used in complex systems is the computing network under development by the Advanced Research Projects Agency (ARPA). ARPA is an agency of the U.S. Government that has funded the development of advanced computing systems in various universities and research establishments in the United States. These include early time-sharing systems such as TSS at the System Development corporation in California, the TX-2 experimental computer at the MIT Lincoln Labs in Massachusetts, and the ILLIAC computers at the University of Illinois. These sites, and others, have developed elaborate software, under ARPA's sponsorship, on a list of computers which covers virtually every major manufacturer in the United States. This work represents a huge pool of computing knowledge and capability, but it is spread over a wide geographic area and is, in general, available only to people in the immediate location of each site. Time-sharing does allow many users to simultaneously access the facilities, but does not let one user have access to the total facilities developed by ARPA. It would be prohibitively expensive to bring all ARPA developed software to each site and translate it to run on the computers available at that site, and equally uneconomical to provide each user with communications for direct access to each of the 20 or so computer sites.

The solution which is now in the process of implementation provides users in widely separated locations with easy access to a great variety of computing facilities. The technique is of considerable generality and may well be the way large computing systems of the future are built. The principle is to provide high-speed communication paths between all computers in the network, and use mini-computers to standardize the network control disciplines. Figure 2 shows a diagram

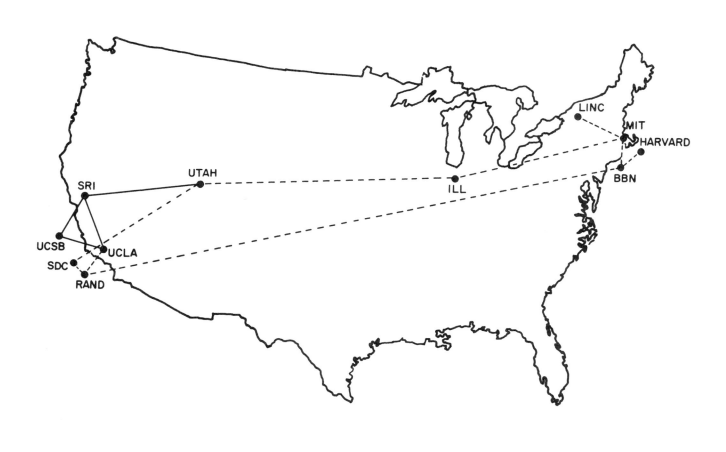

FIGURE 2   ARPA Network

of the network, and Figure 3 indicates how the Interface Message Processors (IMP's) are connected to the Host computers. With a large variety of Host computers covering both different word lengths and code sets, the simplest procedure would be to treat messages be-

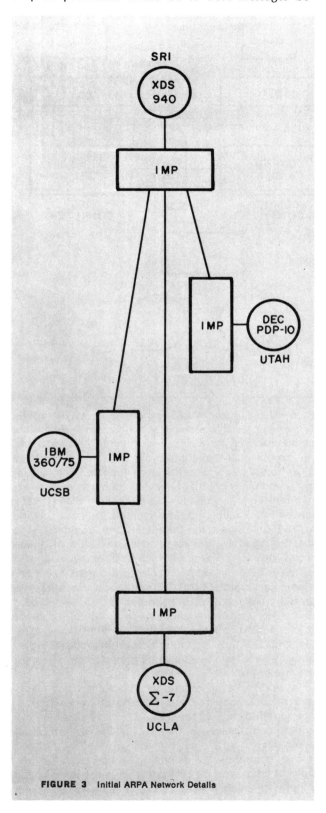

FIGURE 3 Initial ARPA Network Details

tween Host computers as bit streams. A Host computer wishing to communicate with another Host simply prepares a message which has a header with the destination Host number and the requesting user number. This is then passed to the IMP which formats the message in a "packet," which can be up to 8,095 bits long. This packet is then transferred over 50 kilobaud circuits from IMP to IMP on a store-and-forward basis until it reaches an IMP that recognizes the message as destined for its own Host. The final IMP then removes the network control information and passes the packet over to the Host computer. On its way through the network, the packet may pass through as many as five or six IMP's before it reaches its destination. At each one, strict controls are maintained on message integrity, and retransmission requests are made if an error occurs. Dynamic routing is employed to get each packet through the network with minimum delay. Each IMP continuously estimates the delay that messages are encountering in passing through its part of the network, and about twice each second it informs its neighbors of this delay estimate. Each IMP then automatically reconfigures its routing table to achieve an estimated minimum delay for messages. This means that the routing will be automatically adjusted to IMP failures or line failures without the need for manual intervention. The use of 50 kilobaud communication circuits and dynamic routing procedures allows the average short message transfer time to be kept in the region of 0.2 seconds. This means that a programmer sitting at a terminal connected to an SDS 940 computer in Palo Alto can request a running of programs on, for instance, the PDP-10 in Salt Lake City and receive responses virtually as rapidly as if they were being run on his local computer. Similarly, the files in a local computer can be transferred to a remote computer for processing and returned to the local computer for subsequent printing on the user's terminal. Thus, a huge amount of computing power becomes available economically to the general time-sharing system user by employing minicomputers to establish a general purpose computing network.

On a smaller scale, a locally interconnected set of mini-computers can provide quite sophisticated computing power with a number of significant advantages over large general purpose machines. The Honeywell H1648 time-sharing system is a first step towards a powerful computing facility which can be developed to meet increasing requirements. Figure 4 shows a block diagram of how the computers are connected. The Communications Computer handles the line traffic from as many as 48 simultaneous users, and passes valid character streams to the Control Computer. This machine acts as the system executive and, under command from the user terminals, constructs files on the disks. When a user has finished constructing and editing his files, he can then request that they be processed in whatever system language he is using, e.g., FORTRAN, BASIC, COBOL, etc. On receiving this command, the Control Computer schedules the request for execution on the Job Computer. The Job Computer is

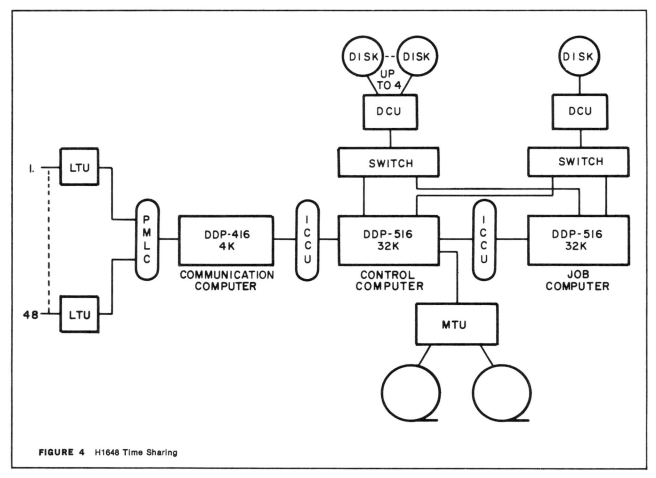

FIGURE 4 H1648 Time Sharing

not multiprogrammed, but simply processes one program at a time, allowing it to run for a predetermined period, approximately one second, and then swapping it onto the system disk if it has not been completed. It then resumes processing a previously swapped program, or a new one which has been scheduled by the Control Computer. This separation of tasks between three computers allows considerable processing power to be obtained from small machines. An obvious development to obtain more power is to add another Job Computer having perhaps longer word length and floating-point hardware. Computing tasks could then be scheduled for the appropriate Job Computer and a powerful time-sharing service would be available.

It is also important to note that the software development in a multi-computer time-sharing system is much simpler than in a single-computer system. In particular, the executive in the Job Computer can be quite simple since it only has to process tasks handed to it by the Control Computer. Similarly, the Control Computer does not have to be concerned with time slicing or swapping, and it simply handles the basic file building functions for a user and schedules computing and compilation tasks for the Job Computers.

I believe it is true to say that mini-computers are being accepted as significant members of the computer community, and that they are capable of providing real advantages over their big brothers in many situa-tions. These occur mainly where large tasks can be broken into easily separable subtasks with fairly limited communication between them. It then becomes simpler to use many small machines rather than one large one. Considerable benefits are gained in simplicity of programming, potential fail safe capability, ease of expansion, and (frequently) lower cost. It is important, however, for mini-computer manufacturers to provide a level of support for their machines comparable to that provided by the larger scale machine manufacturers. It is vital that good, high-performance standard software be provided to enable applications to be implemented rapidly. Large, all embracing operating systems are not required, but simple, high-speed standard executives are badly needed. These should provide high-speed handling of interrupts, simple task dispatching, and clearly defined interfaces with application programs. The system must also be modular and allow for easy expansion.

In addition, manufacturers should provide high-quality documentation, application assistance when required, effective field service and maintenance support, and a comprehensive training in the use of mini-computers.

Mini-computers are beginning to mature, but if their full potential is to be realized, they must be sold and supported as sophisticated computing modules and not as laboratory toys.

EDITOR'S BIOGRAPHY

Fred F. Coury was born in Detroit, Mich., on October 22, 1940. He received the B.S.E. degree in science engineering and the M.S. degree in systems engineering from the University of Michigan, Ann Arbor, in 1963 and 1969, respectively.

He worked as a Research Assistant at the University of Michigan Brain Research Laboratory from 1963 to 1967, where he developed analog and digital systems for on-line analysis and control of behavioral research experiments. From 1967 to 1969 he was an Associate Research Engineer and Lecturer in the Department of Electrical Engineering, University of Michigan. During that time he was involved in the design and implementation of the data concentrator at the University's Computing Center. He was also the principal investigator on an industry-sponsored development project in the University's Industrial Sciences Group. He developed and taught courses, and developed laboratory facilities in the Digital Systems area of the Department of Electrical Engineering at the University of Michigan. He has done private consulting and has participated in the faculty of seminars in the minicomputer area. Since 1969 he has been employed by the Hewlett-Packard Company, Cupertino, Calif., recently as Project Manager of the HP 2100A Digital Computer project, and currently as Minicomputer Section Manager.